DOING FIELDWORK

DOING FIELDWORK
Warnings and Advice

Rosalie H. Wax

The University of Chicago Press
Chicago and London

International Standard Book Number: 0-226-86949-0 (clothbound)
0-226-86950-4 (paperbound)
Library of Congress Catalog Card Number: 73-167940
The University of Chicago Press, Chicago 60637
The University of Chicago Press, Ltd., London
© 1971 by The University of Chicago
All rights reserved
Published 1971. Second Impression 1975
Printed in the United States of America

To Emanuel Geltman

CONTENTS

PREFACE

When, in 1946, I wrote a detailed account of my fieldwork in the centers where the Japanese Americans were confined during World War II, Robert Redfield and Alfonso Villa Rojas suggested that I try to get it published. After several publishers had rejected the manuscript as "fascinating but unpublishable," I set it aside. In 1963 I wrote a similar but shorter account of fieldwork on the Thrashing Buffalo reservation. Once again I approached a publisher with the suggestion that I prepare a book on fieldwork and once again I was discouraged. But in 1966 a publisher's agent named Emanuel Geltman *asked* me to write a book on fieldwork. One possible moral: *Nicht Kunst und Wissenschaft allein,/Geduld will bei dem Werke sein* [Not only art and science but patience must be part of all].

I cannot remember the names of all the people who helped me learn what I have tried to say in this book. I do, however, wish particularly to thank the following: Joseph Yoshisuke Kurihara and Roselyn HolyRock because they taught me so much; Abraham M. Halpern and Anselm Strauss, who read the first draft of the description of fieldwork in the Japanese centers; Everett C. and Helen M. Hughes, who read the first draft of the Thrashing Buffalo account; Robert L. Bee and Harry M. Lindquist, who, as students, urged me to write a book about the more personal and practical aspects of fieldwork; McKim Marriott and Gerald Suttles, who read the entire final draft and contributed many helpful suggestions; Murray Wax, who assisted me over many rough spots, and Mary Wolken and Barbara Johnson, who typed the manuscript.

As Everett C. Hughes has remarked, it is confusing to encounter in a text a reference which suggests that Durkheim (Tarde, Boas, etc.) published a cited statement in 1964. Accordingly, when I have been obliged to make references to later editions of particular works, I have put in brackets the date when the work was first published, e.g. (Evans-Pritchard [1951] 1964:23). Then, in the bibliography I have put that date of the first publication at the beginning of the reference and, when necessary, the date of the edition cited in this book at the end of the reference.

The autobiographical materials herein are intended as type cases for pedagogical purposes in training future generations of field-workers. I have not attempted to describe these cases in a balanced fashion—in the round—as I might do, or have done, in an academic presentation, but rather to describe the nature of my personal experiences in the field. Out of courtesy, and out of respect for the privacy of the individuals involved, I have employed pseudonyms for the individuals, groups, peoples, and locations mentioned in the book, except in those instances where concealment was unnecessary or futile or would excessively obscure the narrative. In two instances, out of admiration for the individuals involved, and after they personally gave me permission to do so, I have used the actual names of the participants: Joseph Kurihara and George Kuratomi. I suppose that even a third-rate amateur detective could with a little trouble find the real locations and groups where the fieldwork was conducted. However, I must warn this detective that I have tried to shield personal identities, and he might be in trouble if he leaped to conclusions about individuals. On the other hand, I suppose that I ought to add that if anyone thinks he recognizes himself in one of my portraits and is troubled by this, preferring to be revealed more openly or hidden more thoroughly, I invite his correspondence and, if there should be future editions of the book, I will endeavor to alter the text or take other appropriate action.

PART ONE Introduction

1　Theoretical Presuppositions of Fieldwork

There are some social scientists who see taking an *insider's* view as a precondition of research. They take it for granted that "to understand a people's thought one has to be able to think in their symbols" (Evans-Pritchard [1951] 1964:79). Or they assert that, as researchers, they secure their data "within the mediums, symbols, and experiental worlds which have meaning to [their] respondents" (Vidich 1955:354). It is these researchers who define field work as does Powdermaker (1966:9): "To understand a society, the anthropologist has traditionally immersed himself in it, learning, as far as possible, to think, see, feel, and sometimes act as a member of its culture and at the same time as a trained anthropologist from another culture," or like Pehrson (1957:iv), when he told the Lapps, "I want to become a Lapp so that my people may learn something of your people."

Obtaining something of the understanding of an insider is, for most researchers, only a first step. They expect, in time, to become capable of thinking and acting within the perspective of two quite different groups, the one in which they were reared and—to some degree—the one they are studying. They will also, at times, be able to assume a mental position peripheral to both, a position from which they will be able to perceive and, hopefully, describe those relationships, systems, and patterns of which an inextricably involved (and perhaps thoroughly socialized) insider is not likely to be consciously aware. For what the social scientist realizes is that while the outsider simply does not know the meanings or the patterns, the insider is so immersed that he may be oblivious to the fact that patterns exist. Thus, most native speakers of a language do not realize that their speech is governed by a unique phonemic pattern, or, indeed, that the music to which they listen is governed by particular scales, rhythms, or other patterns. What fieldworkers eventually produce out of the tension developed by this ability to shift their point of view depends on their sophistication, ability, and training. Their task, in any case, is to realize what they have experienced and learned and to communicate this in terms that will illumine significant areas of the

3

social sciences. Hortense Powdermaker (1966:19) refers to this process in graphic terms as "stepping in and out of society." She tells us (1966:228–29) that in one particularly difficult field situation she was not able to accomplish an objective analysis because she was not able to step inside the roles of the people she was studying and in consequence she was never able to step outside. Everett Hughes (1960:x) expresses the complementary view when he suggests that "it is doubtful whether one can become a good social reporter [on an alien society] unless he has been able to look, in a reporting mood, at the social world in which he was reared."

There are other social scientists who assert that research consists of building models. Primarily they are interested in working with data that can be manipulated according to formula or mechanical rules and so require a minimum of involvement in the experiential worlds of the people being studied. Demographers or census takers, for example, do not need to have a deep understanding of their respondents' language, art, etiquette, or laws, in order to know what their answers mean. Linguists can subject a language to a phonemic analysis without themselves knowing precisely what the words mean (or, indeed, knowing anything about the society or culture of the people who speak the language). Lévi-Strauss ([1962] 1966:35–74) can point out that tribal peoples bring order to their worlds by dividing phenomena into categories, without giving us a clear idea of what these categories mean to the people who created and employ them. Some behavioral psychologists claim that they study behavior without regard to meaning.

Researchers disposed to acquire an insider's view tend to emphasize the importance of learning new forms of communication, new definitions of good behavior and evil behavior, new social roles, new meanings for the phenomena of everyday life. Researchers who wish to construct models try to structure their work so that they (or their assistants and respondents) will not need to do any interpreting. Data, for them, are materials collected in such a manner that they do not require meaningful understanding; or, more precisely, data are data only when collected according to a series of invariable rules which, in themselves, provide the framework for interpretation. Other researchers are not so sectarian. They may seek an inside view but also enjoy working with models. Or they may see themselves as model builders, but enjoy stepping inside a society or culture in an attempt to understand what the models mean to the people who use them. Still others (among whom I count myself) may get so interested in a body of data, a problem, or a hypothesis, that they will learn new languages, play various roles, take on obligations, interview, administer tests, live inside or outside a community, or, as Groucho Marx once put it, "wrestle anyone in the house" if they think this will help them find out what they want to know.

Some researchers who assert that they are objective, uninvolved model builders are, in actuality, crypto-insiders, whose strategy is concealed because their studies are conducted among their own peoples. They need not consciously concern themselves with understanding or getting an insider's view, because they have been reared in the society they are studying and they already understand many of its meanings. Thus, a young, middle-class housewife who interviews other middle-class housewives on their preference in detergent almost always "understands" what her respondents mean by their answers. But if she tried to administer the same interview to Tibetan women or Puerto Rican men, the likelihood is that neither she nor her employer would know what to make of the responses. Similarly, students who study people from their own ethnic background do not need to familiarize themselves with the understandings of the people on whom they are reporting, though they may need to become consciously aware of some of them.

Moreover, many professional fieldworkers who emphasize the importance of obtaining an insider's view frequently use the techniques favored by the model builders in order to supplement or facilitate their participation and observation. For example, Powdermaker defines an anthropologist's "systematic work" as interviewing (model builder's technique), participating, and observing (insider's techniques). In Indianola, she tells us (1966:155) there was hardly a day in which she did not combine all three. We ourselves followed much the same procedure in Thrashing Buffalo, combining structured and unstructured interviews, orally administered questionnaires and written schedules, and even thematic apperception tests, as well as participation and observation. In the Japanese relocation centers I was instructed to do what many sociologists and anthropologists of today would call participant observation (no one used the term to me then), though I, had I been asked, would have said that I was trying to work like a local reporter. In any case, my friendly remarks and queries and my assurances that I was a student doing research were received with cool stares and knowing smiles. Most people took it for granted that I was a "spy for the administration." As a last and desperate resort I decided to act as if I were collecting the materials for a model builder and I invented several innocuous research projects and structured questionnaires. After months of administering the questionnaires, some of the people I had interviewed began to accept me as a reasonably trustworthy acquaintance. Thus, I was forced to use formal interviews to help me learn how to get "inside," so that eventually I would be able to associate with, observe, and understand the people I was supposed to study. As I gradually gained a greater understanding of how the confined Japanese Americans felt, I was able, more and more easily, to select, solicit, and develop the additional relationships or techniques which, in time, were to give me something like an insider's view. For the first time I began to understand many of the responses people had made to my formal questions.

Again, on the Indian reservation I found that my Indian guide and interpreter had given most of her friends and relatives the impression that my job consisted of asking Indian parents a specific series of questions about the schools. In consequence, whenever she and I called on a new "respondent," the Indian lady would sit up straight and brace herself, and I was obliged to pull out my questionnaire and administer it, whether I wanted to or not. Clearly, a woman whom I did not "subject" to an interview would feel slighted. This task accomplished, I could put away my notebook, pencil, and schedule, and we ladies could relax and "really talk," as the Indians put it, discussing what the woman thought about the schools, the teachers, her children's future, and any other current news, gossip, or scandal.

DISADVANTAGES OF RIGIDITY

A rigid and uncompromising self-definition—as a model builder or an understander—limits the areas in which a student may do research. Thus, a researcher who is determined or ordered to do nothing but administer and analyze sample surveys can work only with respondents who live in the same world of meaning as he does, that is, with "people who speak the same language." This means, almost always, that he can work only within the society or the social class in which he had been reared. He knows how to approach and how to treat these people. He knows who will submit to mechanistic or highly artificial types of investigation, who will fill out a long mailed questionnaire or respond to a structured interview before a tape recorder, and, conversely, he knows who is likely to use his ten-page questionnaire for scratch paper or slam the door in his face. Moreover, because he and his respondents speak the same language, he is usually able to *understand* or interpret correctly a great deal of what they say. But if such a researcher carries his sample surveys into a different culture, group, or class, he may get no "data" at all, or the "data" he gets will be blurred or misleading.

Similarly, the researcher who insists on equating understanding with intense and intimate participation—who believes that he can do field research only if he lives with his hosts, shares in all their activities, and refrains absolutely from asking questions—may find himself thrown out on his ear, or, a less harsh lot, simply unable to carry on his work. Had Evans-Pritchard ([1940] 1960:15) insisted on following to the letter that dictum of Malinowski's that an anthropologist must camp right in the native village, he would not have produced his great work on the Azande, as these people would not permit him to live with them as an equal. Powdermaker found that she was unable to participate or even observe much of the life of the people she studied in Hollywood. Important and powerful people would communicate with her only through formally arranged interviews.

Or again, a dedicated would-be participant may find that the powers-that-be will not permit him to live with or even near the people he wishes to study. Powdermaker did not dare to live in the Negro section of the small Mississippi town she was studying. In Rhodesia, the white administrators would not permit her to live in the section where the mine workers were housed. Had I suggested to the U.S. army or the War Relocation Authority that I live in the same section as the "disloyal" Japanese Americans at the Tule Lake center, they would most certainly have asked me to terminate my study. Another very common obstacle to living on intimate terms with a people is the plain fact that many people are made uncomfortable by the presence of an outsider. Another is that the people one may wish to study are extremely poor and there is simply no unoccupied living space. Indeed, the scarcity of housing is one of the most difficult (and least discussed) practical problems in participant observation. Ethnographers have tended to bring their own dwellings with them or they have paid natives to build them special

7

houses. While this is often the only way one can survive a field trip, it keeps one from learning many important things about the people's daily life. If one attempts participation and observation in the slums of a large city or in a depressed rural area, one may have an even harder time. There is literally no room—or there is no spot on which the law will permit one to tent.[1]

Some situations are peculiarly favorable to researchers who wish to make surveys or administer questionnaires, whereas others almost cry out for the individual who wants to engage in all-out participation and observation. Certain classes or distinct groups within a society or an institution seem to enjoy submitting to arduous interviewing sessions. A number of young married couples who attended university with me seemed to feel that they had scored a point in the status race because they had been selected as respondents to the Kinsey report. They might have reacted quite differently had they been asked to include the interviewer as a participant in their sexual activities and give him a real insider's view; but, on the other hand, they might not. Conversely, many of the institutions of a great society are specifically structured to receive participants and turn them into insiders. Almost anyone of the right age and sex can, with little effort, get into a hospital, a prison, a night school class, an insane asylum, or the army, providing he is willing to participate as a patient, pupil, inmate, or private. He will, moreover, have no trouble learning the ropes and acquiring an insider's view, because the people who run these institutions are experts at shaping-up or resocializing the men and women for whom they are responsible. On the other hand, should he enter any of these institutions as a participant, he may find it impossible to use the model builder's techniques or methods either on the higher-ups or on his peers.

Advantages of Flexibility

When a researcher is not dedicated to the exclusive use of sample survey procedures, amusing contretemps may occur and the intracultural or heterogeneous nature of the situation (and the need for understanding or resocialization) may be revealed. Thus, some twenty years ago, when David Riesman was conducting a study of

---

1. Twenty-five years ago, William F. Whyte moved in with a family to make his study of slum society. They gave him their son's room ([1943] 1955:294–96). A few years ago William Stringfellow, who took up residence in Harlem, found "living conditions" very difficult indeed (1966:2 ff.).

apathy in politics, he had his interviewers administer a long and highly structured questionnaire. When this questionnaire was administered to working-class people, the responses were so meager that the research group decided, tentatively, that the working class must be inarticulate (that is, deficient in the English language). When I heard about this, I exploded, and wrote Riesman an irate and rather pungent letter. Riesman responded by sending me a copy of the questionnaire and suggesting that I do some interviewing. Since I had spent a good deal of my life with working-class people, I shared many of their meanings, which is to say that I had some understanding of how to approach them. The first woman I interviewed gave me responses which ran to over forty typewritten pages. Subsequent interviews were not always so long, but they showed that most working-class people were not inarticulate and that the researchers who had framed the interviews lived in a world of meanings very different from that of the people they called lower or working class. One of the questions on the schedule was "What do you think is the cause of war?" An old woman respondent thought for a long time and then announced, "The star with the tail!" I did not "understand" until I remembered the medieval portents of disaster, among which, of course, were comets. In another interview, a middle-aged woman seemed baffled by the question "Do you get excited about politics?" Turning to a woman friend who had dropped in while the interview was in progress, she asked, "Now what does that mean?" Her friend explained, "It means, do you get excited when you go into a voting booth." The respondent looked blank for a moment and then broke into a bawdy guffaw. Nudging me, she countered with the question "What's there to get excited about in a voting booth?"

Many years later my husband and I found ourselves in a situation similar to that of Riesman when we contracted to administer a specific number of interviews to a random sample of Indian adolescents. With the help of a census report and an old deck of playing cards, we drew our sample and sent out our young Indian interviewers, two of whom had been brought up in the local community. Day after day the Indian interviewers returned with extremely short and uninformative responses. When we questioned them, they said only that the young people did not care to talk about school. Murray and I then personally tried to interview the adolescents. For an entire afternoon I administered questions to teen-age girls and got

9

nothing but squirms, timid or embarrassed glances, smiles, and a few barely audible yesses, noes, or don't knows, and this despite the fact that I was accompanied by a young Indian matron who had known these girls from childhood and did her best to put them at ease. When my Indian friend and interpreter put the questions in the Indian language, she received the same responses as I did: squirms, smiles, and mumbled monosyllables. On the drive home she kept repeating in an exasperated tone: "I don't know what's the matter with those girls."

We experimented with many other devices, and after weeks of hard work we "began to understand" that most Indian adolescents talk fluently and freely only to the members of their own peer group or, on certain occasions, to an older female relative, particularly an aunt. On the other hand, most of the young people were willing to answer a written questionnaire, because communicating in writing apparently did not put them under the strain of social interaction with a threatening stranger or with an Indian "college graduate," before whom they felt embarrassed. In the end we were able to fulfill our contract, though we gained most of our understanding not from these written questionnaires but from the unstructured interviews which our Indian assistants were eventually able to "conduct" after they were permitted to share in some of the activities of the Indian teen-agers.

The above discussion is not intended to derogate all or any of the social scientific methods, techniques, or theories. It is presented in the hope that the student may perceive for himself that strict and rigid adherence to any method, technique, or doctrinaire position may, for the fieldworker, become like confinement in a cage. If he is lucky or very cautious, a fieldworker may formulate a research problem so that he will find all the answers he needs within his cage. But if he finds himself in a field situation where he is limited by a particular method, theory, or technique, he will do well to slip through the bars and try to find out what is really going on.

WHAT IS UNDERSTANDING? [2]

Understanding, as here used, does not refer to a mysterious empathy between human beings. Nor does it refer to an intuitive or

2. The argument in this section is based on a dialogue carried on for four years by Murray Wax and myself. Its first principles were sketched in 1964 in an article on participant observation which appeared in the *International*

rationalistic ascription of motivations. Instead, it is a social phenomenon—a phenomenon of *shared* meanings. Thus, a fieldworker who approaches a strange people soon perceives that these people are saying and doing things which *they* understand but he does not understand. One of the strangers may make a particular gesture, whereupon all the other strangers laugh. They share in the understanding of what the gesture means, but the fieldworker does not. When he does share it, he begins to "understand." He possesses a part of the "insider's" view.

An eloquent example of understanding has been given us by Theodora Kroeber (1961:6–8) in her biography of Ishi, "the last wild Indian in North America." Starving and exhausted, with all his people dead, Ishi was turned over by the Bureau of Indian Affairs to the staff of the museum at the University of California. Sitting in the jail at Oroville, unable to make himself understood or understand anything said to him, he was approached by Professor Waterman, who brought with him a copy of vocabularies in the Yana language.

Waterman found a weary, badgered Indian sitting in his cell, wearing the butcher's apron he had been given at the slaughter house, courteously making what answer he could in his own language to a barrage of questions thrown at him in English, Spanish, and assorted Indian from a miscellaneous set of visitors.

Waterman sat down beside Ishi, and with his phonetically transcribed list of Northern and Central Yana words before him, began to read from it, repeating each word, pronouncing it as well as he knew how. Ishi was attentive but unresponding until, discouragingly far down the list, Waterman said *siwini* which means yellow pine, at the same time tapping the pine framework of the cot on which they sat. Recognition lighted up the Indian's face. Waterman said the magic word again; Ishi repeated it after him, correcting his pronunciation, and for the next few moments the two of them banged at the wood of the cot, telling each other over and over, *siwini, siwini!* . . . After a while Ishi ventured to ask Waterman *I ne ma Yahi?* "Are you an Indian?" Waterman answered that he was. The hunted look left Ishi's eyes—here was a friend. He knew as well as did his friend that Waterman was not an Indian. The question was a tentative and subtle way of reassuring and being reassured, not an easy thing to do when

Encyclopedia of the Social Sciences (1968, vol. 11, 238–41). M. Wax (1967) developed these notions further in "On Misunderstanding Verstehen: A Reply to Abel." I then used the expository section of his article as a framework for the discussion appearing here.

the meaningful shared sounds are few. . . . In the excitement and relief of having someone to talk to, Ishi poured out confidences and recollections which Waterman could by no means comprehend even with the aid of an elaborate pantomime. Ishi's seeming pleasure was not in the recollected event, but was rather a near hysteria induced by human interchange of speech and feelings too long denied.

Paula Verdet (1969) has given us an illuminating description of the process of understanding in the interview situation:

We need to *see* and *hear* respondents struggling with their reality as much as they need to see *us* eager for the insights they can give us. I had a happy experience along these lines in the quiet days of the 1960 campaign. I participated in a pre-election study where my own interest lay in the religious issue. I ended up by taking interviews in areas of which students' parents disapproved, i.e., the worst part of the black ghetto. One of my main questions read, "In your opinion, why is it that religion is more important in Presidential elections than in other elections?" Much to my surprise, I found a great many of my Negro respondents—many of them Baptists, hence not particularly well disposed to the Catholic Church—relating warmly to the Catholic candidate *qua* Catholic. As they perceived it, here was a member of another minority group struggling not only for a breakthrough for his own people, but also in some way against the prejudices directed at *all* underprivileged groups. One of them said, "Even we, who have been treated as the lowest of the low, always we were granted at least our religious freedom. And *he* is denied it!" From such contact with individual respondents I derived a firm insight that the Negroes were not voting for Kennedy *only* because they were Democrats (some of them had voted for Eisenhower); *not* simply because he had shown that he would help them in their fight for equality (not one referred to the release of Martin Luther King from jail); but also as a step in their *own* accession to full rights as citizens. *They* were helping him to make it as he was helping them make it. *They* were in that fight shoulder to shoulder, so to speak. (In a sense, the tremendous popularity in 1968 of the second Kennedy candidate gives further confirmation to the 1960 finding.) I don't think I could ever have arrived at sensing this special type of back lash of the religious issue among Negro Protestants, if I had not heard my respondents reason out their position for me with the fervent conviction they had. In turn this realization awakened me, rather early, to the tremendous transformations which were about to take place within the Negro community.

Understanding in field research is very like the aural learning of a language. The fieldworker begins "outside" the interaction, confronting behaviors he finds bewildering and inexplicable: the actors are oriented to a world of meanings that the observer does not grasp. With a strange language, at first all is mumbo-jumbo; then patterns begin to emerge, and the student proceeds from halting discourse (stumbling over new phonemes and translating inwardly from his mother tongue) to the fluency of one increasingly at home in the language and situation. Likewise, the fieldworker finds initially that he does not understand the meanings of the actions of a strange people, and then gradually he comes to be able to categorize peoples (or relationships) and events: for example, this man who is visiting is a brother-in-law to my host; last week his wife gave mine a gift; today he is expecting some reciprocity. Parallel illustrations might be drawn from historical investigation, where the student first finds that, while he seems to be reading the text of a document, its meanings evade him, and then, as he gains familiarity with the historical period and the peoples involved, the same document speaks more profoundly.

Understanding is not an "operation" or a scientific instrument capable of generating fresh knowledge. It does not generate knowledge about a culture any more than being fluent in a language generates knowledge about it. Rather, it is a *precondition of research*[3] in any social situation. This is more easily apprehended if we consider how understanding is acquired, namely, through socialization—either the primary socialization into one's native culture or the secondary socialization (or resocialization) into an alien culture, or even vicarious socialization.

Some readers may feel that I am giving too much weight to socialization, since it can, after all, be considered simply a form of "learning." One of the reasons for my procedure is that learning, as conceived by most psychologists, is a culturally static procedure (as the learning of nonsense syllables or mazes), whereas socialization implies a participation in the cultural dynamic and a corresponding development or enlargement of the self. Neither a culture nor a language can safely be regarded as a formal and static abstraction, as each is a dynamic system maintained and modified by its bearers or speakers. Because a language or dialect is created and defined by the continual dialogue of its speakers, they are the only authority as to its nature, even though none of them may be able to perform a linguistic analysis of the language or delineate its phonemes or

3. The same point was made by Kroeber (T. Kroeber 1970:165–67) with respect to the study of cultural trait lists.

syntax. The same is true of culture, which, like language, is borne and maintained and created by joint activity. Accordingly, the intra-cultural understanding deriving from primary socialization does yield a knowledge, a species of data, that is as absolute as any in science. What native speakers say and respond to defines their dialect; what natives do, say, and respond to defines their culture and their society.

Secondary socialization (or resocialization) does not supply the fieldworker with the same authority as the native. However intimate and extensive an experience, no period of living within another culture can fully compensate for the lack of childhood experiences therein. Yet, because culture is a dynamic system maintained and modified by its members, participation is the most efficient way to gain as near total a grasp of it as is possible for the alien. In participating as he observes, the fieldworker undergoes a secondary socialization (or resocialization) which allows him to perceive the major categories of objects of the culture and to understand the major types of relationships and interactions. Thus, he gains something of an "insider's" view, a view that is extremely difficult and sometimes impossible to acquire with such secondary devices as structured questionnaires.

Some of the most outstanding achievements in understanding, in gaining and presenting something of an "insider's" view, have been made by individuals who were not formally connected with a specific social science discipline. The writings of Freuchen, who lived for years with the Eskimos, reflect a greater understanding of "shared Eskimo meanings" than do most of the reports prepared by trained ethnographers. Much the same may be said for Doughty, "a crotchety Semitist" (Kroeber, [1923] 1948:317) who, with incredible fortitude and courage, traveled and lived with the Arabs during the latter part of the nineteenth century, or of Codrington, a missionary bishop who lived in Melanesia for more than twenty years and prepared a superb work on the religious beliefs of the natives.

2   The First and Most Uncomfortable Stage of Fieldwork

> The child born into a society may be said
> to go through the same process of socialization
> as the stranger who is finally adopted into a
> new society.   —Robert E. Park

In the previous chapter I suggested, first, that understanding is the precondition of social research and, second, that understanding is achieved during and by means of the experience of (re)socialization. So, in order to understand the ways of an alien people, the social researcher will try, insofar as he and they can agree, either to participate with them as they go about these ways or to associate with them and observe them as they do so; and by being so situated, the researcher places himself in that position where he can be resocialized. Given the interconnectedness of so much of social life, the researcher usually tries to live with or near the people he is studying during the entire round of their living, and it is this process of "living with" an alien people that is termed *fieldwork,* (or in some cases, "participant observation"). But this brief description makes the process look far too simple, for living successfully with an alien people is no easy matter. Moreover, each variety of social intercourse is premised upon different kinds and levels of understanding, and participating by the researcher requires different kinds of socialization. Few groups of people (and few institutions) are so established as to be hospitable to inquiring social researchers. Hence, a researcher cannot simply learn a few basic "rules of fieldwork," drop himself among an alien people like a man from Mars, and then proceed to acquire understanding. As any researcher or explorer, he will fare better if he anticipates what he will confront and prepares himself accordingly. To be quite frank, it was my pedagogical impulse to confront the student as early in this book as possible with the most basic issues, so that even if he gave up its reading after the second chapter, he would still have derived some profit from the exposure.

15

Most field experiences that involve living with or close to the host people fall into three stages. First, there is the stage of initiation or resocialization, when the fieldworker tries to involve himself in the kinds of relationships which will enable him to do his fieldwork—the period during which he and his hosts work out or develop the kinds and varieties of roles which he and they will play. Second, there is the stage during which the fieldworker, having become involved in a variety of relationships, is able to concentrate on and do his fieldwork. Third, there is the post-field stage, when the fieldworker finishes his report and tries to get back in step with, or reattach himself to, his own people.

Most discussions of fieldwork ignore or pass rapidly over the first stage and dwell in great detail on stage two—the period of tangible accomplishments. This is understandable, because the manifest task of the fieldworker is to get his work done. But it is unfortunate, for it is during the first stage that the fieldworker finds, is offered, and accepts the lines of communication and the social vantage points through and from which he will make his observations and will be permitted to participate. It is also during this stage that he will find out whether or not he will be able to do the work he wishes to do. And, quite frequently, it is during this stage that the character, scope, and emphasis of his problem or investigation is determined.

In a field situation where the host people are genial, tactful, patient, and cooperative, a fieldworker may not even be aware that he is passing through a preliminary stage. He finds friends and respondents easily and rapidly; he becomes involved with family groups and organizations; he can begin work almost immediately. If at first he makes mistakes and misinterpretations, these are gradually and naturally cleared away as his knowledge of the culture becomes more thorough and his insight more penetrating. But field situations as ideal as this are rare, and, with the disappearance of the old South Sea cultures, they are becoming rarer.

A fieldworker may also pass through stage one with less difficulty if he has lived or associated for some time with a people before beginning fieldwork with them. Consciously and, more often, unconsciously, he will have learned some etiquette and some proper social responses. Previous association and familiarity may account for the relative ease with which Liebow became involved in Negro street corner society (1967:233–34).[1]

1. On the other hand, a familiarity with basic Indian etiquette and general world view did not keep my husband and myself from getting into an em-

Usually a beginner arrives in the field ready and eager to begin "gathering data." Then, for weeks, and sometimes for months, he gropes and wanders about, trying to involve himself in the various kinds of human or social relationships that he needs, not only in order to acomplish his work but because he is a human being. He tries to make the acquaintance of as many people as possible, and he tries to tell them who he is and what he hopes to do. He may also try to obtain permission to attend meetings or ceremonies, or he may tag along, as a quasi participant, with various groups. He may try to find a good language teacher, a competent interpreter, or, sometimes, a good clerical assistant. All this time, of course, he is trying hardest of all to find some person or persons who will advise, assist, and teach him, introduce him, or, as the Indians put it, "go around with him."

What happens to the fieldworker and his hosts during this involvement-seeking or role-constructing period varies with each fieldworker and each situation. Nancy Lurie (1970), in her study of the Winnebago, seems to have had a remarkably agreeable first field experience, which she ascribes to the instruction and assistance given her by a wonderful old man. William F. Whyte also seems to have been relatively lucky. After several unsuccessful experiments such as knocking on doors and trying to discuss "living conditions" or approaching strangers in a bar and almost being thrown downstairs, he encountered Doc, the leader of a street corner gang. Whyte and Doc thereupon began a relationship which, whatever it meant to Doc, the sponsor-guide, was to be of enormous assistance to Whyte, the student-researcher. Powdermaker ([1966] 1967:58–59) in her first field trip to Melanesia also seems to have made out very well, for she mentions only that for a few hours she felt frightened and isolated.

But initiations so easy as these are, I suspect, rare. Carpenter (1965) tells us that when he began his work with the Eskimo, he felt for months like a mental defective. Gradually, however, his "feelings of stupidity and clumsiness diminished, not as a consequence of learning skills so much as becoming involved with a family, with individuals. If they hadn't accepted me, I would have remained less than an outsider, less than human." I had a similar experience on my first field trip to the Gila center, where it took

barrassing and inconvenient social involvement when we began our study of the Thrashing Buffalo reservation.

me four months to develop any kind of social relationship, not because the Japanese Americans or I were socially maladept, but because almost everyone automatically defined me as "a spy for the
administration." Like Carpenter I often felt like a mental defective,
and for about six weeks I felt as if I were losing my mind. Lowie
(1959) tells us that he learned very little on his first trip to the
Shoshone. Powdermaker ([1966] 1967:138–43), in 1932, had an
extremely difficult time trying to begin her study of caste and class
in a small town in Mississippi, and she also tells us that in
Hollywood (228–29) she was never able to become involved with
any of the persons or groups she studied and, as a result, she was
not able to accomplish a satisfactory piece of work. Schwartz
(1964:87), who did fieldwork in a mental hospital, tells us: "My
initial period at the hospital was one of disorientation, shock, and
disequilibration. It lasted for about three or four weeks and was
highlighted by my need and attempt to find firm ground upon
which to stand and to reconstitute an integrated "self" with which
to operate." Franz Boas's letters from the field contain many complaints about the intractability of his Northwest Coast Indian informants: "For some inexplicable reason I could not get the people
to talk. They evidently think I come with some evil intent. As a result I wasted three hours without accomplishing a thing. . . . In
spite of anything I could say I could get nowhere with them"
(Rohner 1966: 164–65). Or again: "The only way I can get people
is to drag them in by the hair. I am very glad to get away from
here because I cannot work at all. The Indians are so difficult here"
(Rohner 1966: 172–73). Boas's student Margaret Mead had even
more difficulty among the Omaha: "This is a very discouraging job,
ethnologically speaking. You find a man whose father or uncle had
a vision. You go to see him four times, driving eight or ten miles
with an interpreter. The first time he isn't home, the second time
he's drunk, the next time his wife's sick, and the fourth time, on the
advice of the interpreter, you start the interview with a $5 bill, for
which he offers thanks to Wakanda, prays Wakanda to give *him* a
long life, and proceeds to lie steadily for four hours" (Mead 1966:
313–14). Evans-Pritchard (1940) has given us an edifying and
entertaining account of some of the difficulties he encountered while
studying the Nuer, and Malinowski may have endured the most painful research experience of all, for he seems to have lived for three
years with an alien people, "participating" in many of their activities

but, so far as his work and field diaries indicate, avoiding any socially meaningful involvement.

During this first stage of fieldwork, the fieldworker lives in a kind of social limbo, trying to behave as if he "belonged" and as if he knew what he was doing. He may give the superficial appearance of working very hard. He may approach many different people with his carefully composed description of who he is and what he is doing, carrying his list of carefully structured, "inoffensive" questions, and may wonder why they giggle, shake their heads, simply stare at him, or mumble, "I don't know." Or, like a young anthropologist friend of ours, he may energetically explore the paths of his new living quarters, only to find that most of them lead to his neighbors' privies. Or, in his enthusiasm to participate in the lives of his hosts, he may settle down unwittingly, as Murray and I did, with a family notorious for its skill in relieving unsuspecting strangers of their money. He may, as we did, take extremely voluminous notes (sometimes because he has nothing else to do), and months later find that a good part of these early notes consist of amateurish observations that could have been made by any outsider—naïve hypotheses about the meaning of things various people did or said, pseudo-gallant or pseudo-jocular complaints about living conditions or the peculiarities of his hosts, or, when all else fails, long and detailed descriptions of the scenery. Indeed, it is no accident that the few professionals who tell us anything about their first-stage, preinvolvement experiences, almost always adopt a comic or whimsical style. Painful and humiliating experiences are easier to talk about if one does not take them too seriously, and it is less distressing to picture oneself as a clown or figure of fun than as a dolt or a neurotic.

The process by which a fieldworker moves out, and is moved out, of this uncomfortable and frustrating first stage is complicated, and it varies with each situation and each individual fieldworker. It may be as complicated and variable as the process by which an individual infant becomes a socialized and civilized member of his community. It resembles the latter process in that, among other things, it involves a great deal of learning or socialization (or, better, *relearning* and *resocialization*) on the part of the fieldworker (and sometimes of his hosts) and the mutual desire and ability to establish reciprocal relationships of the kind that will help the fieldworker learn what he wishes to learn and do what he wishes to do. Frequently it is during this period that the fieldworker also discovers that he cannot possibly do what he had hoped to do and, simultaneously, that there are many unsuspected avenues of investigation open to him.

Once the fieldworker has managed to establish some reciprocal relationships with his hosts, he will find, sometimes very suddenly, that his anxieties and his feelings of incompetence and stupidity have decreased to a marked degree and that he is able to work on a new and very encouraging level of competence. Indeed, the process of involvement is circular and cumulative. The less anxious a fieldworker is, the better he works, and, as he becomes aware that he is doing good work, he becomes less anxious. Usually the essential factor in this transformation is the assistance and support—the reciprocal social response—given him by some of his hosts. It is in their company that he begins to do the kind of "participation and observation" that enables him to "understand" what is going on about him at his own speed and at his own level of competence. It is his hosts who will let him know when he behaves stupidly or offensively, and will reassure him when he thinks he has made some gross blunder. It is they who will help him meet the people who can assist him in his work, and it is they who will tell him when his life is in danger and when it is not. As this process continues, the fieldworker often becomes quite skillful and self-confident in his own right. He no longer lies awake at night tormenting himself over the question of whether or not he hurt this or that person's feelings or overlooked some particular opportunity. He finds himself doing with assurance many things over which, previously, he hesitated and worried for days. He learns how to behave in the presence of old people, young women, children, and infants. He begins to learn how to accept obligations and how to repay them, when to ask questions and when to keep his mouth shut—in short, how to stay out of the most obvious kinds of trouble. Indeed, in the literal, ancient, and comforting sense of the phrase, he now begins "to know what he is doing."

The student who expects to be told precisely how to construct this kind of field relationship would do well to read a number of the available descriptions carefully. If he has the wit to be a good fieldworker, he will perceive how different were each of these situations and he may also understand why honest and experienced fieldworkers frequently tell beginners that there is not much they can tell them, because each situation differs from every other.

3 A Historical Sketch of Fieldwork

Descriptive reporting of the customs, inclinations, and accomplishments of foreign peoples is almost as old as writing itself. In the fifth century B.C. Herodotus was instructing and entertaining his Hellenic readers with accounts of the Persians and the Scythians; the former, he reported, regarded themselves as superior to all the rest of mankind (though they were quite willing to adopt novel foreign customs like pederasty); while the latter collected the scalps of their enemies, made drinking cups of their skulls, and had an extreme hatred of all foreign countries (Dundes 1968:614).

The Romans continued this practice, but their writers of descriptive or ethnographic works—at least those who come most quickly to mind—tended to take a more sober and polemical stance. Thus Josephus (ca. A.D. 37–95), the Jew who became a Roman army officer, wrote a detailed account of the siege of Jerusalem by the Romans, in which he demonstrated that the Jews possessed many of the characteritics held in high esteem by their conquerors. Or again, Tacitus (A.D. 55–120), a Roman who admired the Teutonic tribes, wrote a remarkable account of their customs in an effort to show his fellow countrymen that they, in contrast, were becoming effete and unmanly. In the fifth century Fa-hsien, a Chinese Buddhist pilgrim, wrote extensively on his observations in India (Reischauer and Fairbank 1958:146) and, some three centuries later, Chinese annalists were recording careful descriptions of the material culture and ceremonies of the Tibetans (Snellgrove and Richardson 1968:64–65).

With the rise of the Islamic empires, their traders and ambassadors began to visit foreign lands and record what they had seen and heard. In 921–22 Ahmed Ibn Fadlān journeyed from Baghdad to Bulgaria and subsequently wrote a remarkable description of the Swedish Vikings he encountered on the Volga: "tall as palm trees, and florid and ruddy of complexion," tattooed from finger tip to neck, and "the filthiest race that God ever created" (Dundes 1968:14–22). Ibn Fadlān must have had the disposition of an amateur ethnographer of high caliber, for though some of the

Vikings' customs disgusted him, he took the trouble to attend and describe meticulously the funeral of a chief (who was cremated in his ship along with his dog, two horses, a cock, a hen, and a slave girl who had volunteered for the honor). Then, when he observed that one of the Northmen was haranguing his interpreter, he had the speech translated and learned that the Northman was telling the interpreter how superior were his peoples' funeral customs to those of the Arabs.[1]

The first Europeans to collect and record genuinely useful ethnographic data about alien people were missionaries of the Catholic church and certain ambitious and imaginative merchants. Between 1245 and 1255 John of Piano Carpini and William of Rubruck visited Mongolia: Piano Carpini observed and described how the Mongols elected their Great Khan and how princes of the house of Chingiz came from all over the world to participate. Rubruck left a fascinating description of how he in company with a learned Moslem and a Buddhist were invited to expound their respective beliefs before the great Khan Mangu. Polo, the Venetian traveler and merchant, lived in the Mongol-Chinese empire for many years, became a member of Kublai Khan's administrative staff, and wrote a most useful and informative account which, it seems, many people did not believe. Indeed, one might do worse than nominate Polo as the first participant observer.[2]

A thorough reading of Herodotus, Ibn Fadlān, or Marco Polo would not necessarily improve the field techniques of a modern student. Nevertheless, their bald revelations of their own biases and those of their subjects—their depictions of how differently members of one culture view members of another—are fascinating, while their

1. For other interesting accounts of encounters between Moors and Norsemen, see Jones 1968:214–15, 250, 255. Students interested in reading the accounts of Herodotus, Josephus, Tacitus, Polo, or Rubruck will find translations listed in the bibliography.

2. The shrewd devices by which Jesuit missionaries got themselves accepted as participants in Chinese society of the seventeenth century may also be listed as a variety of fieldwork. Father Ricci, for example, mastered the classic language, dressed in the garb of a mandarin, discussed problems of science and philosophy with his potential converts, and presented Christianity as the fulfillment of Confucianism. Another Jesuit, Father Adam Schell, demonstrated that the Chinese calendar was inaccurate and was made the director of the Chinese observatory and a minister of state for mathematics. For brief accounts see Chadwick (1964) and Neill (1964).

curiosity, vitality, and sheer stamina are often awe-inspiring. Besides, their accounts are sometimes considerably more interesting than are the pedestrian efforts of some social scientists of today.

During the last quarter of the nineteenth century in Europe there occurred a spectacular efflorescence of ethnographic fieldwork. This was related to the fact that a good many literate and reasonably well-educated men—governmental officials, administrators, missionaries, and political exiles—were obliged to spend many years and sometimes most of their lives living and working with an alien or "backward" people. Most of these men had been trained in the humanities, they liked to write, and some of them took up the study, observation, interpretation, and description of native life with great enthusiasm and diligence. Some of their works, of course, are distorted by a provincial point of view. Others, however, are unsurpassable as field descriptions, for these amateurs (as some later anthropologists were to call them) often lived for many years or even decades with the people they were observing and came to speak the native languages well. Their works are not always easy to find nowadays even in well-stocked libraries, and most of them take a great deal of time to read. Still, the student who feels the urge might try his hand at Codrington's *The Melanesians* (1891), Callaway's *The Religion of the Amazulu* (1870), Doughty's *Travels in Arabia Deserta* (1888), or the accounts of Mikloukho-Maclay's sojourn in Melanesia in 1871–72.[3] A new and abbreviated edition of Bogoras's *The Chukchi* is in press. More accessible are the writings of Nimuendajú, Freuchen's journalistic but insightful works on Eskimo life, and Jaime de Angulo's *Indians in Overalls*. The last three writers worked in the first third of the twentieth century, but their perspective has more in common with that of the old amateurs than with their professional contemporaries.

DOMESTIC RESEARCH IN THE EIGHTEENTH AND NINETEENTH
CENTURIES [4]

Social research involving direct observation of groups or institutions in the researcher's own society was carried on in Britain and France as early as the latter part of the eighteenth century.

3. References to Maclay's journeys may be found in Lawrence (1964:63–67).

4. Much of this sketch of early social research is derived from Lécuyer and Oberschall (1968).

Arthur Young, with the aim of improving agricultural practices, made an extensive study of the actual way of life in the rural areas of England, France, and Ireland. His accounts were published from 1771 to 1793. In France, from 1785 to 1789, a committee consisting of Bailly, Lavoisier, Laplace, and Tenon, made a vast reforming inquiry into the hospitals of France and Europe, basing their conclusions on documents, questionnaires, and direct observation. In Great Britain from 1780 to 1841 there was an enormous amount of fieldwork involving observation. Most of this work was directed at improving the conditions of the poor and the working classes—the idea being to gather data so that the outmoded poor laws and institutions, schools and prisons, could be subjected to intelligent and informed reform. John Howard, a country squire, traveled over 42,-000 miles in Great Britain and Europe, making detailed studies of the life, diet, pastimes, and illnesses of prisoners. In the books he published in 1777 and 1789 he compared treatment of prisoners in various countries and made suggestions for improvement. (His efforts, incidentally, did lead to more humane treatment for prisoners.) In France comparable research appeared somewhat later. Among the most noteworthy was a study of prostitutes and prostitution pursued by Parent-Duchâtelet, in which the researcher used interviews (as well as files and documents) and made personal observations in the field. Research via interviewing was not usual in France at that time, but a friend of Parent-Duchâtelet had remarked that, if one wished to help prostitutes, the first thing one must do was to get to know them. Villermé's monumental study of textile workers (from 1819 to 1843) also merits mention, though he stressed accurate observation rather than interviewing.

It is interesting that all this social research—which was based on the assumption that poverty and human degradation sprang from malfunctioning social institutions which could be corrected by informed and intelligent action—remained outside the university system. It was, of course, undertaken by educated men—lawyers, scientists, doctors, and administrative officials, working singly or in small groups or societies. But, the researchers did not have university appointments, nor did they use the facilities of the universities.

After the middle of the nineteenth century this type of action-oriented research dwindled away. In its place there appeared a great deal of academically oriented research with a quite different perspective—the theories of Social Darwinism. According to this latter view, crime, poverty, and backwardness were assumed to be the result of inherited lacks or defects. Thus, research aimed at the remedying of social ills could be defined not only as futile but as harmful to mankind, since it interfered with the laws of natural selection and might result in a degeneration of the species.

In the 1880s the pendulum swung back, and there was a great revival of reform-oriented research, the most impressive being aimed at improving the situation of the working people of London. The prime mover was Charles Booth, who came from a wealthy family of shipowners. Assisted by a number of able and energetic colleagues, Booth employed a variety of research techniques. So far as I know, his were the first researchers to combine the use of statistical data with extensive interviewing and systematic participant observation. Booth had his researchers observe particular streets and households, and he himself lodged with workingmen's families. The end result was the most detailed and large-scale social description ever achieved. It stirred the contemporary social conscience and eventually led to the Old Age Pension Act of 1908, a legal minimum wage in the "sweated" trades, state provision for the sick and disabled, and the start of unemployment insurance (Lécuyer and Oberschall 1968:44).

Beatrice Potter, who was to become one of Booth's coresearchers, undertook a personal adventure in participant observation in 1883. The daughter of an industrial magnate, she wished to help the working class and she perceived that her knowledge of the people she hoped to help was nil:

> What had been borne into me during my book studies was my utter ignorance of the manual-working class, that is, of four-fifths of my countrymen. . . . How was I to get an opportunity of watching, day by day, in their homes and in their workshops, a sufficient number of normal manual-working families to enable me to visualize the class as a whole; to understand what was meant by chronic poverty and insecurity of livelihood; to ascertain whether such conditions actually existed in any but a small fraction of the great body of the people? [Webb 1926:146,147]

It so happened that Beatrice's maternal grandmother had been the daughter of a power-loom weaver and that Beatrice's mother's nurse (and her grandmother's companion) had come from the same community. The twenty-five-year-old Beatrice thereupon requested the nurse to take her on a visit to these working-class kinfolk. When the nurse pointed out that her friends would not be accustomed to such grand folk as Miss Potter, Beatrice suggested that she come as Miss Jones, a farmer's daughter, and the nurse agreed to carry out "the pious fraud" (Webb 1926:149).

While Miss Potter's first effort was not a notable piece of field-work, she made some observations that are still pertinent today:

> I can't help thinking that it would be well if politicians would live amongst the various classes they legislate for, and find out what are their wishes and ideas. . . . Of course, it would be absurd to general-ize from such a narrow basis; but much that one sees and hears whilst living with the working men and women as one of them, sets one thinking that a little more patient observation might be advisable before carrying out great organic changes, which may or may not be right [Webb 1926:152].

In 1888 Miss Potter sought and obtained employment as a seamstress in a London sweat shop. She has left us a most interesting decription of her experiences as a participant and observer (Webb 1902:1–19).

In 1892 Miss Potter married the social crusader Sydney Webb, and the couple devoted their lives to trying to improve the situation of the working class through the use of social research. Their descriptions and discussions of field methods and techniques merit more attention than they are usually given today. Especially worthy of note is their detailed analytical criticism of their first attempt to use a formal questionnaire (with 120 questions!) and their con-clusion that the only kind of questionnaire that can be used at the beginning of an inquiry is one in which the questions can be answered by plain statements of such recognized facts as dates, numbers, ages, places, etc. (Webb 1932:68–73). They were also, so far as I know, the first researchers to suggest (1932:39) that the fieldworker who knows precisely how to put his questions has also come to know a large proportion of the correct answers. (This maxim, incidentally, seems to have been passed on like folklore, for I have heard it pronounced by young sociologists as if they had originated it.) I find most valuable the Webbs' conception of the attitude with which one should approach fieldwork or, for that matter, any investigation (1932:34)—an attitude which they derive from Heraclitus via Morris Cohen (1931:348):

> The successful investigator is he who is eager to have the conven-tional classification upset, and the orthodox categories transcended.

He has in mind the axiom fathered on Heraclitus, "If ye expect not the unexpected ye shall not find truth." "The progress of science," it has been well said, "always depends upon our questioning the plausible, the respectably accepted, and the seemingly self-evident." Far from ignoring an entirely unexpected fact, or some phenomenon inconsistent with accustomed definitions, he hails it with joy. It is to him a positive pleasure that things should be other than he had supposed them to be; and it is this occasional delight which makes the stir and thrill of the investigator's art.

In Germany social research and fieldwork developed in the context of the universities, not, apparently, because the German philosophers and professors of economics were so partial to fieldwork but because some of them sympathized with the underprivileged classes and believed that they could do research which would assist these people. A great many statistical studies of poverty, crime, and marital and familial problems were conducted; other economic and social data were collected; and a nationwide survey of agrarian problems was performed in the latter part of the nineteenth century. Then, in 1890, Paul Göhre, a student of theology, undertook what may have been the first systematic attempt at participant observation. Pretending to be an apprentice, he worked for three months in a factory and shared, day and night, on the job and off, the life of the workmen. Each night he made a record of his observations (Lécuyer and Oberschall 1968:49). Göhre's published work impressed many people in and out of the universities, notably Max Weber; a year later, Weber (1892) collaborated with Göhre in a study of agricultural laborers. Subsequently (ca. 1909–12) Weber, assisted by other researchers, tried to make a large-scale study of industrial workers in which some of the data were to be obtained from the workers themselves. Weber himself spent a summer observing workers in a textile mill. The research, however, did not prosper, for most of the workers refused to cooperate. (For a detailed discussion of the development of social research in Germany, see Oberschall [1965].)

It is one of the interesting ironies of the social sciences that the British tradition of social research, which was, for so long, entirely extra-academic, took root and flourished in the environment of certain of the American universities, whereas the German tradition of field research, which from its inception was closely related to the universities, made so little impact that many American sociologists of the present day have not been aware that it existed. Perhaps the

American model-building sociologists are partly responsible, for they persist in painting Weber in their own image—as a "pure" theorist with no interest in field research.

EXOTIC RESEARCH IN THE EIGHTEENTH AND NINETEENTH CENTURIES

The eighteenth and nineteenth century philosophers who have been called "pioneers" or "fathers" by subsequent generations of social anthropologists or ethnographers were a varied lot. While most were highly theoretical thinkers interested in the formulation of what they called general principles, a fair number conceived their ultimate goal to be the improvement of human institutions and human society. For example, Saint-Simon (1760–1825) hoped to develop a "positive science of social relations" and insisted that scientists must analyze facts and not concepts (Evans-Pritchard [1951] 1964:23). Scottish philosophers, like David Hume (1711–76) and Adam Smith (1723–90), also asserted that societies must be studied empirically and inductively rather than by the methods of Cartesian rationalism.[5] Their views, however, did not lead any of these thinkers and writers into doing empirical research. In the 1830s and thereafter, certain professional men founded societies to protect and assist the aboriginal peoples (Reining 1962). One of these early "applied anthropologists," Dr. Thomas Hodgkin, wished to study native people and help them "after he had learned how they lived and what they wanted" (Reining 1962). But, so far as I know, none of these well-intentioned folk did any fieldwork, and they accomplished very little.

Writers and scholars of the latter half of the nineteenth century—men like Maine, Bachofen, Fustel de Coulanges, McLennan, Tylor, and Morgan—labored heroically to relate their theories to facts (though only Morgan did what could be called genuine fieldwork). Their major interest lay in theoretical or conjectural history (Evans-Pritchard [1951] 1964:24)—in discovering and tracing the origin and development of salient social institutions like "religion" or the "family." To test or substantiate their very broad and general theories, they used the preserved writings of classic antiquity and the materials collected and recorded by travelers, explorers, missionaries, and members of scientific expeditions. And since their interest in

5. For a collection of the writings of Saint-Simon see Markham (1952). For selected papers of Hume and Smith see Schneider (1967).

origins was so intense, they tended to prize most of all the descriptive accounts of the very primitive or very simple peoples.

It is difficult for contemporary social anthropologists or other dedicated fieldworkers not to become exasperated by the reluctance of these conjectural historians to make use of any but secondhand or derived sources. As Evans-Pritchard ([1951] 1964:71–72) puts it:

> It is indeed surprising that, with the exception of Morgan's study of the Iroquois, not a single anthropologist conducted field studies till the end of the nineteenth century. It is even more remarkable that it does not seem to have occurred to them that a writer on anthropological topics might at least have a look, if only a glimpse, at one or two specimens of what he spent his life writing about. William James tells us that when he asked Sir Jamese Frazer about natives he had known, Frazer exclaimed, "But Heaven forbid!" [6]

Other critics, students of Boas in particular, have been less kind. In my youth I frequently heard men like Frazer and Bachofen called "armchair anthropologists." On the other hand, I submit that this particular criticism of the ninetenth-century writers is unfair and suggests a lack of understanding on the part of the critics that is not seemly in a good fieldworker. These conjectural historians were not professionally interested in a study of the present, in what "natives" or other peoples were really doing, saying, or feeling, except insofar as these phenomena, as survivals, might throw light on the past and illuminate their theories. And, ironically, as I shall point out in my discussion of Boas, neither were most of their critics. The fault for which many of the conjectural historians may justly be criticized is their unquestioning assumption that they, with the nineteenth-century rationalist point of view, could easily interpret and understand the point of view, the institutions, and the mental processes of alien peoples or of "human beings in the first ages of the world." For this assumption they were vigorously criticized by Sir Henry Maine (Evans-Pritchard [1951] 1964:35 citing Maine ([1861] 1912:266–67), but they seem to have paid little attention to him.

There was in the nineteenth century a considerable amount of correspondence and exchange of information between these "historians of mankind" and the missionaries and administrators who carried on their work in areas inhabited by tribal or unsophisticated peoples. Unfortunately, little has been researched or written on the extent to which these theorists and fieldworkers assisted each other, or, for

6. Evans-Pritchard credits Benedict (1948:587) with this anecdote.

that matter, the extent to which they understood each other. Morgan, in the 1860s, was the first ethnographic researcher to use a mailed questionnaire, gathering data on kinship terminologies from numerous American agents in foreign countries. Subsequently, Frazer accumulated data for *The Golden Bough* in the same way.

When, in the late 1890s and early 1900s, some British anthropologists—Haddon, Seligman, Rivers, and Radcliffe-Brown—broke with the earlier academic tradition of working only from derived sources and went into the field to obtain data at first hand, they seem to have carried on their investigations much more like natural scientists than like the fieldworking officials or missionaries from whom the historical theorists had obtained their data. Their funds were meager, their time short, and they were in a hurry. Consequently, they made surveys, looked for and collected interesting or relevant specimens, observed native ceremonies, and questioned native informants as best they could. They would probably not have been able to reside near or with an alien people for any length of time to observe or participate in the on-going cultural and social events even had this method of doing fieldwork occurred to them. And when Boas and his first students and research assistants began their fieldwork among the Indians of North America, they usually proceeded in much the same fashion—even though the goals of their research were quite different.

BOAS AND EARLY AMERICAN ANTHROPOLOGY

Lowie (1937:131) has said that Boas must be understood, first of all, as a fieldworker. I would counter that Boas cannot be understood as a fieldworker without a prior understanding of his views on theory and method. On the study of cultural data, Boas's view closely resembles that held toward linguistic data by a linguist interested in phonemic analysis. No linguist embarking on a phonemic analysis would dream of analyzing a language with the categories that pertain to another. He takes it for granted that each language has its own unique categories, which can be discovered only if the student obtains and analyzes linguistic materials created by a speaker of the language. In like manner, Boas insisted that if anthropologists looked at other cultures with the concepts, categories, and biases of Western culture—that is, with their own *Kulturbrillen*—they would see nothing but distortion.[7] What they had to do instead was collect vast

7. The same point was made by Maine in 1861 and, subsequently, by the French "sociologists" Durkheim and Lévy-Bruhl.

quantities of entirely reliable material *in the native language.* (Boas's attitude toward the collection of ethnographic or cultural data was also very like that of the archeologist, who feels impelled to rescue the artifacts of long dead cultures from the dam and highway builders. Indeed, Margaret Mead [1966:314] shrewdly called this kind of fieldwork "excavating in a culture.")

Boas believed that these native texts—such as myths and tales written down in the native language—would constitute large, petrified, everlasting, and absolutely genuine primary or undistorted expressions of the culture. By pouring over them long enough, students would find the clues or keys for "understanding" the culture. As Smith (1959:54) puts it:

> The exhaustive collection of data which seems at the time to have little or no connection with any specific problem is peculiarly a feature of [Boas's] approach. . . . Masses of data may therefore be worked over with no clear knowledge of what is to be gained at the end. A new hypothesis or a new slant on an old problem will "emerge" or be "revealed" or "suggested." The data will "speak for themselves."

Boas, it would appear, wanted, at one blow, to eradicate from the collection and analysis of data not only the bias of a particular individual but the biases of western culture—and, especially, the theoretical biases of the anthropologically oriented philosophers of history who subscribed to the doctrine of cultural evolution. Accompanying this goal was a very strong sense of the limitations of personal observation. Boas, according to Smith (1959:55–56), was convinced that "people see what they expect to see, and interpret what they see in the light of their previous experiences. . . . Even the trained observer has constantly to be on guard against possible inaccuracies and omissions in his own records." "Boas," she continues, "was always too self-critical to rely completely on his own observations. He needed the documentation of the texts, the family history, to test his own precision."

This primary aspect of Boas's approach explains why he and some of his students believed that materials collected by or written by trained natives in their own tongue might be superior to the textual materials collected by trained ethnographers. Thus, Boas sponsored an enormous amount of high-grade recording by Indians or by white men who lived with Indians and spoke the native language. Several of his students continued this practice. Radin encouraged a Winnebago Indian, Crashing Thunder, to prepare an autobiography; Underhill recorded the autobiographical recollections of Chona, a

31

Papago woman; and Lowie translated from the German the voluminous writings of Curt Nimuendajú, a white man who lived for decades
with, and died among, the Indians of Amazonia.[8]

Boas (1911:60) asserted that a fieldworker ought to have a command of the native language "because much information can be
gained by listening to conversations of the natives and by taking part
in their daily life," and he also remarked that "a thoroughgoing description of all cultural data" was "the sole warrantable scientific
attitude." But he added that these ideals could not usually be
realized.

The fact is that Boas and his students did not customarily spend
a great deal of their time in the field learning the native language
and observing and taking part in native life. The kind of data they
desired did not require this, and, besides, their funds rarely permitted them a field trip of more than a few weeks or, at most, a few
months. What most of them did was try to locate as rapidly as possible a competent informant who was fluent in English and the native
language, knew the old stories and customs, and was willing to dictate and translate texts by the hour, day, week, or month. It is not
surprising that the two hardships about which they complain most
frequently in their letters are (1) wasting valuable time trying to find
or keep a good informant or interpreter and (2) writer's cramp.
They were, of course, interested in observing and recording traditional ceremonies and in watching traditional craftsmen at their work.
But most of them did not really try to do fieldwork in the style in
which it was subsequently done by the British social anthropologists,
and they did not, except for rare exceptions, become even moderately
fluent in the native languages.

Boas himself made thirteen trips to the Northwest Coast. These
trips rarely lasted more than two months and during each trip he
usually visited and worked in a number of locations. All in all, he
seems to have worked in about forty different areas, and his letters
leave no doubt that he regarded fieldwork as hard and uncomfortable work, and sometimes even as drudgery. He found the uncoopera-
tive attitude of many of the Indians thoroughly exasperating, and
complains that they would not talk at all, or that they would work

8. References to many additional works by American Indians may be
found in Lowie (1937:132–33) and Smith (1959). References to other and
more recent examples from African and other cultures may be found in
Dundes (1968:440–68).

for a few hours and then disappear, or that they demanded payment when he wished to photograph their totem poles. But, despite these trials, he returned to the field again and again, not, one suspects, because he liked it or found it financially remunerative; but because he believed that the gathering of firsthand data from the natives themselves was a task of incalculable importance and simply had to be done.

There is little evidence in Boas's letters that he himself did much participant observation or learned any native language well. It is hard to see how he could have done either, given the short duration of his trips. An occasional remark suggests that he found conversation with Indians a waste of time—except insofar as it related to the collection of textual materials—and one sometimes wonders why a man who was so interested in gathering data so that future generations might understand the old cultures "from within" had so little interest in understanding the people who were serving as his informants. For example, there was the informant who insisted on answering Boas's questions in his own way. When Boas asked, "How do you say in Tsetsaut, 'If you don't come the bear will run away'?" the informant responded that his people could not say a thing like that because they were "always there when a bear was to be killed." Boas was very much annoyed. On another occasion (in 1884) we find Boas listening impatiently to a chief's long-drawn-out account of incidents which illustrate his (the chief's) humility. Boas listens but remarks, "It is really interesting to find out how these people think but this does not help my work" (Rohner 1966:182).

Advocates of participant observation may find these remarks bewildering and exasperating, and it is interesting that twenty-seven years later Boas seems to have changed his mind, asserting that one could learn a great deal by listening to the conversation of natives. Still, it can be argued that Boas's intense and urgent interest in preserving "unchanged" relics of the "rapidly dying" Indian cultures so that these cultures might someday, after long analysis, be understood without distortion was as much a study of the past as were the efforts of the conjectural historians. In what was actually going on before their eyes, Boas, and many of the fieldworkers trained by him, evinced relatively little interest.

On the other hand, there can be no doubt that Boas got on reasonably well with the Indians. But this may tell us more about the Indians than about Boas. Thus, the Indians who knew and worked for Boas remember him not only as a collector of information but as a kind man who liked to be among Indian people:

> Well, Dr. Franz Boas was a very kind man. And he really know —know to be amongst the Indian people. He goes around to every house and see—visit them and talk about things what he needs to know. All about the things of the Indians. And he works very well. We like him very much because he was very kind to us. . . . He used to use button blanket and some bark on his head and he was *really* likes to be amongst Indian people. He was very good to us. [Rohner 1966:204]

Only a very few of the American ethnographers who were students of Boas or worked in Boas's tradition have told us anything about how they did their fieldwork. Robert H. Lowie (1959) completed an interesting autobiography shortly before his death. His account of his difficult and not very successful first field experience (pp. 4–14) helps us appreciate why he and his fellow students, anxious to be recognized as professionals, were not eager to publish blow-by-blow accounts of their experiences. Additional firsthand data may be found in Mead's (1966) collection of Benedict's articles and letters. Particularly interesting is Mead's letter to Benedict (313–16) describing her difficulties in obtaining data on the Omaha reservation in 1930, and Jaime de Angulo's letter to Benedict (296–98) in 1925, reproving her for asking him to help her get a Taos Indian informant whom she could take with her "to a safely American place" and there have him tell her about his people's sacred and secret tales and ceremonies. But perhaps the statement most worthy of the young fieldworker's attention is Boas's kind and sensible advice to Mead before her field trip to Samoa (289): "If you find you cannot stand the climate do not be ashamed to come back."

It is my impression (though I voice this suggestion with reservations) that the extent to which Boas's students really got to know and understand the people with whom they worked depended partly on their interests and partly on their personal inclinations. Those, like Lowie and Mead, who were primarily interested in social organization or cultural dynamics, became observers and participants without giving it a second thought. Gifted and independent individuals, like Jaime de Angulo, lived with the people they studied as a matter of course, though some of de Angulo's practices, like getting drunk with a shaman, were looked at askance by his sober-minded supervisors and colleagues.

34

Kroeber and Lowie never said anything about their own fieldwork in the classes or seminars I attended from 1939 to 1942. Once, during the Second World War, Kroeber gave us a session on fieldwork in which he played the part of an American Indian "informant" who, with sly wit, parried all the questions of a student who tried to interrogate him. I gained most of my impressions of what good fieldwork was like by indirection. Lowie made it clear that he believed that Nimuendajú was a superlative fieldworker—and Nimuendajú was a German who, to all intents and purposes, became an Amazonian Indian, living and dying with the people who adopted him. When I asked Lowie how I ought to prepare for my predoctoral examination in German, he suggested that I read the ethnographic reports like those of Nordenskiöld (which were then available in German but not in English). From works like these, with dictionary in hand, I learned that fieldwork was a rough, uncomfortable, dangerous, and sometimes brutal business; that it might entail anything from living on a starvation diet to getting sick on native brew.

MALINOWSKI AND HIS INFLUENCE

Bronislaw Malinowski (1884–1942) claims to have been the first British social anthropologist to pitch his tent in a native village and observe and record what was actually going on. Thus, as he explains, he was able to compare what his informants told him with what they did in the course of their daily life. He seems to have adopted this hitherto unprofessional practice not as the result of deliberate forethought but because of circumstances over which he had no control. Like all the ethnographers of those days he went into the field with meager funds. (His mentor, Professor Seligman, had to finagle him a free passage from England to Australia.) Immediately after his arrival in New Guinea World War I began. Formerly classified as an enemy national, Malinowski found it difficult to engage in any but local travel and so was obliged to remain in Australia or the nearby islands until the end of the war in 1918. During this period he made three long field trips to the Islands: September 1914 to March 1915; June 1915 to May 1916; and October 1917 to October 1918.

Malinowski was also the first professional anthropologist to give his readers a relatively detailed account of how he got his data and a relatively straightforward and comprehensive picture of what intensive fieldwork was really like. His description (first published in 1922,

cited from 1961:4) of fieldwork is all the more remarkable because
for twenty years no social researcher except the Webbs cared or dared
to follow his example.

> Imagine yourself suddenly set down surrounded by all your gear,
> alone on a tropical beach close to a native village, while the launch
> or dinghy which has brought you sails away out of sight. Since you
> take up your abode in the compound of some neighbouring white
> man, trader or missionary, you have nothing to do, but to start at
> once on your ethnographic work. Imagine further that you are a
> beginner, without previous experience, with nothing to guide you
> and no one to help you. For the white man is temporarily absent, or
> else unable or unwilling to waste any of his time on you. This exactly
> describes my first initiation into field work on the south coast of
> New Guinea. I well remember the long visits I paid to the villages
> during the first weeks; the feeling of hopelessness and despair, after
> many obstinate but futile attempts had entirely failed to bring me
> into real touch with the natives, or supply me with any material. I
> had periods of despondency, when I buried myself in the reading of
> novels, as a man might take to drink in a fit of tropical depression
> and boredom.

Malinowski's romantic enthusiasm for this "new method" radiates
from his account and it is still capable of striking a responsive chord
in anyone who has done fieldwork. He tells us how the anthropologist who lives in the village gets to know the natives, sits and talks
with them as social beings, develops some feeling for native etiquette,
and is present during the intimate scenes of family and community
life. Thus he sees for himself what is going on instead of being told
about it subsequently. But Malinowski does not tell us how or why
he hit upon this radically new procedure; nor does he, so far as I
know, refer to the fact that his method, as such, was novel only to
the academically oriented social anthropologists or sociologists. It
would not have seemed new to Vladimir Bogoras or Marco Polo.

Ironically, in terms of health, temperament, and intellectual background, Malinowski seems to have been particularly unsuited to
undertake the kind of expeditions he lived through and recommended
so highly to others. Neither in his publications nor in his intimate
diary (1967) is there the slightest indication that he ever relished
or even mildly enjoyed any aspect of fieldwork except, perhaps, the
beauty of the landscape. That he managed to endure what he did is
a marvel.

The degree to which Malinowski succeeded in doing all he claimed
to do by living with the natives for an extended period is still a

subject of debate. Nonetheless, his fieldwork won high praise from some of Boas's students. Lowie (1937:231) remarks that Malinowski reformed British field methods and praises his techniques as conforming to Boas's standards because he learnt the Trobianders' tongue, tried to live their life, garnered concrete rather than abstract statements from his informants, and recorded them in the vernacular.

Malinowski also developed what he considered a radically new theoretical approach, which he called functionalism. (The subsequent debates between functionalists and historical conjecturers, between functionalists and the students of Boas, and between functionalist and functionalist need not concern us here.) What I find interesting is the possibility that Malinowski developed this new theoretical school partly as an academic justification for his monumental and, professionally speaking, highly unusual piece of fieldwork. In addition, and much more significantly, Malinowski convinced his social anthropologist colleagues and his students that they ought to do intensive studies of contemporary native communities; that they should and could live in native communities, learn the native language, and penetrate the native "mental attitude." Fired with enthusiasm to explore these new horizons, some of Malinowski's and Radcliffe-Brown's students went into the field and followed this ideal procedure. They and students trained by them produced many of the most valuable and influential ethnographic monographs of the second quarter of the twentieth century.

Only a few of these highly trained and experienced fieldworkers have told us anything about their experiences or their methods. Among these the most notable are the writings of Evans-Pritchard, who in 1940 published a brief but brilliant description of the difficulties he experienced doing fieldwork among the Nuer of Africa in the early 1930s. Later (Evans-Pritchard [1951] 1964) he delivered a series of lectures on social anthropology for the BBC, in the course of which he made some very cogent and illuminating statements about fieldwork. In 1954, Laura Bohannan, using the pseudonym Elenore Smith Bowen, published an account of fieldwork in Africa which has received many favorable comments, although it may be a fictionalized pastiche composed of the tales of several persons and numerous trips. In 1966, Hortense Powdermaker, who studied with Malinowski in the late 1920s, published a detailed description of her four different field investigations, ranging from a study of a Melanesian village (April 1929 to February 1930) to an investigation of the effect of mass media on mine workers in Rhodesia (1953–54). In my opinion, Powdermaker's (1967:138–43) description of how she tried to begin fieldwork in a small town in Mississippi in 1932 is one of the most interesting and valuable accounts of what fieldwork may entail, and I recommend it heartily. In 1969 and 1970, several collections of fieldworkers' accounts of their experiences were published (Freilich 1970) (Golde 1970) (Henry and Saberwal 1969), some of which are very interesting.

PARTICIPANT OBSERVATION AND THE "CHICAGO SCHOOL"

A restless and inquiring man, Robert Ezra Park (1864–1944) had been a journalist and then had reentered the university world, taking an MA in psychology at Harvard and a PhD in philosophy at Heidelberg. After further experiences, particularly with the social situation of American Negroes, he came to the University of Chicago in 1914, where he joined a Department of Sociology that included Albion W. Small and William I. Thomas. Park saw the central focus of his interests as "the frontier" where people of different ethnic stocks fought and mingled, traded and competed; and the most interesting of these frontiers was the city. He sent his students out into the world, and especially into the city, to study at first hand these processes, and this early generation of "Chicagoans" brought back monographs about the (Jewish) ghetto, the taxi-dance hall, the professional thief, the hobo, the boy's gang, and the like.

Also in 1914, W. I. Thomas (1863–1947) began his collaboration with the Polish sociologist Florian Znaniecki in an enterprise that was to lead to the publication of the monumental *The Polish Peasant in Europe and America*. Much of later sociological response to this research has been in terms of its conceptual and theoretical schemes ("attitudes," "values," and so on), and this has had the unfortunate consequence of diminishing interest in (a) the design of the problem, which focused on the lives of Poles both as peasants in the old country and as urban proletarians in the U.S., and (b) the variety of empirical techniques used in the investigation, including the life history and letters. Moreover, considerable practical guidance could be mined from this report by officials concerned with urban welfare and urban planning, while the process of movement from rural peasant conditions to urban slums has continued steadily and all over the world and has presented to each generation of urban officials a similar constellation of difficulties.

Despite their graduate studies in Europe, the researches of Park and Thomas and their students were more closely affiliated to the English investigations of Mayhew, Booth, and the Webbs. The text by the Webbs, *Methods of Social Study* (1932), was assigned by Park to his students (and it may still be read with profit by anyone planning research in modern society). Students were encouraged and expected to get their hands dirty in field experiences. At the same time, and notwithstanding the criticisms of later generations of sociologists, there was not an antipathy to theory. Students were expected to familiarize themselves with the major social theorists of the time (German and French as well as American), as is evident from the contents of the introductory text (1921) assembled by Park and Burgess. Perhaps the difference was that these men were less concerned with sociology as an autonomous and pure science than they were with discovering what was occurring in the world and with utilizing whatever lay to hand in the form of sociological or other concepts in order to analyze it. Park, for example, was very attracted by the conceptual system of ecology, and, while some of his students proceeded to utilize those concepts in a mechanical and shortsighted fashion, some of Park's own essays have genuine value today in a time when ecology has again become a pressing concern of administrators, planners, and intellectuals generally.

One of Park's students, Everett Cherrington Hughes, went to Quebec, where he studied the mingling and conflicting of French and English in the context of a small town that he labeled "Cantonville" (1943). Returning to Chicago in 1938, he too directed his students into field researches within the modern world. Most of these students were taking graduate work as part of the process of social mobility and emancipation from the ethnic groups and occupations of their parents, and together with some of his colleagues Hughes abetted and exploited this process by directing their attention to their social roots. Thus there emerged a sheaf of fascinating reports on ethnic enclaves, on religious communities, and on occupations ranging from janitor to physician.[9] Other students exploited the work they performed in order to earn their way through the graduate program, so that they derived intellectual as well as pecuniary and aesthetic

9. In this respect these Jewish, Negro, Polish, and Japanese sociologists resemble the American Indians whom Boas and his students turned into ethnographic reporters. It must, however, be admitted that the sociologists more frequently were given professional status for their efforts.

39

satisfactions from being jazz musicians or taxi drivers; and still others transformed such apparent disabilities as being a patient confined to a tuberculosis ward into the subject matter of doctoral dissertations.

Park and Thomas had tended to be eclectic in their research techniques, drawing heavily from persons such as Booth and the Webbs, who had made use of both participant observation and survey work with questionnaire schedules. But the rise in reputation of public opinion polling and its close association with academic sociologists such as Paul F. Lazarsfeld and Robert K. Merton provided a major challenge. The disciples of the new survey sample research, with their emphasis upon statistical techniques, formal experimental designs, and mechanical data processing, argued that theirs was the scientific sociology. Moreover, these technical innovations were supported by a reintroduction of continental sociological theory, so that Durkheim's *Suicide,* which had been regarded by Chicagoans as of minor value, being an armchair exercise based on dubious data (cf. Douglas), was now presented as the veritable model for sociological investigation. Faced with this challenge, a cluster of Chicagoans came to scrutinize their methodology more closely and to reconceptualize it around the term "participant observation" (others have spoken of "community study" and still others retain the generic "fieldwork"). Thus, when a cluster of "Chicagoans" (E. C. Hughes, Howard S. Becker, Blanche Geer, Anselm Strauss) produced a study of a medical school, they felt impelled to explain and justify their research procedures, both in journal articles and within the monographic report.

By focusing upon "participant observation," the Chicago sociologists have emphasized their linkage to the tradition of ethnographic fieldwork from Malinowski onward. And they have been led also to seek and reemphasize the uniqueness of subgroups within the modern world. Where survey sample methods are premised on a mass society (mass production, mass media, mass politics), and where its sampling procedures are premised on the notion of individuals as social atoms (to be selected for interviewing as are balls drawn from the statistician's urn), the Chicagoans see natural social groupings, whether residential communities, occupational associations, ethnic enclaves, or total institutions. And they see the sociological fieldworker as embarking on a process of social discovery as he attempts to locate these distinctive microcosms and to enter into them in order to understand and analyze their dynamics. Like Malinowski, they wish to pitch their tents among the dwellings of the natives (even if these be drug addicts, mental patients, medical students, or rabbis).

In speaking as I have of "Chicagoans" and "the Chicago School," I have been engaging in a shorthand that is imprecise. Not all of the Chicago faculty were disciples of this kind of fieldwork, and it is far more accurate to speak of specific men at specific times. More important, the tradition was appealing—even infectious—so that researchers trained elsewhere came to share much of the appreciation of the virtues of fieldwork as a basic research methodology. Where this research was well done (and sometimes it was not), the consequent report had a power and vitality that was influential (see, for example, some of the works of H. S. Becker, E. Goffman, J. Roth, G. D. Suttles, and E. Liebow); critics might contend that the research was the unsystematic product of idiosyncratic genius, but there was no gainsaying the accuracy of the basic findings or the implications for both theory and action. Accordingly, scholars of the caliber of Alvin Gouldner and Maurice Stein came to embrace this research style and to explain, defend, and proselytize it.

But more was involved than the intellectual attractiveness of brilliant research reports. As Malinowski argued, the fieldwork experience itself was transformative. Whatever their graduate training, once men like Maurice Stein or Herbert Gans had personally conducted a field investigation of some depth, they came to have different views of the sociological enterprise. Furthermore, the involvement of the fieldworker undermined his pretence of moral neutrality. After working among opiate addicts, Alfred Lindesmith became a lifelong critic of the harshly repressive laws of the United States and the barbaric procedures of the federal narcotics bureau—just as, at a later date, I and my husband became moral protagonists of Indian communities. This engagement of sociology and moral commitment also proved attractive to some sociology students, while it antagonized those who defined science as pure.

4 The Ambiguities of Fieldwork

It is very difficult to appreciate and understand what goes on in another culture in the terms of the people who live in that culture. It is even more difficult to communicate such an appreciation and understanding—once it is acquired—to members either of one's own culture or of yet a third culture. But it is even more difficult to understand and describe what goes on in a field situation, because many of the most important things that occur are not explicable in terms of the meanings, concepts, or definitions of either culture. One consequence of this is that certain of the more important utterances of fieldworkers about fieldwork may be understood at once by their experienced colleagues, but they may be misleading or ambiguous to inexperienced people who do not know what it is like to live and work in the limbo between two cultures or societies.

IMMERSION

When an experienced participant observer reads that a fieldworker "immerses himself into the native scene" (Lowie 1937:232), "steps into another society" (Powdermaker 1966:19), or becomes "physically and morally a part of the community" (Evans-Pritchard [1951] 1964:77–79), he nods his head in understanding because he knows from personal experience and in depth what these professionals mean by the terms they use. But a person who has never tried to "live with" an alien people does not know what these terms mean, and should he read the existential accounts given us by Whyte, Lowie, Carpenter, and others, he may reasonably conclude that terms like "immersion" or "becoming a member" need a good deal of qualification. For example, a human being may immerse himself in a book, a game of chess, in the study of Arabic, or in a bathtub. He may even, like some great historians, immerse himself in the literature and culture of an ancient people so as to become intimately acquainted with this people's *Weltanschauung* or their world of meanings. But he cannot, by his own will and determination alone, immerse himself in another *living* group or society. If he manages to squeeze, step, or even dip into a group of living people, it is because

42

the people who are already there invite or let him in or, at least, move over and give him a place to stand. Immersion or stepping into, or becoming a member of, a society or culture of living people is always a *joint* process, involving numerous accommodations and adjustments by both the fieldworker and the people who "accept" him.

On another level, many fieldworkers, and especially inexperienced researchers, do "become immersed in" or, perhaps it would be better to say obsessed with the impulse to get themselves totally accepted by, the host people. This, they mistakenly think, is what "developing rapport" means. In extreme form, this obsession may take the form of the fieldworker's trying to divorce himself from his own people and developing the delusion that he is rapidly becoming a native. If there is any value to this practice I have not discovered it. Still, it may be a stage through which novice researchers must pass—just as some adolescents get pimples and some graduate students attack the pet notions of their professors. Perhaps, illusion though it is, the conviction that a fieldworker is "in" may serve as a crutch and comfort during the initial period when he must sometimes live in an almost total social limbo. Later, when he becomes more genuinely "involved," he can dispense with illusions and accept the fact that he is and will always remain a non-native.

There are other and more genuine forms of "immersion." For example, a fieldworker may become so fascinated by the new, exciting, and significant things he is learning, that he may spend months passionately and persistently thinking of nothing else. Simultaneously, he will find himself becoming personally or socially involved in the community, not only because of his developing relationships with acquaintances, employees, and friends, but because, to some degree at least, he is now really beginning to lose touch with his own people and with the world outside. After many months or, perhaps, several years of concentrated study of what was once an "alien community," this activity, for the time being, has become his life. By this time, of course, the community is no longer alien.

The symptoms of this kind of immersion are various. I, for example, find that as soon as I become personally or intellectually involved in a field situation, I cannot concentrate on any problem that does not concern this immediate situation. Each time I have gone into the field I have taken along a box of academic tomes, but I have never read any of them. During the first part of the field trip I was too worried and anxious to concentrate; during the later part I was too busy. My husband, on the other hand, is able to do field-work and also to read and think about many "outside" things. Indeed, at Thrashing Buffalo, during the spells of cold weather that kept us housebound for a week or more, he "surfaced himself" quite easily and rewrote a long paper dealing with a subject which had nothing to do with Indian education. For this feat I still feel a kind of awe.

During my first difficult months at Gila I threw myself so furiously into my attempts to "get data" that I almost forgot the existence of the world outside the center and outside the interests of the Evacuation and Resettlement Study. When the American army invaded Italy, I did not hear the news until a Japanese acquaintance told me about it. This, I realized, was going too far, and I subscribed to a daily newspaper and forced myself to read it at my solitary meals. Twenty years later, when we went to Thrashing Buffalo, I urged my husband to subscribe to a number of newspapers and periodicals. Even so, during the Cold War flareup of late 1962, I was once startled by an Indian grandmother, who, though she could barely speak English, opened our discussion of education by asking in a loud voice, ringing with joyful anticipation: "Has the war started yet?"

There is another and deeper kind of immersion which may occur after a fieldworker has truly become involved with the "living people" in the society he is studying. Indeed, he may be unaware that he is "immersed" until he is given the opportunity to leave the field for a pleasant vacation and finds that he does not want to go. Sometimes, his new and hard-won social ties and relations may mean, or seem to mean, more to him than his ties with his own people. He may even come at times to feel that his own people are "the outsiders." After becoming involved in the political activities at Tule Lake, I found leaving, even for short staff conferences, extremely difficult. Life "outside" had become almost unbearably dull. Leaving Thrashing Buffalo after only seven months of work proved to be almost as much of a wrench, even though I had been complaining loudly and regularly about the "hardships" and the "isolation." William F. Whyte tells us that after he had lived and worked in Cornerville for three years, he applied for another grant of three years, since he felt that there were many important areas of Cornerville life about which he as yet knew little. As Evans-Pritchard remarks, "An anthropologist has failed unless, when he says goodby to the natives there is on both sides the sorrow of parting" ([1951] 1964:77–79).

Perhaps I should digress here to remark that every time I have been in the field and become truly involved I have had to struggle with an impulse to stay longer than I should have stayed. By this I mean that I felt an almost irresistible urge to gather more data rather than face the grim task of organizing and reporting on the data I had. But in every case, the longer I stayed, the less time I had to write, and the poorer became my final report. Indeed, most of the data gathered at the expense of the time I had allowed for writing is still languishing in my files. It is a horrid but inescapable fact that it usually takes *more* time to organize, write, and present material well than it takes to gather it. The notion that one can work in the field for a year and then write a good report while one is carrying a full- or part-time teaching load is idiotic. (People do write in this fashion, but this is one reason why so many monographs are uninspired.) The sensible researcher will allow as much free time to write his report as he spent in the field. If he is really astute and can get away with it, he will allow himself more.

MEMBERSHIP

Some enthusiastic participant observers assert or imply that a field worker must become a member or, at least, a quasi member of the group which he expects to study. Like the notion of immersion, this notion of membership can be ambiguous and misleading. It ignores or glosses over two crucial facts: (1) that it is the group that defines the terms of acceptance or rejection of new members; (2) that groups vary enormously in the ways in and the extent to which they will permit an outsider to "become one of them." In a complex culture there are groups or societies that solicit membership, and a fieldworker will have no trouble at all in becoming a participating member if he is willing to pay the expected price of money or time. There are also many aggregates or categories into which an un-fortunate or unaggressive person may be pushed. Thus, a researcher who loses his job may join the unemployed, he may become sick and study a hospital, he may get himself arrested and imprisoned and study a prison. Complex societies also offer a variety of jobs, occupations, or statuses into which a fieldworker may be admitted in whole or in part, if he learns the ropes, keeps to the codes, and behaves with reasonable circumspection. But they also contain

45

many groups, organizations and professions which grant membership only after a long and arduous apprenticeship (which virtually no fieldworker can endure or afford to undergo), and they contain at least some ethnic and religious groups into which one must be born and reared in order to be accepted as "one of us." Folk or tribal societies may not be quite so complicated, but they vary a great deal in their practices of accepting an outsider as a member. Some peoples seem to have a tolerant or casual attitude toward "outsiders." They may accept a fieldworker, not as one of themselves to be sure, but as an outsider who is willing to learn, understand, and respect their ways. Other tribal societies may permit an outsider to live near or even with them, provided that he comport himself discreetly, like a wise cat in a house full of dogs; but they would consider ludicrous and contrary to nature the idea that he might become "one of them." Still other peoples define any outsider as an enemy, and the fieldworker who tries to push his way in and "join" them is asking for disaster.

Moreover—and this is a point which most people who write about fieldwork do not sufficiently emphasize—many tribal or folk societies not only maintain a strict division of labor between the sexes and ages, but the people who fall into these different categories do not converse freely or spontaneously with each other even when they eat, sleep, and live in the same dwelling. For example, a young male anthropologist might live in an Indian household and even carry on with the Indian girls and yet learn very little about what women—old or young—think, say, or do. Similarly, William Foote Whyte, in his study of a street corner society, seems to have learned a very great deal about the young men, but he tells us virtually nothing about the Italian girls or about local family life. Conversely, I, as a middle-aged woman, was never able to converse openly or informally with either the old or the young Indian men at Thrashing Buffalo. The older men, even when I knew them fairly well, would tend to deliver lectures to me; the younger men, as was proper, were always too bashful or formally respectful to say much. With the Indian matrons, on the other hand, I could talk for hours.

Since this is what groups or societies are like, the researcher who wishes to do at least some participating will do well to bear in mind that the quality and depth of his participation or his "membership" will be determined by a series of understandings, agreements, and new situations, worked out by his hosts and by himself. If he joins a group that welcomes new members, he may find himself pressured into acts or undertakings in which he does not wish to involve himself and find it necessary to insist that he can be only a partial or incomplete participant. If he joins a group that admits useful hangers-on, he may be pressured into roles that contribute very little to his research, for example, rich feast-giver, upaid taxi-driver, pampered and secluded guest. If he tries to obtain membership in an elite group, like physicians, big business executives, Orthodox Jews, or American Indians, he will soon "observe" that most doors are firmly closed in his face. If he is permitted to attach himself to a suppressed, subordinate, or persecuted group, he will find that he must reciprocate by keeping his mouth shut. But whatever the area or depth of his research, he will, as he gains experience and trust, be offered opportunities to enlarge the scope of his participation and his "membership," and this usually means that he will be able to enlarge the scope of his investigation.

IDENTITY

Perhaps the most egregious error that a fieldworker can commit is to assume that he can win the immediate regard of his hosts by telling them that he wants to "become one of them" or by implying, by word or act, that the fact that they tolerate his presence means that he *is* one of them. Indeed, this is the mistake that all experienced fieldworkers warn against.

William F. Whyte ([1943] 1955:304) tells us that early in his investigation he tried to enter into the spirit of his friends' conversation by cutting loose with a string of obscenities and profanity. The boys looked at him in surprise. Doc shook his head and said: "Bill, you're not supposed to talk like that. That doesn't sound like you." "I tried to explain that I was using terms that were common on the street corner. Doc insisted, however, that I was different and they wanted me to be that way."

Powdermaker (1966:263) does not seem to have suffered from the impulse to assume a native identity. But she gives us several examples of how foolish and impractical the notion is. Africans, she emphasizes, do not expect any European to become an African or to follow tribal customs. But they want to be treated "properly," with respect. "The absence of this attitude in many Europeans caused bitterness and hostility." She relates how, on one occasion when she was driving in the compound, the hat of an African riding a bicycle blew off and fell directly in front of her car. She stopped her car, whereupon the African retrieved his hat, saying, "You are a proper European." By proper he meant "someone who treated others with respect and had a sense of etiquette, i.e. politeness and good taste; it was a valued trait in tribal society." She also tells us a pertinent anecdote (1966:119) about a couple of anthropologists who worked in South America:

> The wife decided that she wanted to "go native" and left her husband for a short time to live with an Indian family. She slept in their house, dressed as they did, ate the same food, and, in general, tried to live the native life. At the end of an agreed-upon period, her husband and his colleague called for her. As she climbed into the truck with a sigh of relief, her Indian host winked broadly at her husband. He and his family had been humoring her play-acting.

Ned Polsky, (1967:124) who has done fieldwork among hustlers, beats, and other persons classed as criminals, speaks with even more emphasis against trying to "become one of them":

> In doing field research on criminals you damned well better *not* pretend to be "one of them," because they will test this claim out and one of two things will happen: either you will . . . get sucked into "participant" observation of the sort you would rather not undertake, or you will be exposed, with still greater negative consequences. You must let the criminals know who you are; and if it is done properly . . . , it does not sabotage the research.

William Stringfellow (1966:24–25), a young white lawyer who took up residence in the Harlem slums, tells us that, after he had lived there several weeks, a Negro acquaintance from the neighborhood suggested that they have a cup of coffee. Over the coffee, the Negro remarked that Stringfellow was still shining his shoes. "He said that he knew that this represented the continuation, in my new life in Harlem, of the life that I had formerly lived and he added that he was glad of it, because it meant that I had remained myself and had not contrived to change, just because I had moved into a different environment." Stringfellow interpreted these words to mean that "to be accepted by others, a man must first of all know himself and accept himself and be himself wherever he happens to be. In that way, others are also free to be themselves."

These comments and examples suggest that the wise and well-balanced fieldworker strives to maintain a consciousness and respect for *what he is* and a consciousness and respect for *what his hosts are*.

48

Clumsy and amateurish attempts to alter or adjust his identity make him look silly, phony, and mendacious. Besides, many people will interpret his assurances that he is one of them as rude, presumptuous, insulting, or threatening.

Perhaps good fieldwork is more like play or playacting than most of us are willing to admit. Respondents rarely resent a fieldworker's "acting like them" or "learning their ways" so long as the fieldworker makes it clear that he knows that he is only playing a part and that his newly acquired skills do not entitle him to any privileges which they are not willing to offer him. What people do resent—sometimes very deeply—is the amateurish notion that the acquisition of a few tricks or a sentimental statement about universal brotherhood will, almost automatically, turn a clumsy and ignorant outsider into an experienced, hardened, expert, or sacred person like themselves.

Among our acquaintances are a number of men who have put much effort into establishing an identity as an American Indian. They convince many white people that they are Indians, but, rarely, if ever, do they convince the Indians. The latter tell humorous anecdotes about them and laugh behind their backs. Ironically, another white man, married to an Indian woman, is sometimes affectionately called an Indian by his Indian relatives (Wax, Wax, and Dumont 1964:56), for, though he makes no claims to Indian status, he talks to all of the Indians in friendly and unassuming fashion. Indeed, his mother-in-law remarks that he is "just as much an Indian" as her daughter "even though he is a white man."

The disposition to assume an identity with the people of quite a different society or culture is, I suspect, related to the fact that our complex contemporary culture contains so many groups or societies that permit or encourage "joining" or voluntary membership. Besides, our notion of progress is closely related to the notion that man changes his "self" (though not his identity), and from infancy we are taught not only that we can but that we must change and "develop" ourselves. In consequence—even if we take many courses in anthropology or sociology—it is difficult for most of us to grasp the point of view of peoples who are unable to conceive of the idea of the changing self.[1] On the other hand, many of the young people in our contemporary society are undergoing "a crisis of identity"

1. Illuminating discussions of conceptions of the self may be found in Lee (1949) and Wright (1966).

and do not know what they are. Some of these young folk search for their missing sense of identity in a strange or alien group. To what degree their search helps them I do not know. But I doubt that it helps the host group or contributes much to a general knowledge and understanding of mankind.

ATTACHED OR INSTRUMENTAL MEMBERSHIP

With rare exceptions a fieldworker cannot become an autochthonous, aboriginal, or organic member of a tribal or ethnic group. Nor, except in rare cases, can he slip neatly into a long-established traditional role. Nevertheless, there is a special sense in which a fieldworker who lives near or with the people he is studying does become a member of the group. But what he becomes is an attached or instrumental member, a person who, though he always *is* and *remains* an outsider or non-native, may function *in the society* in a manner that is useful and agreeable to his hosts. An excellent example of this kind of instrumental membership is the case of Peter Freuchen. Freuchen lived with the Eskimos, off and on, for half a century. He took an Eskimo wife and had children by her. His Eskimo "friends" called him "the man who thinks for us," and, in many ways, treated him as *if* he were one of them. He played many useful roles in the community, serving his hosts as trader, explorer, arbitrator, and as mediator between them and the white men. But these roles, it should be noted, were not those of the traditional Eskimo man. Nor is there any indication in Freuchen's voluminous writings that the Eskimo ever came to regard him as a fellow Eskimo or that he ever thought of himself as an Eskimo.

An extremely perceptive and helpful discussion of what it means to be an attached member, a friend, but always an outsider, is given us by Elliot Liebow in his study of Negro street corner men. He tells us (1967:248–51) that the

> brute fact of color, as they understood it in their experience and as I understood it in mine, irrevocably and absolutely relegated me to the status of outsider. I am not certain, but I have a hunch that they were more continuously aware of the color difference than I was. . . .
>
> Whenever the fact of my being white was openly introduced, it pointed up the distance between me and the other person, even when the intent of introducing it was, I believe, to narrow that distance. . . .
>
> Once I was with Richard in his hometown. It was his first visit in five years. We arrived in the middle of the night and had to leave before daybreak because Richard was wanted by the local police. We were in his grandmother's house. Besides Richard, there were his

grandmother, his aunt, and two unrelated men, both long-time friends of Richard.

The group was discussing the possibility of Richard's coming home to stay and weighing the probable consequences. In the middle of the discussion, Richard interrupted and nodded at me. "Now Ellix here is white, as you can see, but he's one of my best friends. Him and me are real tight. You can say anything you want, right to his face. He's real nice." "Well," said his Aunt Pearl, "I always did say there are some nice white people."

Though Murray and I lived on the Thrashing Buffalo reservation for only seven months, our Indian neighbors gently or not so gently nudged us into roles for which, in their opinion, we were particularly suited. To begin with, of course, we were "claimed" by one family and propelled into the already well-established role of white thrill seekers or Indian lovers who would pay their hosts large sums of money for the opportunity to participate in "genuine fullblood life." Having escaped from this cul-de-sac, we were "adopted" by and established a more edifying relationship with one of the reputable families of the community, playing the role of eccentric but reasonably decent employers. Other reputable and not so reputable families then made overtures to us, letting us know that they too had bright sons or daughters who knew how to type or who had graduated from high school. We hired some of these young people as we needed them, and if this caused any conflict within the community, we did not hear of it. (Though had we given a good job to any rival of the ChargingBear family there might have been trouble.) Other families called on us, sometimes as a formal courtesy, sometimes out of curiosity, and more frequently to sell us beadwork. We bought a good deal of beadwork, partly because our neighbors needed a little cash, and our purchases were a way by which we could share our wealth and yet maintain a principle of reciprocity. Besides, the beadwork was often very beautiful. We also learned much because we attended most of the ceremonial events, dances, weddings, bingo parties, giveaways, and even the forty-year-old movies (which were shown by an itinerant missionary lady from the Crow reservation). We were tolerably welcome at these events because we minded our manners, did not "poke fun" (laugh at Indian ways), were not shocked by bingo playing or lively jokes, and because, like well-mannered rich visitors, we shared with the community by making seemly gifts and contributions. Besides, by attending these affairs we showed our respect for the community and unostentatiously demonstrated that we were not like "the other stuck-up white people and mixedbloods" who pointedly avoided appearing at fullblood ceremonials or events. In a sense, Murray came, in a small way, to act as a "chief" in the traditional Indian pattern of patronage, but not, of course in the sense of the moral leader or organizer. He also began to be approached by people in the community who wanted expert advice on how their children, now in high school, might obtain the kind of higher education they desired, for this, everyone conceded, was the area in which he was truly knowledgeable.

We also learned much because we allowed the schoolchildren of our local community to wait inside our house for the school bus. They soon began to arrive long before the bus was due, and they often stopped in for a return visit in the afternoon. These visits were sometimes hard on us, but they provided an opportunity to observe the children in a situation where no adult was organizing or controlling them. We also learned many interesting things because we were the only white people for miles around who would let Indian neighbors use their telephone. In this way we were apprised of local scandals, travels, and accidents (though of course I learned most of these through visiting the women), and we were also able to observe how the fullblood Indians use the Indian police force. On the other hand, we learned relatively little by functioning as chauffeur for some of our neighbors, though our willingness to pick up people and help them in an emergency gave us a general reputation as generous folk, and the Thrashing Buffalo, unlike some other peoples, do not despise casual or unconditional generosity.

ROLE PLAYING

Some experienced fieldworkers speak of role playing in fieldwork as if the fieldworker's roles were ready and waiting for him in the society he wishes to study. All he has to do is find the roles and "assume" them. In point of fact, in the field, many of the researcher's most useful roles are spontaneously invented and developed by the combined efforts of his respondents and himself. These new relationships are sometimes peculiar or even fantastic, and they rarely fit precisely into the social structure of either of the participants. But hybrid devices though they may be, they serve as social ties which the involved parties find mutually profitable and satisfactory.[2]

2. Readers interested in this point will enjoy a perceptive article by R. O. Haak (1970). Haak suggests that "when groups are forced into confrontation

I would not have been able to do fieldwork in Gila and Tule Lake if my respondents and I had not been able, jointly, to invent and maintain many of these relationships. Some Japanese Americans felt more comfortable if they could treat me like a sympathetic newspaper reporter. I knew very little about how a reporter behaved (indeed, I had never seen or spoken with one), but I responded and we were able to converse more easily. In Tule Lake the super-patriots and agitators found it easier to talk to me once they had convinced themselves that I was a German "Nisei," "full of the courageous German spirit." I found this fantasy personally embarrassing, but I did not make a point of denying my German ancestry. Finally, I was not a geisha, even though a shrewd Issei once suggested that it was because I functioned as one that I was able to find out so much of what happened at Tule Lake. His explanation was that Japanese men—and especially Japanese politicians—do not discuss their plans or achievements with other men or with their wives, but they are culturally conditioned to speak of such matters with intelligent and witty women. Though vanity has tempted me to accept the Issei's hypothesis, I think it would be more accurate to say that the Japanese agitators and I developed a new role which fitted their temperaments and mine. This role had no precise place in either the Japanese or the American culture, but in Tule Lake it permitted us to converse with considerable mutual satisfaction and enlightenment.

During the course of my fieldwork, respondents and I have spontaneously constructed many of these mutually profitable roles. But the experience I remember most vividly is one that occurred before I attended a university or became interested in anthropology.

During the depression, from about 1930 to 1938, my family—two brothers, two sisters, my mother, and myself—lived in a Mexican neighborhood in Los Angeles. We met several pleasant Mexican youths at a settlement house and invited them to join us at our house for some sessions of poker. We played for stakes of atomic minuteness, but even so, we soon became aware that our new friends were cheating. Embarrassed, we pointed out that we didn't play that

---

each takes what it needs from that confrontation and does not perceive it in the same way even when both are moving toward a satisfactory rapprochement. Far from representing this as a lapse in communication, I would generalize that a happy outcome requires each faction to salvage its self-esteem under the common umbrella of mutual misunderstanding."

way. The Mexican boys smiled amiably and said, "But this is the way we always play. We can't play any other way." So we *gringos* held a discussion and decided that we too would cheat. But this worked out very badly for us because we were very clumsy cheaters. Besides, we had played our kind of poker for so long that we could not really enjoy cheating even when we got away with it. So we held another discussion. This time the Mexican boys suggested that we all play as usual. They would cheat with might and main and we would play fair. But if one of us caught one of them cheating, the catcher would get all the cheater's chips. This new set of rules worked marvelously well. The Mexicans outdid themselves in clever deceptions, and we, in the course of many sessions, became phenomenally expert at detecting "aberrations" in their play. Best of all, the new system evened out the odds, so that neither of us won consistently from the other. Occasionally, fascinating moral dilemmas arose. Our dog once snapped at the seat of a Mexican youth's pants just as he was sliding an ace between himself and his chair. My sister contended that she should get the pot by reason of the alertness of our dog; the Mexican youth contended that she ought to be penalized because her dog had not behaved like a sportsman. The debate was so wonderfully entertaining and lasted so long a time that I do not remember how it was resolved.

I do not intend to suggest that roles in most field situations are developed as easily and with as much open discussion as was the procedure in this culturally mixed poker game. Nevertheless, the fundamental principles and mutual assumptions of both situations are similar. While the two parties may be willing to play together, yet each carries with himself a set of habits or skills that he is unwilling or unable to abandon. The very process of their interaction may lead to the emergence of a new game with new rules. (The situation in a cross-cultural schoolroom or in cross-cultural medical practice seems to me to be quite similar. Dumont [1971] remarks that, in a successful classroom, "cooperaton was lodged within this framework and the development of it required an environment in which choice and compromise was the norm." See also Marriott [1955].)

Perhaps the most useful thing to say about involvement, membership, or role playing in an alien community is that the value of a role, for the participant observer or social scientist, does not depend on its traditional genuineness or *Echtheit* but on the vantage point that it gives to the observer or participant who plays it. If the role gives him the opportunity to observe what he wishes to observe, to communicate with and understand the people about whom he wishes to learn, in a manner and fashion to which they do not object, it is a *good* role.

PART TWO

Fieldwork in the Japanese American Relocation Centers, 1943-1945

5   Background

In the spring following the Japanese attack on the U.S. fleet at Pearl Harbor, all of the Japanese Americans residing on the Pacific Coast were incarcerated by order of the U.S. government. Numbering some 110,000 persons, and consisting both of citizens and enemy nationals, these people constituted a vexatious problem for governmental and military authorities. They had not committed any acts of treason or espionage, and indeed there was never any evidence that they included in their ranks any individuals who contemplated such activities, but they were the object of venomous propaganda from powerful political organizations, politicians, and newspaper columnists,[1] and their removal and incarceration was more a capitulation to the anti-Japanese campaigners than it was a rational assessment of military necessities. After keeping them jammed in assembly centers in California, the authorities decided to ship them to relocation centers in isolated sections of the West and Midwest until circumstances should permit their release or some other expedient should present itself.

These people were not inclined to welcome the presence of a fieldworker who wished to record their opinions, words, or deeds. Citizen or alien, they had been forced to leave their homes and occupations and to remain in confinement behind barbed wire fences patrolled by armed soldiers. They had been slandered and vilified in the press. Many had suffered irreparable economic losses. On

This narrative contains only those parts of the history of the evacuation essential to an understanding of the problems entailed in doing fieldwork in this situation. For a full account see Thomas and Nishimoto (1946), Grodzins (1949), R. H. Wax (1950), U.S. Army (1943).

1. Henry McLemore suggested in the San Francisco Examiner of January 29, 1942: "Herd 'em up, pack 'em off and give 'em the inside room in the badlands. Let 'em be pinched, hurt, hungry and dead against it . . . let us have no patience with the enemy or with anyone whose veins carry his blood. . . . Personally, I hate the Japanese. And that goes for all of them." Westbrook Pegler on February 16, 1942, urged that "the Japanese in California should be under armed guard to the last man and woman right now and to hell with habeas corpus until the danger is over." (See also Thomas and Nishimoto 1946, pp. 17–20, and Grodzins 1949.)

arrival at the relocation centers, they found that the "apartments" provided by the War Relocation Authority (WRA), the civilian organization set up to administer the centers, consisted of one barn-like room, twenty feet square, within which families of six to eight people were to live. Having been instructed to sell their furniture, they found that the only furnishings provided were an unshaded electric drop light and one army cot per person. Forbidden to cook in their apartments, they were offered cheaply prepared, wartime, institutional food within the mess halls attached to each "block" of barracklike apartments. A public latrine was provided for each block, but there were no partitions between the toilet stools. In time, some of these basic physical discomforts were mitigated. People built furniture from packing boxes, put up partitions in the latrines, and even cooked in their apartments when they could get away with it. But insofar as center life developed a pattern, it was a pattern of constriction, monotony, and exasperating, petty discomforts, broken at intervals by a humiliating experience with a Caucasian supervisor or social worker, or by some new bureaucratic foul-up— as when stoves for heating the evacuee apartments did not arrive until winter was well under way.

More subtle irritations were provided by the WRA's attempt to instruct the Japanese Americans in the principles and practices of democracy and community government. In each center the residents were invited to elect a representative council, but with the humilitating proviso that they elect only Nisei, that is, Japanese Americans born in the United States. Since the Nisei constituted the younger generation and were, in the main, youthful and inexperienced, it was insulting that they be set in authority over their elders; but, of course, the deeper truth was that the center administrations had no intentions of giving the evacuee councils any power. Consequently, the young men who took office found themselves in the uncomfortable position of lacking status in the eyes both of the residents and of the WRA. Meanwhile, any evacuee who bought and read newspapers (radios were forbidden) could learn that the armed forces of Japan were proceeding from victory to victory, and they would also learn that some American columnists felt that "the dirty Japs in the centers" were being coddled, when they ought, by rights, to be beaten and starved.

In this situation, most of the Japanese Americans tended to view their future with what today would be called a wait-and-see attitude:

they decided to say little, be prudent, offend neither the Japanese nor the American government, and see how things turned out. Many of the younger people remained openly and passionately attached to the United States. Many of the older people retained a sentimental attachment to their native land, and a few of them openly expressed their allegiance to Japan and saw their future, such as it was, in a return to their country. Most people, however, waited and vacillated, swayed by events, news, and rumors, but preferring to keep their opinions within the small circle of people they could trust.

Had I, like the other research assistants hired by the study, entered the centers at the beginning of the evacuation (early 1942), I would have found fieldwork difficult. But I started work in July of 1943, after the evacuees had been subjected to experiences which made fieldwork by an outsider almost impossible. The most important of these experiences was the so-called *registration,* the attempt on the part of the U.S. army and the WRA to separate the "good Japanese" (those willing to assert that they were loyal to the United States) from the "bad Japanese" (those willing to assert that they were loyal to Japan).

What happened was something like this.[2]

The army had moved the Japanese into centers distant from the Pacific Coast. The WRA, bearing in mind what had happened to the federal government in the case of the American Indians, now devoted itself to getting the Japanese out of the centers. The idea was to relocate the "good Japanese" to areas of the country other than the Pacific Coast. But the problem was how to convince the American public that the people being "released" or "relocated" were "good" and "loyal" Japanese, and that, conversely, all the "bad" or "disloyal" Japanese were being safely confined until they could be sent back to Japan.

By the spring of 1943, a year after the evacuation, the various authorities had devised a plan. All of the evacuees eighteen years of age or older were to be required to fill out a questionnaire prepared by the U.S. army. Citizens, both male and female, were asked whether they would be willing to serve in the armed forces of the

2. For a detailed account of the registration and subsequent segregation, see Thomas and Nishimoto (1946: 53–112. See also Morris Opler's outstanding unpublished report, "Studies of Segregants at Manzanar," available at the Bancroft Library at the University of California at Berkeley.

United States and whether they would foreswear any allegiance to the Japanese emperor. Noncitizens were asked to swear unqualified allegiance to the United States and foreswear any allegiance to the Japanese emperor. Apparently the authorities assumed that almost all the evacuees would answer these questions in the affirmative and that this display of loyalty would make a wholesome impression on the American public. Then the young male evacuees could be drafted into the U.S. army, and their families moved to civilian areas where they might contribute to the war effort. The relocation centers and the barbed wire could be torn down, and the soldiers who now guarded the centers could be sent to more useful stations. The few evacuees who refused to declare themselves loyal to the United States would be moved to a separate detention center under the jurisdiction of the Department of Justice and, hopefully, shipped to Japan as soon as possible.

But this well-intentioned plan went awry. In many centers the demand for an unequivocal commitment—to the United States or to Japan—resulted in an uproar. Spontaneous mass meetings were held at which some of the younger people argued passionately that the only sensible policy was to express loyalty to the United States. Other Nisei were quick to point out that the intent of the questionnaire was "to draft us from behind the barbed wire." Issei (first generation) pointed out that if they renounced their allegiance to the emperor they would be people without a country, for the United States had forbidden them to apply for American citizenship. Some persons held that the evacuees ought to refuse to express loyalty to the United States until the United States gave an indication that it would make amends. Tension and hostility rose so high that in some centers (including the Gila center, where I began my fieldwork) a few men who expressed strong "pro-American" views were waylaid at night and beaten. The authorities thereupon arrested the most vocal of those who spoke against the questionnaire and removed them to a separate detention center managed by the Department of Justice. Immediately rumors circulated that these men had been betrayed to the administrators by *inu* ("dog," i.e. "stool pigeon"), and, correctly or incorrectly, various unfortunates were branded as the informers.

To be stigmatized as an *inu* brought social ostracism, which, in the crowded and confined life of the centers, was painful in the extreme. A suspected man, seating himself in the mess hall, was met with an uncomfortable silence and meaningful glances. If he entered a latrine or boiler room, the common gathering places for gossip and discussion, friendly talk or argument ceased with his appearance. Because of the lack of privacy imposed by camp conditions, he could find no escape and was reminded of his despised status many times a day. Moreover, camp life offered almost no resources in which an ostracized individual might find temporary escape. The administration frowned on fraternization between Caucasian staff members and the Japanese. Marked friendliness with Caucasians would, in any case, corroborate the suspicions of the community. When tension between the administration and the residents became grave, the man marked as *inu* was liable to be attacked and beaten. Understandably, most people avoided doing or saying anything which might cause them to be suspected of being *inu*.

Needless to say, any person who claimed to be a research worker and not a WRA staff member was almost certain to be taken for a federal investigator looking for people who expressed "un-American" or "pro-Japanese" sentiments. Any Japanese who talked to such a person would put himself in danger of being called an *inu*.

After two or three months, excitement began to die down. Some young men who had boldly expressed their loyalty to the United States volunteered for service in the army. Their families were among the first to be permitted to "relocate"—to leave the centers for those parts of the United States where Japanese were allowed to reside. Thus, the people who remained in the centers when I arrived were the large body of less venturesome "loyals," most of whom wished "to sit here quietly in the center for a while," plus, of course, those "disloyal" folk who had said "no" to the army questionnaire.

Like many fieldworkers I went into the field ill prepared, technically and intellectually. I was hired to work as a participant observer in one of the relocation centers, but I knew very little about the Japanese—American or otherwise—and I had not, in college or university, learned a blessed thing about how to study living, breathing, and thinking people. The director of the study was a sociologist, a specialist in rural sociology, demography, and statistics. What she wanted from me, as an employee, was detailed accounts of what the detained Japanese Americans were doing and detailed—if possible, verbatim—accounts of what they were saying. I, on the other hand, had never read or been told anything about participant observation or interviewing, had never heard of symbolic interaction, social structure, value systems, or ambivalence, and did not know even the rudiments of statistical method. What I did know something about was diffusion, invention, kinship systems, and "primitive" societies. I had also read Darwin, Tylor, Morgan, Boas, Coon, Childe, and, of course, Kroeber and Lowie. With the help of a fellow graduate student in anthropology I had collected a great many variants of a current ghost story and had even published a paper. But these experiences were not of much value in understanding life in the detention centers, and, besides, whenever I tried to put them to use, the director of the study, Dorothy Swaine Thomas, made discouraging and sometimes even caustic comments.

What had fitted me well for fieldwork was my pre-college life experiences. For eight years, from age twenty to twenty-eight, I had lived through the Great Depression. I had solicited and done housework by the day, applied for and received relief (a gunny sack of starchy groceries per week), worked on several WPA projects, and with my family I had lived for eight years in one of the Mexican-American slums of Los Angeles. During this period I had come to accept hard work as one of the essential elements of life and I had also developed an imperviousness to obstacles, disappointments, and discouragements. If I thought a task worth doing and finishing, I would stick with it.

When I completed junior college (at about age twenty-seven), I applied for and received a tiny Phoebe Hearst scholarship to the University of California at Berkeley. At Berkeley, Professor Lowie was cordial and kind to me. When he helped me register, he chuckled, and asked me why my grades ranged from *A* in physics to *D* in hockey. At first I saw very little of Professor Kroeber. This was my doing, because some of the graduate students talked a good deal about Kroeber's hostility to the idea of women becoming anthropologists. According to this gossip, Kroeber discouraged women graduate students because jobs were hard to get—even for men. The prospect of not getting a job did not bother me because I was used to it. But I kept away from Kroeber for a year or so because I was afraid he would tell me to get out of the department. When I did take courses with him, I worked like a demon and he seemed to find my phenomenal energy both baffling and amusing. He never made an attempt to discourage my interest in anthropology.

The Japanese bombed Pearl Harbor during my first semester of graduate work. Most of the male graduate students entered the armed services, and I myself might have become an officer in the Waves, as they wanted a qualified woman to write naval history, but I was rejected because my eyesight was not 20–20. This irritated me, not because I wanted the job but because I hated to be rejected as a physically inferior being. Though I continued to work very hard, I became increasingly restless and reckless. In consequence, when, in the spring of 1943 Kroeber called me to his office and told me that I might wish to apply for a position as research worker in the Japanese relocation centers, I was much attracted by the idea.

What happened was this. When the evacuation of the Japanese Americans had been proposed, a group of social scientists had seen in it a splendid opportunity for interdisciplinary research. Social anthropologists, political scientists, social psychologists, and economists at the University of California had cooperated in a research proposal and received generous financial support (Thomas and Nishimoto, 1946). But the war gradually drew all of the male planners out of the study, and its directorship fell upon Dorothy Swaine Thomas, who was then a lecturer in sociology for the Gianini foundation and a professor of rural sociology. All but one of the fieldworkers for the study had been recruited from Japanese American students, who were themselves about to undergo relocation and confinement. The one exception was Robert Spencer, then a graduate student in the Department of Anthropology. Spencer had resigned, and it was for his job that I applied.

I prepared for my entrance into the field by listening to the advice and instruction given by Dr. Thomas, reading the field notes submitted by the field assistants, and enrolling in a course in the Japanese language. As things turned out, none of these was particularly helpful. The one point that Dr. Thomas made perfectly clear was that I was on no account to give any information or "data" to the WRA. (Some of the Japanese fieldworkers employed by the study had been accused by their fellow evacuees of being informers or "spies for the administration." Some were made so uncomfortable that they left the centers soon after the registration crisis.) As for the field notes, they were so voluminous and various that they bewildered me. The teacher of the language course was a Korean (all Japanese being gone) who taught us to write *Kanji* and speak a few words in a Korean accent.

When I paid my farewell call on Professor Kroeber, he asked me whether I knew anyone in the centers and whether there was anyone to whom I could go if I needed help. I told him cheerfully that Mr. Spencer had recommended two of his Japanese informants and a friendly WRA staff worker. This did not seem to impress Kroeber very much. He emphasized several times that the heat of the southern Arizona desert in July would be like nothing I had ever experienced and that it might well make me ill. He warned me about the dysentery and asked if I were taking along proper medicines. But I was bursting with real and assumed enthusiasm and told him that I was taking along a bottle of vitamin B tablets, which would help me adjust to the heat. "I think you may need more than vitamin B," said Kroeber. Professor Kroeber, I now suspect, was dubious about my taking this assignment, not because he doubted my capabilities, but because he felt responsible for me and had the insight and experience to see that the task would be terribly difficult. I, on the other hand, felt a little offended that Kroeber should choose to talk about such mundane matters as heat, dysentery, and loneliness, instead of sending me off with words of profound intellectual counsel and inspiring cheer.

I knew, of course, that the living conditions at the Gila center would be unpleasant. Dr. Thomas and Mr. Spencer had warned me that the food—even in the Caucasian mess halls—was "awful." Kroeber had warned me that the heat would be extreme. I did not know a living soul—either on the WRA staff or among the evacuees. But I was determined to endure these unpleasantnesses, make friends and acquaintances, find or make a reasonably comfortable place to live, and proceed with my work.

I arrived in Phoenix, Arizona, early in the morning and stepped off an air-conditioned train into an early morning temperature of 110°. I found that the bus to Sacaton—a hamlet in the desert where I was to be picked up by a truck and conveyed to the camp—did not leave until the early afternoon. Having little money, I carried my bags the mile to the bus station and sweltered there as the temperature gradually rose to 120°. Finally, the bus—an extraordinary vehicle, resembling the ramshackle affairs in which migrant agricultural workers are transported—took off, bearing me and four or five rotund Pima Indians to Sacaton, an area marked by an abandoned gas station and nothing else save a large building (an Indian school) in the distance. The Indians walked off, and I sat down in a tiny but all-important bit of shade on the dirty cement stoop of the defunct gas station. After a while, a great dust cloud appeared in the distance. From it emerged a GI truck driven by a Japanese American who had been sent to pick me up. Since I had not talked to a soul all day, I tried to tell the truck driver why I had come to the Gila center and something about my job. He answered in curt mono-syllables or grunts which seemed to imply that it was none of his business why I had come there. So I turned my attention to the landscape. It looked like the skin of some cosmic reptile, an ocean of coarse grit, studded at repulsively regular intervals with regularly shaped projections. Some people might call them hills. Every stone, every piece of cactus, looked bleached and tired. The sky also looked bleached and tired. After some twenty hot, dusty, and identical miles we came to a barbed wire cattle fence outside of which (I later learned) the Japanese Americans were forbidden to go—unless, of course, they had a special pass as did the man who had come after me. After several additional delays we arrived at the administrative offices of the WRA. Here I was instructed that no quarters were available in the particular camp Dr. Thomas wished me to study, so that, like it or not, I would have to live in the other and smaller camp, six miles away. (The Gila center at this time numbered about twelve thousand persons. It was divided into two "camps"—a larger one where Mr. Spencer had carried on the work I was supposed to continue and a smaller one where the WRA administration had put me.) I knew that this would not suit Dr. Thomas at all and that I would somehow have to get into the larger camp. But since I had to have a place to sleep that night, I waited in stupified resignation for another army truck and, in a heat I now found incredible, I was driven to the staff quarters of the smaller camp. This proved to be an army barracks building sub-divided into tiny cells. Since no one was around, all the staff still being at work, I found the cell assigned to me by a process of elimination.

It contained four dingy and dilapidated articles of furniture: an iron double bedstead, a dirty mattress (which took up more than half the room), a chest of drawers, and a tiny writing table—and it was hotter than the hinges of Hades. Since there was no one around to ask where I might get a chair, I sat down on the hot mattress, took a deep breath, and cried. I was too far gone to be consciously aware

that I was isolated or to wonder why I had left a beautiful and comfortable university town to stick myself in this oven of a concentration camp. Like some lost two-year-old I only knew that I was
miserable. After a while, I found the room at the end of the barrack
that contained two toilets and a couple of wash basins. I washed my
face and told myself I would feel better the next day. I was wrong.

6   I Begin to Work

Several things might have helped ease the trouble that lay ahead of me. Had I been more experienced, I would have realized that I had three, four, or perhaps even five months of uncomfortable and frustrating resocialization ahead of me before I could expect to function as even a clumsy or pseudo-participant observer in this particular situation.[1] I might also have understood how the Japanese felt about their future and I would not have expected them to talk to me about "loyalty" or "disloyalty" in a frank or open fashion. Had Dr. Thomas understood either of these matters, she might not have kept asking me, with a regularity I found dismaying, why I was not sending her the kind of voluminous data about attitudes and events that she desired.

As it was, I called first on a few high-ranking WRA officials, introduced myself, and learned that there was an administrative regulation forbidding evacuees to visit the staff barracks. This meant that I would have to seek out my informants in their own quarters or in the administrative offices in which they worked. Next I called on the Issei informant who had been recommended by Mr. Spencer. He proved to be a solemn and worried man, and he made a few guarded remarks which I carefully noted down and sent to Dr. Thomas. (He never did help me very much, and I found out later he was suspected of being an *inu*. Moreover, the study had been paying him a small stipend, which was cut off when I began to work.) Next I called on the WRA staff worker recommended by Mr. Spencer as a person of sensitivity and insight. He was a tall, nervous-looking man, who invited me to his apartment to meet his wife. But when I arrived, he sent his wife out on an errand and began to pat me on the rump. I did not like this man, and so I lost another potential informant.

1. A first-rate discussion of difficult field situations has just been published by Berk and Adams in an article entitled "Establishing rapport with deviant groups." Students may find it useful to compare the advice given in this article with my experiences when I first tried to study the suspicious and fearful Japanese Americans.

During the succeeding weeks I did my level best to strike up an acquaintance with any Japanese who would exchange a few words with me. I introduced myself as a student of anthropology, working for a group of professors who had no connection with the administration. I explained that the object of my employers was to obtain and publish a true picture of the evacuation and of life within the centers. I emphasized the confidential nature of "our data" and added a description of some phase of the study which was likely to meet with the approval of my listeners, for example, that a study of Japanese financial losses due to evacuation was under consideration.

I knew that the status of student carried considerable prestige with the Japanese, and I anticipated that the academic objective would meet with approval, reasoning that the evacuees would be pleased with a correction of the inaccuracies previously published by ill-informed and prejudiced persons. Above all, I expected that the fact that the study had no connection with the WRA administration would facilitate gaining rapport. Most people listened politely but did not say anything. When I asked a specific question about attitudes in the center, they professed ignorance or made bland and innocuous comments. Thus, at the conclusion of a month of work I had obtained almost no data of the type that Dr. Thomas considered valuable. Indeed, the only person in the entire center who talked at all openly with me was Gordon Brown, an anthropologist who, like myself, had just arrived to do work very similar to mine, but for the WRA administration.

I discussed my difficulties in obtaining "data" with Dr. Brown, who had done fieldwork in Africa and Samoa. He laughed at my conscientiousness, pointing out that he was obtaining even less "data" than I. Nevertheless, I knew that I was not conforming to Dr. Thomas's expectations and I became very discouraged and depressed. I became even more depressed when I received a letter from Berkeley instructing me to avoid too close an association with Dr. Brown or his wife lest they get my "data" and pass it on to the administration.

In mid-July of 1943 the WRA issued an administrative instruction stating that all the "disloyal" evacuees were to be removed from the relocation centers and segregated in the Tule Lake center in northern California. It was my task to find out and record how the "loyals" or "yes-yes," as they called themselves, felt about the imminent segregation and to observe and record their behavior before, during, and after this event. (As for the "disloyals" or "no-noes," I do not recall being given any instruction. It is my impression that we assumed they would be so bitter and alienated that they would not talk to a stranger.) What none of us experienced and inexperienced social scientists understood or, perhaps, cared to face up to, was that it was precisely the people now defined as "loyal" who had good reason to fear that an honest expression of sentiment or opinion might get them into serious trouble.

Nevertheless, I did my inexperienced best. All day long I approached people, explained my job, exchanged some polite remarks, and then asked them what they thought about the impending segregation. At this point most of them looked sad or uncomfortable and remarked that they did not know any of "those people" well. Some looked down and said it was a sad or unfortunate business. Being a raw newcomer, terribly anxious to behave like a social scientist, I did not realize that it was stupid and callous to ask these harassed folk to express their views about the United States to a stranger who might well be a "spy for the administration." Nor had I yet begun to grasp what the segregation meant to most of these people: that they had gambled their own and their children's future on cards which would not be turned up till the end of the war; that many of them had quarreled bitterly with friends and relatives who held different views and from whom they were now parted; that many of them, even now, were by no means certain that in asserting their loyalty to the United States they had made the wise decision. On the other hand, I was not so insensitive that I did not perceive that most of the people with whom I tried to scrape up an acquaintance were troubled in mind and wanted to be left alone. But if I acted like a decent human being and left them alone, how was I to earn my salary as a researcher?

Week followed week without any noticeable improvement in my "rapport" or my reports. Every letter I received from Dr. Thomas made it clear that I was not doing what she expected me to do. There was no one I could talk to in any meaningful fashion—except Dr. Brown to whom I was not supposed to talk—and after about two months I began to see myself as a total failure. The anxiety I suffered was so agonizing that I still find it hard to describe. Every time I returned to my stifling room after a series of futile "interviews," I sat down and cried. I took long walks in the desert in temperatures of 110°–120°, and cried. For several weeks, I refused to associate with the Caucasian staff members, hoping that this rudeness to members of the administration would make me more acceptable to the Japanese. I welcomed the administration's request that I move from the overcrowded staff dormitory to a room in the ruder type of barracks assigned to the Japanese. This cut me off still more sharply from the staff and gave me the opportunity to share what I conceived to be the discomforts of my "informants": the incredible heat of the barracks rooms, where one often could not fall asleep till two or three in the morning; the mosquitoes that entered, since the unscreened doors and windows had to be opened at night if one was to sleep at all; a severe attack of dysentery with the latrine a block distant. Though I was far from stoical about these hardships, I took a masochistic satisfaction in them, naïvely hoping that my misery would increase my rapport with the Japanese Americans. Meanwhile, I fought a losing battle with an obsessive desire to eat. For several weeks I alternately stuffed and starved myself. Finally I surrendered and ate almost all the time—good meals, poor meals, cans of spam, stale cookies, warm soda pop, whole boxes of crackers bought at the PX; anything remotely digestible went inside to fill the void that stretched around me. That the temperature might stand at 120° did not mitigate my appetite. I ate in a kind of desperation—until the sweat rolled down my face and body. In three months I gained thirty pounds.

In late August, a few weeks before the actual segregation took place, I ran into Dr. Brown. (He was always jovial and friendly to me, though I, following instructions, was always, at this time, curt and close-mouthed with him.) Brown remarked that he himself was learning a good deal about how the "loyals" and "disloyals" felt by attending the hearings to which some of the avowedly disloyal were being subjected. (These hearings were designed to give some of the potential segregants the opportunity to recant.) Brown said he would try to obtain administrative permission for me to attend these hearings, but he was refused. It was then that I conceived the desperate but original idea of trying to approach not the "loyals" but the "disloyals." I thereupon asked Brown to let me look at his carbon copy of the list of people who were to be "shipped out." He let me have this list for a few hours, and I copied as many names and addresses as I could. Then I walked through the center, knocking on doors, asking for specific people. When I found them, I introduced myself as a student making a study for the University of California. I explained that my professors were interested in knowing why people wished to go to Tule Lake and that I suspected that many of the things "other people" were saying about the segregants were not true. Therefore I had called on them in the hope that they would tell me the truth. If they did not wish to talk to me, I would go away, but if they felt like telling me why they had made their decision, I would be grateful.

More than half the people I approached in this fashion told me they did not wish to talk to me. But some invited me to come in and sit down, waited for me to open my notebook, and proceeded to answer all my questions in detail. Some talked for hours, telling me again and again that they were not disloyal but they had lost faith in America and felt that they had no future in this country. Some became so distressed they could barely hold back their tears. Others put on a bold front, saying: "Heck—I'm going to Tule Lake anyway, so why shouldn't I say what I think?" Some denounced the American government for its treatment of the Nisei and its abrogation of democratic principles. Some urged me to come and see them again before the "entrainment," and one young man even wrote a long essay for me, describing how he had once felt toward the United States and how he felt toward it now.

To this day I am not sure why some of these people talked to me so freely. I do not think that it was because I represented the classic "uninvolved stranger" whom they never expected to see again, for some of them clearly wanted to see me again. My guess is that they had defined their decision as a moral stand—a stand which I, as an "indignant stranger," might understand. In point of fact, I did not at that time understand much of what they said, but I listened, wrote it all down, and began to learn.

Perhaps if I had gone about the camps asking the loyal people why they had decided to *stay* in the United States, some of them might also have talked to me. But it never occurred to me to do this, because I simple-mindedly took it for granted that a "loyal" citizen of a nation did not go about asking other loyal citizens why they were loyal. I sent these interviews and essays to Berkeley along with a detailed description of the "entrainment," and many "statements" from Caucasian staff members, some of whom had a great deal to say about the (to them) incredible and inexplicable behavior of the segregants. Dr. Thomas seemed to think my report adequate, but this was small comfort to me, since the few people who had shown a willingness to talk to me at length were now being removed from the center.

It was at this point that I received a visit from Mr. Nishimoto, an Issei who had recently joined the study. He was accompanied by a young Japanese woman who, like myself, was an anthropologist and who, also like me, worried Dr. Thomas because she sent in so few field notes. I told Nishimoto and Miss K. what little I knew of what was going on in Gila, and they told me many interesting things about the Poston center. It was so wonderful to have someone to whom I could talk freely that I babbled for hours without a break. Then Nishimoto remarked that he disagreed with one of the statements in my report on the segregation. This was a section in which I told how the Caucasian chief of police, during a dinner at the mess hall, had expressed the opinion that most of the "disloyal Japs" were going to Tule Lake to escape the draft. (I had become very angry when I heard this remark, but I had dutifully put it in my report with the comment that it was nonsense.) Nishimoto, however, asserted that this remark was not nonsense but the plain truth. I listened carefully while he explained that most of the Japanese had made the decision which categorized them as "loyal" or "disloyal" with sensible or practical considerations in mind, even though many might insist that they had answered the military questionnaires in a spirit of exalted idealism. Most of the WRA staff members believed that the evacuees' decision had been idealistic, and in consequence, they were not able to understand what the evacuees said or did. He added that I was not to feel too bad about this, because most of the members of the study, including Dr. Thomas and the Japanese research assistants, labored under the same limited view. They refused, he said, to see what the evacuees were really like. He implied that I was not doing too badly as a fieldworker, considering what I had to contend with. Besides, he would introduce me to some Japanese friends in Gila who he thought would help me. (Much later Nishimoto told me that on this occasion he had been sent to Gila by Dr. Thomas to report on whether or not I should be fired.)

Though it took me several weeks to appreciate and digest some of the things Nishimoto had told me, I was much heartened by his visit. Moreover, his friends, Mr. and Mrs. Murakami, were kind and courteous folk of about my own age, and I arranged to visit them one evening a week to take a lesson in the Japanese language.[2] (In this way I would have a reason for calling on them regularly, and they would be less likely to be called *inu.*) Simultaneously, Mrs. Brown went out of her way to draw me out of the neurotic, Caucasian-avoiding shell into which I had retired. She called on me in my dismal barrack room and invited me to dinner. I enjoyed myself so much that I took to visiting the Browns regularly, and we became very good friends. (It was from Gordon that I learned my first and best, uncensored, folk songs, including *William and Mary* and *They're Moving Father's Bones to Lay a Sewer.*) The kindness of the Murakamis and their considerate attempts to initiate me into an understanding of the attitudes which most of the center residents thought right and proper, coupled with my growing fondness for the civilized and human Browns and their two young sons, gradually helped shape me once again into the semblance of a social being.

Nishimoto's visit also strengthened my slowly developing realization that I simply could not do the kind of participant observation desired by Dr. Thomas, at least in this period of investigation. The "disloyal" people, who, as one of them put it, had "nothing to lose," had talked to me as they might have talked to a sympathetic newspaper reporter. But the loyal people were not going to talk to me with any degree of freedom until they were convinced that I was the kind of person they could trust. Accordingly, it was my job somehow to convince them that I was this kind of person (see Berk and Adams 1970:106).

As a first step in this new program I undertook simultaneously a number of sociological and anthropological studies which had no connection with the delicate center attitudes and very little connection with the kind of data I was supposed to be getting. I began, in short, to behave much more like a formal interviewer than like a participant and observer. I invented questionnaires and interviewed women on how they thought evacuation had altered their way of life. I interviewed parents on what they thought evacuation had done to their

2. It was not imperative that I learn Japanese, since most evacuees could carry on a fluent conversation in English if they chose to do so. On rare occasions I used an interpreter. On the whole, however, I found it more practical to use Issei informants who spoke some English. If they were ashamed of their English, I demonstrated my difficulties in attempting to learn Japanese, which almost invariably put them at ease.

children. I interviewed anyone at all for information and attitudes on social stratification in Japan and the United States. I talked to the secretary of the cooperative on the proposed co-op education program and to the officers of the community council on what they thought about juvenile delinquency. Almost all of these interviews were arranged by recommendation from one informant to another, except for officers of organizations, who could be approached directly.

These red-herring studies had many advantages besides the primary one of becoming acquainted with many people of different ages, backgrounds, and opinions. They provided an excellent opportunity to become familiar with the pattern of center life and constituted an entree which none but the most timorous of evacuees could have refused without discourtesy. They presented me in the role of a conscientious scholar, collecting data on relatively harmless matters. They also provided the opportunity for a return visit to discuss specific problems which appeared as my investigations were pursued. They gave respondents a reasonable story to tell to curious neighbors.

This device would not have been nearly so effective in a normal community as it was in the camps. The extreme monotony of life there, the scarcity of recreation, and the fact that few evacuees were ever too busy to begrudge the time for a chat provided an ideal background for interviews and conversations. Even employed evacuees rarely had anything to do in the evening but sit and talk. It is likely that some respondents were not deceived by my ruse, but once they were assured that I was not going to ask foolish or nosey questions and that, to some degree at least, I was beginning to understand their plight, they did not usually mind my visits.

Nevertheless, many of my calls were fruitless. Some people did not attempt to hide their suspicion that I was a dissembling spy. Others were more courteous but confined their comments to the questions pertinent to the interview or to long stories of the painful experiences of themselves, their friends, or the Japanese in general. I persevered, however, and, in time, some of the people who had served me as respondents began to treat me as a friend.

When some of these friendly individuals began to be of marked assistance, giving a considerable amount of their time, I offered to pay them for their trouble. These offers were politely refused. (Refusal to accept payment sprang in part from the fact that it would have stigmatized the informant as an *inu.*) Mr. Murakami refused to accept payment for the Japanese lessons, and he did so in a manner which implied that the suggestion was in poor taste. One did not accept payment for talking to a friend. This produced a situation—created by respondents—which gradually turned me into a kind of participant. My respondents had indicated that they were willing to accept me as a friend or friendly acquaintance but not as an employer. This put me under an unverbalized obligation. They and I knew that I was getting information on the strength of an intimate social relationship. I had no means of recompensing them except by returning their friendship and accepting the obligations it implied, the most important of which was to learn to keep my mouth shut. In the words of Robert E. Park ([1939] 1952:260) I was beginning to "feel the pressure of the customs and expectations of the society by which I was surrounded." I was becoming resocialized.

Meanwhile, I was gradually pushed into the role of a willing learner. Instead of giving information to a stranger who dominated a somewhat formal interview, friendly respondents now began to instruct me in some of the less confidential aspects and attitudes of center life as well as the rudiments of Japanese etiquette. Issei men were most inclined to do this. My inferior age and sex status made them less hesitant to give instruction and offer advice. At first, this instruction consisted chiefly of dissertations on Japanese customs and other matters on which the younger generation was ill informed. The respectful attention with which this instruction was received often put respondents in a mellow mood, and they might proceed to informative, though still cautious, discussions of current center attitudes or even to advice on gaining rapport. This advice was often given by implication. A respondent might remark that the Japanese were "very suspicious people." One quoted a Japanese proverb, "Look upon every stranger as if he were a thief," thereby implying that if I expected to get information I must exercise great caution, patience, and discretion.

One of the most valuable pieces of advice was the repeated statement, "Japanese seldom lie; but they will seldom tell you anything to your face." More sophisticated friends expressed the same idea by remarking that Japanese prefer to make significant statements briefly and by implication. They added that if the hearer has the intelligence to understand the suggestion, well and good; if not, it is his misfortune. I took this advice to heart but was not able to apply it capably until I had learned far more about the center attitudes, because I could not always recognize the hints when they were given to me.

The inferior role of learner did not cause me to lose status as a scholar, for, as I learned from informants, the ideal Japanese scholar is a modest and self-effacing individual. Moreover, the task of "understanding the Japanese" was one which every Japanese believed ought to be approached with modesty by an ignorant Caucasian even if he had a university degree.

In any case, I acquired skill at small talk and gossip and at making the proper responses to a recital of grievances. I also acquired some familiarity with tabooed subjects and gained some skill at showing no curiosity about them. For instance, I found that an academic interest in Japanese culture was flattering, but interest in what anyone thought of the Japanese emperor or the American government was taboo.

When I began to make modest progress in the Japanese language, some respondents drilled me in simple phrases and were pleased when I remembered their instructions. With my exuberant and energetic personality I could not even attempt to conform to the ideal standards of Japanese female behavior, but my forceful remarks were not resented if they were covered with a veneer of self-deprecation and if, as was good manners, they were accompanied by apologies for anything which conceivably merited an apology. Gradually, I became familiar with the cynical and ironic humor which permeated the camp and concerned itself chiefly with the hardships of center life, meanwhile aiming its sarcasms at unpopular staff members or suspected *inu*. With practice I found it possible to take a modest part in such byplay.

It should be stressed that the salient advantage of the role of learner did not lie so much in the semiformal instruction given but rather in the increased intimacy of the relationship and the mutual and largely unconscious imparting of attitudes. The red-herring studies and the role of learner also provided the Japanese evacuees with an opportunity for conversing with a Caucasian on equal terms or with the Caucasian in the quasi-subordinate position of learner. Many of the evacuee contacts with WRA staff were on the basis of employer to employee or of the Japanese as petitioner and the Caucasian as the potential donor or withholder. It was, therefore, a rare experience for an evacuee to be approached as a social equal or as an authority capable of instructing a "stuck-up Caucasian." (Roles which bypassed or broke the formal and informal administrative rules of power and status proved very efficient in this situation, for the Japanese Americans saw themselves as a people oppressed by an unjust authority. Such roles or such equalitarian behavior might prove fruitless or foolish in situations where authority is demanded and revered. See, for example, Marriott [1955:263], Evans-Pritchard [1940:15].)

When my respondents were teaching me how to be a competent friend and fieldworker, I—though I did not recognize this at the time —was teaching them how to be competent and useful respondents. This involved my showing and convincing them that I was the kind of person who could understand them and whom they could trust. It also involved demonstrating to them that I could learn to play the complicated games of social and conversational concealment and cueing, which is to say that I could act and talk something like a member of the "in-group" even though I was an outsider. It also involved instructing them in just the kind of thing I wanted to learn. How I taught my respondents this I do not know. Indeed, at the time I was not aware that I was doing this. But the fact is that my more intelligent and kindly friends gradually found that I liked to hear about how people were responding to current events, and, when I called, they would sit back and regale me with detailed stories of what was going on in the block or at meetings. This, however, did not happen until I had been living in the center for five or six months.

As I proceeded with the four-faceted role of conscientious investigator of scholarly subjects, willing learner, half-accepted friend, and subconscious teacher, I was able to gain skill at the most fundamental technique of all—alleviating suspicion. (This sounds as if fieldwork consists only of learning and applying techniques. I did learn techniques which I then applied consciously and conscientiously. But I also had changed, in the sense that by undergoing this gradual process of instruction and resocialization I had found out things about the Japanese Americans and their situation which made it impossible that I ever again approach or talk to them in the way I had approached and talked to them three or four months before. In this sense I had become a different person, a person who could never go back to being what she had been before.)

The primary importance of presenting myself as a trustworthy person had of course, been clear to me from the beginning of the study. It was obvious, for instance, that I ought to avoid dangerous or delicate topics, at least until relations with a respondent were well established. However, it was difficult to find out what these delicate topics were, without understanding the center life. Moreover, there were subtle gradations in danger and delicacy, depending on circumstances and the degree of intimacy. In an early interview, hinting brashly that I understood the significance of certain taboos was poor policy; it might be interpreted as an effort to extract embarrassing or even incriminating information. But as our acquaintanceship deepened, my respondents began to take it for granted that I had some familiarity with touchy matters. In time, I could ask about some things openly and give no offense. Other topics could never be introduced. For example, I never attempted to identify any Japanese whom an informant was discussing, for this was what governmental investigators were supposed to do.

I was just beginning to conclude that I had developed considerable skill as a fieldworker, when I committed a crude error. By good fortune I was able to perceive the error immediately, for a friendly informant had remarked, during an earlier interview, that one could always tell when Japanese were under emotional strain "because they get so quiet." The error developed during a visit with the Murakamis. A group of their friends were visiting, and the conversation turned to the possible fate of the people who had recently been sent to Tule Lake. One of the visitors remarked that he had just received a letter from Tule Lake. I was extremely curious as to what might be going on in the newly established center for "disloyal" Japanese. Relying on my rapport with the Murakamis, I remarked that I would like to see the letter. The silence that fell on the chatting group was almost palpable, and the embarrassment of the Murakamis was painful to see. The faux pas was not that of asking to see a letter, for letters were passed about rather freely. It rested on the fact that one did not give a Caucasian a letter in which the "disloyal" statement of a friend might be expressed. I felt very bad, because the Murakamis had treated me with candor and affection and had assisted me greatly. Now I repaid them by embarrassing them before their friends and giving the impression that they were consorting with a spying Caucasian. I immediately apologized for attempting to pry into private correspondence, and the tension eased. Fortunately, the Murakamis trusted me sufficiently to interpret the incident correctly.

After this experience I redoubled my efforts to control my enthusiasm and to approach delicate matters obliquely, if at all. The error, in fact, was eventually turned to good account. I found that a delicate topic might be approached by degrees. If a hint of the silent tension manifested itself, the subject could be dropped. The overwhelming importance of patience was reemphasized. Until *all* the people present trusted me, I could show no curiosity about those matters on which the study most urgently required data. Indeed, I sometimes found it good policy to show no special interest if a respondent began to skirt a delicate topic. Weeks later, he might bring it up again and give more details.

For several months I followed this program, collecting much information but, as yet, very few spontaneously expressed verbatim statements about current events. I doggedly submitted my red-herring studies to Berkeley and described the attempts I was making to reach the point where I could get the kind of information needed. As the return letters grew increasingly critical, I grew increasingly stubborn. I knew I was not doing a good job, and this distressed me very much. But in my more optimistic moments I hoped I was making progress.

Then, in early December 1943, the camp was shaken by an event of the type on which the study particularly desired data. An adolescent Nisei boy, who was later diagnosed as schizophrenic by his physician, had for many months been attempting to obtain permission to leave camp and continue his education. He had answered the military questionnaire in the negative and, like many other Nisei, had later decided to change his answer to affirmative, which meant that he wanted to change from a disloyal to a loyal status. He was given a hearing before the project attorney, a man with a singular lack of insight into the evacuees' behavior and its motivations. The boy explained that he had become angry over the evacuation and the abrogation of his rights as a citizen, so that, moved by illogical emotion, he had answered in the negative. The attorney insisted that, if the boy had had the sentiments of a loyal American, he would have taken legal means to right the injustice done him. The boy attempted to explain that his emotional state, his ignorance of the law, and his loss of faith in the intentions of America precluded such calm behavior. The attorney dismissed this explanation as irrelevant, held that the boy was disloyal to the United States and a liar, and recommended that he continue to be classed as disloyal. The boy did not know of this negative recommendation, although he probably suspected it. Months passed. His parents prepared to relocate, although their son's status was still undetermined. The young man brooded on his predicament and became more and more irritable and depressed. One evening, he went to the army-patrolled camp entrance, paid no attention to the sentry's challenge, walked out of the gate, and was shot. In a few hours the news spread, and the camp buzzed with excitement.

I immediately made a round of visits. To my surprise, little effort was needed to obtain data on the rapid "development of attitudes." Acquaintances or friends, individually or in family groups, did not censor their excited comments. With new respondents such as the injured boy's physician, his pastor, and his neighbors, no introduction was needed. Detailed opinions and explanations were freely offered; some people did not even conceal the fact that a certain group of hot-heads were counseling a meeting "to make something of the shooting." The officers of the community council appeared glad to explain their plans for controlling the situation and for presenting the administration with certain requests which, if acceded to, might quiet the excited residents. In short, I found it possible for the first time to prepare a detailed, reasonably accurate, and well-balanced report, which presented a comprehensive picture of the dynamics of an event and the attitudes it produced.

Just as I was finishing this report, I received a letter from Dr. Thomas sternly and, it seemed to me, even harshly ordering me to abandon my time-wasting interest in the Japanese language and Japanese customs (e.g. in one red-herring study I had been collecting material on the *eta* or pariah caste) and to report what was going on. This letter made me very angry. But then I composed myself and remembered that the report I had just completed was good. So I wrote in reply that I would not defend my strange field techniques but would allow the enclosed report to justify them. Dr. Thomas praised the report and did not again complain about my field techniques.

The crisis involved in the shooting of the Japanese boy crystallized the attitudes of my respondents toward me and my attitudes toward them and toward the field situation. I became aware that my hesitant experiments and precautions had fallen into a coherent pattern, so that I could now proceed boldly where previously I had crept. As for my friends and respondents, it is possible that up to this time many of them had not been conscious of the fact that they trusted me. Previously they had given me casual assistance. Now, for the first time, my need for data was specific and obvious. They were forced to make a choice. Either they must cut me off coldly, or they must accept me as the kind of person to whom they might speak their minds. Almost all chose the latter course. Now more and more people began to regard me as a friend who looked to them for clarification and interpretation of current issues, and they came to expect that I would call on them for enlightenment. This was an ideal situation and offered exactly the type of data the study required. Needless to say, the knowledge that I had prepared a good report also did wonders for my self-confidence and morale (Wax 1957).

From this point forward it was relatively easy to keep informed on the salient political and social developments. All that was required was to maintain the existing rapport, pick up the issues as they came along, and ask questions about them if attitudes permitted or, if they did not, merely keep my ears open. Rapport was so well established in some families that an important issue was bound to be brought up and discussed before me almost as if I myself were an evacuee.

7 The Difficult Field Situation: Case Histories and Discussion

In the Gila center I usually made four, five, or six visits extending over a period of three or four months before a potential respondent began to talk to me in anything like a relaxed and natural manner. In point of fact, I doubt if either the respondent or I were ever relaxed, for I always had to be careful lest I inadvertently say something rude or threatening, while my respondent never forgot that he (or she) was talking to someone whose country was at war with Japan. It may be useful to present some case histories of how this kind of repetitive interviewing friendship was developed. I will begin with what might be called a very difficult prospect.

Mrs. Sato

Mrs. Sato was a handsome Nisei woman in her late thirties. The center administration considered her an "incorrigible troublemaker." She was married to an Issei who had been interned by the Department of Justice because (according to rumor) he, and several other men, had celebrated a Japanese holiday by putting on ceremonial kimonos and singing the Japanese national anthem. Mrs. Sato had been introduced to me by her brother, one of the outspoken "disloyals" on whose door I had knocked before he was "segregated" and sent to Tule Lake. Having learned not to rush people, I waited several weeks before calling on her. She was suspicious and said little. With some encouragement, however, she began to describe the hardships of the evacuation and life in the assembly centers. I responded with scathing remarks about the race baiters, couched not in my old "liberal" phraseology but in the terms used by evacuees. She then began an eloquent denunciation of the food served in the mess halls, with which I was able to agree because I had eaten in the evacuee mess halls many times. At the close of the interview she had given me no "data" with which Dr. Thomas was not already well supplied, and there was little indication that "rapport" had been improved. However, I had not tried to pump her on any delicate topic and I had listened to her harangues with sympathetic attention. When I asked if I might call again, she replied with an unenthusiastic yes.

Since Mrs. Sato had been so suspicious, I let a month pass before I visited her again. At this second visit, we again exchanged polite and innocuous remarks, after which she began a long and profane denunciation of the head of the social welfare department because (she said) he had reduced her and her children's clothing allowance from twenty-four to ten dollars a month. Fortunately, I was able to respond with similar stories told me recently by other women. At my third visit we exchanged more gossip about the inadequate or stupid behavior of the administration in general and of certain staff members in particular. (By this time—mid-December—I had, on several occasions, sat by while the Murakamis gossiped with friends, and I had learned how much the evacuees relished stories about the stupidities and incompetencies of their Caucasian supervisors. One staff member achieved so great a reputation for "dumbness" that people laughed at the mere mention of his name.) At the fourth visit Mrs. Sato became a little bolder and, for the first time, began to discuss her fellow evacuees. She expressed her disgust with the "fence-sitters," the Japanese who could not make up their minds whether to go to Japan or stay in America. "They are not good for any country," she said, and added, "I know my mind. I am going to Japan." As she began to speak with increasing bitterness of her resentment against the United States, I interrupted her, saying, "You are right, but a person has to be very careful what he says in this camp full of fence-sitters and *inu.*" Mrs. Sato looked at me with the "inscrutable expression" which Japanese may adopt when they are surprised, moved, or at a loss. I had tried to stop her from making statements which might prove dangerous to her.

At our next visit, her manner was distinctly different. She was cordial and gracious, treating me like a lady instead of like an impersonal investigator of the abuses and incompetencies of the WRA. She told me she was learning to play a Japanese musical instrument, which she showed me, and I told her I was studying Japanese. I added that I had recently heard a beautiful Japanese song at a center gathering and that I would very much like to learn it. She immediately produced a song book; I sang the melody, and she taught me the words. She observed (but did not comment on the fact) that I was a novice in the Japanese language but was not feigning an interest or competence in music. Then we began to talk about Japanese culture, etiquette, and table manners. She showed me how a woman should hold a rice bowl, and ended by inviting me to lunch with her in her apartment where we would eat some "real Japanese food." During that luncheon she announced rather dramatically that she was going to Tule Lake. (Her brother and his family were already there, and her husband would also be sent there from the internment camp where he had been confined.) "I'm tired of looking at these gutless people in Gila—tired of watching them cringing and groveling in front of those Okies!" I nodded and said, *"Ikujinashi."* (*Ikujinashi* ["spineless"] was center slang for Japanese who meekly accepted every hardship and insult. "Okies," of course, was the term generally applied to poor and ill-educated white migrants from the southern part of the United States.) Mrs. Sato then gave me her version of a knock-down, drag-out fight that had occurred in her block the week before, and then began to tell me about her husband. "Before evacuation he worked me like a dog. When I was pregnant I worked so hard [in the field] I nearly busted." But now, because of his internment, she had tasted freedom. "I'm never going back to the old arrangement. Either he behaves himself or I'm leaving. He's never going to boss me around again. . . . When I get back to Japan I'm going to Manchuria and have a decent life. . . . I *told* my husband to be careful when he was always talking here in camp about being loyal to Japan. I told him, 'These people are not worth it.' But he told me, 'You Nisei—you have no feeling for Japan.' Well, look what happened. He went and blabbed in the mess hall and a week later the FBI picked him up and took him to Santa Fe. What good is he now? He thinks that when he gets back to Japan the Japanese government is going to give him a medal and lots of money." Then she added with exaggerated sarcasm, "I can just see the way he thinks he'll be going around to his friends in Japan and be bragging and bragging. But I told him, 'Do you think the Japanese government is going to bother about you? Heck no!' " (Wax 1944:24 February).

This time, when we said our good-byes, Mrs. Sato cautioned me to be careful in my speech, lest I be arrested by the FBI and my work in the centers stopped. She was to be proved right, but I did not suspect at the time that this could possibly happen.

Winning Mrs. Sato's confidence was one of the more difficult tasks I attempted in the Gila center, and it exemplifies many of the points I have previously made. My acquaintance with her brother provided me with a logical reason for calling on her. When she criticized the administration, I either said what I thought or replied with the stories other people were telling me. When she made a rash statement, I warned her about the ears in the walls and then waited several weeks before calling again, so that she could be sure I had not reported her. As we became acquainted, I was able to show my respect for and interest in certain aspects of Japanese culture, and she responded by teaching me some basic etiquette and making the significant social gesture of inviting me to eat with her. After this intimacy she felt sufficiently responsible for me to warn me that I was heading for trouble. Over and above these "field techniques" stood the fact that Mrs. Sato was a lonely woman. Her husband was interned and her brother was in Tule Lake. She was avoided by her block neighbors because of her outspoken antiadministration attitudes and because of gossip relating to the absence of her husband. She did not desire to go to Japan, but she had forced herself into a synthetic enthusiasm for Japanese culture by the need to put a good face on her situation and the fact that without this enthusiasm she might be obliged to relocate alone. In brief, she needed a friend even more than I did. (After about a year's residence in Tule Lake her brother was permitted to relocate, and she went with him. I'm not sure what happened to the Issei husband.)

It should be emphasized that participating in this kind of relationship involved far more than learning the center argot, a few Japanese catchwords, or becoming acquainted with a few center attitudes or sentiments. It involved not so much *"acting* like" as it did *interacting* like a Caucasian who knew the score and could be trusted to behave with circumspection. The explanations I offered about what I was doing in the center, the roles I learned, the fact that I knew certain rules of the game, were relatively unimportant. What was important was that I was learning to play the game—and play it relatively well in a series of ever-varying situations in which one error might mean that I was "out," at least as far as a particular respondent was concerned. A fieldworker cannot tell himself too often that his respondents or potential respondents are judging him by what he *is* and what he *does,* and not by what he *says* he is or says he will do. The words he utters are important only if he says them at the right place, the right time, and to the right people.

MR. SAKAMOTO

Early in December I was able to establish a friendly relationship with one of the most influential men in the center. This was Mr. Sakamoto, an Issei fifty years of age, a stalwart, heavy-boned man with an enormous beard. He had, I was later to learn, taken an oath that he would not shave until the Japanese Americans were released from the camps. His philosophy is best expressed in his own words: "I feel no personal pride over any very plain guy in the hill-billy country. To me everybody's human and the same." No one had referred me to Mr. Sakamoto, because, like the ideal Japanese leader, he preferred to work through other people. I first became aware of his influence after the Nisei had been shot by the sentry. A center council meeting was called at which Mr. Bennett, the project director, was invited to speak. Mr. Bennett made a regretful and conciliatory speech, which was received in a terrible and awe-inspiring silence. Having finished, he began to leave the barrack room in which council meetings were held, when Mr. Sakamoto, who in the many previous meetings I had attended had said almost nothing, stood up and said loudly and with calm authority: "Mr. Bennett, sit down." The project director returned to his seat and sat down. Mr. Sakamoto then made a long speech in broken but eloquent English, pointing out that the Japanese people did not blame the soldier, because he had acted under orders. But they felt that the administration and the army should remember that none of the evacuees had any weapons whatsoever. He then made a number of simple and feasible suggestions which (he said) the WRA ought to follow henceforth, so that incidents like this would not be repeated. Mr. Bennett agreed to carry out the suggestions. Immediately the tension in the room dissipated.

I was impressed by the political astuteness of this speech, and a few days later I approached Mr. Sakamoto and asked him if he would help me. He said I could come to see him any time I wished and added that he was accustomed to tell the truth without fear of the consequences or concern over the status of the listener. Thenceforward he was of great assistance to me, for he would give an unvarnished answer to any sensible question. Even better, he understood and could explain the intricacies of center politics. With regard to the segregation and the attitudes of the evacuees, he pointed out that one of the main troubles was that the administration was "too idealistic" and refused to see the people as they really were. Most people, he explained, were in a state of indecision: "They are undecided about whether their future in the United States will be better or worse." Only a very few had genuinely made up their minds to go to Japan or stay in the United States. Once one accepted these plain facts, he told me, most of what the people did made sense.

Mr. Sakamoto had also played an important role in a center labor difficulty. The WRA had decided to build a high school auditorium. After construction was begun, the evacuee carpenters, discouraged by the hard work and low wages (eighteen dollars per month), stopped work and requested transfer to less arduous jobs. For a while, it looked as if construction would stop. Sakamoto, however, felt that the young people needed a hall for their recreational activities, and he undertook the recruitment of a work crew. He succeeded by promising to work as foreman, though he had little knowledge of carpentry. The auditorium was finished.

I grew to respect and like Mr. Sakamoto very much and looked forward to my talks with him. I surmise that he enjoyed the talks also. In any case, at one visit he asked me if I disapproved of drinking. When my response was appropriate, he reached behind his rocking chair and brought forth a quart milk bottle containing a repulsive looking black liquid. This proved to be a home brew, strictly forbidden by the authorities. After this interview, I noted that my teeth had turned black.

THE DIFFICULT FIELD SITUATION

I have been told that human beings who are artifically deprived of all sensory stimulation tend to hallucinate. But when, like space trainees, they are told in advance that they will be so deprived and will therefore tend to feel disoriented, they usually manage to cope quite well with their physical and mental discomforts. Indeed, my informant asserts that the space trainees' level of competence and alertness is raised by the awareness of the nature of their ordeal. I have never been in space, but I know from personal experience that a fieldworker placed in a situation where his communication with "friendly" or "predictable" human beings is very limited, or where he can communicate only with other hallucinating human beings, will also tend to develop symptoms of "psychological mal-adjustment." On the other hand, if he knows which of his miseries are a part of what he has bargained for, and that other competent and intelligent professionals have experienced misfortunes very like his, he may accept his difficulties as evidence, not of failure, stupidity, or incipient mental breakdown, but of the fact that he is beginning to come real as a fieldworker.

Loneliness, boredom, frustration, and eventual resocialization are intrinsic to the field situation. The most that can be said for them is that they may be easier to bear if one is aware that all great field-workers have experienced them. But other miseries common to fieldwork are related not to reality but to misinformation or to false notions of what good or proper fieldwork is like.

Perhaps the most crippling and disorganizing notion a fieldworker can take with him into the field is the assumption that he will be able to get his work underway, that he will be able to begin the collection of the kind of material or "data" he desires, within a few weeks. Thus, he may brace himself for loneliness, for physical discomfort, for "cultural shock," and for some initial shyness or suspicion on the part of his hosts. But he usually does not prepare himself to face the possibility that he may at first accomplish nothing that resembles professional work; that weeks and months of his precious research time may slip away and he may still have nothing to show for all of his effort and ingenuity; or, most heartbreaking of all, he may begin to get his work underway only to be ejected from the field by some authority whom he has inadvertently threatened. This, he tells himself, is the kind of thing that happens to *other* field-workers, like Evans-Pritchard among the Nuer or Stanley Diamond in Nigeria. It is not the kind of thing that can happen to him.

The fact is that we do not know what proportion of field situations might be called extremely difficult or even impossible, and what proportion might be called easy. Indeed, most anthropologists who have written detailed, descriptive accounts of their experiences indicate that they usually had a great deal of trouble getting their research well started, and some do not conceal the fact that on some expeditions they were never able—even after months of effort—to establish a professionally adequate working situation. We have already referred to the difficulties encountered by Boas, Lowie, Powdermaker, Evans-Pritchard and Mead (see chapter 2). To these we might add Berreman's account (1968) of his fieldwork among the Paharis, where, it would seem, he lived for many months without getting to know the people in any but the most superficial manner. Another anthropologist, whom I shall not name, told me that he spent six months living in an Indian household in the Peruvian highlands and that during that time his Indian landlord never spoke to him. Maybury-Lewis's account (1965) of his eight dreary and depressing months among the Sherente of Brazil suggests that he was rarely, if ever, able to work in a satisfying or even mildly rewarding manner. Among the Thrashing Buffalo, Murray and I struggled for ten weeks before we felt we were really beginning to get our proposed research underway. In Ottawa we encountered all manner of obstacles and, after seven months' work, were denounced by powerful politicians as social activists or communists who were "making trouble among the poor, ignorant Indians."

Most of the experienced anthropologists who have described their field experiences in detail, seem to feel that their difficulties were extraordinary. Other anthropologists, they seem to imply, were able to gather their data in an easy, rapid, and orderly fashion from an agreeable and reliable people, but look at what I had to go through! But after coming upon so many accounts of "extraordinary," difficult experiences and so few accounts of "ordinary," smooth-running, reasonably easy expeditions, I am beginning to wonder whether, perhaps, the reasonably easy expeditions are not the exceptional ones. Then I remind myself that we possess only a handful of detailed accounts of the preliminary stages of fieldwork. Until we accumulate more data, it might be wise for beginning fieldworkers and their employers and supervisors to assume that a fieldworker is *likely* to encounter a great deal of difficulty getting his work underway and that even the most able and ingenious investigator will probably take several months to get "organized." If this assumption proves wrong and he meets with little trouble, he may congratulate himself not for his intelligence or competence but for his good fortune.

One reason that going into the field with the expectation of starting to work immediately on a concrete and accomplishable task can be so crippling is that many beginners seem to regard their first performance in the field as the supreme criterion of their professional competence. This, for them, is "the final test," and, since they wish to confirm that they are intelligent, able, and well trained, they expect to pass this test as they have passed all others. When, after weeks and months of effort, they perceive that they have "failed," they can be terribly shaken. At this stage in their career, their professional competence may comprise a large part of their self-image, and if this image becomes marred, they cannot function as human beings. (The reader will note that, in recounting my own mental difficulties at Gila, I say that the one thing I did not *dare* to admit to myself was that I was not doing good work.)

The strain of trying to maintain a high standard of professional competence in a situation where he is scarcely able to work at all is particularly hard to endure, because the newly arrived fieldworker is existing in an abnormal situation, an alien limbo, cut off both from the supports and refuges of his own society and from those of the society in which he is vainly trying to "immerse" himself. To make matters worse, the anxiety which automatically arises when the self is threatened can, in many normal social situations, be relieved by hard work, for hard, systematic work is one of the major psychological refuges of the student. But when a researcher is suffering from extreme anxiety because he cannot find a way to begin to do the work he knows he ought to be doing, and he has no friend to whom he can go for advice or comfort, he is truly up a creek.

While most fieldworkers who have described their field experiences show marked concern over the fact that they were unable to "cover certain areas of their assignment" or get some types of data, very few comment on the demoralizing effect of facing the possibility that they could not work at all, or that they had undertaken a task that was beyond them or was foredoomed to failure. Perhaps this is because many of these fieldworkers had already passed through one or more successful and untraumatic field experiences. They *knew* they were competent professionals and they could correctly assume that the difficulties they were encountering were situational and not personal. Powdermaker had worked successfully with the Melanesians before she had to cope with the white power structure of a Mississippi town; Evans-Pritchard had worked with the Azande before he tried the difficult Nuer; Mead had worked with the Samoans before she went to the Omaha. On the other hand, we know so little about this aspect of fieldwork that we can only call for more discussion.

I can personally vouch for the fact that a fieldworker, caught in this kind of difficult situation, will tend to deny, even to himself, that he cannot do his work. I also, on the Thrashing Buffalo reservation, saw my husband pass through a much milder form of what I had experienced twenty years before. After we had lived on the reservation for about ten weeks and had accomplished very little—at least according to the program of our expectations—and after we had been thoroughly hoodwinked by our redoubtable Indian hosts, I returned one evening from an interviewing session and found my husband doubled up with laughter. Since he had been anxious and ill and had not laughed happily for weeks, I was much moved, and I wondered what had happened. Laughing so hard he could barely speak, he waved a paperback book at me, saying, "The same thing happened to him! The same thing happened to him!"

The book was Turnbull's *The Forest People.* Murray had been reading about how Turnbull was repeatedly told (by the pygmies) about some remarkable experience which was in store for him, only to find that the reality was tiring, boring, and performed with a casual and offhand air that was extremely disconcerting (1968: 23–24). Seeing how profoundly Murray was affected by the knowledge that he was not the first fieldworker to have this kind of trouble, I decided that if I ever wrote a book on fieldwork I would emphasize strongly that even the most able and competent of fieldworkers encounter a great deal of trouble "getting started." I also resolved to tell fieldbound novices who asked me for advice that they could do worse than take with them several accounts of difficult field trips.

8   First Visit to Tule Lake

After the segregants had left Gila for the Tule Lake center, I corresponded occasionally with a few of the people who had been most open with me. Then, in early November 1943, the newspapers printed lurid accounts of "Jap riots" at Tule Lake. Thousands of Japanese, readers were told, had surrounded the administration buildings, the army had been called in, and the mob had been dispersed with tear gas. For several weeks I received no letters from my "disloyal" friends. But one day a Japanese friend told me that one of his friends had just been transferred from Tule Lake to the Gila center [1] and that he would not mind talking to me. This man was spilling over with the story of what had "really gone on" in Tule Lake, and, though he was classed as a "loyal," he was heart and soul behind the strikers. His account differed so markedly from the newspaper accounts and WRA rumors that I conceived a great desire to study and make an accurate report of this strange uprising. Then I began to receive letters from my friends at Tule Lake, explaining that there had been no riot and giving various accounts of what had happened. At Christmas time I sent some of my friends modest boxes of candy, and I was surprised to receive moving expressions of gratitude. One young man stated that he would not forget this kindness as long as he lived. I did not at that time realize that these people had been participating in a long-drawn-out and hopeless strike, that there had been no holiday celebrations in the center, that no one had any money for gifts, that "everything," as one transferee put it, "seems and looks cold and still and melancoline" (Thomas and Nishimoto, 1946:177), and that a small friendly gesture from an "outsider" might strike sensitive individuals with peculiar force.

In late January of 1944 Dr. Thomas asked me whether I would be willing to make an exploratory visit to the Tule Lake center.

1. This man was a key worker in one of the center management crews. Though classified as "loyal" he had been asked to remain at Tule Lake and help in the complicated task of moving the "loyal" population out and the "disloyal" population in.

Apparently the WRA had informed her that the center was now functioning so smoothly that she might send an observer from the study. I surmise that I was the only possible candidate for this job, since all the other field assistants were "loyal" Japanese Americans, whose entrance into the "disloyal" center would have been improper. I was very eager to go, since, as I have explained, I was intensely curious about what had gone on during the much publicized "riots" of November. I made my first visit on 2 and 3 February. My account of this experience will make more sense to the reader if he has some idea of what had happened in the center since the arrival of the segregants in September and October of 1943.

To begin with, it is important (though confusing) to keep in mind that Tule Lake had originally been a relocation center. When it was decided to conduct a segregation, the "loyal" residents of Tule Lake had, supposedly, been transferred to other centers, and the "disloyal" had been permitted to remain. It was generally believed that many of the people who remained in Tule Lake had said they were "disloyal" so that they might escape the discomforts of being moved once again, and that, in addition, many who were technically "loyal" had simply refused to leave. (Subsequently I tried to find out how many technically "loyal" people had remained in the center, but this proved impossible. A high-ranking administrator assured me that the WRA simply did not have accurate records and could not be sure.) In any case, these folk soon became known as "Old Tuleans," as distinct from the new arrivals.

Many of the incoming segregants told me later that they had been dismayed at the sight of the "man-proof fence"—crowned with barbed wire and guarded by watchtowers and armed soldiers —with which the authorities thought it necessary to surround the new segregation center, and by the impressive (but obsolete) tanks which had been placed so that the segregants could see them. They were also dismayed at the quarters provided. Many of the vacant "apartments" (the single barrack rooms provided for families) were extremely dirty, and some had been stripped of wall board and stoves by the Old Tuleans. Some rooms, presumed to be "vacant," were occupied by Old Tuleans who had moved into the vacated areas without administrative permission. The newcomers found almost all the facilities of their new home "inferior" to those at the centers from which they had come; the food was poor, the latrines and laundry rooms dirty, even the weather was bad, and complaints were heard on all sides. The only facility that was judged "better" was the Co-operative Enterprises—the general stores or canteens popularly called "the Co-op."

Meanwhile, the project farm was continuing in operation, and segregants were transported every day by truck to labor in the fields. On 15 October (just two weeks after the first trainload of newcomers had arrived) one of these farm trucks turned over. Thirty men were injured, and one died within a few days. Many segregants were shocked and indignant, and those who had been serving as farm laborers refused to return to work. Acting with that speed which authorities and administrators always find so incredible, the people held block meetings and set up a *Daihyo Sha Kai* ("Representative Body"), chosen, in large part, from among the men who had attained prestige as leaders in the relocation centers. Faithfully reflecting the discontent of the population, this body decided to use the farm work stoppage as a means of mitigating or alleviating the people's grievances. In a remarkable explosion of parliamentary procedure, the *Daihyo Sha Kai* appointed numerous subcommittees (to investigate sanitation, the hospital, the schools, the food in the mess halls, the farm accident), and it also appointed a central committee of seven men (one for each ward), which was to organize the materials submitted by the investigating committees and present them to the administration. These seven men came to be known as "the negotiating committee."

When it was announced that one of the injured farm laborers had died, several committees of segregants approached the administration and requested permission to hold a public funeral. Permission was refused. In defiance of this administrative veto a public funeral was ceremonially conducted on a platform stage customarily used for outdoor entertainment. The administration countered by turning off the power to the public address system, and the funeral service could not be heard.

On 26 October the project director met with the negotiating committee of the *Daihyo Sha Kai,* listened to their list of grievances, and promised to do what he could to relieve the situation. Meanwhile, he was recruiting additional farm laborers from among the "loyal" Japanese of nearby relocation centers and so was preparing to harvest the crop and thus deprive the strikers of their only important bargaining point. On 1 November, the national director of the WRA, Dillon Myer, visited the center. Seizing this opportunity to appeal directly to the highest authority, the negotiating committee engineered a mass demonstration, during which several thousand segregants surrounded the administrative buildings. Most of the demonstrators behaved in an extremely orderly fashion. However, a group of young Japanese toughs entered the hospital and urged the Japanese staff to join the demonstration. When the chief medical officer —a generally unpopular man—ordered them to leave, they attacked him and beat him severely. Order was restored; the negotiating committee presented its list of grievances; Mr. Myer promised he would investigate the complaints and take justifiable action; and the crowd then dispersed quickly. That night, all over the country, newspapers carried headlines about the spectacular Jap riots at Tule Lake.

Three nights later (4 November) a fight broke out between a group of young Japanese and a few Caucasian WRA employees who, the Japanese thought, were attempting to transport food from the project warehouses to the strike breakers. According to the WRA report, the project director feared he was about to be kidnapped, and he turned the jurisdiction of the camp over to the army. These events took place late at night and most of the residents did not know that anything unusual had happened. The next morning, therefore, about a thousand of the Japanese began walking as usual to their work in the administrative section (for only the farm workers had stopped working at this time). In the area between the administrative and the evacuee sections, they encountered a cordon of soldiers who could only assume that these converging Orientals were the vanguard of another demonstration. The would-be workers were met with a barrage of tear gas, and, bewildered and indignant, they fled to their quarters. The army then began to build a fence between the administrative area and the large section of the center where the segregants lived.

This unprovoked attack on the Japanese working staff greatly exacerbated the situation. Without Japanese workers—doctors, nurse's aides, typists, bookkeepers, warehouse men, police, and garbage, coal and mess crews—the center could not function, and so some means had to be found of getting at least some of the people back to work. On the other hand, some work crews had been overstaffed, since the WRA, until the segregation, had followed a policy of spreading employment. The fortuitous work stoppage gave the lieutenant colonel and the high-ranking associates of the

WRA the opportunity to cut these crews drastically and so purge them of persons with antiadministration sentiments. The coal crew, for example, was to be cut from 300 to 90. The negotiating committee vigorously resisted these suggestions, and, after several abortive meetings between the committee and the army, it was decided to hold a mass meeting at which representatives of the army, the WRA, and the negotiating committee would speak and explain the situation to the people. But when the members of the negotiating committee relayed this decision to the *Daihyo Sha Kai,* there was much discontent. After a stormy session lasting far into the night it was decided to cancel the proposed mass meetings. The next morning, announcements to this effect were made in the Japanese mess halls. But no one, it seems, remembered or had the nerve to inform the army or the WRA that there was to be no meeting. A few minutes before 2 P.M. (the appointed time), the colonel and a WRA field director entered the center with a strong escort of armored cars and jeeps. Thirty soldiers surrounded the open-air stage and fixed bayonets; other soldiers in military vehicles patrolled the nearby areas. But not one Japanese was to be seen. Thereupon the colonel delivered his address, announcing to the empty firebreak that the center was under complete military control, that a curfew would be enforced between the hours of 7 P.M. and 6 A.M., and that no ingoing or outgoing telephone or telegraph messages could be made without the approval of the military.

The next day (14 November) the army began to arrest and confine the members of the negotiating committee and other men suspected of being leaders of the farm strike. These arrests and, perhaps, the formidable searches that accompanied them seem to have stiffened the resistance of even the less irate or aggressive segregants, for now many people asserted that they would not return to work until the apprehended men had been released. The army responded by arresting still more alleged leaders and agitators. (By January more than two hundred men had been apprehended, and a special stockade, complete with a new man-proof fence and watchtower was built to house them.)

Meanwhile, the army and the WRA personnel were becoming increasingly uncomfortable. The army wanted to get rid of the job of running the center, and the WRA wanted its job back. But before this could occur, the center would have to return to what the administrators called "normalcy." The army and the WRA thereupon made advances to the only Japanese Americans in the center who were inclined to take a collaborating attitude—the officers of the Co-op, Old Tuleans who managed the highly successful and profitable general stores or canteens. With the help of these few men the army and the WRA arranged a popular referendum (on 11 January) in which the residents voted whether they would maintain the strike or return to work. By the barest majority—a plurality of 473 out of 8,713—the residents voted to abandon the strike.

Many people now returned to work after first having been "cleared" and accorded a pass which they were obliged to present daily to the sentries guarding the gate to the administrative quarters. On the other hand, almost half of the residents had voted to continue the strike, and these persisted in asserting that their still-confined representatives had been betrayed and that those who had negotiated the truce and referendum—a group that now took the name of "coordinating committee"—were "a bunch of *inu.*" Hostility and distrust toward Caucasians and hatred of the *inu* were intense. The fear of becoming known as an *inu* was all-pervading. A Caucasian who entered the Japanese section of the camp without a legitimate reason was commonly thought to have only one motive—to spy; a Japanese who received a Caucasian in his barrack was at once labeled an *inu*. This was the state of affairs when I first visited the Tule Lake center in February of 1944.

When I made this first visit, I did not, of course, know whether I would be able to talk to people in a camp where martial law had just been withdrawn. But my spirits were high, and I was determined to make off with any information I could garner. I had written to my segregant friends, telling them I was coming. Moreover, when my friends in Gila heard I was going to visit Tule Lake, many asked me to call on their "disloyal" friends and relatives. So I went with a list of more than a dozen people to whom I had been warmly recommended.

The first things I saw were the bristling, barbed-wire-topped "man-proof" fence and the great watchtowers manned by armed soldiers and equipped with powerful searchlights. I walked past the sentries at the gate and entered a little building where I was given a visitor's pass by a soldier, who first telephoned his superior officer to verify my statement that the project director had invited me to visit the center. Then I walked about a quarter-mile farther to another little building where I was given still another pass, admitting me into the Tule Lake military area. Then I was driven to the large administration building where I met an assistant project director who told me that I would not be permitted to enter "the colony" unless I took a soldier with me as a bodyguard, although, if I preferred, I could have particular "colonists" brought to me under armed guard. My protests were of no avail; the policy would not be mitigated. So I decided to speak to the project director.

While I was waiting in the director's office, I was approached by another man who introduced himself as Dr. Marvin Opler, the community analyst. (He occupied the same position at Tule Lake that Gordon Brown occupied in Gila.) Dr. Opler told me that he was ready to accompany me immediately on my visits inside the colony. I told him that I would go neither with him nor with a soldier, but, if my Japanese friends wanted to see him, I would take him with me the next day. Meanwhile, another assistant director, a Mr. Penn, whom I had once met in the Gila Center, noticed me and asked me to step into his office. He closed the door and quietly advised me not to try to get the regulation about bodyguards set aside. Instead, he suggested that I do as he did: take a plainclothes man from the Internal Security (the WRA police) rather than a soldier, and ask him to sit outside in the car while I made my visits.

After lunch I finally saw the project director. By this time I was angry. I told him that I disapproved of his bringing me all the way to Tule Lake and then subjecting me to crippling restrictions. It was asinine (I said) to expect me to talk to evacuee friends with a soldier breathing down my neck. The project director apologized and said that the WRA had not wished Dr. Thomas to know that matters at Tule Lake were still so critical. Besides, they had expected that Dr. Thomas would send a man. I refrained from commenting on these remarks, and he ended our meeting by suggesting that I see what Dr. Opler could do for me.

So I returned to Dr. Opler and told him that the project director had said that I could enter the colony accompanied by a member of the Internal Security. (He had not specifically said this, but I was tired of arguing.) Dr. Opler courteously made the arrangements for me. My escort turned out to be a soft-spoken and well-mannered policeman, who had himself just arrived at the center. He drove me to yet another man-proof fence with a gate guarded by five armed soldiers, through which we drove without showing our passes.

My escort explained that he knew the corporal on duty. Once within the "colony," I perceived that my guide did not know his way around; so I frequently got out of the car and asked the Japanese for directions. By the time we located the first address on my list, he cheerfully accepted the three paperback mystery novels I offered him, and remained in the car, remarking that he was grateful for the chance to get into the colony and look around. (Later, he volunteered that the residents did not look like bad people.)

My segregant friends seemed most happy to see me, and I was moved by the fact that all of them, poor as they were, had managed to scrounge some refreshments. One family served me cocoa and puffed rice; another, by some miracle, had managed to procure a cake. Many were eager to give me their versions of what had happened, and correctly anticipated that I would wish to record their long accounts and explanations in my notebook. I fared almost as well with most of the folk who had been referred to me by Japanese friends living in Gila. (I had, of course, prepared myself with a list of topics and questions which I hoped to get clarified—a list which kept growing and changing as my informants filled in or added details.) In the day and a half I spent working, I had long talks with eleven Japanese. In the evenings I talked with Mr. Penn and Dr. Opler, each of whom helped me very much. When I left, I had forty pages of typewritten notes.

Most of the segregants talked a great deal about what had happened to them during the exciting period of the demonstrations and the dreary period of the strike. Many said that "the people now wanted peace"—that they "wanted to be left alone." Others assured me that the center would not really settle down until the men still held in the stockade were released. When I asked my friends about the new coordinating committee, some said they knew nothing about them. Others said that they must be *inu*. Not until many months later did some of these friends tell me that they had been very worried by my visit (lest they be considered *inu*) and had taken the precaution of announcing to their neighbors that a Caucasian friend from the relocation centers was going to pay them a purely social call.

By happenstance, I met the executive secretary of the coordinating committee, Mr. Sasaki. Mrs. Murakami, the wife of my Japanese teacher in Gila, had asked me to call on a girlfriend of hers, and this friend proved to be Mr. Sasaki's secretary. When I tried to locate her, I was referred to his office. Mr. Sasaki was too busy to be interviewed, but his secretary told me, with surprising frankness, that Sasaki and the other members of the committee were caught in a very uncomfortable situation. They had not been elected by the people but *selected* by the administration, and "the people just had to take it or else." The committee hoped to resign as soon as possible in favor of an elected body. She then added nervously, "The people say that we're *inu.*"

The only people I had real difficulty talking to were some of the young Nisei. One young man, whose "loyal" girlfriend had asked me to call on him, was now living in a barracklike apartment with fifteen other fellows. He invited me in and offered me a seat, but then turned his back on me in embarrassment. Two or three Nisei girls on whom I called would talk of nothing but how boring life at Tule Lake was. "Nothing ever happens."

During this first visit I met Joe Kurihara, the man who was to become my best informant and my friend. Mr. Kurihara was a Hawaiian Nisei about fifty years old. In 1915 he had come to California, and in 1917 he had enlisted in the U.S. army and served abroad. After the war he had gone to night school and become a certified public accountant. Unable to find employment, he then learned navigation and, until the outbreak of World War II, had worked as a navigator on a tuna-fishing boat. In January of 1942 he tried to enter the merchant marine but was refused. He then tried to obtain employment in two shipbuilding firms but was again refused. He gave the following account of his encounter with the port master of San Diego:

> I went to see the Port Master in San Diego to get a permit to sail the sea. Seeing that I was a Japanese, he said, "No permit for any Jap." We argued awhile. Losing his temper he said, "Get out or I'll throw you out." So I told him, "Say, officer, I wore that uniform when you were still unborn. I served in the U.S. Army and fought for democracy. I may be a Jap in feature but I am an American. Understand!" I saw fire in his eyes, but he had no further words to say. [Thomas and Nishimoto, 1946:367]

At the Manzanar center, Kurihara became known for his out-spoken criticism of the WRA administration. He also denounced the young Nisei leaders who, he thought, had meekly submitted to the evacuation and cooperated with the authorities. When one of the Nisei leaders at Manzanar was beaten and his accused assailant jailed, the residents of Manzanar staged a demonstration which culminated in the project director's calling in the army. Kurihara and a number of other men suspected of being agitators were arrested and then reconfined in a special isolation camp. In December 1943, having answered the military questionnaire in the negative, he was sent to Tule Lake. While undergoing these experiences, Kurihara had written several articles denouncing the evacuation, the living conditions of the centers, and the treatment that the Nisei had received from the United States government. He sent these to *The Saturday Evening Post* and *Collier's,* and they were rejected. He then gave them to Mr. Penn (the man who had advised me to take a policeman instead of a soldier with me), and Mr. Penn sent them to Dr. Thomas.

Kurihara was short, stocky, and partly bald. He spoke with simplicity and force and gave an impression of great integrity. After I explained the object of the study, he asked me for my personal opinion of his articles. I groped vainly for a tactful comment on these fiery denunciations of the treatment accorded the Japanese Americans. Finally I blurted out: "I thought the man who wrote those articles was honest. He must either be very courageous or crazy." Kurihara laughed and we got on well from that time on.

ANALYTIC COMMENT

As, twenty-three years later, I read over the field notes covering my first visit to Tule Lake, I am abashed and a little amazed. Students may well wonder whether I am recommending that they too adopt so arrogant a manner toward officials and bureaucrats. They may also wonder how, in a few months, I managed to change from a timid, fumbling amateur who cried every day—and who, for a while, thought she was going out of her mind—into a formidable female snoop who knew when to be arrogant, when to be tricky, and when to be honest.

The fact is that while my notes give a fairly accurate picture of what I did, they do not give a true picture of how I felt. I was arrogant, deceptive, and, perhaps, even brave, but I *felt* completely sure of myself. I knew I was doing a job that no one else in the world could, at this moment, do so well as I. So I worked and thought as hard as I could, playing each new situation by ear.

I had exchanged no more than a few words with the soldiers and the WRA employees when I realized that they were living in a world of fantasy, frightening themselves with shadows. To find

103

oneself in a situation where everyone around you is afraid to do what you know you can do safely and skillfully, is exhilarating and intoxicating. Besides, I had been invited to visit the center for only two days, and no one had said anything about another visit. Thus, while I did not try to hurt anyone's feelings, I was under no pressure to behave in such a way that I would be permitted to return.

9 Second Visit to Tule Lake

In the following detailed account of my experiences in a difficult field situation, the reader should note that, as I assumed certain obligations toward my Japanese American respondents (or associates), I discarded certain obligations toward my own people. Yet the obligations and involvements which I was entering into—as I acquired understanding—did not affect adversely my efficiency and productivity as a fieldworker. As I became more and more involved with the people I was supposed to be detachedly observing, I began to understand more and more of their real feelings and to comprehend the details of their factional plottings; and, as this happened, I, in turn, eventually became as ruthless and hard-minded as some of my Japanese associates.

After my visit to Tule Lake, the Gila center seemed quiet and dull. Most of my Japanese friends were marking time until the end of the war or waiting for a good opportunity to relocate. Obligingly they furnished me with all manner of information (which I dutifully wrote down and mailed to Berkeley), but, on the whole, they were as bored as I. In consequence, when Dr. Thomas asked me to return to Tule Lake for a visit of ten days (14–23 March), I was happy to go.

On my first visit to Tule Lake I had been allowed to sleep in a "high status" barrack, sharing quarters with a visiting journalist from *Fortune* magazine. But on this second visit I was told that there was no room for me on the project. After trying without success to obtain a hotel room at Klamath Falls, the city nearest to Tule Lake, I proceeded to the center, hoping that Mr. Penn or Dr. Opler might find a corner for me. If need be, I was prepared to sleep on the floor. At lunch I sat with a group of women staff members, one of whom told me I might sleep in her room if I could get a cot; Mr. Penn furnished the cot.

The general situation at the center had not changed much in six weeks. Though most of the high-ranking staff members assured me that things were getting better every day, they did not sound as if they believed it. I asked one of them why, if things had improved so much, I was still required to take an armed guard into the center. He explained that WRA employees no longer needed a guard, but I was an outsider. The stockade was still very much in evidence. On one occasion I walked past the colony fence and saw several clusters of people, mostly women and children, standing with arms upraised, slowly waving their arms and bodies from side to side. I looked over to the distant stockade and saw several prisoners doing the same thing. A soldier patrolling the fence paid no attention. On another occasion I was being driven through the area where the WRA staff resided when I noticed several Japanese carpenters working at the construction of new barracks. These workers were surrounded by armed guards. Puzzled, I asked my escort whether the stockade detainees were being put to work in this manner. He explained that the carpenters were not detainees but were being watched so that they did not communicate with the men in the stockade.

I found my segregant friends less anxious and less subdued than they had been in February—which is to say that they were more open in their complaints and criticisms of the WRA and the coordinating committee. Indeed, the boldness with which even moderate and "unradical" people denounced the committee surprised me. "That bunch is a bunch of *inu*," said a friend from Gila, "and Sasaki is the biggest *inu* of them all. He'll probably get his brains beat out one of these days" (Wax 1944: March). Another friend told me that he thought the committee was trying hard, but that he felt that "another big trouble" was brewing because the people were still so strongly divided into "status-quo" and "anti-status-quo." (People were called "status-quo" if they had voted to continue the strike. This usually meant that they had supported the *Daihyo Sha Kai* and that they still favored a defiant and morally indignant attitude toward the administration, so long, at least, as the "people's representatives" were imprisoned in the stockade.) Radical "status-quoers" made open avowals of their loyalty to Japan and insisted that the disloyal Nisei ought to be given the opportunity to renounce their American citizenship. They also insisted that all people who were still "loyal" to the United States ought to be forced to leave the center. "Anti-status-quoers" wanted only peace, quiet, and order. As one put it: "Let us roam around here and feed us three times a day. . . . Nobody likes trouble. If they'll treat us like human beings and not like dogs, nobody starts kicking." Many of the anti-status-quoers were covert fence-sitters, in the sense that they wanted a refuge where they could live in reasonable comfort until the end of the war. Others intended to go to Japan but were convinced that agitation and troublemaking at Tule Lake only increased the hardships of the segregants and that this kind of "rowdyism" would not win the approval of the Japanese government. Most "anti-status-quoers" also insisted vociferously that the "loyal" ought to be ejected from the center (even though they themselves might be classed as "loyal" on the administrative records). There were, however, two points on which almost everyone agreed: the WRA could not be trusted, and the members of the coordinating committee were stooges or *inu*.

Joe Kurihara, who had not been in Tule Lake at the time of the "riot," was more level-headed than most folk and more able to appreciate the impossible bind into which the coordinating committee had been forced. He told me soberly:

> The coordinating committee, I think, is the unconscious tool of either the army or the WRA. If Sasaki could wriggle out of the committee, all right. But if he waits longer, some day it's going to be too late. . . . If he keeps on and sticks at it, even if he's really for the Japanese, he's going to be branded an *inu* and blamed for working with the WRA. [Wax 1944: March]

I asked my friends and acquaintances a great many questions about what had happened at various periods during the uprising: Had they attended the farmer's funeral? Had they attended the meetings at which the *Daihyo Sha Kai* were elected or selected? Had they attended the demonstrations of 1 November, when Dillon Myer, the national director of WRA, "had talked to the people"? How had they felt when the army searched the camp? and so forth. I was interested not so much in obtaining an accurate chronological history of events as in gaining some insight into how they themselves had felt during various stages of the process. I particularly wanted to check on the statements of some of the WRA staff members—that the negotiating committee's claim to popular support was false, that the strike was the work of a few "rabid", pro-Japanese agitators, and that the residents had been forced to come to the demonstration by Japanese "goon-squads." Most of the information given me suggested that popular support of the strike and of the *Daihyo Sha Kai* had been very strong during the early period of the uprising. But as the strike dragged on and the remnants of the *Daihyo Sha Kai* made progressively more desperate suggestions—one being that everyone in the center go on a hunger strike—popular support for the "representatives" had dwindled. On the other hand, no one seemed happy that the strike had failed, and most people felt that the men in the stockade ought to be released. Even the officers of the Co-op assured me that the people had supported the *Daihyo Sha Kai* and that the men in the stockade should be released, though one older man half-jokingly told me that, so far as he was concerned, the "chronic agitators" could be kept there for the rest of their lives.

The fact that I was supposed to gather information in two areas, past history and current issues or events, was a great help to me. If I visited a friend at a time when he was reluctant to talk about current happenings, we could discuss some aspect of the strike. Such friends sometimes waited until the end of a visit and then asked *me* a question which revealed the nature of their current anxiety. Conversely, if we were discussing some "historical event" and wandered too near a topic which my respondent wished to avoid, he could shift the subject to some innocuous event of current interest.

When I called on Mr. Sasaki (executive secretary of the coordinating committee), he looked as if he had aged ten years. He had also lost his voice and could talk only in a whisper. Indeed, all of the young Japanese working or standing about the committee's office were on edge. Since we could not converse in this uncomfortable atmosphere, I asked Sasaki if he and his secretary would come to see me at my quarters in the administrative section. (Since I did not think it wise that we talk in front of my roommate, I planned to ask a sympathetic staff member if she would let me use her room for a few hours. I had discovered, both at Gila and Tule Lake, that each project had a few disaffected employees who disliked the WRA and were always ready to do anything that seemed to sidestep the "regulations." I tried not to take advantage of these persons, but on a few occasions they helped me a great deal.)

When Mr. Sasaki and his secretary arrived, I served crackers and cheese (all I could buy at the army PX) and asked him what the committee had accomplished in the six weeks since I had last seen him. "Nothing whatever," he said. I asked many other questions but received few answers that made sense in the light of what I knew was going on. Perhaps Sasaki had reached the state of mind where he trusted nobody. Or again, as Kurihara had told me, he might not have been able to communicate well in spoken English. He did, how-

ever, give me copies of the minutes of meetings between the coordinating committee and the WRA, and he told me that he was
working on an English translation of the minutes of the *Daihyo Sha
Kai* and would give me copies when he had finished. He kept his
word, and I have always felt that I owe Mr. Sasaki an unpaid debt.
The minutes demonstrated that the coordinating committee had accepted its uncomfortable and difficult assignment with the clear understanding that the WRA would support its publicly proclaimed
policies of "full employment and justifiable release of stockade detainees." They showed also that the committee had tried to get the
support of the imprisoned leaders of the *Daihyo Sha Kai* even before
the referendum vote of 11 January and that for this act of initiative
they had been sharply rebuked by the WRA. And they showed that
for two months the committee had been begging the WRA to create
more jobs, to speed up the "clearance" through which job-seekers
were supposed to pass, and to release at least some of the detainees.
These desperate requests were, for the most part, met only with
promises. Indeed, on 18 March (three months after the referendum
vote), Mr. Myer told the committee that the WRA had to do a
great deal of paperwork to get a man released from the stockade and
that the committee should "withhold too many recommendations
which are inclined to embarrass the administration." The facts, then,
were that some persons had gone back to work, but very few had
been released from the stockade, and meanwhile, still others had
been put there (Thomas and Nishimoto 1946: 184–220).

The one "big event" that had occurred during my absence was the
arrival, in late February, of the "disloyal contingent" of segregants
from the Manzanar center. The coordinating committee and the
WRA had tried very hard to make these new arrivals comfortable,
assigning them to new barracks and even lighting fires in the apartments before they arrived. Mr. Sasaki, on behalf of the committee,
had welcomed the newcomers with a mimeographed appeal for co-
operation:

> None of us know how long will our stay in Tule Lake be. All Tuleans
> have been trying to make it a better place to live under the circum-
> stances. Yet they have no other desire than to live in peace and
> happiness for the duration. Our ideal is Utopia. Ideal of Utopia may
> not be attained, however, we must strive to attain that goal as much
> as we can for ideal is like a North Star. Sailor never reaches North
> Star, yet without North Star he cannot come to the port.

We appeal to you, MANZANITES!! Now you are in the same boat with us. Let's make the best of it and lay up for the future happiness.

This appeal was immediately followed up by a counterblast from the underground supporters of the *Daihyo Sha Kai*. Working secretly, these "pro-status-quo" folk mimeographed a pamphlet in which they accused the WRA of refusing to clarify the status of the Nisei and thus of trying to convert disloyal segregants into loyals. (They had a point here, for the "disloyal" Nisei were still, technically, citizens of the United States.) The U.S. army, they asserted, had employed a "suppressive policy" upon the segregants, using "even motor trucks and tanks and fired great number of ammunitions. During the incident over 200 innocent ones were picked up and every apartment was searched, for which even a mere child of three years of age was indignant." The "pro-status-quoers" claimed that the army had withdrawn from the center because of a "stiff protest" by "the Imperial Government repeatedly," and they denounced the coordinating committee and the executives of the Co-op as participants in a "dark stream of sinister plot" to deceive the colonists and discredit the *Daihyo Sha Kai,* asserting that the committee and its supporters were "betrayers of the Fatherland," gamblers, bootleggers, and shameless egotists. Finally they claimed that the WRA had hired *inu* "with excellent salary" to help them "carry out their damnable policy."

What the new arrivals from Manzanar thought about these pamphlets I do not know, for I was not then well enough acquainted with any of them to find out. Segregants from other centers who had experienced the strike did not seem much impressed by either of the broadsides. They tended to dismiss Mr. Sasaki's statement as "softsoaping the people" and to see the pamphlet from the underground as the work of "crazy radicals." What really vexed them, as one woman put it, was the "unfair" treatment that had been given to the "Manzanites," that is, the new mops, the clean wall board, the neat latrines, and the brooms.

During this visit, I had my first and only conversation with Dillon Myer. Immediately afterward, I had my first talks with members of the "pro-Japanese" underground group, the "crazy radicals." These events were related, and they came about because I was drawn into an administrative debate about what ought to be done with regard to the anomalous position of the coordinating committee.

On 14 March, when I had asked Mr. Penn for an army cot, he had asked me to try to find out what could be done to mitigate the hatred and suspicion that the segregants felt toward the administration. I liked and respected Mr. Penn, first because he had helped me and, second, because he seemed to be the only member of the administrative staff who was really interested in what was going on in the center. Moreover, I knew that Joe Kurihara trusted him. So I told Mr. Penn that I would talk to people and, in a week or so, tell him what I decently could. Six days later, Mr. Penn came to my quarters and asked me if I would mind talking to Mr. Myer, who had suddenly arrived on the project. I was not enthusiastic because I had heard Myer talk to a general staff meeting, and he had asserted that "the WRA had passed its worst crisis," that everything was going to be all right because "things are on the beam now" (Wax 1944:17 March). Myer's attitude of radiant and benevolent optimism shocked me, not because I thought he was lying (which would have made him sound like a politician) but because he sounded as if he believed what he was saying (which made him sound like a fool). So I told Mr. Penn that Mr. Myer probably would not like to hear what I had to say. But Penn urged me to describe the situation exactly as I saw it, so I said I would try.

Mr. Myer was over half-an-hour late for our appointment. While Mr. Penn and I waited, I told Mr. Penn how the people in the center felt about the coordinating committee, and I added jokingly that almost all my friends seemed to respect Penn except the officers of the coordinating committee. "Do you know why?" asked Penn. "It's because I have kept up my contacts with the other group." "What other group?" I asked. Penn then told me that there was an underground group in the colony who were trying to find a better method of representation than the coordinating committee, and that this group had been in touch with him. He would however, tell me nothing more.

When Myer arrived, I told him that I had been surprised at his speech because, so far as I could see, the situation within the center was deteriorating. Though the people were going back to work, they did so in a state of sour disillusionment. Many people who were not "agitators" said that the members of the coordinating committee were stool pigeons and grafters, and many people, radical or moderate, still felt that their true representatives "were sitting in the stockade." When I sensed that Mr. Myer was not impressed by

111

my remarks, I tried to convey my uneasiness about the situation by remarking that beaten, disillusioned, and hate-filled people can be more dangerous than loud and hopeful demonstrators.

But Myer tolerantly ignored my prophetic outburst and told me that he may have sounded a little overoptimistic in his talk to the staff, but he felt that the worst hump had been passed when the people went back to work. Then, with a glance at Mr. Penn, he said, "I feel that it is futile to attempt to get relations with the colony when the appointed staff are not able to agree among themselves. I rely chiefly on Mr. Penn to accomplish this. I believe this is a more important and pressing task than the establishment of personal contacts in the colony." I gathered that Mr. Penn was being rebuked for his contacts with the agitators, and so I bluntly asked Mr. Myer what he planned to do about the 137 men in the stockade. He said their release was being pushed as rapidly as possible. He added that he now felt that the administration had erred in November when it had refused to recognize the *Daihyo Sha Kai* as the people's representatives.

When I talked to Penn that evening, he suggested that I myself might find it interesting to talk to some of the members of the "underground group." I might call on Mrs. Hyacinth Tsuchikawa, at whose home the secret meetings were being held, but he asked me not to use his name as an introduction. He further suggested that I talk to Henry Yamaguchi, a young Nisei who had been a member of the *Daihyo Sha Kai,* had been put into the stockade, but had recently been cleared and released. Penn agreed to ask this young man whether I might call on him.

Calling on a resident of Tule Lake without a recommendation from a friend or relative was never easy, and I anticipated that calling on a member of the underground would be very difficult. Here, however, I was wrong. Mrs. Tsuchikawa opened her door, holding a little girl in her arms who looked as if she had been snatched from a nap when I knocked on the door. The mother invited me in, asked me to be seated, and then sat down opposite me, still holding the girl on her lap. Mrs. Tsuchikawa looked and spoke so much like Mrs. Sato (the aggrieved wife of the Issei agitator in Gila, see chap. 6) that I gambled on approaching her in the same manner. I told her that I was a member of a university study and that we hoped, at the end of the war, to publish an accurate account of what had happened in the centers. I added that I had heard her name from a member of the coordinating committee (which was not true but plausible) but that, so far as I could see, many of the people did not trust the committee. I said that I hoped at some future time to find out what had occurred at the time of the strike, but that I suspected that I would never get the whole truth from the WRA or from the coordinating committee. I encouraged her to make inquiries about me, so that, when she found out what kind of person I was, she might decide to talk to me. Mrs. Tsuchikawa loudly and shrilly denied any connection with the *Daihyo Sha Kai* and said repeatedly that she was only a high school graduate standing up for her rights. Her brother, she told me, had been put in the stockade for no reason at all, and she was tired of being grilled by the Internal Security. She added that she was glad that I did not act like the police. When I rose to go, she asked me to stay a while, and we discussed democracy, freedom of speech, and other "safe" topics.

I was not favorably impressed with Mrs. Tsuchikawa. She seemed bossy and hysterical, and I suspected that, when push came to shove, she would not be particularly scrupulous. (I learned later that other segregants referred to her as Madame Chiang Kai-shek.) Besides, I could not warm to a mother who, at first hint of danger, picked up her child and held it in front of her.

Harry Yamaguchi, the ex-member of the *Daihyo Sha Kai,* was a different kind of person. Though young, he was dignified and outspoken, and, unlike many Nisei, he did not complain. He told me much about the farm strike, the farmer's funeral, the election of the *Daihyo Sha Kai,* and the long painful struggle between the WRA, the army, and the dwindling "representatives of the people." As he put it: "At that time everybody believed in the *Daihyo Sha Kai,* because we all had one camp and were trying to make it livable."

When he began to tell me how the block representatives had been elected, his mother, who was sitting nearby, spoke to him sharply in Japanese, warning him not to tell "that *keto*" too much. (*Keto* is a derogatory term for Caucasian—a rough translation being "hairy ape.") He replied (in Japanese), "She is a German Nisei." I did not know what to say, for I had not told these people that I knew a little Japanese. Besides, though I spoke German fairly well, I was not a German Nisei (second generation) but a third-generation American of German, Polish, and Scandinavian ancestry. Subsequently, the rumor that I was a German Nisei spread through the underground group. Whether it helped me win the confidence of some of these people, I do not know. The fact is that I sometimes became a little tired of being complimented for my German "virtues."

Harry Yamaguchi told me that he believed that the coordinating committee had tried very hard to get the detainees out of the stockade, but that they did not have the backing either of the WRA or of the people. He also told me that he had gone alone to talk with Mr. Penn (a polite way of letting me know that I would waste my time asking about his confederates) and had told Mr. Penn that the coordinating committee did not have the backing of the people and that the *Daihyo Sha Kai* had petered out. The only way to have the center return to a "normal basis" was to "dispose of the coordinating committee" and have a real election—have each block elect two representatives. Then, he added, the WRA would have *evidence* that the people approved of their representatives. He then asked me if Mr. Penn had told me about this meeting. I replied that Mr. Penn had mentioned a meeting, but that he had not given me any of the details. Thereupon, Harry said he would tell me nothing more. If Mr. Penn wished to tell me, it would be all right.

Since I was scheduled to leave Tule Lake on the evening train, I hurried to Mr. Penn's office to see if he would tell me more about the meeting. He did so, after I had promised to use the information with discretion. In mid-January, about a week after the people had voted to abandon the strike, Mr. Penn received a frantic telephone call asking him to come into the colony and talk to the block manager of Block 11. This man referred him to a young man who lived in Block 6 (Harry Yamaguchi), who, in turn, asked him to attend a secret meeting of the remnants of the *Daihyo Sha Kai*. At this meeting Mr. Penn spoke to some six men, all strangers to him, who asked what they could do to bring about the release of the men held in the stockade. Mr. Penn pointed out that nothing much could be accomplished so long as the people were divided into two hostile factions. They would either have to combine and work together or there would have to be another segregation. He further suggested that the people might be able to elect a group of representatives who could work together, provided that the leaders, now detained in the stockade, formally resigned.

The underground group tentatively accepted this plan, leaving Mr. Penn with the task of convincing the imprisoned members of the negotiating committee that they should resign. Without informing the project director, Penn had the members of the negotiating committee brought to his office and laid the plan before them. George Kuratomi, the spokesman, replied, "If you'll promise me that we'll eventually get out of the stockade, we'll go for that plan." Kuratomi further stated that he himself would go into the colony and urge the people to elect new representatives. Mr. Penn told me that he had then reported these matters to the project director but that no action had been taken—except that one of the men with whom he had talked at the meeting had been picked up and confined in the stockade.

ANALYTIC COMMENT

These developments in fieldwork suggest that no technique or talent is quite so valuable as luck and that the way luck operates can be very complicated. Mr. Penn thought I could help him influence the higher echelons of the WRA to adopt a policy that would put an end to the stockade and bring about the election of a genuine people's representative body. He also considered me a person of discretion. When his ploy failed, he recommended me to Mrs. Tsuchikawa, who later was to introduce me to the real leaders of the "superpatriots," the pro-Japanese agitators that eventually set up a regime of terror in the camp.

The encounter between Myer, Penn, and myself illustrates how difficult it is for people who operate at different levels of a complex situation to communicate with and understand each other, especially if they come from different backgrounds and are employed by different institutions. Myer's task, as he saw it, was to keep Tule Lake on the quiescent track which it seemed to have taken with the abandonment of the strike, and to do nothing which might jeopardize the WRA's plan of getting the loyal Japanese out of the relocation centers and off the hands of the federal government. As for Tule Lake, from the very beginning of the segregation the Washington office had assumed that the "disloyal" people would not be permitted to engage in self-government.[1] It had been expected that in time the segregants would be permitted to select an advisory council, which, of course, they now had in the form of the coordinating committee. Indeed, at this time, the Washington office was not yet

1. Whyte (1967) has presented an illuminating discussion of the various definitions of this type of situation.

115

sure what it was going to do with the segregants, and, until major policy decisions were made by the Departments of the Interior and Justice, the WRA could do nothing but stall. Meanwhile, any obvious "concessions" to the open and vocal "disloyals" had to be avoided, for such concessions might once again draw the attention of the press and of a congressional investigation committee.

Mr. Penn, the only higher-ranking member of the administration who seemed deeply concerned over what was going on in the center, felt that this policy would lead to a local disaster. I, in my political naïveté, could not accept as final, unalterable, and *real,* any policy which subjected the segregants to such immoral and unjust procedures. The idea that my own government would continue to behave so unfairly to *any* people under its jurisdiction—especially when these people had striven to act honestly, peaceably, and democratically—was a notion which I could not quite grasp.

My college education had not made me aware that high-ranking officials of the government (and, indeed, most professional men) tend to conceal or disguise many of the motives for their decisions and actions. In my innocence I thought that only cheap politicians did this. Thus, I concluded that many of the WRA decisions and statements were merely stupid, when, stupid or not, they were based on a point of view I did not understand. When, for example, Mr. Myer referred to his appearance before the Dies committee (House Committee on Un-American Activities, then headed by Congressman Martin Dies) as "a good-natured rough-and-tumble," I thought him an idiot (and I still think it a silly statement). My views on these matters were very like those of the segregants and even like the agitators. We tended to blame what we considered unjust or stupid administrative acts on particular staff members or, sometimes, on the local WRA. The notion that the federal officials would refuse to abide by the basic principles of democracy was unthinkable.

Holding to this point of view I conscientiously gathered a great deal of data about the mechanics of the selection of the *Daihyo Sha Kai,* because I took it for granted that the question of whether or not the representatives truly represented the people was very important. It was very important—to the people—but I did not see for a long time that it was of little or no importance to the WRA or the Department of the Interior. Another consequence of my political simplicity was that I did not, until several years later, appreciate the profound absurdity of the situation in which the WRA, the army, and the "disloyal" segregants were involved. Ever since Pearl Harbor, the Japanese Americans had been meek and obedient. On the whole, they had done very little to defend their rights as American citizens. But as soon as the "disloyals" were put into a separate center, they began to behave like genuine democrats, choosing a body of representatives, staging a demonstration, and demanding an alleviation of their grievances. To these phenomena the authorities had responded with a policy of suppression, going so far as to arrest and confine American citizens without charge and without trial. Now the WRA's only contact with the disillusioned, distrustful, and intimidated population was a body of accommodators who were regarded as stooges or quasi informers by almost everyone. Meanwhile, the members of the pro-Japanese underground were beginning to spice their discussions with references to "civil rights," "freedom of speech," and "unlawful search and seizure."

10 The Resegregation Petition

In April I made another visit to Tule Lake, this time for six days (12–17 April). On arrival I found the higher-ranking administrators in a state of crisis. Even the secretaries seemed tense and anxious. People who had never noticed me before called me into their private offices and asked my opinions. Since I did not know what had happened, my opinions were not worth much, but I had no difficulty in finding out what had generated the excitement.

Like many crises, this one had a fairly long history. Early in February the underground "pro-status-quo" group (the "radicals" who had approached Mr. Penn) had written a letter to Attorney General Biddle and to the Spanish embassy, asking for permission to circulate a petition for the signatures of those residents who wished to go to Japan as soon as possible and who, meanwhile, wished to be "resegregated" in Tule Lake from those not so inclined. This request was not so fantastic as might first appear, for, at the time of the strike, the army had fenced off a section of the center in which "troublemaking" families would, if necessary, be confined. In any case, the letter requesting permission to circulate the petition was passed from the Attorney General to the Secretary of the Interior, thence to the national director of the WRA, and thence to Mr. Best, the project director at Tule Lake. Best, who was about to leave the project on official business, passed the letter on to Mr. Black, the assistant project director in charge of housing and social welfare. Black, who, it would seem, had some training in sociology, decided to allow not a petition but a *survey,* structured to obtain the names of the following two types of persons:

> 1. Persons and families who have applied for repatriation or expatriation, who wish to return to Japan at the earliest opportunity, and who wish to live in a designated section of the center among others of like inclination.
> 2. Persons and families who have not applied for repatriation or expatriation, who have reached no conclusion with respect to an early return to Japan, and who wish to live in a section of the center not specifically designated for persons and families of the first group.[1]

1. Letter, Black to Ishikawa, March 1944.

Black took special pains to emphasize that this survey was to be made "with the entire liberty of choice resting with the subject interviewed." He added:

> It is further understood that the survey will be made without commitment on the part of the administration, either stated or implied, that the result of the survey will be made the basis of administrative action beyond that which is already established for housing adjustments through the Housing Office.[2]

Gratified at having won this degree of recognition, the underground group disregarded the notion of a survey and Black's qualifying clauses and proceeded to approach the center residents with a draft of their original petition. The text urged all "who wish resegregation because they desire the opportunity to board an exchange ship . . . to sign this petition of your own free will and judgment." Moreover, in their Japanese translation of Black's last sentence, they conveyed the impression that the results of the petition *would* be made the basis for further administrative action (Thomas and Nishimoto 1946: 231–32).

The circulation of the petition between 7 and 9 April threw many of the center residents into a state of great anxiety. The long-suffering coordinating committee, whom Black had not consulted about the "survey," took this convenient opportunity to submit their resignations. The administrators, with no responsible Japanese to help them, now had only rumors to rely on, and most of these were alarming. Even level-headed and relatively well-informed men like Mr. Penn anticipated that another demonstration or "riot" might occur at any moment.

I made a round of visits and found that the Japanese were, on the whole, in far less panic that the administrators. Men who followed center "politics" closely—like Kurihara, Yamaguchi, or George Wakida, my ex-agitator friend from Gila—had realized almost immediately that the people behind the petition represented what they called "would-be big shots," "people with a narrow point of view," or "a radical goon-squad business." George remarked that such people thought, if "they try to segregate two or three Japanese in this center, that make them very popular when they get to Japan." My outspoken friend Bob Tsuruda told me: "What do I care about *Dai Nippon* (the Great Japanese Empire)! I came here to lead a peaceful life until the war's over."

2. Ibid.

On the other hand, since the petition seemed to have administrative sanction, most of the people had, at first, been very worried. Some interpreted the petition as the first administrative step in another segregation, and they harangued me with rather incoherent assertions that the "loyal people" and those who did not really want to go back to Japan ought to get out of the center. Some added, "Trouble like this is occurring because there are too many *inu*."

I felt sorry for these people because I suspected that most of them had not applied for repatriation, and I knew that the issue of immediate loyalty meant very little to them. What they wanted was to be left alone until the end of the war. Three or four days later, when I called on them again, they told me they had found out that the petition was not sanctioned by the administration and they were much relieved.

Interestingly, almost every person to whom I spoke ignored the major point made in the petition—the issue of a resegregation *within* the center. What they emphasized instead was that the "yes-yes people" (those who had stated that they were loyal to the United States) should be taken *out of* the center or there would be serious trouble. As one friend remarked: "There's been a lot of talk about dog (*inu*) hunting with baseball bats. If there's any trouble here in the next five or six months, it's going to be because of keeping the yes-yes in camp." (Since so many people made this assertion, I asked Mr. Penn how many yes-yes people there were in the center. He told me that it would be difficult to find out, because the administration had not kept accurate records.)

I had a long talk with Mrs. Tsuchikawa, the "lady agitator." Though in bed with a heavy cold, she insisted that I remain and visit. For half an hour or more, she told me how, on various occasions, she had been roughly or rudely treated by the Internal Security. She also told me how one of her brothers had been beaten by the police on the night of the warehouse fracas (4 November), and this was a pretty grisly story. Another of her brothers was serving in the United States army. I took careful notes on all these matters and I then remarked that many people were talking about a petition, and asked her what she could tell me about it. At once she sat erect and spoke as if she were delivering an address:

> Since we came here, we call ourselves the real expatriates and repatriates seeking to go back to Japan and be with her in everything, win or lose, as her subjects. We've been denied all privileges in the

United States. We're going to go to a place where our children can
become somebody.

When we came, much to our dismay, we find many loyal [to U.S.]
are still here, although they put up a front of expatriation or repatriation. They did it as a means of escaping the draft or leaving the
camps since Tule Lake won't close. . . . A lot of draft evaders come
here. It's nothing but a dump! They [draft evaders] are disloyal
Japanese, but they do not have any future thoughts about bringing up
their children, but would face on either side of the fence as the war
progresses.

She continued in a tone of passionate exultation:

We don't care which wins or loses. We're going to stick to Japan!
We cannot raise our children overnight to become Japanese subjects.
We can't do this because there are so many elements here. Those
guys [the fence-sitters] are always double-crossing us!

I agreed with Mrs. Tsuchikawa that there were many fence-sitters
in the center, and I respectfully asked her how her group could be
sure they could distinguish between people who truly wished to return to Japan and those who did not. She replied:

We put up a question. Those who like to go back to Japan at the
first opportunity is the ones who *really* want to go back. They don't
want to stay here until they see what happens. We asked them, "We
might be given a bad place to live—would you go?" They said: "Yes,
we'll die there as Japanese!" Those who won't say yes to this are the
guys who are going to stay here!

Since I already knew that most of the people in the center felt
threatened by the petition, I remarked that I had heard that there
were thousands of people who had not signed it and I did not think
all of these people were *inu*. What was to be their fate? Mrs. Tsuchikawa replied with scorn: "They didn't stick up for us in the crisis.
It's not our business to worry about them." Then she made a curious
statement, "We're holding ourselves in. We tell them over and over
it's not time. We don't want the community to see us forget ourselves." I did not know what she meant by this, and the tight-lipped
fury with which she spoke kept me from asking. Months later, I was
to hear much the same phrase from her male counterparts among the
underground leaders. It meant that they were keeping their strong-
arm boys from beating up the people who spoke against them but
that they could not, of course, be expected to maintain this restraint
indefinitely.

121

When I called on Mr. Sasaki, formerly the executive secretary of the recently resigned coordinating committee, I found him a changed man. In March he had not been able to speak above a whisper and had barely been able to put one word after another. Now he was relaxed and almost garrulous. He told me that, despite the committee's resignation, the administration was insisting that it "continue" until official permission to elect another representative body had been received. (Mr. Penn had told me that permission to proceed with an election had been received from Washington the day before, but, apparently, no one had informed Mr. Sasaki.) He also volunteered a good deal of information on the cavalier way in which the administrators had treated the committee, and he told me that the petition for a resegregation had caused a good deal of trouble in his block. He believed that some of the signatures on the petition were not proper, since many people had signed not only their own names but the names of their minor children.

In the six days I spent at Tule Lake on this April visit I conducted twenty-three visits or interviews, eleven with Japanese. My most significant talks, however, were the two I had with Mr. Kurihara. When I told him that members of the administration had been very concerned about the petition and that some of them even feared another uprising, he smiled and remarked that the administration did not have to fear any action against *them*. Instead, the plain fact was that from here on the Japanese in the center were going to fight each other. If the administrators wished to avert this coming trouble, they could do one of two things, either get the yes-yes people out of the center or have the army patrol the camp by day and by night.

Kurihara told me that the petition had been presented in a "haphazard manner" with no "clear cut explanation," and that many people now regretted having signed it. "I think they [the petitioners] should have explained it so thoroughly that even a child could understand it. But their attitude was take it or leave it. It was too much of a high-pressure group."

I had given Mr. Kurihara a working copy of my first report on the strike and the demonstration and had asked for his comments and criticisms. He said he wished to criticize only one item. I had mentioned that some of the WRA administrators had believed that certain leaders of the November uprising had conspired to seize political control of Tule Lake even before the segregation—that is, they had laid their plans in the relocation centers. Kurihara explained that administrators always tend to think this way and they are usually mistaken. "A thing of this nature happens spontaneously." As a case in point he cited his own experience as spokesman for the people in the Manzanar riot (Thomas and Nishimoto 1946: 49–52). All in all, he concluded, my paper had surprised him. He could not understand how anyone could have learned so much about the situation.

COMMENTS ON FIELD TECHNIQUE

By April of 1944 I had a good working relationship with more than a dozen of the segregated residents of Tule Lake. Almost all of these relationships had developed out of the carefully nurtured recommendation of a mutual friend or acquaintance. Though I asked most people the same questions, I rarely interviewed anyone in a formal way and, by and large, I behaved much more like a journalist than like the stereotyped social scientist. This procedure was efficient and it suited my respondents who, of course, knew I was "gathering material" on the uprising and its suppression, and also knew that I was intensely interested in current events. Most of my respondents, without any overt suggestion on my part, were beginning to collect materials for me, telling me what happened in their block, what they heard had happened in other wards, and what people were saying about these things.

At this time most people seemed to enjoy or, at least, to get satisfaction out of my visits. It gave them the opportunity to play the role of expert and express their views before an appreciative person who, they had convinced themselves, would keep her mouth shut. I think some people also welcomed my visits because center life in Tule Lake was dull and atomizing. There was little employment, and most people had nothing to do with their time. The situation was such that most people did not dare to talk or socialize with neighbors or even with friends. It was too easy to get into trouble because of a careless or misrepresented expression. How close-mouthed people were about these matters is illustrated by the fact that I called on two families for over a year, and, though they were friends to each other, neither ever mentioned my visits to the other. We eventually discovered our "connection" through an accident. Though I was an outsider before whom a guard always had to be maintained, I could, in this peculiar situation, sometimes be told things that could not safely be expressed to a fellow Japanese. Another reason that people sometimes welcomed my visits was that I could be used as an informant and advisor.

123

Though I was not privy to the counsels of the administration, I could find out the answers to many questions, and I probably did more visiting and knew more about what people in general were saying than anyone else in the center.

At this time and later, most of my respondents fell into three categories: those who avoided or tried to give the impression that they were avoiding politics, those who were intensely interested but not active in politics, and those who were actively involved in politics. In the first category were the numerous people for whom politics was not a major life interest. The traumata of the past few months had convinced them that their safety lay in keeping their heads down—in knowing, saying, and doing nothing. While they gossiped and fretted interminably, they rarely took the trouble to find out precisely what was going on. In justice to them, getting information was not easy. For example, anyone who went to the administrative area to ask a question might be accused of being an *inu*. In the second category—those interested but not active—were men like Mr. Kurihara and Mr. Wakida, who, at one time or another, had sought or been pushed into positions of leadership. Both Kurihara and Wakida had been arrested and placed in isolation centers, and, having promised the authorities that they would take no active part in politics, they were transferred to the Tule Lake center. Here they maintained an intense interest in what was going on in the center, and they tried, as best they could, to keep up with outside events. They made splendid informants because they knew what was going on and did not mince words. Other respondents in the second category were men like Mr. Tsuruda and Mr. Kurusu (who will be referred to later in this account)—persons who were not activists but tried to keep up with events and who, like Tsuruda, loved to talk. In retrospect I am impressed by the frankness with which these and other men like them talked with me. Though they usually refrained from mentioning names or saying anything that would get anyone into trouble, they never, so far as I can see, knowingly gave me misleading information. In the third category, of course, were people like Mr. Sasaki and his secretary and Mrs. Tsuchikawa and other members of the underground pressure group.

Perhaps I exaggerate the difference between the "political afficionados" and the ordinary folk, but the fact is that the former, when presented with the petition for resegregation, either knew immediately that its source was a small pressure group or they knew where to find out. The latter (unless they belonged to the few hundred people who really wanted to go to Japan on the first exchange boat) were thrown into a state of frantic anxiety, reasoning that, if they signed, they would be shipped off to Japan immediately, and, if they did not sign, they would be drafted or forced to relocate somewhere in the hostile United States.

I MOVE TO TULE LAKE

In the middle of May I packed my belongings (by now reduced to an archaic portable typewriter and whatever else would fit into two suitcases) and moved to Tule Lake. I regretted leaving the Browns, the Murakami's, Mr. Sakamoto, and my other friends, but I knew there was going to be trouble at Tule Lake and I wanted to be there when it happened. This time when I arrived my fingerprints were taken, for I was going to be a "permanent resident." Then I was given a police pass marked "good until revoked" and assigned a room in the staff barracks.

My expectations of turmoil and excitement were not fulfilled. The WRA staff members were relaxed and optimistic. Mr. Penn and Dr. Opler told me that the project director, Mr. Best, had been putting himself out to be agreeable to the colonists. There had been a half-holiday on the emperor's birthday, and the director had even thrown the first baseball at the game celebrating this event. Japanese schoolchildren had been permitted to visit the project farm, outside of the main barbed-wire fence. Most of the men in the stockade had been released, leaving only about twenty-five prisoners. The fence that had divided the Japanese "colony" into two sections (and had raised the hopes of the underground pro-resegregation group) had been torn down.

Most of the Japanese also were in good spirits. Some people told me with smiling irony that they were now getting one egg a day per person in the mess. They also told me that the *"inu* hate" was dying down and that people were forgetting the coordinating committee and Mr. Sasaki. Young people told me about the newly initiated entertainments and athletic events—movies, block entertainments, baseball, and basketball. But the best event of all was the removal of the fence. When the Japanese told me about this, their faces lit up.

My politically oriented friends corroborated this picture. Kurihara remarked that "right now things are simmering down pretty fast." My block manager friend from Gila quipped: "All Quiet on the

Western Front," and told me how the block managers were going to ask the Spanish Consul to get them divided washbowls for the latrines and screens for the barracks. George Wakida, my ex-agitator friend from Gila, told me that he was devoting himself to sponsoring athletic activities and entertainments for the Issei, adding philosophically, "If you do good for the people you get put in the stockade. If you do good for WRA you get called *inu*. So I'm going to play baseball." The only unhappy voice I heard was that of a soldier, loudly berating a Japanese worker because he was not wearing his large, red identification button in the proper manner. As I approached the gate to leave the center, many Japanese passed me on their way home from work, and the soldiers yelled at all of them: "Wear your button on the left lapel! Wear your button on the left lapel!" These buttons, two and a half inches in diameter, were part of a new army regulation requiring evacuee workers to carry a blue work card, an identification tag, and wear a numbered button on the left lapel. I was not able to find out why all of these items of identification were necessary.

I MEET THE "PRO-JAPANESE" AGITATOR, MR. YAMASHITA

On 20 May Mr. Penn's secretary told me that Mrs. Tsuchikawa (the ardent lady resegregationist) had telephoned, requesting that I call on her. I went that same afternoon and found Mrs. Tsuchikawa very cordial. She gave me an account of trouble in block 54 involving two Japanese members of the police force. (Like most of the other divisions of the center, the police force was manned by Caucasians, assisted by Japanese. The Caucasians were paid a standard wage. The Japanese, though they might be experts or professional persons, were paid sixteen or nineteen dollars per month.) The Japanese policemen (whom she called *inu*) had reprimanded some young men for doing physical exercises. (She did not tell me that these exercises were patterned on those of the Japanese army.) Then, according to Mrs. Tsuchikawa, the young men had called the Japanese policemen *inu* and "un-Japanese," whereupon the policemen had reported the incident to Internal Security. Now the people in the block were demanding that the *"inu"* policemen and their families leave the block.

Mrs. Tsuchikawa also told me that she had been visited by a young man who claimed "that he was really working for the Germans and Norwegians." She assured me, however, that she had immediately recognized him as "FBI." One of the things he had told her was that she and the Japanese in Tule Lake were behaving foolishly, for if they were really loyal to Japan they would say they were loyal to the United States, leave the camp, and commit sabotage. To this suggestion Mrs. Tsuchikawa had replied that she had a brother serving in the United States army.

As I was preparing to leave, Mrs. Tsuchikawa remarked that the man she wanted me to meet was a certain Mr. Yamashita who had just arrived in the center from Santa Fe (the internment center for Issei who were considered "pro-Japanese agitators"). She suggested that I call on him the next morning, which I did.

Mr. Yamashita was about forty years old. His wife was very elegant and handsome. Their apartment was well furnished; in fact, it was the best looking evacuee apartment I had seen, and there were so many people present that it looked as if the Yamashitas were holding a reception. All of these people were listening to Mr. Yamashita with the appearance of great respect. Seated near me was a striking looking man almost six feet tall. He was introduced to me as Mr. Tada. I pricked up my ears, for Tada was the ex–chief of police who had been a member of the negotiating committee of the *Daihyo Sha Kai* and had for a long time been imprisoned in the stockade. He was also, rumor had it, the camp's vice king, running a gambling establishment and controlling the bootleg sake market.

At intervals other men and women called, stayed briefly, and then withdrew, engaging with Mrs. Yamashita in some of the most elaborate bowing rituals that I had even seen. After this had been going on for about half an hour, Mr. Yamashita addressed me in English, telling me that he was a graduate of Stanford University and that he approved of our study. He explained the high aims and ideals of the resegregation group in pompous, and excessively erudite language (which was sometimes very difficult for me to understand) and he closed with the solemn assertion that "every man in this room is going to be an important man in Japan some day and it will be very fine to have a record of what we have done in Tule Lake." (This record, I surmised, was to be kept by me.) In this and in all of our subsequent conversations he spoke very slowly, so that I would have the opportunity to write down every word he said.

Much of the conversation was carried on in Japanese, and I understood very little except that everyone present was treating Mr. Yamashita with great deference. Once, when Yamashita was called away for a few minutes, I ventured to address Mr. Tada and tell him that I was pleased to meet him and that I hoped some day to discuss

127

certain aspects of the early history of the center with him. Tada replied suavely with some fluent but carefully worded statements about the "riot" of 4 November. I thanked him and remarked that some day I hoped to learn the inside story of that important event. Meanwhile, I suggested that he watch my activities until he was sure that I could be trusted. Tada made no reply. But eight months later, when I was finally able to talk to him, he told me that this statement had impressed him. "When you said that, I knew you weren't so dumb."

Perhaps I seemed less dumb than I was, because I sat there most of the morning looking alert, interested, and respectful, while Mr. Yamashita talked to Tada and to many other visitors, trying to get allies for a powerful new resegregation movement which he hoped to organize. Tada, as the one available member of the old negotiating committee (the others were still in the stockade), was being asked to join the movement and help obtain the sanction and support of the still imprisoned members of the old negotiating committee, and he was politely refusing to do this. Yamashita, on his part, was refusing to join Tada in an attempt to appeal to the American Civil Liberties Union in behalf of the American citizens imprisoned in the stockade. Of all this I understood nothing, because I did not know enough Japanese. But I learned about it eight months later from Mr. Tada.

Still more people came to call on Mr. Yamashita, and it was obvious that many people had come to regard him as an important man. "He sat still while the people came to see him." The apartment became very crowded, and I rose to leave. But the Yamashitas would not hear of this and insisted that I stay and eat Sunday dinner with them in the mess hall. The dinner was unusually good for camp fare —much better than meals at Gila—and I remarked on this. But Mr. and Mrs. Yamashita assured me that everything was much better in the internment camps for Americans in Japan. I made no comment. At the end of the dinner Yamashita drew himself up with dignity, invited me to call again, and said: "Be sure you have the Rockefeller Foundation send me a copy of the book you plan to publish when I am in Japan. They can well afford it."

THE ABORTIVE ATTEMPT TO NOMINATE A REPRESENTATIVE COMMITTEE

The most important non-happening of mid-May 1944 was the administration's attempt to arrange for the nomination of a permanent representative committee. The initiation of this procedure was kept so secret by the WRA that even I, snoop that I was, did not find out that it had failed until the next day, when several Japanese friends remarked, almost parenthetically, that the block managers had tried unsuccessfully to call block meetings to nominate candidates for the new representative committee. That same evening I called on Dr. Opler and asked him what was going on. He gave me the preliminary results which were that, out of the seventy-four blocks in the center, only fifteen had nominated representatives.

During the next three days I made as many calls as I could. What people gave me, for the most part, were expressions of oblique or ironic satisfaction. They seemed to feel that they had put the administration down with considerable finesse. For the first and only time during my stay at Tule Lake I saw some people in really good spirits. A few of my friends laughed and joked with me and each other in the style that they had sometimes done in Gila. George Wakida gave me and several ladies a comic recital of what had happened in his block. At first there had been no quorum. Then the block manager had gone about begging people to come. So George went and, of course, was nominated. He declined the nomination, pointing out that as an ex-internee he was not permitted to engage in politics. By the time George had finished arguing, about ten people had left the meeting. Thereupon he pointed out that the quorum no longer existed, so that his nomination was not valid. I asked George whether his block manager would not get into trouble trying so hard to comply with an administrative suggestion. "Oh well," he said, chuckling, "he's an old man and is going to die soon anyway." The ladies laughed, and each began to relate with gusto how the nomination meetings in her block had failed. But the hostess topped them all, for in her block the people had met and all shouted, "No, no, no, no, no!"

Bob Tsuruda, my cynical respondent from Gila pointed out that the suggestion to nominate representatives had come from the WRA and therefore "had a rank odor." Besides, people were catching on to the fact that block managers could act as liaison men between the people and the administration without standing in danger of being imprisoned in the stockade as agitators. "You can't yank a liaison man for what he reports. The people are starting to realize it would be a smart thing to have a good block manager and let them do all the 'representing' because they can't be yanked."

An Issei friend said much the same thing: "If we elect more representatives, they will only put more people in the stockade. Everybody said, 'What the heck! We don't want to send any more people to the stockade.' "

Mr. Kurihara, on the other hand, was concerned over the failure of the nominations. He pointed out that the agitators—the fanatical resegregationists—would take credit for the debacle, whereas the fact was that the people were striking back at the administration. Dr. Opler told me that Mr. Best had taken the news with equanimity. If the people felt that an election was premature, he would try again later.

COMMENT

Though almost all of the WRA staff members and, I suspect, many of the segregants felt optimistic about the situation in the center, I continued to feel apprehensive. What worried me was not the presence of such determined and self-righteous agitators as Mr. Yamashita or Mrs. Tsuchikawa, but the fact that most of the people I talked to, despite their pleasure in baseball games or center entertainments, or their childish satisfaction in putting the administration down in the matter of the nomination of representatives, were, at bottom, apathetic and frightened. They had accepted the fact that anyone who spoke up or made a fuss would be confined in the stockade, and most of them believed that there was nothing they could do to help themselves or improve their situation. People in this state of mind would react to any threat by panic.

11 Shooting, Beatings, and Murder

In the evening of 24 May, a staff member knocked on my door and told me that a Japanese had been shot by a soldier on guard duty at the gate. Soon after, another staff worker, a high school teacher, came in and told me that she had been ordered out of her night school class by her supervisor and told to return to the administrative section. She was sputtering with rage because the male teachers had been permitted to remain.

I knew I could learn little by running about exchanging rumors; so I decided to wait until morning. I was then able to have a word with Mr. Penn. Penn told me that one of his maintenance workers returning from work had been shot in the abdomen by a sentry—apparently at a range of less than three feet. He also told me that the Japanese construction crews had not come to work and that many other workers were not showing up.

After lunch I called on Mr. Kurihara. I did not, of course, feel comfortable doing this, but I hoped that Kurihara would advise me whether or not it was proper or decent for me to visit people at this time. Kurihara was unusually gentle and serene, and I did not realize that he was in a state of shock. He told me that the people were very calm. "We must be fair," he said, "Mr. Best is not responsible. We had an announcement here at noon. . . . As I say, the Japanese could take it. They'll take it more than any race." I asked how the injured man was doing, and Kurihara told me that the man was dead. Then he began to cry, and I realized this was the announcement he had just heard. I did not want to sit and watch my friend cry, and so I expressed my sympathy and left.

I think I might have stopped visiting people at this period had I not been obliged to keep an appointment with my secretary, a Nisei girl who lived in the same block as Mr. Kurihara. This young woman was so relieved to see me and so eager to tell me what everyone was saying that I concluded that she found my visit reassuring. Thereupon I called on several other friends and was also well received. What I found was that my friends were not only shocked and angry, but afraid—afraid that there might be another riot and that this

131

time the soldiers might shoot them as they had just shot Mr. Okamoto, the dead man. That I had walked safely past the soldiers and visited them was a normal and somewhat reassuring phenomenon.

That evening, however, as I sat in my room and typed up my notes, I suddenly fell into a state of shame and rage. With a little encouragement I would have hollered and howled. But since there was no one to whom I could holler, I stamped up and down and cried. Finally my eye was caught by my old Bible, the only book I had brought with me, and I sat down and began to read Isaiah. These ancient assertions of an ultimate justice made me feel a little better.

In the weeks that followed Mr. Okamoto's death, the people behaved much as they always do after a shocking event. At first there was a great deal of wild talk—so much, in fact, that Bob Tsuruda, my garrulous friend from Gila, told me that "if all hell should break loose" I was to come and stay with him and his family in the center, where, he assured me, I would be safe. Many people predicted that there would be trouble if the soldier were not punished, but some added, cynically, that "these things are always whitewashed." And when the WRA issued statements to the effect that the shooting was the responsibility of the army and not the WRA, some people asked me anxiously, "If the WRA isn't responsible for the safety of the people, who is responsible?"

The edge was taken from many a person's resentment by the seemly and sensible behavior of the high-ranking members of the administration, even though it was recognized as expedient. Immediately after Mr. Okamoto's death, Secretary of the Interior Ickes issued a press release stating that the shooting was "completely unwarranted and without provocation on the part of the victim." Members of the WRA police force, both Caucasian and Japanese, were stationed at the gates with the army sentries, who, I observed, did not make a show of carrying arms. Mr. Best and the three assistant project directors called on the dead man's family and made arrangements for a public funeral. Mr. Best himself attended the funeral and gave a memorial address. As Bob Tsuruda put it:

I will give the man [Mr. Best] credit. He really has done his best. He attended the funeral and called the half-holiday, and [in his speech] he said just enough—no more. . . . Regardless of *why* he did it, the fact stands that he *did* do it. It couldn't all have been prompted through selfishness.

The leaders of the underground resegregation group, of course, were openly sarcastic, but few people seemed to pay much attention to them.

During June of 1944, my fieldwork proceeded very well, and I was able, through recommendations, to acquire half a dozen additional respondents. I made frequent and regular calls on people of varied ages, interests, and political points of view, and many of these people (and I myself) began to regard these visits as partly social and partly as "my job." The only other Caucasian who did this kind of visiting was Mr. Penn. I mention this fact because several of my respondents remarked upon it and added that if the director or some of the other staff members "walked around the center and talked to people like you and Mr. Penn do," they would have a much better idea of what was going on. I concluded that though my visits might put some people in fear of being thought *inu,* they were also reassuring. That I walked about the center showed that I trusted people and that I believed they were responsible human beings. My visits also helped to relieve one of the most exasperating and depressing aspects of center life—the uncertainty. In many matters (such as the resegregation petition) I knew what the administration's policy was, and I could pass on correct information and scotch frightening rumors (see Shibutani 1966). In addition, my visits were also to some degree social events, and the segregants had no other opportunity at all to play host to any one living on the other side of the fence.

During June I had some conversations I will never forget. One was with Bob Tsuruda, who told me that he had decided to take his family and get out of Tule Lake. How much he was motivated toward this decision by the fact that his Caucasian WRA supervisor had found him a good job "on the outside" and how much by the news of German reverses he probably did not know himself.

> The only reason I consider relocation is that I've got a pretty good thing coming up. As you should know by this time, the majority of the Nisei—myself included—came in here because they didn't want to go into the army. If they had treated us differently, I would have volunteered. Now, seeing as how they're deferring people over twenty-six, I think I might take a chance.

He added that the war might last another three years and then he would be in Tule Lake until he was thirty-three:

133

. . . Then I get deported to Japan. It'll take me ten years to get on my feet. It seems to me Germany is going to pull a flopperoo. I wouldn't want to be here when that happens. I don't care if Japan has seventeen kinds of *Yamato Damashii* (the Japanese Spirit), she isn't going to be able to buck fighting three big nations.

More and more people in the center, he assured me, were behaving in an unrealistic and even an unbalanced fashion:

Believe it or not, a fellow told me the other day that Japan was going to have a decisive victory and the war would be over in seven days! . . . A lot of the old men are getting goofier and goofier. They stand around in the latrines and mutter to themselves. I think they're losing their minds. . . . the trouble is they expect you to act like a damn radical and go out and kill every *hakujin* [Caucasian] on the other side of the fence, and when you don't act like that you are an *inu*. [Wax 1944:25 June]

I asked other respondents whether the Nisei were being influenced by the reports of Allied victories, and I was assured that they were. Mrs. Wakida, who taught Japanese in the segregant organized language school said that her pupils were very much disturbed. " '*Sensei* [teacher],' they say to me, 'What's going to become of us?' " But Mr. Kurihara, while admitting that many Nisei were having second thoughts about their "disloyal" status, asserted that he had no use for people who changed their minds:

These persons who will change their minds now are no good to either country. . . . You'll find there are many of that kind. . . . They just want to wait and see how it turns out. If Japan wins they want to go to Japan and if the United States wins they want to stay here. It's disgraceful. It makes me ashamed of the Japanese race . . . . I've talked to many of them. They say, "I'm going back to Japan." Then I ask, "Then why aren't you studying?" They're not studying. They're just fooling around and gambling and having a good time.

At this time I also began a cordial relationship with Mr. Itabashi, a gentle and scholarly man of about sixty. Mr. Itabashi (to whom I was referred by Mr. Kurihara) was a rare being, a good man who was both practical and brave, a kind of Japanese Erasmus. He told me that he had written a long letter to the project director, suggesting that the administration treat the segregants fairly and decently and not look upon them as "traitors or criminals to be deported"; that the project director attend meetings in the center and "not depend entirely on his subordinates for information"; that more jobs be provided; and that the hospital have one visiting hour per day—instead of the current system which permitted only a brief visit on Sundays.

Mr. Itabashi also told me that, when he was repatriated to Japan, he planned to go on a lecture tour and speak about all the good things that America had done for the Japanese people in the past. Today, he told me, the Japanese think only of the bad things the United States had done, and this, Itabashi felt, was neither fair nor correct.

Given the atmosphere at Tule Lake, Mr. Itabashi's words sounded a little mad. But they were the voice of reason, and I was beginning to appreciate that, in a mad situation, reason may sound mad.

THE INU HUNT

As I have remarked, any Japanese who was friendly with Caucasian staff members was likely to be called an *inu*. Most of my respondents, except the leaders of the resegregation group, risked being called *inu* because of my visits. Dr. Opler's Japanese assistants were also called *inu,* and the office they occupied was dubbed *"Inu* Headquarters." Most of the members of the coordinating committee and the men who held administrative positions in the Co-op were also called *inu.* Men like Mr. Sasaki, chairman of the coordinating committee, or Noma and Watanabe of the Co-op, who made no secret of their accommodating attitude toward the administration, were called "Public *Inu* Number One." The fact, of course, was that anyone might be called an *inu* by a suspicious or spiteful neighbor, and the charge would be believed and repeated—at least by some people. Moreover, many people felt that if they denounced the *inu* strongly enough, they themselves would be less likely to be called *inu.* In April, when the resegregation group circulated its repatriation-expatriation petition, most people began or ended their distracted complaints with the statement: "The main trouble is that this camp is full of *inu* and .yes-yes." It is interesting that in May, during the brief period of optimism and good feeling, I heard very little about the *inu.* In fact, no one mentioned them except the ardent resegregationists, Mrs. Tsuchikawa and Mr. Yamashita.

But soon after the shooting and death of Okamoto everyone once again began to talk about the *inu.* Some people retold the story about the Issei policemen in block 54 who had tried to stop the young men

135

in their block from doing morning exercises. These men, I was told, were *inu*. The Co-op board of directors were called *inu* because, according to rumor, they were enriching themselves at the expense of the residents. Even Mr. Tada, the ex–chief of police who had been released from the stockade, was called an *inu* because, it was said, he "went to the administration section too often." The stories and rumors became increasingly unreal and fantastic. When, for example, I called on Bob Tsuruda's wife, she and her sister told me, "When we came here we thought we would be through with them [*inus*], but there are more of them than ever. Every place you look you can see one!"

Then the beatings began. On 12 June a man was waylaid at night and beaten so severely that he suffered concussion. It was reported that he might lose his eyesight. This unfortunate was the brother of Mr. Noma, the general manager of the Co-op, and rumor soon had it that the beaten man had been mistaken for his brother. The next night one of the Issei who had tried to stop the Japanese militaristic exercises in block 54 was beaten. People said his skull had been fractured, and though most of them knew little or nothing about the incident, they assumed that he must have been beaten because he was an informer. A few days later another man, the chief eyewitness of the Okamoto shooting, narrowly escaped a beating. Once again people figured that he must have been an *inu*—the theory being that he had given testimony unfavorable to Okamoto. On 21 June a mentally deranged elderly man attacked his roommate with a hammer, almost killing him. Some people said that the old man must have "found out that his friend was acting like an *inu*."

Most people, including myself, found the news of these beatings exciting and somehow gratifying. As Mr. Kurihara put it, "The majority of the people are enjoying the beatings. . . . The Japanese have grievances against the administration, but they know as a fact that they're helpless. Naturally, the only thing they can think of doing is how to get back at those who spy on them." But as the beatings continued and the stories about graft in the Co-op grew more and more fantastic, many people began to feel uneasy. Mrs. Tsuruda, who had happily complained about the *inu* on 4 June, looked shaken and sick when I called on her on 24 June. "I think everybody is nervous in here," she told me. "This place gives me the willies." Even the strong-minded Mr. Kurihara became anxious. On 26 June he told me: "If the agitators and spies get out of here we'll be united. But it wouldn't matter if we didn't have unity, so long as we have peace."

The administrators, of course, were by now well aware that the situation within the center was desperate. They tried to interest the residents in the nomination of a police commissioner, but no one went to the meetings. "Who wants to be a legalized *inu?*" said some of my respondents. The administrators also, on 28 June, transferred nineteen Issei from Tule Lake to the Santa Fe internment camp operated by the Department of Justice. Some of these men were taken from the stockade and some from the center. The resegregation group leaders were furious, and many other people remarked that "this might cause a lot of trouble."

On 29 June another man was waylaid and beaten at night. People said he too was beaten because he was a friend of Public *Inu* Number One. A few nights later a third man, this time one of the genuine Number One *Inu* of the old coordinating committee, was beaten, though not severely. On 2 July I asked Kurihara why none of the men who had been attacked had been really notorious *inu*. "You should know," he said. "The big ones are too well guarded. But the guard will slip up some time."

By this time I had had about all I could take. I called on Mr. Penn, intending, once again, to stress that the situation in the center—and especially, the people's attitude toward the men who ran the Co-op—was pathological. Mr. Penn told me that he had already recommended that the Co-op issue a dividend immediately, but he implied that the Co-op managers had been slow to take action because their books had recently been audited and had been found impeccable. I felt like wringing my hands and saying that the Japanese Co-op managers and their Caucasian advisors ought to know by now that innocence did not protect one against fanaticism, but I did not do so because Mr. Penn knew this as well as I did. Then Mr. Penn told me that on the night before members of the resegregation group had approached him and told him that the removal of the Issei to the Santa Fe detention center had been "the last straw." They no longer could or would restrain their "strong arm boys." Future attacks might not be restricted to beatings. They might result in murder.

The following night Mr. Noma, the general manager of the Co-op, was found lying on his brother's doorstep with a knife pushed through his larynx to the base of his brain.

The news of the murder produced a general state of panic. All of the members of the Japanese police force and the key officials of the Co-op resigned. Some, who feared they might be "next on the list," were taken from the center and housed in the administrative area. People rushed to the Co-op to stock up on food supplies, for they feared it would be closed. The administrators decided that the murder was the result of a conspiracy between the stockade detainees and the resegregation group. So they attached large pieces of plaster board to that section of the stockade fence which faced "the colony" and stopped mail to and from the stockade. In the middle of this turmoil, a representative of the American Civil Liberties Union arrived at Tule Lake and insisted that he be allowed to consult with his clients—the Japanese American citizens detained in the stockade.

At this point I decided that the best thing I could do was disappear, lest some frantic member of the administration set eyes on me and decide that I ought to be put off the project. So I returned to Berkeley. In Berkeley I received a letter from Mr. Kurihara advising me to stay out of the center for a while. Later, Kurihara explained that it was not his but my life he was concerned about. Immediately after Noma was killed, some fanatics had spread the rumor that "a Caucasian would be next."

But I was not able to endure the dreariness of wartime Berkeley. All I could think and talk about was Tule Lake, and no one in Berkeley, not even the members of our study, wanted to listen to me. My graduate student friends were in the armed services, and I had nothing to do but sit in an office and write a report of the Noma murder. After a week of this I talked Dr. Thomas into letting me go back, arguing that I could get a good deal of data even if I were not permitted to go into the Japanese quarters. This proved to be the case, for Mr. Penn and Dr. Opler helped me keep up with the administration's attempts to reorganize the Co-op and the Japanese police force, and I was there when the administration threatened some of the stockade detainees with indictment for the Noma murder, and when the detainees, in desperate retaliation, went on a hunger strike. More important, I was able to talk to a number of my Japanese friends who worked in the administrative section and came to see me during their lunch hour, and I corresponded with others. On 14 July Mr. Kurihara sent me a formal note saying that I might call on him at my convenience. The next day Mrs. Wakida invited me to come and see the painting job she and George had done on their apartment. Mr. Itabashi, the elderly man who was gathering material on the good things that the United States had done, also permitted me to visit him. But all of my other friends and acquaintances—even Mrs. Tsuchikawa—suggested that I wait "until things settled down." I lost some respondents entirely, for, as they explained apologetically, there were too many hot-headed people in their block, and I had better not come to see them anymore.

Though I was not aware of it at this time, the murder altered my relationships with many respondents. Mr. Kurihara, Mr. Itabashi, and the Wakidas became more friendly to me and began quite openly to express their disapproval of the resegregation group leaders. Other respondents—and particularly those who were fence-sitters—also spoke more openly, but they were afraid to be seen with me. The people who really intended to go to Japan and who were, perhaps, already sympathetic to the stated ideals of the resegregation group, were most afraid to be seen with me, and it was with people of this mind that I lost most of my acquaintance. But the resegregation group leaders, of course, were more cordial than ever, particularly after the administration had threatened some of them with indictment for the Noma murder.

I Become a Fanatic

I think I should pause here to remark that during this period— from mid-June, when the *inu*-fear hit the center, until mid-September, or thereabouts—I once again went a little crazy. I came to believe that observing and recording what went on at Tule Lake was my transcendental task, and I went about this task with an unflagging energy and relish that today seems rather frightening. I did not think or have fantasies about being killed. But I *knew* I might be killed, and this knowledge made me feel happy and well. At the same time, I was often very much afraid; however, the thing I feared was that the administration might find out how much I was learning and order me off the project. I do not think that this manic or "battle-mad" state hampered my fieldwork or distorted my observations. Indeed, I probably would not have been able to live and work at Tule Lake had I been entirely in my right mind.

Along with this bravado, I developed an unpleasant sense of self-righteousness. When, for example, my sensible and cynical friend Bob Tsuruda told me that he did not give a damn about *Yamato Damashii* and that he had come to the center to escape the draft, I

139

felt shocked and somewhat repelled. And when my young Nisei acquaintances told me that Tule Lake was a dull place and they wished that their parents had not made them come, I thought to myself that they were rather spiritless creatures. When I heard that Mr. Noma had been murdered, I experienced a cruel and self-righteous satisfaction, for—as I told myself—the WRA and the Japanese accommodators had been asking for it for a long time, and now they had gotten it. When I saw the wretched Mr. Sasaki and his secretary, the Co-op directors and their families, sitting in a room in the hospital, staring mutely at each other like frightened animals, I thought this served them right for having cooperated with the administration.

Since then I have often tried to understand, not very successfully, what happened to me. I suspect that I suffered from an exaggerated case of an occupational disease which often afflicts fieldworkers who find themselves involved in a desperate factional struggle and have accumulated just enough knowledge to think that they are "really involved." Naïvely, I had taken the side of "the oppressed," and, as part of my protective self-deception, I had constructed an ideal model of "true Japanese" behavior—for the Japanese and for myself—and I proceeded (in my own mind) to criticize and despise anyone who deviated from this model. That my model was melodramatic and unreal I did not then perceive. Nor did it occur to me that as a social scientist I had no business sitting in judgment on myself or on the people I was supposed to be studying and understanding. My behavior, perhaps, was not unlike that of some ethnologists I have seen at American Indian ceremonials who complain bitterly that the participants are not wearing traditional garb—by which they mean the kind of garb the ancestors of these Indians were wearing in 1850, 1750, or, perhaps, 1492. It may also resemble the practice of certain sociologists who write long articles and even books devoted to the not very startling observation that the people they study do not practice what they preach. It bears an even closer resemblance to the experience which Powdermaker (1967:209–25, 291) had when she did her study of Hollywood. As she so astutely suggests: ideological centricity can be far more difficult to surmount than ethnocentricity.

I do not think that fieldworkers can escape this kind of bias by course work, psychoanalysis, or an act of will. Indeed, it may be that catching the disease, recognizing it, and recovering from it is a part of professional maturation. On the other hand, it may be comforting to know that this bias need not distort the field notes of a well-trained individual. Scrupulously I took down each day precisely what my friends and respondents said or did, whether or not I liked it, approved of it, or understood it. Then and now these notes make a great deal of sense, whereas my parenthetical comments or current reports are sometimes misleading or pathetic. Once in a while my reports advance interpretations and then support them with verbatim quotes which say just the opposite.

A fieldworker may take some comfort in the knowledge that it is possible to train himself to the point where he may be an accurate observer and reporter—even when he is in the grip of a bias or a fanatical "ideological centricity." He might be likened to a well-trained musician or linguist who can put down an accurate record of a song or dialect, even though he may consider the material he is recording to be defective, disgusting, or atypical. When he recovers from his bias, he will have his notes and his honest memories—for one cannot really fool oneself eternally about what one has seen or heard—on which to base his report. The fieldworker may also think twice about following the example of those would-be ethnographers who assert or boast that they take few field notes or no notes at all. The fact is that most of the people who say that they are able to get along without taking notes do not write anything worth reading.

It may also be helpful to remark that I recovered from my bias, not by a process of self-analysis nor professional resolution, nor by paying heed to the frequent and justified criticism that Dr. Thomas made of my reports. What cured me was continuing my fieldwork, talking to as many people as possible, and *listening* to what they said. The recovery took time, and it was not until late August or early September that I began to suspect that the disposition to denigrate or look down on people who did not behave like "true Japanese" was silly and immature. Perhaps I was helped by a particularly bizarre incident. Leaving my room one night, I ran violently into the pouring spout of the large oil can from which we filled our oil-burning stoves, and my leg was cut so severely that I knew it would have to be stitched. At the hospital I found that the only doctor on duty was Dr. Noguchi. My heart sank, for I knew that Dr. Noguchi had good reason to dislike Caucasians. Before he left the Gila Center for Tule Lake, the authorities had forced him to hand over his grandchild, whom he had reared from infancy, to the child's wastrel father. The father was "loyal" and Noguchi was "disloyal." When I lay down on the operating table I pulled up my skirt a few inches. Noguchi pulled it down, remarking curtly, "It will wash." I remembered all the stories I had heard about the Japanese contempt for cowardice, and I determined to be brave. Noguchi gave me the opportunity, for he selected an improper needle, and though he was able to stick it into my leg he could not pull it out. Noguchi tugged at the needle several times and I saw the nurse's aides glance anxiously at each other. Then he asked me, "Does it pain?" "No," I replied. He thereupon ordered one of the nurses to go and get a cutting needle. When she returned he deftly sewed up the cut. (Though the cut required seven stitches, the fact was that it did not hurt me very much, then or later.)

I did not know that the story of what had happened at the hospital had spread among the Japanese. A few days later when I was hobbling about, I ran into Mr. Yamashita and remarked that I would be over to see him again as soon as my leg healed. "Yes," said Mr. Yamashita in a loud, admiring tone, "We have all very much admired your *German* courage." I gulped and said nothing, for by German courage Mr. Yamashita meant that I had behaved like a true Nazi. After this I gave up trying to behave like a "true Japanese" and began to meditate on the complexities of the images that we think we are presenting to other people.

12 Fieldwork in a Factionalized Community

Immediately after the murder there was an outburst of approving and satisfied statements. Many people said they thought that Noma had gotten what he deserved. "Never have I seen such pleasant reactions to a murder in all my life," wrote Kurihara. "This might sound awfully heartless," said a Nisei girl, "but nobody has any sympathy for Noma." Yet the temper of the people changed after a few weeks. Some expressed remorse and bewilderment over the way they and other people had reacted to the murder:

> I never understood why Mr. Noma had to be killed. My parents knew him and felt sorry for him. I can't feel one bit of this hate that made someone stab him. Nobody seems to know why he was killed.
>
> In camp there were so many rumors at that time. People believed what they heard was true. To prove its credibility they always said, "My friends say it." It made almost everybody believe the story.

Rumors about the evil doings of the *inu* subsided; indeed, I do not think I ever again heard a non-resegregationist denounce the stool-pigeons. The resegregationist leaders, of course, continued to call anyone who opposed them an *inu*, but, so far as I could see, these stories did not spread outside of the membership. First covertly and then overtly, many people began to express dissatisfaction with the unending tension and, as some termed it, the gangsterism and hoodlumism that permeated the center. With increasing frequency they wished aloud that there might be some "peace and order." No one, however, dared to suggest that anyone ought to inform or assist the administration. Instead, individuals pointed out (Wax 1944: 24 July) that "troublemakers" were disgracing the Japanese and were acting contrary to the desires of the Japanese government.

Most of the residents (and some of the administrators) suspected that the Noma murder had been committed by a small group of fanatics or "gangsters" belonging to or connected with the resegregation group. But although the administration threatened a number of people (resegregationists and stockade detainees) with indictment on charges of murder and conspiracy to murder, the murderers were

143

never apprehended. The Japanese police force was never properly reconstituted. For a few weeks there were no police except for a handful of Caucasian Internal Security men, and the center was filled with rumors of rape and violence. Finally, the administrators prevailed upon the residents to elect "block wardens," but only about 60 percent of the blocks did so. Moreover, the new and reluctant wardens announced that they would serve only so long as they were not asked to work as agents of the administration or take action in any "political matter." What this meant, of course, was that they would not interfere in any of the activities of the resegregation group. It is significant that the Manzanar section, where the resegregation group was very powerful, elected a full corps of wardens—all members of the resegregation group.

The resegregationist leaders were now more confident than they had ever been before. Since April of 1944 they, as Mr. Yamashita put it, "had been working in secret and awaiting the moment" (Wax 1944: 17 August).[1] They also hoped to join forces with the imprisoned but still respected leaders of the *Daihyo Sha Kai,* especially the Reverend Abe and George Kuratomi, in order to form a formal organization of such strength that the WRA administration in Washington would no longer be able to resist their demands for a separate center or area of residence whence they might be expatriated or repatriated to Japan with the prestige accruing to a group that had made a courageous and positive stand for the Empire. In July the stockade detainees finally obtained the assistance of the American Civil Liberties Union, which threatened that it would have the WRA served with a writ of habeas corpus in order to gain the release of American citizens confined without trial. Simultaneously the stockade detainees went on a hunger strike during whose course all of them had to be hospitalized. When this first hunger strike brought them no relief, they went on another. On 14 August the administration finally gave way, and from 14 to 24 August all the men who had been imprisoned in the stockade were released.

While these events were going on, Yamashita and other resegrega-

1. In mid-July their hopes for an eventual resegregation were raised when the Congress of the United States passed the denationalization bill, opening the way for the renunciation of American citizenship, and from this point forward they made the renunciation of citizenship an important plank in their program.

tionist leaders had been delivering "educational lectures" at small block meetings. They assured their listeners that Japan was winning the war and interpreted the various reverses as a strategic trap into which the American forces were being drawn. They further emphasized that, "for those who desire to return to Japan, the discipline and education of our children adapted to the system of wartime Motherland are absolutely necessary" and they asserted that they hoped, with the consent of the WRA, to form organizations which would provide such discipline and education. I was not invited to these lectures, but Mr. Yamashita told me he was giving them without permission from the administration and that he would continue to give them "for the sake of the people." Simultaneously a group of residents headed by a young Buddhist priest approached the administration and received permission to use the high school auditorium for a series of lectures on Japanese history and culture. Yamashita and the other leaders were using the priest as a front or even as a cat's-paw, but, so far as I was able to find out, neither the administrators nor most of the residents were aware of this. The priest and other speakers announced that the purpose of the meeting was to form a centerwide Young Men's Association for the Study of the Mother Country (the *Sokoku Kenkyu Seinen-dan*). The expressed aims of this organization were to prepare the members to be useful citizens of Japan after their expatriation through a series of lectures and classes on the Japanese language, history, and political ideology. Within a few weeks about five hundred young men had joined the ostensibly educational *Sokoku*.

But if the organization of the *Sokoku* was a success, the resegregationists' attempt to join forces with the more influential and prestigious leaders of the November uprising was not. Abe, Kuratomi, and Tada (the alleged vice king and ex–chief of police) remained aloof. Yamashita and the other resegregation group leaders did not like this, but at this time they said and did nothing about it.

From this point forward, my fieldwork became increasingly interesting and demanding. Working in an almost anarchic community, where several polarized groups were struggling for control, I was acquainted with and able to interview and converse with most of the leaders at least some of the time. Simultaneously I was able to keep in touch with a good number of people whom the resegrega-

145

tionists called "fence-sitters" (a category that really included most of the population) and to elicit their reactions to what the "would-be big shots" said and did.

On 20 July, less than three weeks after the murder, Mr. Kurihara casually suggested that I might find it instructive to call on a certain Mr. Kira. Kurihara advised me not to use his name as a recommendation, and he warned me that Kira might use insulting language. He did not tell me that he had known Kira for many years and that he considered him an irresponsible man adept at getting other people into trouble while himself posing as an innocent and law-abiding citizen. I, for my part, did not tell Kurihara I had heard whispers that Kira was the leader of a gang that called themselves the Black Tigers, had signed their names in blood, and would do anything Kira told them to do. I also suspected that Kira was a member of the upper-level leadership of the resegregation group but was keeping this relationship undercover.

Kira replied to my respectful letter with a curt note, telling me that he would see me at his office (he was a block manager) at 7:30 in the evening. This was awkward, for the administration strongly disapproved of unescorted women entering the center at night. Moreover, Kira's office was over two miles from the gate, and the center, as I have remarked, was full of rumors about gangs of toughs attacking women. During these weeks, I was told, Japanese women rarely left the barracks after sundown.

But I was so irritated by the rude tone of Kira's letter that I kept the appointment. Kira was a small, soft-looking man with a closely shaved head and a Van Dyke beard, and, though night had fallen, he wore dark glasses. He sat stiffly behind his desk and seated me so that I faced the large painted Japanese flag that had been fastened to the wall behind him. I smiled and set out to give him the impression that he was a great and important man. This was not difficult because he had the same objective.

Kira was far more cautious than Yamashita and made no open admission of interest in the resegregation group. But he tipped his hand by giving me a long account of a talk he had had with the project director in which (if he was to be believed) he had arrogantly instructed him as to what was wrong with the center. What he claimed to have said was resegregationist propaganda, and I concluded that Mr. Kira was connected with the underground group but was too canny to say so. I also decided to see him only occasionally, lest I arouse his suspicions, for if what people said of him were true, he was no one to fool with.

By August of 1944, when the resegregationist leaders decided to organize the innocent appearing young men's group to study the culture of Japan, I was on very good terms with Mrs. Tsuchikawa and the Yamashitas. I had been given many minor confidences and had kept them. Each time I was thus tested, my rapport increased. From the questions they now were asking of me, and from their denunciation of administrative policies in my presence, I was able to glean a great deal of what was going on. When, for instance, the young men's organization was initiated, I discovered almost immediately that the nominal founder, the young Buddhist priest, was not the true organizer, because Mrs. Tsuchikawa could not resist telling me that her husband was doing most of the work. Likewise, the Yamashitas' anxious questions as to how the administration was viewing the organization made it obvious that they were intimately concerned.

Keeping track of the gradual development of hostile feelings between the leaders of the resegregation group and the most important and influential leaders of the *Daihyo Sha Kai* (the Reverend Abe and George Kuratomi) was a more delicate matter. For many months I myself had been waiting for the release of the imprisoned leaders, not only because I felt that they ought to be released, but because there were many things about the strike and its organization that only they could tell me. (I knew, of course, that they might not choose to tell me, but it would do no harm to ask.) At first I had no suspicion that these leaders were not on good terms with the resegregationists, and, had not Mrs. Tsuchikawa and Mrs. Yamashita begun to make snide remarks about the "unwise attitudes" of Reverend Abe, George Kuratomi, and Mr. Tada, I might have become involved in serious difficulties.

As it turned out, my eagerness to obtain data worked to my advantage. I tried to talk to Abe and Kuratomi immediately after they were released, and since the resegregationists had been openly voicing their respect and regard for these men for many months, it was natural and proper that I ask Mrs. Tsuchikawa to arrange interviews with them. The resegregationists and the farm strike leaders were still on reasonably good terms at this time, and Mrs. Tsuchikawa complied, arranging for an interview with Mr. Kuratomi, chairman of the negotiating committee.

147

I called on Mr. Kuratomi but found him out. At his apartment, instead, was a young man of extremely powerful physique. Later I learned he was a black-belt judo man. This man, Mr. Yamada, had also been a leader of the farm strike and he suggested that I call on a certain Mr. Kato, who had been secretary to the *Daihyo Sha Kai* and was also well acquainted with many matters on which I desired information. I expressed my appreciation, and Yamada made the appointment for me.

The interview with Kato and Yamada was my first meeting with the notorious "riot leaders" (except, of course, for my brief chat with Mr. Tada). With exemplary propriety, the young men had arranged to have two Issei ladies present at the interview—presumably to serve as chaperones. I explained how long I had been waiting for this opportunity to learn the truth about the organizational activities which had been carried on before and during the farm strike uprising and how grateful I was for the chance to talk to people who could speak on these matters with authority. The two young men were visibly pleased, and Kato immediately launched into a description of the very first meeting of the farmers—a meeting that until then I had not been able to learn anything about. He was a rather good-looking fellow who had once attended San Francisco State College, and he talked fluently for two hours, telling of events about which the WRA knew nothing, explaining the organization which had preceded the public funeral, and relating some of his experiences in the stockade. By this time he was hoarse. Not wishing to exhaust so eager an informant, I suggested that we stop. "But I've only told you a little bit," said Mr. Kato. We thereupon made an appointment to meet four days later. Kato said he had more time in the evenings and suggested that we meet at the apartment of his future parents-in-law.

At our next talk Kato produced his minutes of the early meetings, the originals of the petitions signed by the residents indicating their support of the farm strike representative body, and the original copy of the hunger strike pledge signed in the stockade. He also gave me the diary he had kept in the stockade and, with apologies for the vulgarity, he told me how, during the early period of imprisonment, the detainees had been followed even to the latrine by armed soldiers who held a gun to their bellies—a circumstance which made the performance of natural functions somewhat difficult. Kato lent me these and many other documents so that I might copy them. About 10:30 in the evening I decided that I dared not stay any longer lest I incur the disapproval of the administration for remaining in the center so late, and said that I must leave. Kato and Yamada offered to escort me to the gate. Flanked with this very capable bodyguard I proceeded toward the sentry post, carrying on an animated discussion of the evils of British imperialism, initiated by Mr. Kato. "I sure wish they'd start some night school classes here," said Mr. Yamada, the black-belt man, who was carrying my typewriter as if it were an orange, "I've always wanted to get some education." Within a hundred yards of the sentry I sent my escorts back, lest I be observed in the company of men who had been accused of threatening to kill the project director.

At this time I was too busy copying documents by day and by night to wonder about why these young men were so eager to give them to me. I did not think of what it must have been like to be locked up for nine months, collecting materials and recollecting experiences, hoping that someone, someday, would take them seriously. I did realize, of course, that Kato wanted very much to be regarded as a formidable agitator, or what today would be called an "activist," but that, being young and not particularly clever, he had been overshadowed by older and abler men like Abe and Kuratomi.

A few days later I met Mr. Kuratomi, the chairman of the negotiating committee and the man who had been spokesman at the confrontation with Dillon Myer during the mass demonstration of 1 November. Kuratomi was tall, slender, high-strung, and very handsome; but with me, in contrast to Kato and Yamada, he was reserved and diffident. At our first meeting he was very worried about the indictment threat hanging over his head, and I had no difficulty in expressing my sincere conviction that he had nothing to do with the murder of Mr. Noma. He seemed to appreciate this and began to tell me about his first impressions of the center in October of 1943 and why he had then been moved to take so prominent a part in the uprising. After we had been talking for about an hour, I began to wonder why he had made no mention of the resegregation group, and, in Japanese fashion, I referred to them indirectly. Kuratomi smiled and said that he would make a prediction for my private benefit. Before the passage of many weeks there would be a split in that organization. I responded with the under-standing smile which such an obliquity demanded and inwardly wondered what was going on.

I did not have to wait long to find out. A few days later Mrs. Tsu-chikawa told me in her dramatic way that Kuratomi was now an outcast. Indeed, she added, the resegregationists had cut off all relationships with the Reverend Abe and George Kuratomi and with their wives. When I asked how this had come about, she told me that Abe and Kuratomi had not shown sufficient gratitude to the resegregationist leaders for their unceasing attempts to get them out of the stockade, and they had also tried to borrow money from them to assist the evil Mr. Tada in fighting the indictment for murder.

I was now faced with the task of staying on reasonably good terms with the touchy and temperamental leaders of two hostile factions. But since I had lived in the centers for over a year and had, so to speak, learned the rudiments of center etiquette, I found the situa-tion not too difficult. I knew that it was very unlikely that the leaders of either faction would compare notes on how I viewed them, or that they would believe each other's statements if they were to do so. Therefore I allowed the resegregationists to believe that I thought Kuratomi an unwise young man and that, as far as my knowledge extended, their policies appeared superior to his. I did not have to express this opinion in words. It was sufficient to listen to their statements with an expression of sympathy and occasional nods of approval. If questioned on the matter, I replied truthfully that I saw Kuratomi only at rare intervals because my studies neces-sitated obtaining the data he could give me on the early period of center history. The resegregationists did not press me for details. Nor did they ask me with which faction my sympathies lay or what Kuratomi was telling me.[2]

Kuratomi himself was more cautious and seldom made direct reference to the resegregationists. He knew, of course, that I was well acquainted with Mrs. Tsuchikawa and Mr. Yamashita, and he contented himself with oblique remarks about "certain groups" which the administration "did not know how to handle." I listened with at-

2. It will be noted how very differently the members of the Six Friendly Tribes establishment behaved toward my husband and myself, insisting that we make a public pronouncement that we stood with them as against their enemies (see chap. 24).

tention and tried to give the impression that I was open-minded on the subject and that his remarks made good sense.

I also made it a practice never to criticize one factional leader to another, beyond the mild implication that my investigations were leading me to the conclusion that the policy of the rivals was not, perhaps, entirely wise. I did not make personal comments on the rival leaders. I did not repeat any remarks made by one leader to another, even when the men belonged to the same faction. After all, I never knew when two men who had appeared to be on the best of terms might quarrel and become bitter enemies.

I avoided giving even the slightest impression that I was playing one faction against another. For instance, to say to Mr. Kuratomi, "Mr. Yamashita tells me that you are too friendly with that notorious gambler, Mr. Tada," would not only have been uncouth but would have given Mr. Kuratomi the dangerous impression that I was discussing him with Mr. Yamashita. For that one interview Kuratomi might become angry enough to say some harsh things about Mr. Yamashita. More probably, however, he would have smiled and said, "Is that so?" meanwhile thinking I must consider him a fool to try to needle him in so clumsy a manner.

In truth, by this time I had a hunch that the resegregationists were riding for a fall. I had excellent rapport with them and did not wish to lose it. I therefore gambled on the possibility that, once their power began to diminish, Kuratomi, if he had come to trust me, would tell me a great deal. So I restrained my impatience, listened to long and valuable explanations of Kuratomi's farm strike activities, and exchanged veiled and oblique remarks with him on current events.

I had to be equally careful but less devious with Mr. Kato. He and Mr. Yamada had become staunch allies of the resegregation group and, I suspected, of Mr. Kira and his strong-arm boys. Kato was so eager to impress me with his growing importance and prestige as an agitator that he sometimes tried to tell me things he should not have. When I suggested that he be more discreet, this only seemed to make him trust me more. I was glad when I heard that he was about to be married because I thought, incorrectly as it turned out, that marriage might make him less rambunctious.

13   I Become an Antifanatic

On 21 September I was extraordinarily lucky. I paid a casual call on the Yamashitas and found the gentleman absentminded and distraught. After quizzing me mercilessly on the current activities of the project director and the Caucasian chief of police, he began to ask me whether I had heard of any repercussions among the members of the administration regarding a speech which he had delivered before the young men's group (the *Sokoku*) on 8 September. He seemed very worried about this, and I assured him truthfully that I had heard nothing. He then bumbled along awkwardly for a while, asking questions so obtuse and involved that I was unable to understand him. Finally, his wife who had been sitting quietly and knitting, spoke up sharply, "Why don't you tell her the truth? You know you can trust her." Mr. Yamashita looked nonplussed but decided to follow his wife's advice. He struck an attitude and stated solemnly, "The philosophy of the majority of the residents here and hereafter will be changed."

"How is that?" I asked.

Yamashita thereupon produced a copy of a new petition which the resegregationists were planning to put before the residents. It was a long document in both English and Japanese, offering the signer the opportunity to express his willingness for an immediate return to Japan. Yamashita asked whether the presentation of such a petition would be followed by the arrest of its sponsors. Since this was a very difficult question to answer, I carefully reread the petition (memorizing as much of it as possible) and then said that, as far as I could determine, there was no great difference between this petition and the previous one of April which the administration had given permission to circulate. On the other hand, it was difficult to predict exactly how the administration would react to something like this.

This answer appeared to satisfy Yamashita, who then went on to explain how the resegregationists had worked underground for a long time and how he and his group intended to use social pressure to obtain their ends:

Those who refuse to sign this will have people asking them, "Are you loyal to Japan or not? If you are not loyal why don't you go out [relocate]?"

They will have to sign this. . . . If they don't sign this they will be known to be not loyal to Japan and will be told in public, "You are not Japanese."

Of course, many people who don't want to go back to Japan will sign this, but then they will go in a corner and keep quiet. [Wax 1964:21 Sept.]

I thanked Yamashita for the trust he had placed in me, and assured him that I would mention the matter to no one. Seeing that he was suffering great anxiety, I asked him about the ancient tale of Banzuin no Chōbe, a notoriously brave bandit-gambler, who incurred the enmity of a tyrannical lord Mizuno. The tale contains some wonderful dramatic episodes. For example, Yamashita told me how Mizuno had ordered his men to catch a five-foot carp, by which, of course, he meant Banzuin. Having captured Banzuin, they laid him on a board—just as a carp is laid before it is sliced up alive to make *osashimi* (a raw fish dish). One of Mizuno's warriors raised his sword to begin the slicing, but Banzuin looked at him so bravely and unfalteringly that the man could not bring down his sword. Yamashita enthusiastically gave me a long account of this story and placed particular emphasis on an aspect which is seldom stressed: "Banzuin no Chōbe spent his energies helping the common people. . . . The *samurai* were very dogmatic. They considered themselves the only human beings. Other people were treated as worms. . . . Banzuin was such a brave man that he fought whenever he saw them oppressing the innocent people. Lots of times he risked his life."

Having told this tale with much expression, Yamashita clearly felt better. I left, feeling both elated and sad—elated, because I had been forewarned about the petition and could now do a first-rate job observing how the people reacted—and sad because I pitied Mr. Yamashita. I knew that he thought he was behaving in a very courageous and public-spirited manner, but suspected that most of the people in the center would not appreciate his efforts.

My suspicions proved more than correct, for I had not expected the petition to be quite so much of a flop as it was. Most people had just about had it, and the suggestion that they commit themselves to an immediate return to Japan and an immediate renunciation of citizenship was received with irritation and exasperation. My non-resegregationist friends told me that they wished the agitators and the superpatriots would leave them alone. Some assured me that those who signed the petition did so out of intimidation or ignorance. Mr. Kurihara said the resegregationists were threatening to use force and that if they did so he would not "stay quiet" even if they called him an *inu*. Mr. Wakida, who was now teaching in the Japanese language school, was very angry. "I'm Japanese— no matter what they say!" he insisted to me. "If we swear to be Japanese we are Japanese. We don't show it by signing petition!"

The resegregationists were disappointed with the reception of their petition, but they put on a bold face. Mrs. Tsuchikawa assured me that "their group" had received a letter from the Department of Justice, advising them to hold on, that everything was going smoothly, and that they would be notified when the renunciation of citizenship forms were ready. "We're going ahead as we were," she assured me, "even if the people squawk."

So the resegregationists went ahead. They secured a staff office and covered the walls with Japanese flags and patriotic mottoes. Among these was one stating that any person speaking English in the office would be fined at the rate of one cent a word. They published mimeographed weekly and monthly newssheets. The *Sokoku* (Young Men's Organization) began a program of predawn exercises including judo practice, goose-stepping, and running to a rhythmic shout of *Wash-sho! Wash-sho!* (Hip hip! Hip hip!) Leaders and members spread the rumor that the center was soon to be taken over by the Department of Justice, at which time, they insisted, all those who had not signed the petition would be obliged to relocate. They further insisted that those young men who did not join the *Sokoku* would be drafted, and that adults who did not sign the petition were not true Japanese. In some blocks they set up morning exercises for the children and refused to let the children of non-resegregants participate, which, as some parents told me, made the children feel ashamed. Some of the leaders (I was told) made speeches in which they threatened people who did not sign. For example, the Buddhist priest—the nominal head of the *Sokoku* and a fiery and exuberant orator—is supposed to have said, "We have killers in our organization." It may be that these rash words worried the older and more sober resegregationist leaders, for the next week I heard that the priest had resigned and that the leadership of the

Sokoku had been given to Mr. Yamada, the stalwart black-belt *judo* man who had introduced me to Mr. Kato.

In fairness to the resegregationists it should be noted that their hopes were by no means based on thin air. Representatives of the Departments of Justice and the Interior had been working on a plan whereby the residents of Tule Lake would be given the opportunity (as U.S. citizens) to renounce their citizenship or (as Japanese nationals) to reaffirm their desire to be repatriated. Those who renounced or reaffirmed were to go under the jurisdiction of the Department of Justice until they could be sent to Japan. But the details of the plans and procedures had not yet been worked out.

VIOLENCE AND RESISTANCE

On 21 October, Mr. Kira, who had now openly assumed a high position in the resegregationist organization, told the young men at a *Sokoku* rally that if they engaged in violence he would see that they came to no harm. He quoted a Japanese proverb, which some people translated as, "To help the great cause we have to kill those who stand in its way." Many people also translated it as, "The little bugs must die so that the big bugs may live."

Despite widespread disapproval of the resegregationist activities, very few people dared to speak openly against them. They remembered all too well what had happened to Mr. Noma, and they were also aware that the Japanese wardens (the police) had pledged themselves not to interfere in "political matters." But among the few men who did voice their disapproval openly were the leaders of a faith-healing sect to which my benevolent and reasonable respondent, Mr. Itabashi, belonged. On 10 October Itabashi told me that he had spoken up at a meeting and exhorted the young men to follow the higher ideals of Japan, which, he stated, were not compatible with agitation or violence. "I said that this camp is no place for young men to make trouble. They should study. I said, 'Young men, behave yourselves!'" He also told me that he was telling the resegregationist leaders, "The Japanese government is not so narrow-minded as you." Kira, he remarked, was a selfish and dangerous man who wished only to become a big shot. I was moved to caution Itabashi, for he was, after all, a frail little man and no match for Kira's gangsters. So I remarked that there were some very dangerous men in camp. But Itabashi laughed and said I was not to worry about him. "These people are cowards. . . . When the Japanese talk big they don't bite." But five nights later, when Mr. Itabashi and two other older men were leaving a church meeting, they were assaulted and badly beaten.

I heard about these beatings almost immediately (from the head of WRA Internal Security), but ten days passed before I discovered that one of the victims was my friend. None of my friends seemed interested in discussing the assault, though Mrs. Yamashita told me that some stubborn and foolish people had been beaten up, adding, in a disappointed tone, "But they weren't killed." I also, at this time, became preoccupied with another problem: Mr. Kato, one of my most helpful respondents, told me that he did not love his wife. He added that he admired spirited and courageous women like me and not those who were meek and docile.

I did not know what to say. I was under a considerable obligation to Kato, for he had managed to preserve and give me all manner of valuable documents, and he and I had spent many hours enlarging and correcting my historical account of what had happened before and during the strike. Moreover, Kato was my best informant on the less edifying activities of the resegregation group, he was on excellent terms with Mr. Kira (to whom he stood somewhat in the relationship of lieutenant), and he told me how he and his gang had terrorized or planned to terrorize those center residents who opposed the leaders of the resegregation group. He interspersed these confidences with remarks of how, when he returned to Japan, he planned to devote himself to the establishment of democratic principles, including the liberation of women. In short, he saw himself as a brave, idealistic, and attractive young man.

I thought very hard that evening and the next day and I decided that I would try to find some courteous way to say no to Mr. Kato, see him less frequently, and take my chances.

I then called on Mr. Kira to see whether he would let anything slip—either about the beating or about his connection with the resegregation group. He had now covered the walls of his office with Japanese flags and mottoes, and he sat in state behind a handsome desk. Two brawny and solemn-faced young men stood on either side of him. Another well-muscled youth stood at the door. Making a mental note of the bodyguards, I opened the conversation with a question—far removed from what I really wanted to find out—about a recent squabble between a resident of his block and the WRA office of social welfare. Thereupon Kira gave me a long and boastful account of how he had threatened the project director, telling him, "Go ahead! Call in the army! We'd rather have the army control the center than the WRA!" He then told me that the resegregationists' "group repatriation plan" was his idea, but that some foolish people were objecting to his proposal.

Having found out what I wanted to know, I made several other visits and then—since I had not seen him for ten days—I called on Mr. Kurihara. Kurihara seemed absent-minded and did not respond to my remarks as cordially as usual. Even when I told him about my talk with Kira, he did not say much. But when I told him about Kira's threats, he interrupted me rather curtly and said: "These things are going on because the administration lacks a strong hand. If the administration acts at the right moment, I think they could bring these people into line. They try to appease them too much."

I was taken aback, because, by "superpatriot" standards, Mr. Kurihara was talking like an *inu*. But, without waiting for a reply, he continued in a shaking voice, telling me how the three old men had been beaten with clubs and a hammer because they refused to sign the resegregationist petition and, especially, because they had advised other people not to sign it. "It was the act of a bunch of cowards. . . . One of them you know, Mr. Itabashi."

At this I felt my face grow cold, and, though I continued to hear Mr. Kurihara's voice, all I saw was a picture of myself running to the Manzanar section like a berserk and beating up Mr. Kira. Still, I am ashamed to say, I continued to take down Mr. Kurihara's words verbatim:

> I went to see Mr. Itabashi on Tuesday. He requested me to let the thing die out. They [the beaten men] fear that neither they nor their families will be safe if I carry out my intentions. One of our friends when he heard of it, was going right over to beat up Kira all alone, but we restrained him.

I confessed that I too had the urge to beat up Kira, and Mr. Kurihara laughed, opining that, strong as I was, I probably could. I then asked, rather stupidly, whether the old strike leaders, Abe and Kuratomi—who, everyone knew, were now on bad terms with the resegregationist group leaders—might not denounce Kira to the authorities. But Kurihara said he did not think so.

> The people of this camp must choose if they want such terrorism to exist or else cast that leader [Kira] out. They are just trying to

beat the people into line. If those persons [Itabashi and his friends] had not asked me not to carry out my intentions, I would have done it. I'm afraid there's going to be serious trouble here.

I JOIN THE RESISTANCE

I find that this is the only place in my field notes where I say that I am afraid—afraid that Kira's gang would beat up or kill Mr Kurihara. As for myself, I had privately decided to do all that I could to stop Kira's (and Kato's) policy of terrorism and violence. And I also decided that, if I ever got the opportunity, I would pay Kira back. If anyone had told me that I was about to "interfere" in a field situation and that I was thereby breaking a primary rule of scientific procedure, I think I would have laughed or, perhaps, told the admonisher to go to hell. Meanwhile, another member of Kira's gang knifed the son of a man who, it was said, had criticized Kira. This time the knifer was arrested, but Yamashita and Kira attended his trial and spoke eloquently in his favor, and he was sentenced to ninety days in jail. Yamashita and Kira boasted that they were responsible for this light sentence.

On 27 October I replied to Mr. Kato's declaration of admiration. I did this by remarking that I had been reading a book on *bushido*, the code of the *samurai*. I praised these stern moral precepts and I expressed my admiration for the Japanese heroes who had maintained their honor even at the price of great personal sacrifice. Ambiguous as my remarks were, Kato got the point. He never again referred to his lack of affection for his wife. (Later I learned that *bushido* does not apply to this kind of a relationship between a man and a woman, but Kato, apparently, did not know this. Still, the fact remains that we were able to communicate without humiliating each other—even though we did so with the vocabulary of a code which neither of us understood.)

A few days later I once again called on Mr. Kurihara and found him much upset over the war news. The newspapers were claiming great victories for the American forces in the Pacific. Diffidently, he showed me some poems which he had just composed. They were passionate expression of his confidence in an ultimate victory for Japan. But they contained many grammatical errors, and Mr. Kurihara's use of rhyme made them sound childish. I asked why he had used rhyme, and he explained that his schoolteacher in Hawaii had told him that a poem had to rhyme. I suggested that he try blank verse, and we experimented with some of the lines. The results delighted him so much that I left him hard at work composing a poem in the new style. It was titled "Smile, Japanese, Smile!"

On 9 November my beaten friend Mr. Itabashi invited me to come to see him. The big cut in his head had healed beautifully and he was chipper and talkative. He told me about the assault but expressed no rancor toward the assailants. Of Kira, he said, "Give him plenty of rope and he'll hang himself up."

Cheered by Mr. Itabashi's recovery, I plucked up my courage and called on Mr. Kato. Kato opened the conversation by apologizing for the fact that he had not yet been able to show me any "real trouble" in camp. He explained that he had conceived a grand plan by which his "boys" would beat up twelve *inu* in one night. If this happened, "the people in Washington" would realize that Mr. Best was an incompetent, and when the center was taken over by the Department of Justice the Department would be certain to appoint a new director. But when Kato approached Yamashita with this plan, Yamashita demurred, pointing out that if the resegregationists were involved in this kind of violence, he himself would be arrested and sent back to the Santa Fe internment center. Kato was disgusted with Yamashita's timidity and assured me that on the next day he was going to Mr. Kira with his plan.

I said nothing, not because I was practicing objectivity or non-directive interviewing, but because I did not know what I could safely say.

Kato then told me that the people in his block were complaining about him and that some *inu* had met and talked of circulating a petition to get him out of the block. If they did this, Kato assured me, he "would bring his boys and beat up the whole block!" He had two hundred boys (he said), and ten of these had sworn to die for him. These ten had even made and given him their wills—in case they died for him or were sent to the electric chair. "Only five other people in camp—and you—know about this," he added. Kato did not show me the wills, but he did show me a letter from an older Japanese still interned in Santa Fe, in which the older man sternly told Kato to quiet down and behave himself and also, interestingly, advised Kato not to renounce his American citizenship. Kato sneered at this letter and remarked once again that older Japanese

159

were too cautious. He then obligingly spent more than an hour clearing up various obscurities in the minutes of the meetings of the *Daihyo Sha Kai*.[1]

While I suspected that Kato was exaggerating his power and prestige as a gang leader, I also suspected that he and his roughneck followers were on the verge of doing something very violent and dramatic. Moreover, Kira, who was much more dangerous and more clever than Kato, had talked to me in the same slightly crazy tone of arrogance. In any case, I felt so sure that the gang leaders were about to start another series of beatings that I went to call on Mr. Penn. I did not know what could be done, but I felt that he ought to be warned. But Mr. Penn seemed sad and defeated. He told me that the Washington office was convinced that Tule Lake was now in an ideal state of peace and quite. True, there was some squabbling between factions, but "nothing in the way of trouble is anticipated." He also told me that the project director had had a talk with Mr. Kato and that the director was convinced that Kato had settled down and would behave himself.

Feeling very desperate, I went to call on Mr. Kurihara. He said he was glad to see me, since, the situation being what it was, he was purposely staying at home. He also told me that he had taken the precaution of sending an account of Kira's misdeeds to some friends outside the center, with the instruction that if anything happened to him (Kurihara) his friends were to turn over the information to the proper authorities. I asked whether he was sure that his denunciation of Kira was in capable hands. If Kurihara were murdered, would his friends have the guts to turn Kira in? Kurihara said he thought they would. I then told Kurihara as much as I knew about Kato's plans, without, of course, mentioning Kato's name. Wouldn't it be better, I asked, to denounce Kira to the authorities before his gang beat or murdered any more people? "No," said Kurihara. He explained that he was laying a trap for Kira. He had let one of Kira's spies know that he went out two evenings a week to a class on old Japanese songs. If any of Kira's men ambushed him, they would die too. Then

1. The typewritten translation of these minutes had been given to me by Mr. Sasaki. In October and November of 1944, Kato gave me his elaborations and emendations, and in March of 1945 I was able to get even more assistance from Mr. Kuratomi, the spokesman for the negotiating committee. But in November I could not have called on Kuratomi without alienating the resegregationists.

he opened a drawer of his desk and showed me a curious weapon, a stout club, about six inches long, to which a pipe joint was attached by a leather thong.

I left, still feeling very apprehensive, but, as it turned out, I had underestimated Kurihara. A few days later a rumor filtered through the center that Mr. Kira had resigned his office with the resegregation group. I checked the rumor with Mrs. Tsuchikawa, who explained that Mr. Kira's health was poor and that he was obliged to give up some of his numerous duties. I then visited Kato and found him very depressed. "I'm fed up with this camp," he told me in a disgusted tone. "There isn't going to be any trouble for a long time." The older leaders, he implied, had once again ordered him to wait and "play a gentleman act."

It took some time to discover what Kurihara had done. He himself would not tell me much, perhaps because he thought that doing so would sound vainglorious. Mr. Itabashi and Mr. Wakida supplied the information. Kurihara had sent word to Kira that he wished to talk to him. Kira had sent two of his men. The men had argued with Kurihara for five hours (according to Mr. Itabashi), telling him, "Why should you care what we do in the center so long as we let you alone?" Kurihara told Kira's go-betweens that he had concern for all the people in the center, recounted some of Kira's misdeeds, and told them to take Kira his ultimatum: if there were another beating in the center, he himself would denounce Kira. There were no more beatings in the center.

But while Kurihara did not wish to talk about what he had done, he did want to know how I had found out that a series of beatings was in the wind. I hesitated to tell him, for while I had squared my betrayal of Kato with myself, I was afraid that the stern-principled Kurihara would think I had behaved like a sneak. But, when I told him, he said, "Do you think I will scold you when you saved my life?" Then he smiled and added, "Young men are certainly foolish."

I was somewhat concerned that the resegregationist leaders or Kato might discover that Kurihara, Itabashi, and I were friends. Apparently, they never did.

The third of November is the anniversary of the beginning of the Meiji Dynasty, and most blocks in the center—and the Japanese language school—were planning to hold some kind of solemn, patriotic ceremony. The resegregationists, however, planned a grand ceremony of their own and secured permission to hold it before the outdoor stage of the main firebreak. Mr. Yamashita invited me to attend and I did so. I did not know that the administration had ordered all Caucasians but the police to stay out of the center on that day.

The stage was decorated with yellow and white chrysanthemums, behind which hung a large white cloth. About six hundred young men wearing their best suits marched up to the firebreak and arranged themselves in rows before the stage. About twice as many older people stood behind them. Though the day was bitterly cold, none of the young men wore an overcoat. Those who carried overcoats laid them on the ground. The ceremony proceeded with great solemnity and reverence. There were many long speeches. After one of these speeches everyone faced the rising sun and bowed, maintaining a bowed position for about three minutes. Meanwhile the *Sokoku* buglers inexpertly played what I took to be Japanese patriotic anthems. The sun glowered dimly from behind rain-swollen clouds. The situation was at once so ludicrous and so pathetic that I was moved. One of the *Sokoku* boys fainted and was carried off the field. Finally, Mr. Yamashita told the boys to put on their overcoats, and all joined in singing the Japanese national anthem. Then they bowed deeply and shouted: *"Dai Nippon Teikoku Banzai! Banzai! Banzai!*

Returning to the administrative section I found myself stumbling. I had become so numb with cold that I could not walk properly.

14   The Debacle

From the beginning of their underground activity in January of 1944, the resegregationist leaders had striven to give the impression that they were on the best terms with the prestigious leaders of the November strike. Indeed, they announced that obtaining the release of the detained leaders was their prime objective. But, as I have explained (see chap. 9), the resegregationist leaders refused to help the detainees when they appealed to the American Civil Liberties Union. And when the ACLU did bring about the release of the strike leaders, the relationship between them and the resegregationists remained polite but guarded. Though the Reverend Abe, George Kuratomi, and many of their friends were nominally members of the resegregationist organization (the *Sokuji Kikoku*), they did not participate actively and they declined the positions offered them.

In mid-November of 1944, with the imminence of the renunciation of citizenship and the "take-over" by the Department of Justice, the resegregation group leaders decided to institute a membership purge. They posted statements in the latrines and laundry rooms which, in effect, said the following: True Japanese life was austere and full of sacrifice; people who could not do without American luxuries such as rich food, liquor, or cosmetics, and people who were addicted to degenerate vices such as gambling and *sake* drinking, had no place in postwar Japan or in the membership rolls of the resegregation group. Having defined the "true Japanese" and the "not Japanese" in this manner, the leaders sent curt notices of expulsion to some of their more moderate charter members and to a number of the friends of Abe, Kuratomi, and Tada.

Though the expelled members had not approved of many of the policies and activities of the resegregation group, they resented being cast off in this rude manner and being derogated as "not Japanese." Some also feared that their removal from the membership list might make them ineligible for repatriation. There now emerged the potential of a confrontation between the two groups, and, as usual, the warrior champions were the initiators. When a crowd of several hundred people had gathered on the evening of 19 November to bid farewell to a number of families who were on their way to join interned members in the Department of Justice camp at Crystal City, Tetsuo Kodama, a noted *judo* champion and a close friend of Kuratomi and Tada, approached Mr. Yamada (also a *judo* champion and leader of the *Hokoku* [1]) and accused Yamada of having called him an *inu*. This was a challenge to fight, which Yamada ignored.

This open and aggressive defiance thoroughly upset the resegregationists. Mrs. Tsuchikawa told me that young men of the *Hokoku* were guarding the apartments of the resegregationist leaders night and day. On the other hand, many of the residents (those who disapproved of the resegregationists) were intrigued by the prospect of a feud between the superpatriots and the members of the Abe-Kuratomi-Tada faction. Mr. Kurihara voiced the hope that in the event of a violent fight or a gang war the administration would be forced to imprison the resegregationist leaders, "and then the people could get rid of the gambling group." (Many of the members expelled were young men who spent a great deal of their time playing cards. According to rumor, they also drank bootleg *sake* provided by the enterprising Mr. Tada. People called them "the gamblers," and it is my suspicion that they constituted a kind of young men's peer society.) As part of their new austerity program, all the male members of the resegregation group shaved their heads to an egg-like smoothness, in imitation, they said, of the Japanese army. Conversely, the friends of Kuratomi, Kodama, and Tada let their hair flourish luxuriously. People began to refer to the former as "shavedheads" or, more derogatorily, "baldheads," and to the latter as "longhairs."

On 15 December, the anticipated fight broke out. A certain Mr. Hamaguchi went to the resegregationist headquarters in block 54, discreetly accompanied or followed by fellow members of the long-haired faction. Hamaguchi accosted the head of the *Sokuji Kikoku Hoshi-dan,* demanding the reasons for his expulsion, and the *Sokuji* official gave him a rude reply. Hamaguchi then seized a long piece

---

1. As part of the new program the Sokuku changed its name to *Hokoku Seinen-dan* ("Young Men's Organization to Serve Our Mother Country"), that is, from a group that "studied" the culture of Japan to a group that "served" Japan. They now participated in military exercises every morning and they were commonly called the "the *Hokoku.*"

of wood from a nearby woodpile, the official grabbed a mop, and the two men had at it in what must have been a strange parody of a *samurai* sword duel. Meanwhile, Mr. Kodama, the *judo* champion, and several other longhairs also armed themselves from the wood-pile and guarded the combatants, to see, as they later put it, that there would be fair play. Many strong-arm boys of the *Hokoku* and several hundred other spectators came running to the scene; but no one, apparently, dared to challenge the longhairs. After the fight, which lasted only a few minutes, Mr. Hamaguchi addressed the assembled crowd, denouncing the *Hokoku* for gangster tactics and for the degradation of the true spirit of Japan.

This attack put the resegregationists into a very awkward situation. If they ignored the attack they would lose face. If they responded with open violence they might be arrested, and all their elaborate plans for impressing the Department of Justice and achieving a resegregation and repatriation might go astray. So they drew up a legal complaint against Hamaguchi and ten other men and presented it to the project attorney. Forthwith, eleven longhairs were arrested by the Caucasian police and taken to the jail at Klamath Falls. Then the resegregationists plastered latrines and laundry rooms with mimeographed statements to the effect that their peaceful organization had been attacked by gangsters. To me they voiced vicious threats of what they would do if they were not given justice.

The trial, which took place four days later, was a peculiar event. Kuratomi and Tada had asked for and received permission to act as quasi attorneys for the defendants. The project attorney carried on the case for the plaintiffs. Mr. Yamashita attended every session and interrupted frequently. The eleven defendants were all neatly dressed in what appeared to be their best suits. Their hair was noticeably long, and they bore themselves with something of the air of college boys about to be reprimanded for a prank. The resegregationist plaintiffs and witnesses were dressed in the *Hokoku* uniform, a grey sweat shirt imprinted with the emblem of the rising sun. Their heads were newly shaved and they glared at the longhairs with baleful eyes. Whether of one side or the other, the witnesses seemed to suffer from some optical defect. When the man for whom they were testifying had been struck, they had seen it. But when he had struck someone, they had momentarily glanced away, gone to the latrine, or just not noticed.

165

Ten days later the verdict was announced: Hamaguchi was given a light sentence; two other defendants were given suspended sentences; the rest were acquitted.

The resegregation group leaders were enraged. They denounced American justice and made terrible threats of reprisals. "Bombs and tanks won't stop our boys now if we give them the word," said Mrs. Yamashita.

As a fieldworker and a peculiarly involved participant I regret that this conflict between the puritanical resegregationists and the moderate and somewhat hedonistic gamblers or longhairs was not allowed to work itself out. The fight and its aftermath significantly weakened the position of the superpatriots, and some people even began to submit their resignations. But it was at this time that the representative of the Department of Justice, John Burling, arrived at the center, to open the hearings for the renunciants.

THE RENUNCIATION OF CITIZENSHIP

With Burling's arrival the resegregationists intensified their demonstrative activities, holding their noisy predawn militaristic exercises as close to the fence as possible and blowing their bugles louder than ever. Clearly, they hoped to impress the representative of the Department of Justice with their true Japanese character and their passionate desire for an immediate renunciation of citizenship, resegregation, and expatriation. Burling was impressed, but in a way that neither the resegregationist leaders nor the WRA administration had anticipated. He told the resegregation group leaders and their followers (and also announced to all the residents) that such Japanese militaristic activities were subversive and that if they did not abandon them at once they would be interned in a Department of Justice camp for potentially dangerous enemy aliens. He also took a very critical attitude toward the WRA for permitting young men living under their charge to drill themselves for service in the Japanese army.

The resegregationists ignored these warnings and drilled more ostentatiously than ever, and, on 27 December, the Department of Justice interned seventy of the leaders and officers. (Mr. Yamashita wrote a farewell note to his followers on a strip of toilet paper, apparently the only stationery available, exhorting them to stand firm and continue their true Japanese activities.) This act of official recognition seemed to encourage the membership. They gave their leaders a spectacular demonstration of farewell, sang Japanese patriotic songs, and shouted "Banzai!" They also immediately elected a new slate of officers to replace those interned. Under this new leadership the activities of the resegregationists became fantastic. They stepped up their bugling, goose-stepping, morning drills, and *Wash-sho* chants. Elderly people and little children stood in rigid and motionless prayer in the bitter cold and sometimes marched with the boys so that, as a friend of mine put it, "even the old ladies are running around in slacks yelling "Wash-sho!" *Hokoku* boys taunted nonmembers as follows:

"They say they are glad to be picked up. They say we, who are left behind in camp, are going to be kicked around, while they will be safe and sound in an internment camp" (R. Wax 1945: 3 Jan.).

On 5 January, the WRA released and distributed to all the residents an official pamphlet in which Dillon Myer reaffirmed that it was the WRA's intention to close all of the relocation centers by returning all of the evacuees to "private life in normal communities." The WRA had announced this policy once before, in mid-December, but at that time most of the evacuees to whom I talked told me that they were sure that it did not apply to them. Now, however, many people who had been dubious about the wisdom of renouncing their citizenship—or urging their Nisei children to renounce—began to fear that if they or their children did not renounce they would shortly be expelled into hostile and, by now, very unfamiliar American communities. Newspaper reports in which relocated Japanese Americans or Nisei soldiers were threatened, attacked, shot at, or had their homes burned, were quoted to me. As Bob Tsuruda's sister remarked, "What do they want us to do—go back to California and get filled full of lead? I'm going to sit here and watch" (R. Wax 1945: 14 Jan.).

Meanwhile, the resegregationists, with exultant fanaticism, spread rumors that the families of the men sent to Santa Fe would soon be sent to join them. Members of the *Hokoku* who received notices from Washington approving their applications for denationalization waved them in front of nonrenunciants and urged them to make their own applications without delay. Renunciation became a mass movement. During January, 3,400 young persons (40 percent of the citizen population) applied for denationalization. The Department of Justice became alarmed. Burling tried to stem the flood by asking the national officials of the WRA to declare Tule Lake a "refuge center" from which no one would be forced to relocate for the duration of the war, and by trying to stamp out the resegregationist organizations. At this time, he also held a consultation with Dr. Thomas in Berkeley. But the WRA refused to yield in the matter of forced resettlement, and the only concession made was that "those who do not wish to leave the Tule Lake center *at this time* are not required to do so and may continue to live here or at some similar center until January 1, 1946" (Thomas and Nishimoto 1946: 356, italics theirs). The Department of Justice continued its internments of resegregationists. On 26 January, 171 men were interned, on 11 February, 650, on 4 March, 125.

On 16 March the WRA belatedly announced that all resegregationist activities were unlawful and punishable by imprisonment. But none of these repressive measures stopped the flood of renunciations. In all, 70 percent of those eligible renounced their citizenship.

I remained at the Tule Lake center during this period of renunciation and internments and for about two months thereafter. I took my usual detailed notes about what my friends said, and this became more and more painful, as, week by week, they worried whether their renunciations would be accepted, or, if they had not renounced, they worried about being "pushed out." Some who had renounced kept justifying their decisions to me and to themselves, but told me that they had stopped reading the newspapers.

During the internments I did two very unprofessional deeds. When I heard that my friend Mr. Wakida, the ex-agitator from Gila and one of the outspoken opponents of the resegregation group, had been notified that he too was about to be interned along with a contingent of *Hokoku* boys, I went to the Department of Justice staff and protested. Wakida, I told them, had opposed the resegregation from the beginning, and, besides, his opposition was so well known that interning him would put him into grave physical danger. He was not interned, though he and his wife had, of course, applied for renunciation of citizenship. Again, after the first internment, I found out that Mr. Kira had not applied for denationalization. This surprised me, for Kira had been one of the most vigorous exponents of the renunciation of citizenship—for other people. Thereupon I once again talked to the Justice Department's investigators and suggested that they call in Mr. Kira and question him about his loyalties in the presence of some of the young *Hokoku* officers. Mr. Kira applied for denationalization. Subsequently, he was sent to Japan.

with the other expatriates, and they were all once again confined in a "center," this time by the Japanese government. Many months later, a friend sent me a clipping from a California newspaper. The clipping told how a certain expatriate, Stanley Masanobu Kira, confined in a detention area in Japan, had appealed to the American army to remove him because certain of the young men confined with him were threatening to kill him.

During February, March, and April of 1945 I also became well acquainted with George Kuratomi and his wife, and received a great deal of helpful information from him. Kuratomi arranged for me to have a long talk with Mr. Tada, who hospitably opened our discussion by pouring out for me a large water tumbler of distilled *sake,* which, I soon discovered, had about the same potency as a strong brandy. But I had a very good head for liquor then and I came away with a fine interview, though I noticed later that my handwriting had become larger and larger as the interview progressed.

In the middle of May, Dr. Thomas telephoned me and ordered me to leave Tule Lake immediately without letting anyone know that I was departing. I packed my few belongings and got out that night, assisted by one of the few staff members I could trust, a minister. Arriving in Berkeley the next morning I learned that a Washington official of the WRA had called on Dr. Thomas and insisted that I be removed from the center. He backed up this demand with a list of impressive accusations: I had consorted with pro-Japanese agitators and attended ceremonies devoted to the worship of the Japanese emperor. I had had immoral (sex) relations with a number of Japanese Americans. I had made disrespectful remarks about the project director. I had been a general troublemaker and had tried to subvert WRA policies. I was by temperament an anarchist, and, since my mother had been abused by members of the Los Angeles police force, I had no respect for the law. I had communicated with the Department of Justice.

So far as I can remember (for I took no notes), Dr. Thomas did not pay much heed to these accusations. Her attitude was that if she made any fuss about my expulsion it might create a scandal and jeopardize the research project and the reception of the eventual publications that would issue from it. Therefore, the best thing for me to do was to get out of Tule Lake and keep my mouth shut. I myself had very mixed reactions. I was not sorry to leave Tule Lake, for, with the renunciation of citizenship and the imminent defeat of the Japanese armed forces, it had become a tragic place to be. But there was no other place I wanted to be either. I applied for a fellowship in the Department of Anthropology at the University of Chicago, but I did not much care whether or not I got it. I found most of the WRA's accusations amusing, and I was surprised that the officials, once they had decided to expel me, did not seem to know about any of the colorful and prohibited things I had really done.

THE STUDY OF FACTIONS

When several factions are engaged in a state of violent opposition to each other, keeping on good terms with each of the leadership groups would seem to be a task of extraordinary difficulty, and yet I found it not only possible but even enjoyable. One reason I could do it was that agitators, activists, idealists, and patriots desperately need an admiring and respectful audience—especially an audience that does not try to argue with them or criticize them. Often, these men think of themselves as performing on "the stage of history," and a fieldworker, if he is able and lucky, can sometimes come to be taken as the small advance guard of the historical audience. Hence, some of the leaders of the Pro-Japanese underground were willing to present their plans to me in detail, long before they really trusted me to keep the information from the center administration or from their rival factions among the Japanese Americans. Most of the leaders knew I was visiting and conversing with these rivals, and, as the conflict intensified, they denounced each other to me at length and in detail. Yet, such was the understanding that had been developed concerning my role, that they never asked me for information about their rivals, and I, in turn, never volunteered any (except when I told Kurihara what Kato was planning). Throughout, I maintained the attitude of one willing to be convinced that the person addressing me was on the side of right and justice. I assumed—as, indeed, every fieldworker should assume about every human being—that he had good justification for his position, and, following this assumption, I listened to, recorded, and tried to understand his reasoning.

To hold oneself open in this fashion, as the reporter for future texts of history, is to avoid two other roles, which appear similar but which each hold significant dangers. One role is that of the person who so allows himself to be "convinced" that he is moved to act. As will be seen elsewhere in this volume (chap. 14), such action is not only unnecessary but may violate the moral code of the fieldworker and bring him into grave personal danger (cf. Whyte 1965, Polsky 1967). The other role is to hold himself in a position of rigid "neutrality." As I have remarked:

> Recently, I heard a fieldworker studying a political pressure group complain of difficulties with leaders. He reported that when they questioned him about his sentiments he replied that he was neutral. I think he was making an error. Leaders of a social movement gain nothing by expressing their views before a neutral or ostentatiously fair-minded audience, determined at the outset not to take sides. If there is no chance whatever that the listener may change his mind, the leader is wasting his time.
>
> I do not advise an interviewer to pretend to adopt views of which he does not approve. He will, however, do well to remember that a coquette is in a much better situation to learn about men than a nun. [R. Wax 1952:37]

Before a fieldworker can achieve that happy state of being regarded as the reporter for history, he must be well prepared for the requirements of the situation (see Berk and Adams 1970). No agitator can afford to talk tactics with a person who does not know the players, the game, and the score. Here the terrible initiation of my first months at the Gila center had furnished me with an invaluable training. I had learned how to approach and open a conversation with Japanese of all ages, sexes, and conditions of "loyalty" or "disloyalty." I had learned from participation and observation what center life was like and how most Japanese felt about it. I had become an expert at playing the role of a sympathetic, intensely interested reporter who had no attachment or obligation to the WRA. I had developed an intuitive ability for sensing when I ought to work with relentless energy (sometimes I literally worked day and night), and when I ought to let people alone. In addition, at Tule Lake I had for several months the status of an expert visitor, and, even more advantageous, a visitor who, though an outsider, could understand what people were telling him. The result was that when, in May of 1944, I became a "permanent" resident, I was already well acquainted with and had made a reasonably good impression on a great variety of people, including leaders and members of the several factions. I could approach and talk to almost anyone except the men who were confined in the stockade (and I got to them as soon as I could).

As the factionalism progressed, I was able to modify my conduct and continue my interviewing without any marked difficulty, simply because I doggedly kept on talking to as many people as I could. In consequence, I kept up with what was going on and could keep out of serious trouble.

While the factionalism of the Tule Lake center was extreme, almost any human group or community will contain factions at odds with each other. Unhappily, most of the literature on community studies and much of the advice proffered to fieldworkers tends to view factionalism as an abnormal or pathological state. Accordingly, the fieldworker is mentally prepared for a community where all is peace and harmony, so that he can "immerse himself in" or "step into" its society as he might into a quiet pool. When, instead, he finds himself adrift in a raging torrent and torn by conflicting currents, he is likely to go into a state of panic or of depression and apathy, attach himself to one faction and ignore or discredit the others.

No matter what he studies within a group or community context, the fieldworker must therefore expect to encounter factions, and he should be prepared that a most important aspect of his resocialization into the life of the community is his becoming aware of the lines of cleavage and the forms of struggle. This does not mean that the fieldworker should necessarily involve himself with these factional struggles to the extent to which I did in Tule Lake. Given the political focus of the project as a whole, it was a major part of my job as a researcher to discover and record the maneuvers of the various factional groupings. Years later, on the Thrashing Buffalo reservation, my work did not require that I become deeply involved in the ancient familial factions of the Indian community, though I picked up a good deal of knowledge about them during the course of my participation and observation. But had I attempted to start a demonstration school at Thrashing Buffalo—or, indeed, attempted anything that required the cooperative effort of the important families —I would have been obliged to put a great deal of time into the study and understanding of the various factions.

A SMALL DEATH

When I began to work on this book, I asked a young anthropologist who had just returned from a difficult field expedition in Melanesia what, in his opinion, was the most important thing to tell students who had never been in the field. He replied: "Tell them to keep a personal diary in addition to their field notes and tell them that returning to your own society can be as difficult as trying to enter a strange one."

I was impressed by this response, because it corresponded to my own experience after leaving Tule Lake and also, though to a lesser degree, after leaving Thrashing Buffalo. For the first few weeks after I left Tule Lake I was dazed. I tried to concentrate on writing a report about the renunciation of citizenship, but I had little success. All my close friends and relatives had left Berkeley during the war. My younger brother, to whom I had always been much attached, had suffered a breakdown after three years of uninterrupted army service in North Africa and India. When the atomic bombs were dropped on Hiroshima and Nagasaki, I received several terrible denunciatory letters from Mr. Kurihara, to which I could not bring myself to reply. Shortly thereafter the denationalized and "disloyal" Japanese Americans were shipped to Japan. Before embarking, Mr. Kurihara sent me a postcard on which he had written, in blank verse, a poem bidding farewell to a friend.

Largely because of Kroeber's recommendation, the University of Chicago did award me a fellowship. But for a year or more I felt almost as disoriented at Chicago as I had at Berkeley. The graduate courses I took and the undergraduate course in which I assisted seemed, for the most part, pretentious, pointless, and boring. After a few months I became so dismayed and restless that I tried to find work in what was then called "race relations." But everyone I approached told me to return to the university and get a PhD. Gradually I found that life as a student and, later, as an instructor and assistant professor could be tolerable and sometimes even enjoyable. Nonetheless, for many years I felt as if I were walking around with some vital part missing. My discomfort may have been all the more acute because the community which had become my world was gone.

The situation in Tule Lake was in some respects significantly different from that of most field situations and, the role I took upon myself was one that fieldworkers have seldom been called upon to assume. When the Japanese Americans were first confined in the centers, they were a subordinate and oppressed people only slightly different from many other Americans. But, as a result of their experience within the centers, some of them evolved quite a different way of life, which, in Tule Lake, developed into a complicated political and quasi-military struggle. I, as a fieldworker, came to

173

participate in this struggle, and my behavior and attitudes, especially after Mr. Itabashi was beaten, came to resemble those of a fighter in a resistance movement. Taking part in the attempt to stop the terrorist tactics of the "superpatriot" gangs was the most exciting and vitalizing experience of my life, but the letdown was awful.

I do not wish to overemphasize the pangs of reentering one's own society, especially since many fieldworkers make no mention of it. Perhaps if one has not involved oneself too deeply or changed oneself too much, and if one has a warm and familiar world to which one can return, the transition from the field to home territory is not so painful.

PART THREE

Fieldwork on the Thrashing Buffalo Reservation, 1962-1963

15　We Decide to Study Indian Education

Studying formal education in an American Indian community by *doing fieldwork in that community* was my husband's idea. In the early 1960s he had heard on good authority that the Department of Health, Education, and Welfare wished to interest more sociologists and anthropologists in the study of educational problems and that relatively large sums of money were available for research. Forthwith, he conceived the notion of studying Indian schools, not by the usual method of composing questionnaires to be administered by teachers in the classrooms, but by going to the reservation himself, living there with the people whose children were attending (or playing hookey from) the schools, observing what happened in the classrooms, and talking with their teachers. At the same time, or subsequently, he planned to administer structured questionnaires and interviews. Thus he hoped to combine the participating and observing methods of the ethnographer with the techniques of the model builder and the market researcher.

Since Murray and I had for two summers been directors of a workshop for American Indian college students, we did not have to search for a problem. In our work with these Indian students we had been puzzled by the fact that some of them had attained college status without, apparently, being able to speak or write coherent English. Many showed a singular disposition to be obedient and passive, and were dismayed if we asked their opinion about anything. Some reproved us because we suggested that there might be more efficient and effective ways of coping with the "greater society" than hard work, saving money, and getting to work on time. Some even scolded because we did not forbid the students to drink beer. Thus (though we did not put it quite so bluntly in our research application), one of our major interests was finding out how these young people could graduate from high school and even attend a college or university, and still be so marvelously "out of it"—so innocent of scholastic and academic matters and so misinformed about the society in which they were living.

Murray spent several months writing a research proposal. In it

177

he asked for funds to do a thorough study of the educational situation of three different Indian tribal groups—a study which would last for three years and involve the collaboration of several colleagues and many research assistants. When this proposal was turned down, he was discouraged and somewhat annoyed. I was not annoyed, because I had not expected that he would get the grant, though of course I did not tell him this. (Later, when we discovered the work and trouble entailed in conducting but one research project on but one reservation, we were glad that our ambitious proposal had been rejected.) In any case, Murray began to compose another proposal, this time to study only the Thrashing Buffalo. He was attracted to the Thrashing Buffalo because they were a numerous people and their educational achievement was extremely low. Besides, from what he had read, they were living in a particularly difficult economic situation.

It was at about this stage in the grant-getting period that I began to feel uneasy. I began to suspect that HEW might give Murray this more modest grant, and I did not want to live on an Indian Reservation—even for a period of six months. The thought of once again becoming involved with human beings so as to make an objective record of the hardship, suffering, and disintegration for which my own people were largely responsible, made me sick at the stomach. Besides, during the several years that Murray and I had lived and worked in Florida, I had become addicted to deep sea fishing, and the thought of giving up this beloved activity for even a short while was almost more than I could bear. Indeed, several of my fishing cronies assured me that if *their* spouses had decided to work in the North, the spouses would be told to go and freeze alone. Finally, I was by this time fifty years old, and while I was in no way frail or ill, the prospect of a really rugged field trip was not as attractive as it would have been twenty or even ten years before.

On the other hand, I was torn by the fact that Murray had his heart set on getting the grant and trying his hand at this challenging research. I suspected that he wanted to go to Thrashing Buffalo even more than I wanted to fish, which is a very strong statement. As the day of the announcement of acceptance or rejection drew near, Murray grew more and more nervous. One night he dreamed that the project had been approved. Two days later, he received a phone call telling him that he had been given the grant. I consoled myself as best I could with the thought that his prophetic gifts might prove useful in the field.

On several occasions Murray tried to get me to put my misgivings into words. I took refuge in North European silence, and eventually pointed out that when my people go into a hopeless conflict they stand and fight until they die. Going to Thrashing Buffalo was, for me, like joining a handful of people making a last stand. Murray could not understand this at all and, shaking his head, remarked: *"Mann kann gehärget werden,"* by which he meant that a person who thought as I did could get himself killed.

My ambivalence about leaving Florida was resolved by the behavior of some of the administrative members of the university to which we were attached. We had expected that our receiving a large research grant would increase the regard in which we were held. Instead, we found that at least some of the administrators were annoyed. One, of high rank, told Murray that "the university loses money on all of these research deals." When Murray suggested that we might be wise to transfer our services—and the grant—to another university, I was for it. This meant that I would have to give up my deep sea fishing entirely, but, so far as I was concerned, this was the lesser of two evils.

Once we knew we were going on a minor expedition—and "living out on the reservation" was just that—there was a great deal to think about and a great deal to do. Where, for example, would we find housing in an area where more than half of the heads of families are out of work and the mean annual income of 60 percent of family heads is less than $1,000. Was it possible to find a location where we would not be bothered day in and day out by roving bands of aggressive drunks—about whom our experienced friends had told us many hair-raising stories? We had been told that roads were terrible, but we did not know how terrible. Should we buy a jeep? a small truck? or could we get by in our "compact" station wagon? What kind of clothes would we need for the winter, when temperatures sometimes dropped to thirty or forty below? Was it possible to learn a little of the native language, while we planned and packed? We had funds for two research assistants, and we hoped to hire two young Indians. We found this difficult because the few young Thrashing Buffalo who had had even a little training in the social sciences already had jobs paying them more than we could afford.

We wrote many letters asking for advice and for copies of recent researches, but on the whole we learned very little. We did find out that almost all of the people who had studied the Thrashing Buffalo had lived in and carried on their work from the agency town, where, of course, living conditions were different from those out on the reservation. This made us even more determined to find a base away from the town. We also received a peculiar and disturbing message. A retired missionary who had lived on the reservation for many years told an educated Indian friend to tell us: "If Mr. Wax and an interpreter are going into the field together without Mrs. Wax, to get information from Indian people who live in remote villages, you most certainly must have a man as your interpreter and, further, one who is not too closely affiliated with either the tribal council or the local branch of the Bureau of Indian Affairs." I am ashamed to say that I interpreted this message as an expression of puritanical bigotry. Later, when we were in trouble up to our ears, we realized that it was the most valuable piece of advice anyone could have given us.

If, like all of our academic predecessors, we had stayed in the agency town, lived in the fairly comfortable administration housing area, and limited our investigations to interviews with white and Indian bureau employees, and a few amiable and relatively "acculturated" mixedbloods, we would probably have saved ourselves a great deal of trouble. But we wanted to get to know the people that nobody really knew much about—the poor and unprominent folk who lived "way out" on the prairies in one-room cabins, shacks, or tents, and we wanted to find out what they thought about their children's education. We knew that these so-called "fullbloods" were shy and suspicious and would not talk to outsiders until they had become used to them. So we reasoned that the wisest course was to coax some fairly reputable local fullblood family to take us in as visitors or tenants. And since we were arriving in August, this would mean their letting us camp on their land or letting us rent some nearby shack. (We were experienced, hard-nosed campers and were fairly sure that we could make out for two or three months in this fashion.) Gradually, we hoped, people would get accustomed to having us around, would begin to take us for granted, and would talk to us.

If we had hired white research assistants, we might also have avoided trouble, simply because we would probably never have become so deeply and personally involved in the life of the community. The practice of working with members of a host people as colleagues rather than "informants" is well established among sociologists, but at this time (1962) it had seldom been attempted by anthropologists. We wanted to hire young Indians as apprentices rather than as helpers, because we knew that this kind of experience, in which an intelligent and perceptive younger person watches a professional work, plan, flounder, and (sometimes) succeed, is one of the most efficient means of education. We thought that if a couple of young and educated Indians were given a fair notion of how to go about studying a community—if they actually saw it done before their eyes —they might, in the long run, help their people more than would any number of reports written by outsiders.

These two plans—to live near the people and use Indian assistants —were sound and correct. The only hitch was that Murray and I did not realize that we had a great deal to learn before we could live and work intimately with Indians as neighbors or as research assistants. Having had them as students in the summer workshops, we knew fairly well both of the young men whom we eventually hired. One, Walter GoodHorse, was a college graduate, recommended to us because he was one of the rare college graduate students who came from a fullblood family. (This implied that his people were conservatives, favored Indian ways, spoke the native language—had not, in short, joined the white man in the white man's attempt to shape up the Indians.) Walter, we knew, was no great shakes as a scholar, but then few young Indians are. But he was good-looking, cheerful, and willing, and he was no fool.

Our other assistant, Victor Hibou, was a young bachelor from a reservation in Montana. Vic, as he preferred to be called, was a tall, slender, small-featured fellow, with the longest feet I have ever seen on a man. He spoke only English, said that he wanted to be a writer, and told us that he had no interest in the social sciences. Nevertheless, I favored hiring him because in his classwork he had displayed a fearless honesty and rare perceptiveness. I thought he would learn more from working with us than any other young Indian of our acquaintance.

We formally employed Walter before we expected to arrive on the reservation. We asked him to find us a place to live and record some elementary Indian words and phrases on a tape recorder. After a few weeks he wrote that housing was almost impossible to find on the reservation but that we would be welcome to live with his folks, where we could become acquainted with fullblood Indian ways. Apparently he had had a great deal of trouble finding a tape recorder, and, when the tapes finally reached us (about two days before we left home), they emitted nothing but squeaks. They had been recorded on the wrong type of machine.

Before heading for Thrashing Buffalo we made a detour to Colorado, where we lectured at the workshop for American Indian college students and consulted with people who had recently been doing some field research among American Indian groups. At one of these consultations another disturbing thing happened. A friend who had lived at Thrashing Buffalo asked us where we were going to stay. When we replied that we were planning to stay with Walter's folks for a while, this friend looked alarmed and urgently suggested that we not do this. His reasons were curiously vague, but we had known him for many years and we suspected that he had some good reason for his advice. So we telephoned Walter and explained that we did not want to impose on him or his family and that we would look around for a place to live after we got to the reservation.

Murray and I arrived at Thrashing Buffalo a few days before the beginning of the Sun Dance, once an annual religious ceremony, and recently revived as a bewildering mixture of the sacred, the social, and the profane. Some people take the ceremony seriously; most come because it is one of the great social gatherings of the year; while the tribal council tries to make money out of the tourists. We found a room in the run-down motel in the agency town. The motel owners were mixedbloods, amiable and obliging folk, who spoke of the people out on the reservation as "those Indians," implying that they (the motel owners) were a different breed of human. We took several walks through the little town, visited the post office, and had lunch at the one restaurant. All in all, what we saw of the people lifted our spirits. The Indians, standing or sitting around the major highway intersection, watching the traffic go by, gossiping in front of the various bureau or tribal offices, going in or out of the two grocery stores or the post office, or driving their battered and sag-axled cars, were not, at first glance, impressive. On the other hand, they did not look particularly miserable, depraved, withdrawn, or pathetic. They looked just like Indians minding or going about their business. Many of the men wore the big hats, jeans, dark shirts and boots of the working cowboy. Many of the older women wore rather long, shapeless dresses, which looked like hand-me-downs from a white woman who had neither a shape nor a sense of style. (Later, when I became well acquainted with some of these matrons, they assured me that their dresses constituted proper, modest "Indian" garments. I gathered that this was what the white teachers and the missionaries had told them twenty or thirty years ago.) The young girls, of course, dressed according to the notions of modishness that had filtered into the reservation from the nearby small towns and the movie magazines. Sometimes the effect was pleasant, and sometimes (when it involved bleached hair and skin tight slacks on a splendid and stalwart rump) it was startling.

No one had told us what the landscape was like, and we had braced ourselves for the ultimate in geographic dreariness. Instead, there were long, gently and elegantly rolling hills. Many of the summits bore clusters of dwarf pines, and some were topped by curious perpendicular clay outcroppings. In a dim light these looked like the abandoned fortresses of an extinct race. Though the land was crowded with people—compared to the much more sparsely populated ranch country outside the reservation—it still had the pleasant, bitter smell of wild places, for most of it has never been put to the plow. The stream beds ran deep, six or more feet below bank level, so that the cottonwoods that lined them seem to peer over the edges of the arroyos like lurking warriors in green or golden headdresses. In October and November, when each level of valley or hillside took on a different hue of beige, garnet, buckskin, or deep brown, the land became even more beautiful. (These are the things you put in your field diary when you run out of things to say about people. Nonetheless, I counted the beauty of the landscape a blessing, though it might be too austere for some tastes.)

We spent these first days having long talks with Walter and Victor, calling on high-ranking administrators, and fretting over the problem of where to live. Our meetings with the administrators went reasonably well. This, I suspect, was not because we impressed them with the value of our proposed research, but because they had received communications from the Commissioner of Indian Affairs, a man who had himself earned a doctorate in anthropology from our alma mater. We did less well in our attempt to find a place to live. Our "old friend," the man who had advised us not to move in with Walter's folks, was planning to come to Thrashing Buffalo for the Sun Dance. At that time, he assured us, he would help us settle down near some good, quiet, fullblood Indian family. We had come equipped to camp out, and, if we could find a good location, we thought we might rent or buy a trailer house when the weather got cold. Walter, on the other hand, obviously wanted us to move in with his folks, where, as he once again told us, his parents and other relatives could help us get accustomed to Indian ways and then gradually introduce us into the community. He also warned us that he would not be able to help us much if we located in another district of the reservation (which was what our "old friend" was advising), because he (Walter) had ties with only the people who lived in his own *tiyospaye,* that is, the people with whom his folks were ceremonially related. The upshot of all this was that we stalled until our friend got there for the Sun Dance. Then, to our dismay, we were obliged to stall again, for the business of looking for a future house seemingly could not easily be carried on during the ceremony. We did, however, decide to drive about the reservation, visit Walter's folks, and case the situation.

Our first experience with an Indian road transformed our relationship to our automobile. Leading off the highway lay a dirt trail created by Indian horsemen and wagons. For thirty, or perhaps even fifty years, no one had done anything to this trail but use it. There were three or four pairs of parallel ruts, some of which were ten inches deep. Further along the road were some extremely steep hills, with blind, single-lane summits. (Later, when we were living at Walter's folks' place, Indian cars twice collided on these summits like battling Rocky Mountain sheep. Nobody was hurt except one fellow who got a black eye in the fight that followed one of the accidents.) We noted that whenever a section of the road became impassible, traffic had done what rivers do: flowed to one or the other side. Thus, in especialy rough and low lying sections, one might encounter three or four distinct trails.

As I have remarked, once we started our car down this road, we (and the car) were never the same again, because no sane dweller in the "motor age" could do such a thing. Murray put the car in its lowest gear and we rocked and rolled along with bumpers clanging and the springs groaning like the squashed victims of Ivan the Terrible. Despite our slow speed we raised a great cloud of dust that pursued and pounced on us at every bend or dip. The countryside, which had looked so splendid from the paved highway now became vaguely unfriendly. We saw acres of silvery green and biscuit-colored tall grass combed into whorls by the wind and a few shaggy, scowling Hereford cows and calves and, once, a solitary and thoughtful-looking bull. We also saw and heard some large, noisy, black-and-white birds with tail feathers like enormous rudders. These were the magpies, who (we read) used to kill saddle-sore horses by swooping on them in clouds and tearing their backs to pieces. People watch their horses now, but the magpies are very tough; later I saw one of them brazenly steal food from a half-starved cat. If we had looked up, we might have seen an eagle, but we were in no mood to look up.

The white farmers of this region build their houses to be seen. Indians must build their houses with other things in mind, for they are often very difficult for a white man to find. Most of the houses off the highway are one- or two-room log cabins weathered to a camouflage grey. The low, narrow doors face south or southeast, which exposes them to the sun and shelters them from the wind. Whenever the weather permits, people leave their doors open for light, though, now that I think of it, very few of the Indian houses I was later to visit impressed me as poorly lit. Perhaps, on the prairie, one or two small but well-placed windows let in a good deal of light. Frank Lloyd Wright might have approved of these cabins because they complement the landscape so beautifully. But today most white people find them appalling.

From a distance, the GoodHorse household looked more impressive than most, since there seemed to be at least three or four dwellings. Close by it looked less grand. The largest of the three buildings was a solid, two-room log cabin, about the size of a living room in an average city house. In this cabin lived seven people: Walter's parents, his married brother together with his wife and baby, and his two younger brothers. This (we learned later) was about par for an Indian cabin of this size; sometimes ten or twelve people lived in less space. About ten yards distant was a tiny, neatly painted shack, with red curtains in the tiny windows. In this dwelling, which looked as if it would crowd a brood of chickens, lived Walter and his wife (a girl from another tribe), who was expecting a baby in a few weeks. Fifty yards away was another cabin, so run down that it was not even used for storage. Nevertheless, we learned later that Walter's mother counted this cabin as one of her houses. Close to the main cabin were two army tents: one housed Vic (our other research assistant); the other was used for storage.

185

Before the main house was an arbor or "shade" of dwarf upright pine trunks roofed with pine boughs. The GoodHorse shade was unusually large, sheltering three wooden tables, two defeated-looking cots with their springs partly covered by frayed and dusty quilts, a forty-year-old icebox, under which was lying what looked like a dead black dog, two ancient chests of drawers, two auto seats arranged to serve as sofas, and many other battered objects of furniture difficult to identify. A large yard stretching to the east of the shade, looked, to a city person, like the parking lot of a not too prosperous junk yard. Three cars dominated the area: one ancient car belonging to Walter's father and two middle-aged cars belonging to Walter and Walter's brother. Walter's brother's car, we were told, was in good shape and could make trips to Montana or even Wisconsin without breaking down. The other two vehicles broke down about every fifty miles and were then subjected to bailing-wire repairs. With so much repair work going on, the yard was strewn with cylinder heads, transmissions, gears of all sizes, wrenches, jacks, and other tools. Mixed in with these were the tools or artifacts of sedentary life, an open-air fireplace made of concrete bricks, several old oil drums; iron fence posts (which could be used for pit-cooking, levers, or self-defense), old axes, post-hole diggers, pots, pails, rolls of barbed wire, and five-gallon milk cans. Nearby was an extensive system of clothes lines strung with men's shirts and baby's diapers. (Indian women often wash clothes every day; if there are no clothes on the line a visitor can tell from a distance that no one is at home.) In the prairie near the homestead lay the remains of two cars which, apparently, had died on their tires. Stripped of any useful part, faded and rusting, they lay like great dead and dessicated insects, with the long grass growing through their orifices.

As we drew up, two boys of about eight or nine ran off down the slope toward the distant creek. These, we suspected, were Walter's little brothers. (Later, we found that many country Indian children take to their heels at the sight of a stranger—and especially of a white man. In fact, at some of the isolated homesteads everybody— men, women, and children—run for cover at the approach of an unidentified car.) Nobody seemed about, except Walter's father and, of course, Walter and Vic. Walter told us that his mother was sleeping. (This was not true because I caught a glimpse of her watching us from a window.) I felt very awkward and ill at ease.

We were introduced to Walter's father and shook hands in the gentle, light-fingered Indian fashion, which we were already beginning to pick up. Tom GoodHorse was a skinny but amazingly active little man of sixty, with a big head, a big Indian nose, and a big voice. Though he made every effort to behave with characteristic Indian dignity, there was something about the way he walked and held himself that made him look like Harpo Marx disguised as an Indian. Unlike Harpo, he talked almost all the time. He greeted us in the loud tones used by many older Indian men on formal occasions, and he invited us to sit down. We sat on one of the relocated car seats, and our host struck an attitude and began a speech.

Many Indian men are superb orators. Some have held me spellbound though I could not understand a word they said. Mr. Good-Horse, however, sounded very much like a bag of wind, and I had to bring to bear all of my professional training in order to keep track of and remember what he was saying. Still, I told myself, he was an older man and he seemed to mean well; besides, he was Walter's father. So we listened respectfully to his extensive monologue about the shameful graft in which the "Bureau people" were indulging, and to his long denunciation of mixedbloods and especially of mixedbloods who worked for the Bureau. "All the troubles on this reservation is the fault of those mixedbloods. They grab all the jobs and they never will hire no fullblood boys no matter what good qualifications they have. Mixedbloods are like fish out of water—with no head and no tail." Midway in this speech it began to rain. But it was only a passing shower and the shade protected us fairly well. Mr. GoodHorse continued his oration. The black dog under the ancient ice box came to life, crawled out, and walked away. In his summing up, Mr. GoodHorse startled us into momentary attention by stating that the local high school ought to add French and algebra to its curriculum, so that the young people would be adequately prepared for college. Then we realized that Walter had, no doubt, told him that we were there to study education.

We thanked Walter's father for his observations, explained our aims and needs in some detail, and prepared to depart. As we walked toward our car, Mr. GoodHorse hollered after us, "Remember, when an Indian is your friend, then you have a real friend!" We looked at each other and smiled. "We'll remember," I said.

A few raindrops were still falling, but the road seemed firm and unpuddled; so we started on our way. All in all, the visit had impressed us favorably. The view was beautiful, the air good, and there were no foul odors. Mr. GoodHorse promised to be a bit of a bore, but he seemed naïve and childlike rather than scheming or evil.

187

Suddenly, and with no warning whatever, our car went into an incredible skid. After three zigs and four zags, we lost all traction. I got out and immediately clutched the car door like an amateur ice skater. The sandy-looking surface of the road was like a buttered bathtub. Fortunately, we had traveled only about half a mile from the GoodHorses, and our skid was seen by Walter and Vic. They came toward us carefully, walking only on the grass. With three of us shoving, we managed to sledge the car to a less glassy section of the road. Walter then suggested that thereafter, whenever we come to a low spot, we would do well to drive off the road onto the grass along the margin. We proceeded in this fashion for some time, though the car, in our off-the-road sorties, moved more like a teeter-totter than a wheeled vehicle. Just before we reached the highway we had to cross a creek, and here the road had transformed itself into a morass of puddles and water-filled ruts. I lost my nerve and suggested that we get out and walk the fifteen miles to the motel. But Murray was suddenly possessed by the spirit of some remote warrior ancestor. Shouting "Hoka hey!" (the Sioux equivalent of "Charge!"), he stepped on the gas and steered us straight into the morass. Mud flew in all directions and the car spun around completely. But so great was our momentum that we kept going as we spun, so that the rear wheels came safely to rest on the hard road.[1] Murray, looking marvelously pleased with himself, backed us safely to the highway. I didn't say anything.

As we wiped off the windshield, Murray remarked several times, "Well—I got us out." I could find nothing to say because it was the first time I had seen a Jew act like a Sioux. And I had a presentiment that it was not to be the last. Rather bluntly, I changed the subject and said that if our friend did not succeed in finding us a place to stay, the GoodHorses' did not look so bad to me.

1. The procedure is not quite as reckless as may appear. The trick is to acquire momentum—properly directed—before reaching the slippery place and to release the gas pedal before entry, so that the vehicle slides across like a stone. Most trouble-making skids arise when one rear wheel loses its traction, while the other wheel retains some, and the resultant is a bad (usually unmanageable) twist in the movement of the car. If no power is being transferred from the engine to the rear wheels, then this kind of skid cannot occur, and the car should travel in accordance with its momentum and the nature of the path. The occasion described was the first time I attempted the maneuver, and, as will have been noted, the performance was flawed.—MLW.

16   Still Looking for a Home

We had asked Walter when the Sun Dance ceremony would begin. "At dawn," he replied. The evening paper stated that on 2 August the sun would rise at 4:00 A.M. Dopey, breakfastless, but game, we groped our way out of our motel room at 3:30 and somehow, in the dark, managed to drive to the proper location. In the dim, predawn light we made out a large encampment of canvas army tents and a few trailers, dispersed over the hills. In the center of the encampment was a flat, circular area, the dance ground, enclosed by an annular shade or arbor of posts covered with pine boughs. This area, in turn, was enclosed by a high fence of chicken wire. Not a human soul was to be seen. It was very still. We parked our car and walked around the dance ground, peering through the fence at the ritual tree, a tall cottonwood, which (we had read) was cut down ceremonially, trimmed of its lower branches, and then "replanted" to serve as the focus of the sacrifice. It was still too dark to see the little buffalo figure and the man (who some people say represents the enemy) that were hanging from the tree. But we were able to make out the brush bundle, which scholars say once represented a nest for the Thunder Bird. Rather impressed, we went back to our car, which looked very lonely in the empty visitor's lot. There was almost no noise, although there must have been many hundreds of Indians sleeping all about us. A dog barked; once there was a clang as if someone had knocked an empty pail against a tent stake. The sky turned a light gold and then a faint blue. A pair of yellow-breasted meadow larks flew by. I began to feel sorry for Murray because he really suffers when he misses a meal. But he was busy watching and worrying about three or four Indian boys who suddenly ran up, swarmed over the gates, swung from the supporting poles, and jumped into the speaker's booth. The boys vanished. About five o'clock a tourist drove up with his family. He wore a bright flower-print shirt and carried a shoulder-slung camera. Catching sight of an Indian man walking in the distance, he yelled: "When does the dance start?" "Six o'clock," said the Indian. We sighed. The tourist drove his car and family away.

About seven o'clock two Indian men climbed into the speaker's booth and began to fiddle with the public address system. When they got it working, one announced in Lakota and then in English that everybody ought to get up pretty soon because the dance would start at eight. Murray looked at me and said, "Let's go get some breakfast." By this time it was full daylight, and we were able to drive back to the motel in a few minutes. Here I had cached some milk, fruit, and breakfast cereal. We got back to the dance ground by eight, but the ceremony did not begin until nine.

Eight middle-aged men walked slowly from behind the pine screen that hid the entrance to the sweatbath lodge where they had been secluded all night to purify themselves. Their chests were bare, and they wore what looked like dark, old blankets hanging from their waists. Around their heads and wrists were wreaths of sage—a plant pleasing to spirits of goodwill. Some wore an upright eagle feather above each ear. Two of the men looked very feeble, and one had a pronounced limp. But the man who was going to be pierced was fleshy and plump. The dancers-to-be stood at the margin of the dance ground, looking dazed and patient. About twenty Indian watchers stood around also. The ceremony could not start because the appointed singers had not shown up. Somebody went to round up the singers. At last, everybody was there including the medicine man who was to direct this particular Sun Dance. He was an old man and wore the two braids of the old days; otherwise he was dressed in cowboy work clothes, levis, big, wide-brimmed hat, and rough, dark shirt. Finally, the head singer lifted up his voice in one of the special Sun Dance songs, the other singers chimed in with voice and drum, and the dancers began their ordeal. They danced a very simple little step in place, looking at the sun and blowing rhythmically on little whistles. This went on, hour after hour, except for certain ceremonial rest periods.

It was not the kind of spectacle that would make a sensation on Cinerama. Eight middle-aged men in ragged blankets with sage in their hair, jiggling and making little noises like starving baby birds. But then, the old-time Indians believed that the Great Powers are most inclined to help a miserable, humble, or, as they put it, a *pitiful* person.

About 10:30, helpful Walter arrived looking well fed and cheerful. We didn't have the heart to jump on him since, after all, we had not asked him when to come but when the dance was *supposed* to begin. By this time many Indians had gathered at the dance ground; some sat on the grass and watched the dancers; others leaned against the pine tree trunks that supported the shade; others stood or strolled around outside the fence, visiting, chatting, and joking. Walter introduced Murray to a few older men, and after a while some of these oldsters began to tell Murray that this Sun Dance was not being done properly, according to the old ways. To begin with, it should have started at dawn. Then, too, many people distrusted the tribal official in charge of arrangements and publicity, pointing out that he had recently served a jail sentence for grafting of tribal monies. Some made cynical speculations about how the attendance money would be spent by the tribal council. Finally, one robust old man said contemptuously that the whole Thrashing Buffalo nation was good-for-nothing these days. "In the old days," he said, "they ate buffalo and were strong. Now they eat radishes and they're all sick." "All they come for is to drink," said another old man indignantly. "The bars in Horton will be jammed, and then the jail will be jammed too." Listening to these remarks depressed Murray. Later he was to learn that this kind of lamentation is standard procedure at all Sun Dances. Every medicine man arranges the rites differently, and every year his "version" is rigorously criticized. Indeed, the dance we attended was relatively uneventful because only some sixty or so intoxicated celebrants were put in jail. (This did not dash their spirits, for we heard that they held their own social or Pow-wow inside the jail.) A couple of years ago one of the Sun dancers was bundled off to jail by the police as soon as he had finished his ordeal.

Months later, after we had got to know the Thrashing Buffalo better, we decided that much of what we had seen and heard at the Sun Dance was a display of vitality rather than weakness. A ceremony drawing thousands of people to observe, comment, and criticize, may have more depth and power than one in which the congregation sits in bored acquiescence or does not attend at all. Besides, participants in sacred rites are not infrequently arrested and carried off by the civil authorities.

While Murray listened to the men talk about the Sun Dance, I followed up Walter's hint that his mother wanted to talk to me. I found Beula GoodHorse sitting on the grass, slightly removed from the other spectators. She was holding her only grandchild, Walter's brother's baby. She looked about forty-five (she was forty-seven), and, like many middle-aged Indian women, she was blocky, power-ful, and—by middle-class standards—overweight. But she moved and held herself as if she were an outstandingly handsome young girl. I had exchanged no more than a few sentences with her when I realized that this was the most formidable woman I had ever met. Ruthless, passionate, stubborn, proud, and incredibly strong, she made poor little Mrs. Tsuchikawa look like a thin and dusty bamboo chair. Indeed, I think I would have been afraid of Mrs. GoodHorse, except that I am almost never afraid of people. But I remember thinking, "My God! This is what Medea might have been like, had she lived to be forty-five."

We had no difficulty in conversing, for we both plunged imme-diately into matters which we thought would impress the other.

First I heard about her travels in Europe (the GoodHorses had been among the several Thrashing Buffalo families who had traveled abroad to perform Indian dancing.) I told her about the hurricanes, Miami, University life, and about directing the workshop for Ameri-can Indian college students (much less interesting topics). In Brussels the Thrashing Buffalo had been able to get raw kidneys (an Indian delicacy); they ate funny big bread which the people there did not wrap up; but in Ireland there were big people with red faces who did not speak English, and, when the Thrashing Buffalo danced, these people hollered and clapped; some just stood there and cried. "Why did those Irish people cry when the Indians danced?" Mrs. GoodHorse asked me. I thought I knew why the Irish cried when the Thrashing Buffalo danced, but I wasn't sure I could explain it to her. I did not have to pretend to be impressed by her travels or by the extraordinary fluency of her English (which was far better than that of her college graduate son).

Having defined ourselves as women of the world, we turned to a critical discussion of our immediate kin. Here I naïvely thought I could hold my own because my relatives are a mighty colorful crew. But I soon perceived that Beula GoodHorse was light-years ahead of me—she moved in a different dimension.

First she told me that Gloria, Walter's wife, was trying to turn Walter from an Episcopalian into a Catholic; Walter and Gloria had been married in a Catholic church, and this had distressed Beula so much that she had refused to attend the wedding. Furthermore, Gloria was always telling Walter what to do and making up his mind for him. (This was improper behavior by Thrashing Buffalo standards because, though a woman may scold and nag, a man is supposed to make all the important decisions.) Beula had warned her son that, if he allowed Gloria to behave like this, "people would begin to make fun of her," that is, ridicule her behind her back, but Walter "just laughed." Recently, Gloria, who worked at the hospital, had objected to Walter's calling for her in ordinary clothes (rough cowboy garb) and had nagged him into buying fancy clothes (white shirt, sweater, and slacks). Beula had taunted her son for his uxoriousness, remarking: "Why don't you buy some panties and brassieres for yourself while you're at it?" Again, Walter had only laughed at this maternal reproof, though, as a son, there was nothing else he could do. Finally, Beula lowered her eyelids and voice in embarrassment and whispered that Gloria even flirted with her father-in-law. This made poor Tom so bashful that he didn't know what to do. (This was a dreadful accusation, because conservative Thrashing Buffalo are supposed to "respect" their parents-in-law and, if possible, not even look at or speak to them; to do otherwise is incestuous.)

I did not at this time know what to make of this list of horrid accusations. I had read that Thrashing Buffalo mothers adore their sons and look with a cool eye on their daughters-in-law, but I had, as yet, had no opportunity to find out whether Beula's behavior was customary or extreme. I had also read that Indians are masters of gossip, but I had never before heard anyone but a psychopath blacken a close relative's reputation in so consistent, well-organized, and convincing a manner. (Later I learned that many Indians can do this sort of thing extremely well, but that Beula was a genius. I also observed that Gloria did not "flirt" with her father-in-law or with any other man and that she tried, for the most part, to observe Thrashing Buffalo customs and manners. But she was a young, acculturated, mixedblood girl from another tribe, and she was accustomed to being pleasant, gracious, and a little coy with all men.)

Around noon I excused myself and set out to look for Murray. I found him leaning against a car, listening to Walter's uncle, Bill ChargingBear, a handsome and outspoken man of about sixty-five, with the compact build and slightly stiff walk of a man who has ridden a great deal more than he has walked. Murray had just introduced me to Mr. ChargingBear, when the Sun dancers and singers suddenly quit for the day. Murray was astonished at the abrupt ending of what the ethnographic literature described as a four-day-long ordeal. His face must have shown his surprise, for Mr. ChargingBear explained that most of the people preferred Omaha or Pow-wow dancing and had little use for the holy ceremony. So the Sun dancers would dance in the morning and the Pow-wow dancers in the afternoon.

Omaha or Pow-wow dancing is of recent origin. It is designed to meet the needs of today, when most big affairs given by Indians involve the coming together of a number of tribes. It is exciting and pleasing to sit under the shade with friends and watch the people from the distant plains tribes arrive, don their regalia, and, group by group, join the rotating kaleidoscope of dancers. Every person, man, woman or child, may join the dance when and as he wishes, but each tribe or region tends to have its own style. When a Pow-wow dance goes well, it is a little like a great family reunion, where everybody visits, gossips, makes jokes, and enjoys himself.

We did not see much of the Pow-wow dancing because we were househunting. But we returned to the Sun Dance on the third day to see what Murray called "the bloody business." (The Sun Dance is supposed to last four days, but this time, we were told, the tribal council committee had decided to finish it on the third day.) Since the dance on the first day had begun at nine we came this time at eight. As we entered the wire enclosure, we saw two Indian policemen supporting a green-faced and staggering white man, who, we were told, had fainted. The plump man had already been skewered. He looked in good shape, slowing dancing around the tree. Pulling at the rawhide thong attached to his bloody chest, he looked like a creature, not fully born, trying slowly to detach itself from its mother. There were, today, many hundreds of Indians watching the dancer with sober and expressionless faces. Suddenly a very old lady ululated a faint "war whoop," the shrill noise by which the women traditionally greeted a brave achievement: the skewered man had danced himself free.

Our old friend Bill had arrived on the second day of the Sun Dance, and our spirits were lifted. But he told us that it would be much easier to find a place to live after the dance was over. Then we perceived that his primary interest was in pursuing a beautiful

Indian girl, who, it turned out, he had long been interested in. Apparently, he did not make out very well, for he told us that the girl had demanded that he "go round" the dance area with her (courting couples strolled round and round the edge of the circle in the semidarkness), and that he had refused, adding, half-jokingly, that he did not want to take part in barbarous Thrashing Buffalo customs. We suspected that he did not wish to make a public display of his interest in the girl, whereas this was precisely what she desired. In any case, he dropped the courtship and began to help us look for a landlord. Thus we spent the last three or four days of the Pow-wow either in making long, dusty, fruitless drives over the reservation, or sweltering and fretting in the motel, or, occasionally, watching the dancing. One day we drove forty miserable miles to see a man, only to be told that he had left for parts unknown. Another day we drove for twenty-five miles to see an Indian judge of the tribal court, with whom, however, Murray and I were already acquainted. When Bill described the kind of place *he* thought suitable for us—with a "nice, quiet, peaceful, family that doesn't drink"—the old judge smiled mildly and remarked, "You're asking for paradise." We protested, pointing out that we were not prudes and would not mind a little life and activity. But Bill reminded us that we were greenhorns and did not know "what drunken Thrashing Buffalo were like"; so we subsided. Bill's contacts out on the reservation were soon exhausted. He told us that he had some "adopted relatives" in a small slum village about eight miles from the agency town, but we hesitated to settle there because it was an untypical community. Besides, when he took us to call on his adopted mother, an old, blind lady, she did not seem at all eager to have us around.

By the last day of the Pow-wow I was exhausted, but Murray, restless and desperate, left the motel to see the dancing. He returned earlier than I had expected, and when I saw his face I knew he was in a state of shock. Thinking he might have seen someone killed or might have smashed up the car, I sat him down on the bed and fetched our hidden bottle of whiskey. But he just held the bottle in his hand and looked amazed. "Take a drink," I said. Then, like a man talking under drugs, he said, "Mrs. GoodHorse propositioned me." I sat down on the dust-covered floor and laughed. Finally, we both had a drink. Murray never told me exactly what happened except that Mrs. GoodHorse had climbed into the car with him and refused to get out and that she could not run very fast.[1]

Remaining in the motel was expensive, cramped, hot, and generally uncomfortable. The refrigerator was the noisiest I have ever heard; it woke us up several times every night. In addition, we were slowly going dust-crazy. Daily dust storms can be more irritating than unvarying, humid heat. If we left the door open or went outside, we choked. If we closed the door, we sweated and choked more slowly. As the dust penetrated and accumulated in our eyes, noses, mouths, lungs, hair, etc., we tried to write up our notes and make plans. Some of the notes were not bad—I have used them to write this account—but most of the plans were pointless. Murray developed a tickling cough, which began with the evening dust storms and kept him awake much of the night. Since our double bed sagged like a hammock, it kept me awake also. Nonetheless, Murray remained fairly rational, for he reminded me, between coughs, that there were still people who denounced the Indians because they had refused to put their prairie land to the plow. But thinking of what the dust *would* have been like if the wind had been blowing over plowed fields instead of long, heavy, grass, did not raise my spirits.

For the next five days we redoubled our efforts to find some other place to settle than with the GoodHorses. Every night Murray coughed. (Though we did not know this, there were scores of Indian families who would have been happy to take us in, once they had become acquainted with us and had decided that we would be good neighbors. But we had to put ourselves in a position where they could watch us and decide what kind of people we were.) Finally, we both got so wound up, tired, and unhappy that I began to feel that if we didn't do something positive pretty soon, we would crack

1. After some reflection, I had come to interpret Mrs. GoodHorse's approach as being the result of her anxiety about her son's position with our project and that she had offered herself as a way of obligating me to her, him, and her family. I thought that, when I had indicated my lack of interest in a carnal relationship, while at the same time confirming our interest in Walter, this would have led her to redefine the relationship between her family and ours. Indeed, it seemed to me plausible that some of her anxiety stemmed from our refusal to move out to their place, and that her offering of herself was but a device to induce me to make the move.—MLW.

up. Day by day the GoodHorse abode looked less undesirable. Tom GoodHorse, in friendly fashion, volunteered to get us a big tent and other supplies; Beula, after her one affectionate outburst, behaved herself; Walter, and even Vic, our other research assistant, went about looking gently reproachful. After all (we told each other), while the GoodHorses were not models of middle-class morality, they were not boring, and (except for Beula's remarks about her daughter-in-law) they did not seem to be vicious. Besides, we figured, we were only going to stay a few weeks, during which we would be traveling about a great deal visiting schools and interviewing people. Murray even began to have his doubts about whether he had not misinterpreted Beula's behavior. Perhaps what he had seen as a proposition had been an expression of cordiality. Finally, the idea of camping out on the pleasant-smelling prairie near a cool, tree-edged creek, grew more appealing every time the dust from the streets hit us in the face. Our lungs were beginning to feel like the inside of a dirty vacuum cleaner.

At this point Bill took us to see Mr. BlueCalf, one of the leading citizens of the little Indian slum community near the agency town. Mr. BlueCalf seemed likable, agreeable, and trustworthy, and, moreover, he was willing to lend us a tent and let us camp on his land for a while. While we were not enthusiastic at the location—for extreme poverty seems to become more horrible the more crowded it is—we decided that we would give it a try. On the drive back to the motel, we asked Bill what we should offer to pay for rent and for the use of the tent, but he said, emphatically, that we should not think of paying.

The next evening, while we were packing, Mr. BlueCalf drove up to the motel with his wife and children. They smiled happily at us and we smiled happily at them. Then Mr. BlueCalf asked Murray to lend him fifteen dollars. Murray gave him the money and BlueCalf drove off. I turned back to my packing but stopped when I saw that Murray was white and almost speechless with rage. Murray gets angry so seldom that I have never learned what is best to do. Besides, the few things that enrage him do not usually bother me very much. I assumed that he was angry at Mr. BlueCalf, but in fact he was mad at Bill, who, he figured, had wasted several weeks of our time and, to top it off, had misadvised us.

197

I was by this time not thinking very clearly. Indeed, Murray's rage frightened and distressed me so much that I had to repress a hysterical impulse to run out of the motel and look for a tree big enough to beat my head against. It was in this state that I spoke the fatal words: "Let's move in with the GoodHorses. It can't be as bad as this."

17 Participant Observation at the GoodHorses'

Our first day at the GoodHorses' was fun. Beula and Tom fussed about as we unpacked our gear, helped us put up a big tent (our office and workroom), gave us a wooden table and a chest of drawers (whose drawers turned out to be bottomless), and promised to build a shade for us. We put up our own small, mountain climbers' sleeping tent. Everyone tried hard to make us feel welcome. Vic seemed glad to see us, too, and he and Tom brought us some brushwood for our cooking fire. Tom and Beula worried over the fact that we planned to sleep on the ground. We explained that we had air mattresses and sleeping bags and had used them for weeks in the mountains. But they were not reassured.

When we had finished the essential unpacking, I walked down the hill to the creek and looked around. The stream was narrow, steep-banked, and fairly deep. The cottonwood and willow trees, though not tall, were strong and wind-twisted. There were cattle prints and dried droppings on the path, but no rubbish at all in either the grass or the stream. I felt so good I prayed—that we wouldn't hurt anybody and that things would turn out all right.

I cooked our supper in local style, which means I dug a pit ten inches deep and built the fire in it. The first time you see this done you wonder, Why build a fire in a hole? Half an hour later the wind comes up, and you know why. As we ate we enjoyed the rare sight of a complete sunset, because here, as in mid-ocean, nothing came between us and the horizon. The sky was powdered pink and light blue, enormous night hawks swooped about, and a glowing gold rim outlined the western hills. The first stars let themselves be seen. By the time I had washed up the utensils and burned the garbage, there was´ so much moon- and starlight that one could easily walk by it. A fine Indian voice rose up from the GoodHorse yard a couple of hundred feet away, and we heard people laughing. Strolling over we found Walter, Vic, and the very pregnant Gloria dancing, while a young man we did not know sang and beat the drum. The laughter came from the GoodHorses, watching Vic's first attempts at Indian dancing. We joined in too and found, as we had before, that Indian dancing is more complicated than it looks. Beula danced marvelously; though shaped like a schmoo, she had great style. When we went back to our encampment and crawled into our little red sleeping tent, we were feeling happier than at any time since our arrival on the reservation. Ten minutes later Murray started to cough. He took some cough syrup and it did not help. "I'm almost willing to believe in black magic," he muttered, which was an unusual thing for him to say. Much later he crawled out, found our suitcase, took several aspirins and several slugs of whiskey. He fell asleep. But I listened to the faint hoots of the owls and the distant howls of the wild dogs, the vibrating plonks of the big bull frogs, and the quiet that came between them.

The weeks that followed were a confusion of exasperations, of comedy, and of sudden insights that were almost immediately submerged in new confusions and problems. At first, we were most impressed by the amount of know-how involved in the simplest and humblest of the GoodHorses' activities. Murray was most struck by the skill and experience needed to put up a simple-looking Indian pine bough "shade." When he tried to help, he found there was nothing he could do without getting in the way. I, for my part, knew very little about such elementary matters as washing clothes with creek water or regulating the temperature inside our large tent. We soon adopted the Indian habit of standing back and watching the experts do things. Meanwhile, we thought contemptuously about the white people who live in the agency town and insist that the pattern of Indian life is meager, empty, and degenerate, and that Indians have no "culture."

Actually, we did not do much sitting around. Murray, Walter, and Vic drove off every day to the agency town or elsewhere. They made introductory speeches to the tribal council asking for and receiving permission to pursue the research. Then Murray spent many days trying to find a building that would serve as a project office as well as a place where we could live during the winter. (We were not planning to spend the winter in a tent, though some Indian families still manage to do this.) In time we discovered and managed to rent a one-room schoolhouse called Witkokia. It had been built about the turn of the century and must then have had some style, but it had long since been abandoned as a school building, and, after a term as office for an agricultural extension agent, had been abandoned for official uses. It was now crammed with a miscellaneous collection of things. The structure actually had considerable space, since there was a separate room designed as a kitchen, as well as a foreroom for supplies (into which we moved as much of the litter as possible). The building had been improved by the addition of a single electric circuit and one tap for running cold water; it also had a pot-bellied oil stove, which had evidently been added in replacement for what must once have been a grand heating system constructed about a furnace. To top it off, the building had a phone, which, while not connected, was still physically linked to the antiquated and temperamental local system. That the building was still standing and in reasonable repair was a tribute to the original builders and the system of maintenance characteristic of the BIA. Murray drove about, trying to rent typewriters, desks, filing cases, and other office supplies. This took weeks, because the nearest source of supply was sixty miles away and there was no telephone available.[1] I stayed at the GoodHorses', wrote up many pages of notes, talked to Beula, and puttered away happily, turning my "shade" into a comfortable, snug place, with a tarp floor, an oilcloth-covered table, and a shelf for pans and camping dishes. I even adopted an ugly, starved-looking dog to sit under the shade with me. This dog was the color of dirty slush, had big hairy ears like a piglet and an enormous black nose. Her eyes were glazed with hunger and despair, and I figured that we both needed a friend. Perhaps she was one of the wild dogs. Wild or not, she was tent-broken, quiet, and did everything she was told. I called her Weasel-Bear.

When Murray was not using the car, I drove out twenty miles for groceries and fifteen miles for drinking water, which, as our Indian neighbors did, we kept in a large milk can. We bathed in the creek and used its water for washing dishes or clothing, but nobody drank from it except cattle and birds.

Every day Beula bore down on our quarters for a gossip session. Sometimes her twin boys crept into the tent or under the shade to

---

1. It was very inconvenient to use the Bureau phones, and we had to wait a long time to get the phone at Witkokia connected. In any case, Witkokia was fifteen miles from the GoodHorses', where we lived.

listen. She never seemed to censor her racy remarks because of their presence, but if they began to interrupt or pester her, she shooed them away like chickens.

Whatever else she may have been, Beula was not lazy. She cooked two huge meals every day on her kerosene stove or outdoor fireplace. At midday she usually did a large washing, entirely by hand. In addition, she cared for her seven- or eight-month-old grandchild. I was much taken by the art with which she kept this vigorous baby happy. Whenever possible, she held it on her lap, jiggling it as if her knee were a horse. Once, when she was holding the baby and talking to me, it dropped its little wooden rattle. Beula seemed not to notice, and the baby, after some neck-stretching, became aware that the toy was on the ground. It reached downward with a little grunt, and Beula obligingly lowered it a few inches. The baby reached again and was lowered again. After several more reachings and lowerings, the baby was close enough to touch the rattle. Now Beula—without even interrupting her gossip—kept holding the baby close to the ground, while it looked at the rattle, picked it up, dropped it, picked it up again and finally began to chew on it. Then Beula replaced the baby on her lap. All of this happened twice more within the hour.

Late in the afternoon or early in the evening, Murray might hold a "meeting" with Walter, Vic, Gloria, and myself, in which he explained our proposed research, and we all discussed the ways and means by which we might go about it. Walter suggested that we travel about to the various community fairs and dances, customarily held in August and September, meet people, and let the folks get used to seeing us. But he warned us not to make any attempt to initiate interviews or talk to people, because "the fullbloods were not yet ready to receive us." Sometimes he entertained us with tales about spooks, visions, or medicine sessions. One of his relatives had been warned in a vision that he would be killed by thunder. After that he hid whenever a storm came up. But one day he was not able to reach his house in time and the thunder killed him and his horse. When people found him, one side of his face was all black. Another time Walter told us that some of the things he has seen at medicine ceremonies had made him "wonder if he was living in the twentieth century."

There was a woman who needed more blood. So they held a ceremony and the medicine man put a bowl on the floor. Then it felt as if big eagle wings were flying around over everybody, and when we looked at the bowl it was filled with blood—about a pint. The medicine man said that anyone who wanted to could come and smell the blood or taste it and see whether it was human blood or not.

Twins, Walter explained, are spirits who have decided to come and live with humans awhile. His brothers, for example, were sometimes overheard speaking to each other about riding the rabbits at Bear Butte before they had been born in human shape.

All of the GoodHorses warned us that there was a spook man who walked on the roads at night—but though Murray and I often walked at night we never saw him. On one of our strolls we did come upon the GoodHorses' trash heap. More than half of it consisted of empty beer cans. We said nothing about our discovery, but it was clear that our hosts were putting up a painfully respectable front for our sake, for they never drank beer when we were there. We felt rather guilty about this.

Gradually we found ourselves eating most of our meals at Beula's table. Sometimes this was interesting and even pleasant. Murray and Tom exchanged long, pointless yarns in which anything like communication was entirely accidental. If the talk turned to politics, Tom might say: "Why does a man like Kennedy who already has eleven million dollars want to be president? If I had eleven million dollars I wouldn't take that job." Neither Murray nor I had an answer to this. Once Murray remarked that he had worked in Washington a long time ago. Thereupon Tom announced that he too had once gone to Washington: "Last time we went to Washington to see the president, we went over to the Pentagon building. We walked all through it, and there were nine hundred thousand clerks in the building—three hundred thousand to a floor."

Once Tom came back from a trip to town while the rest of us were at the table. In his ringing and impersonal voice he said: "Some people near Gordon left a little baby in the back of their car and some drunks sat on it and squashed it." Then he added a humorless "Ha Ha Ha." Later, while he ate, he denounced drunken drivers and told us how two of his nephews had killed themselves by driving their cars into bridges. "All this trouble," he concluded, "is the fault of the white man for bringing liquor to the Indians."

Lewis, Walter's married brother, did not talk much at meals, and Lewis's wife, Irene, who seemed to spend most of her life working at the hospital, did not ever say a word. Beula, on the other hand, was very voluble, especially when it came to teasing Vic. She had now several times asked him to drive her to the home of some relative in the community, and when they returned she would remark, for example, that her relatives thought Vic was only sixteen years old. Vic teased her back, by remarking that she was so fat she was bending the axle in his car. This interplay vaguely distressed me, but I filed it under the many incomprehensible irritations of "participant observation." Murray, for his part, hinted strongly, both to Walter and to Beula, that it was I who should be driving Beula about on visits, since it was my particular job to get to know the Indian mothers. But Beula explained that the Indian women were not yet ready to accept a white person. To go with "Vicky" was all right because he was an Indian.

I don't know what Murray and I (or Vic, for that matter) would have done, had we known that Beula was introducing Vic to all of the Indian ladies as her new lover, and that apparently most people believed her. Meanwhile, Vic, in earnest innocence, was delighted to meet the "real fullbloods" and took copious and conscientious ethnographic notes about house furnishings, etiquette, family names and kin connections, and the behavior of children. Some of the matrons, we learned later, thought Beula's behavior particularly shameless, not because Vic was so young but because, living in her household as Walter's peer and friend, he was really her classificatory son. Murray and I, having forgotten the warning of the old missionary, did not even realize that the community was aware of our existence, much less that we were already involved in a glorious scandal.

The food Beula served was not too bad, being about what one would expect in rough circumstances anywhere on the American plains: boiled beans, boiled potatoes, and bannocks. We contributed a good deal of meat, and Tom sometimes got excellent fresh corn, radishes, and cucumbers from the reservation honor farm (where Indian offenders against the law worked out their time). We asked Walter what we should pay his mother for board, but, in this, and on other matters, Walter was vague and evasive. So we brought Beula plenty of food and Murray slipped her some money now and then.

At first we ate only our evening meal at the GoodHorses' table. But after a few days Tom yelled at us to come over for breakfast.

Then, if we did not show up for every meal, we were made to feel that we had been ungracious. This began to get on my nerves, because I enjoy cooking for Murray and I had anticipated at least a few happy and private meals under our pleasant shade. But Beula seemed not to hear my hints that Murray and I would sometimes like to eat by ourselves. Once I boldly announced that Murray wanted me to make him some pancakes, and the next morning we ate under our shade. But the next day Beula, smiling reproachfully, put some thick, lopsided ovoids on the table and announced that these were pancakes.

The same thing happened with our sleeping arrangements. All of the GoodHorses were shocked to learn that we slept on the ground (actually on lightweight foam rubber sleeping mattresses). When Murray's cough continued to trouble him, this was taken as evidence that we were doing the wrong thing. One day, when we returned from a shopping trip, we found two-thirds of the tent we had planned to use as an office filled by an ancient iron bedstead and springs. Tom explained, enthusiastically, that he had hauled the heavy bed a great distance on the top of his car and that it was, in fact, the bed he and Beula had slept in when they were first married. He may have sensed our absence of enthusiasm for he added: "You can use it for nothing and it will save you from having to buy a bed." I now feel that this is where I should have drawn the line. But I didn't.

Like many of the material blessings of the modern world, the bed created more problems than it solved. Since it took up so much of the room of the big tent, we were obliged to move most of our equipment into the little tent where we had been sleeping, and in consequence much of our gear became inaccessible. Then we had somehow to get a mattress, and the nearest town where we could buy a mattress was sixty miles away. So I went to the Goodhorses' junk pile, pushed the old black dog off an ancient, battered, and filthy mattress, dusted it off, slammed it on the bed, and we slept. (I could not dust it very thoroughly because the stuffing fell out of the holes.) It was not bad on Murray's side but it had lost most of its stuffing just where my rump hit the springs. But by now I was getting somewhat dazed; so from then on I slept in a hoop shape.

I continued to spend a good deal of time with Beula without becoming any more comfortable in her presence. Sometimes I asked her about her children and the schools, and on these matters she was quite helpful, telling me precisely what she thought about the situation. But about other people or events she and Walter sometimes told completely different stories. When she directed the conversation, she often talked about her daughters-in-law. She told me that Irene, Walter's brother's wife, was stingy and would not let her wash the baby's diapers. Irene also was too jealous of Lewis, her husband. I felt sorry for Irene, because she came from another tribe and, so far as I could see, she did not have one friend on the reservation. (Later, after we had left the GoodHorses, Vic told me that Beula sometimes taunted Irene, telling her about Lewis's extramarital affairs and then laughing at her.)

But Gloria, whose baby was now due, continued to receive the major part of Beula's malevolence.

"Gloria is really going to have a hard time with her baby," Beula told me.

"So?" I said.

"Gloria is *really* going to have a hard time," repeated Beula, and this time the relish in her voice was stronger than the assumed regret.

"How is that?"

"She keeps eating meat all the time, and she should be eating nothing but soup and watery things . . . Somebody should tell her . . . but then she never listens anyway . . . she's eating all the wrong things." Beula repeated this prophecy several times, and I felt that she wanted me to agree with her because this would help shape the future. So I pretended to misunderstand, and began to comfort her with all the optimistic sayings I could call to mind. Gloria was young and strong, I said, and many doctors said that meat was good for pregnant women. Besides, she came from another tribe . . . But Beula interrupted me and pointed out, with a sigh, that both of her daughters-in-law were Catholics and might turn her sons from their Episcopalian faith. Then her voice became less sad, as, glancing across the yard, she caught sight of Murray. "Mixed marriages don't last," she remarked.

"Oh, I think some people exaggerate that," I said with a bland smile, "Murray and I have been married a long time."

Beula closed her mouth with a snap. Looking at me sidewise, she whispered: "You're a lot older than him, aren't you?"

"Yes," I said, and added grimly, but to myself, "so are you."

206

Murray, on the whole, found life at the GoodHorses' pleasant and even fascinating. He often drove off in the morning with Walter and Vic, to visit or interview important people in the agency town or to buy supplies, and when he returned, in the late afternoon, he enjoyed talking and joking with Beula and Tom, teasing the little boys, and, in general, "observing fullblood Indian life."

But I, after two weeks of spending every day with Beula, watching her work (since she would not allow me to help her), or taking long solitary walks with WeaselBear, was becoming increasingly restless and uneasy. Murray suggested that I use Beula as an informant or get her to teach me Lakota. Beula, however, seemed to be very much aware that this kind of information was worth money. I suggested to Murray that I pay her by the hour to teach me, but he demurred, pointing out that we were already paying Walter a large salary, for which, so far, he had done very little. Once again we suggested to Walter that Beula and I visit the mothers of schoolchildren. This time Walter told us that his father and mother had decided that we should live quietly in their place until early September, when the Standing Man community would hold its annual fair. At this time, Tom, who was a prominent and respected man, would introduce us to all the Indian people of the community in proper ceremonial fashion. Thereafter, Walter assured us, we would "be accepted" and would be able to call on people. This sounded reasonable, so we held our peace. But now and again we wondered why no one ever came to call on the GoodHorses while we were there. For Indians, our hosts seemed remarkably ungregarious.

If I was not happy about my relationship with Beula, Murray was not happy about his relationship with Walter. We had hired Walter because he was one of the few Thrashing Buffalo from a fullblood family who had done graduate work at a university. We paid him an excellent salary as research assistant.[2] We expected

2. We did not know at this time that many reservation Indians believe that any Indian who obtains a year or two of college automatically gets a job paying, six, eight, or ten thousand a year. We also were not aware that a considerable number of Indian college graduates, having been helped by generous scholarship, assume that they will step into soft and very well-paid administrative jobs. This is not an unrealistic expectation, for many do. Thus, the rather casual way in which Walter approached his duties was to be ex-

that he would help us behave decently and correctly to his family and to other Indians and that he would introduce us to respected or knowledgeable elders, for he was, after all, a member of the fullblood community. We also expected him to be acquainted with the fundamentals of social research and learn some of the basic techniques we hoped to employ. After we were reasonably settled, Murray explained several times to Walter and Vic how we hoped to observe classes, interview high school students, and talk to mothers, teachers, and administrators. He then suggested that Walter begin to get a feel for interviewing by talking to some of the young people in his own local band or *tiyospaye* about their educational experiences and attitudes and recording what he could remember of such conversations. So Walter drove off alone for two days, and we congratulated ourselves that we had made a good beginning. On the afternoon of the second day, Walter returned and approached, not Murray, but me, announcing in a happy and triumphant voice that he had interviewed Mr. Blank, one of the high-ranking school administrators. Now Murray had already completed a long and adequate interview with Mr. Blank and could, if he wished, interview him again. What Murray could *not* yet do was talk to the Indian adolescents, the task for which we had hired Walter. Still, I thought, if Walter wanted to cut his teeth on a big shot, that was all right with me. So I told Walter, "That's fine. Why don't you go and write it up?" But Walter did not seem to hear me and, very much like his father, he proceeded to make a long speech in which he tried to present his interpretation of what Mr. Blank had told him. Unfortunately, his oratorical English was almost impossible to un-derderstand (both his father and mother spoke English more coherently), and whenever I asked a question he was visibly upset. But when I listened in attentive silence, he radiated self-satisfaction and energetic goodwill—like some large, good-natured dog. I told Murray about this, and the next day he carefully repeated his original instructions, emphasizing that Walter was to interview Indians between the ages of fourteen and twenty-one and that he was to write the interviews down. After several more attempts to get us to accept interviews with Bureau personnel, Walter did talk

---

pected. Indeed, in these days of graduate scholarships and fat research assistantships, the student *from any background* who works as hard and conscientiously as we, of the older generation, think proper, is an exception.

to a few Indians. In every case, however, these were young people who did *not* belong to the Standing Man community—a highly significant fact, which we, in our experience, did not appreciate. He still, however, insisted on reporting like an orator. When this had happened four or five times, we offered to rent a typewriter for him, only to find that he had one. Finally, finding that Gloria was a bright girl and a fairly competent typist, we hired her to record Walter's interviews. We also began to instruct Walter in Gloria's presence, hoping that she could persuade him to follow at least some of our instructions.

We did not realize at this time that we had hired Walter to do what he was incapable of doing. Or—to state our error in more general terms—we had the misinformed outsider's picture of what the Thrashing Buffalo reservation was like: namely, that there was an integrated and cohesive mixedblood community and an integrated and cohesive fullblood community; and we had assumed that if we hired an educated "member" of this "fullblood community" to act as advisor, guide, and interviewer, we would be in a peculiarly advantageous research position. In reality there was no such fullblood community. Instead, there were local bands or congregations of people—the *tiyospayes*—who, of course, "hated and despised" the mixedbloods but also saw all the other fullbloods from other *tiyospayes* as rivals and competitors. Now Walter's folks, it is true, were a full-fledged and participating family in the *tiyospaye* of the Standing Man district, but, on the other hand, his father and mother (though we did not know this) were notorious not only for cheating and defrauding white people but for cheating and defrauding the more unfortunate and helpless of their fellow Indians. (For example, we were told that Tom might charge a poor old man who spoke no English five or ten dollars for driving him to the hospital or to the agency town.) They were not regarded as what we would call low-status, because they came from reasonably good families and, by reservation standards, they were very well off. But they were thought of as extraordinarily sharp and mean, for, as well-to-do people, they should have been generous. Walter himself was not regarded with the fear and suspicion with which experienced fullbloods looked upon his parents, for he was a reasonably decent and honorable young man and the Thrashing Buffalo tended to judge a man by his deeds rather than by those of his relatives. Still, Walter had been off the reservation attending school for six years, and this meant that he now had no peer group affiliations—no intimates or close male friends. Even worse, because of his long absence, he knew almost nothing about what had gone on in his and the neighboring *tiyospayes* in the past few years: who had died, who had run away from his wife, who had shacked up with whom, who had children of school age, who had been or was in jail, who had been to boarding school and returned. He did not even now know where many people lived. I think Walter was aware that he could not do what we expected of him long before we were, and he probably hoped that his parents would help us in matters where his knowledge failed. And they could, of course, have helped us a great deal, had they wished to do so and had they not been feared and disliked by many people.

Since we were kept so isolated from other "fullbloods," we did not realize that Walter's incoherent English was not the result of a poor education but was an individual defect. Later, we learned that many if not most of the country Indians have superb verbal memories and can give a remarkably accurate, detailed, and fluent account of conversations and events, either in the Indian or in the local Indian-English dialect. We also learned that many Indians considered Walter a poor and turgid speaker in both English and the Indian language, a fact which some of his relatives attributed (with folk etiology) to a head injury suffered at birth. Walter, like many Thrashing Buffalo youths, was inclined to stand back and let other people work. When, for example, his father had put up our shade for us, this involved a day's hard work, beginning with an expedition to the hills where pine trees were felled, then attached to Tom's car, and triumphantly dragged up to the door of our tent in a boiling cloud of dust. Tom, Vic, and an Indian visitor named Jimmy, worked very hard all day, cutting the trees, digging post holes, lopping off branches, and restanding the pine trunks to form a shaded rectangle. Murray tried to help but found that he lacked the know-how and shoulder strength. But stalwart Walter stood around watching, joking, and occasionally pointing to the spot where he thought another post hole might be dug.

It was not hard to find excuses for Walter's difficulty with his work assignments. Gloria was about to be delivered any day, and she had vowed that she would go back to her own tribe and family rather than stay on living in "the chicken coop" with a newborn baby. For months, Walter said, he had been trying to buy some property about three miles from the GoodHorses' place and build a cabin on it. But Tom and Beula wanted Walter to build a four-room house near the highway in which they and all their sons and grand-children would live. Every few days Tom would go almost into a trance, envisaging the family's future life in this great log castle, in which he would sell beer if the law that prohibits the sale of liquor on the reservation were repealed. "Why should those tavern guys in Neuman be taking all that money away from us Indians all the time?" he would intone in the booming voice of a Thrashing Buffalo orator. Sometimes even Murray and I were included in the dream, as tenants in this great Indian castle. Gloria did not like this vision of togetherness at all. Between the badgering of his parents and Gloria's ultimatums, Walter often looked so woebegone that we did not have the heart to ask him why he was doing so little work. (At this time we assumed that Walter was contributing much of the salary we paid him toward the support of his mother and father. This was not an unreasonable assumption, for sharing one's goods with one's rela-tives is the prime moral imperative of the Thrashing Buffalo. But it is possible that Walter was giving his parents little or no money and nonetheless expected them to work for us. If this is so, it explains at least some of the tensions and confusions of our visit.)

As a college-educated Indian, Walter had other problems. Once he told me that the more he went to school off the reservation, the harder it was to come back.

> You got to thinking that the way the teachers and white people felt, they thought the way the Indians live here is pretty poor. But the Indians don't think they're poor or they don't care about it. What they care about mainly is being happy and living together in a nice way. So long as everybody gets along with everybody else and is happy together; that's what they care about. But after I had gone to college for a while—you know, I was away from home for six years— I felt funny about coming back here. It seemed pretty poor and I worried about what the white people would think of me coming back here. It wasn't easy.

Like many Indian men, Walter could radiate enthusiasm and youthful good nature, and, unlike other Indians, he had learned to exert this bewitching power on white people. I had read and heard about emotional contagion and hypnotism but I had never before been so thoroughly exposed to it. Murray and I could be sitting in the doldrums, fretting about all manner of aggravating problems (including Walter's meager work output); Walter would wander over, set his bearlike form on a stump, and tell us a few stories. When he left, we would all be happy, relaxed, and certain that the morrow held splendid things for us. Perhaps we should have hired Walter as a medicine man rather than as an interviewer.

It did not escape our notice that we would have been better off in a number of respects if we had hired Beula instead of her son. She knew all about the community and the attitudes of the people, and, whenever she chose to speak on such matters, her remarks were cogent and illuminating. Though she had finished only the eighth grade, she spoke English very fluently. Moreover, she possessed a formidable intelligence and might likely have learned almost any technique. Walter seemed to have no qualms about referring us to his mother for instruction in the Indian language and for general information, but the situation was awkward because we did not want to pay Walter while his mother performed most of his work.

Our other field assistant, Victor Hibou, was, like us, a newcomer to the reservation, and at first we did not expect much from him. We told him to keep a field diary, attend the high school orientation meetings and take notes, observe the high school classes, and try to interview some of the adolescents. Vic worked extremely hard, giving us rude but informative field notes and even, courageously, attempting and carrying out some interviews. He listened to our suggestions, improvised improvements of his own, and within a few months his observations and interviews were remarkably good. After five or six months they were often superb. Vic was, moreover, a most self-sufficient and self-reliant individual. He might ask for instructions but he rarely asked for help. If he disappeared for a week, we knew he was likely to return with a remarkable and highly useful sheaf of notes. Considering our difficulties with Walter, it is ironic that Murray and I had to give Vic only basic instructions and then turn him loose. With only a little guidance he rapidly, and almost entirely in his own way, became a first-rate fieldworker.

On the other hand, Beula's behavior toward Vic struck us as odd. She showered him with attentions, cooking for him and teaching him Indian words and etiquette. But she often complained to us: "He's confused; he's trying to be an Indian, but he don't know how to be; I'm trying to help him, but he won't let me; he won't act right; I want to help him, I want to do his housekeeping, but he won't let me."

As the weeks passed, I began to feel increasingly ambivalent about the GoodHorse menage, whereas Murray continued to enjoy their company a great deal. He, of course, was spending most of his time driving about the reservation making arrangements and getting supplies, and he found the meals and chats under the shade relaxing and instructive. At least, as he told me, he could talk to *some* Indians. I did not want to deprive him of this bit of fun and, in consequence, I swallowed my misgivings and became more jumpy every day. Perhaps the most disorienting and frightening aspect of my "fits" was that I myself could find no good and sufficient reason for them. I was not being mistreated. Nor was I suffering any intolerable physical discomfort. I was merely living with a group of people who got on my nerves in ways which I could not understand —and, when I could bring myself to complain about something specific, my small-mindedness made me ashamed of myself.

Even when I went fishing in the creek, my fun was dulled by the realization that I would have to go back, that Beula would not cook my fish because fish hurt her medicine, and that I would have to make a fuss if I wanted to cook them privately for Murray. I can remember watching Murray talking to Tom and Beula and feeling ashamed and exasperated because he so clearly believed what they were saying. And yet I had not consciously decided that they were humbugs. The only point on which I was absolutely lucid was that they made me uneasy. Perhaps some inner alarm bell was activated by the eerie immutability of the people and the situation. Ordinarily, as one lives with human beings, one's image of these persons changes and enriches itself with almost every encounter. This is especially so in the early stages of a friendship or acquaintanceship. But the GoodHorses, from Tom and Beula down to the little boys, seemed to have manifested themselves fullblown and remain just as they were when we first met them. That they impressed me like this is not surprising, since they were all play-acting—as a family, they were conspiring to befuddle the naïve white man. Even the youngsters (we later found from Vic's field notes) were ordered by Beula never to say anything in our presence. Another distressing aspect of this highly artificial situation was the fact that neither Murray, Vic, nor I seemed to make any progress whatever in the social graces. So far as we could gather from the GoodHorses, our weeks of intensive participation and observation had left us as ignorant of Indian ways as we had been the first day. Our "stupidity" and "inability to catch

213

on" made us feel insecure and even more dependent on Walter. It did not occur to us that most of the cues to proper behavior were being deliberately withheld.

In late August, just prior to the beginning of the school year, the Bureau school administrators held a week long series of orientation meetings for the teachers, bus drivers, janitors, and matrons. So famished for work were Murray and I that we fell upon these meetings like academic wolves, greedily sitting through whole days of speeches and meetings and filling entire notebooks with verbatim transcriptions. Now, thank God, we were at last collecting "raw data"! Some of these speeches were incredibly dull, and I suspect that no one ever has listened or ever again will listen to them with the attention we gave them. One speech was so uniquely and awe-inspiringly dull that to this day I cannot forget it. It consisted of a description of every type of building and heating unit on the reservation, square foot by square foot and unit by unit—a description pursued with relentless detail and consistency—the point being that the expense of maintaining all this space and equipment was enormous and that the speaker, the head of the Bureau's Department of Building Maintenance, was never given sufficient funds. As the speaker droned on and on, I noted that some of the Indian bus drivers, cooks, and matrons, sitting in the back of the auditorium, had dozed off. I envied them this ability, for I have never been able to sleep sitting up. So I alternately writhed in my seat and took more verbatim notes:

> The government pays $41,000 for electricity here. Forty-one thousand dollars! Now how can we save on this? How can we save and use the money for a better purpose? There are 232 class A buildings (schools and dwellings). They all have light in them. Now if we'd just turn the light out if we're not using it, I wonder how much could be saved?

After forty-five minutes, the speaker looked at the clock. "God be praised!" I thought, "it's almost over." But, on seeing the clock, his face took on the relaxed expression of the lecturer who still has plenty of time. He then told us precisely what happened to each of the triplicate forms filled out whenever anyone made a requisition. This took ten minutes per form. I decided that if I had to do much more work like this I would demand a raise in pay.

214

Trying to get to the teacher-orientation meetings on time taught us an invaluable lesson about reservation life. For though we rose at six, and washed, brushed, and groomed ourselves like mad, we could never get ourselves to look "presentable." The prairie dust covered all of our clothing and toilet articles every day, and we had no closets or heavy trunks, no way to iron creases out of a garment, no really clean water, and, for Murray, no hot water for shaving and no decent mirror. The strain of trying to keep up a respectable, middle-class appearance exhausted us. After a few days we surrendered and moved all of our "city clothing" and toilet articles to Witkokia—the schoolhouse which we planned to turn into an office. Here we had an old gas range, cold running water, and a relatively dustproof closet. Thus, we would rise very early, eat one of Beula's breakfasts, drive to Witkokia, wash and change our clothing, and then drive to the agency town where the high school was located. After our day of note taking and interviewing, we would return to Witkokia, change our clothes and then drive to the Good-Horses'.

We now had a heartfelt understanding of why most people who live "out on the reservation" always look a bit grubby. Or, to put it another way, one *must* have hot running water, electricity, an iron and an ironing board, dustproof closets, and some kind of bathing facility (other than a creek) if one is to present the slickly clean appearance that the schoolteachers thought Indian children should have. We also began to understand why many of the teachers—who had never themselves tried to live without such conveniences—thought that Indian mothers were careless and dirty, and we began to appreciate the desperation of some Indian mothers whose children demand that their mothers dress them in a manner that will win the approval of the teachers.

> My girls [fourth and fifth grade], they have to change anklets every day because when they go [to school] if they don't change anklets they [the other children] say: "Gee, you're lazy, look at your anklets. Where did you get your gray anklets? . . . If I wash their anklets they say they want them clean, like new, really white. They say: "Can't you ever wash the anklets white?" And oh, I get mad at them. And they say: "Can't you iron better? Our dresses are wrinkled and we can't wear them."

It was at this time that Murray began to suffer from dysentery. I say began to, because at first he did not seem very ill. Since Vic

215

and Gloria had recovered rapidly from similar attacks the week before, we did not worry, though old-timers had told us that the summer sickness on the reservation was no laughing matter. Murray stoically drank large quantities of clay and pectate medicines and kept going in several ways, both by day and by night. Since the outhouse was at some distance from our tent, this was tiring. When our large bottle of medicine was gone and Murray was no better, I began to urge him to go to a doctor. I knew how debilitating dysentery could be and how long it could drag on, and he did not. But school was now beginning, and Murray would not hear of wasting one of the precious "first days of school" trying to locate a doctor. He did try to buy some paregoric at the drugstore in the agency town, but the druggist refused to sell it without a prescription. The druggist offered him concentrated Coca-Cola, the favorite local remedy, but this evil-tasting concoction did his bowels no good (and may have done his teeth some harm). Several days passed, during which we all worked extremely hard, doing as much classroom observation as we possibly could. I became annoyed with Murray because I knew he was being foolish and he would not listen to me. He became annoyed with me, because he knew I was annoyed even when I said nothing. The nights were becoming very cold, and he took to putting on his Norwegian underwear, several sweaters, and his parka before going to bed, so that he would not become so chilled going to the outhouse. One particularly nasty and bitterly cold night, a dust storm blew up. We turned out our dusty lantern and crawled into our ever-gritty bed. In the middle of the night Murray made an excursion to the outhouse and returned shaking like a person having a fit. Though he did not know it, he had developed a high fever. He refused to get back into bed, saying: "I think I'll be warmer in the car." This did not make much sense to me, and when he stumbled out and shut himself in the car, I sat up and put on my shoes, intending to go after him. But when I lifted the tent flap to go out, I was so paralyzed by a spasm of helpless and exasperated rage that everything about me disappeared, the car, the shade, the distant outhouse. There was nothing there but horrible prairie, dusty and webby, dead and endless, like the inside of a long unused garbage pail. I heard myself saying, "If he wants to be a damn fool and kill himself, let him." But I also knew that, if I was seeing and saying murderous things, I was having a fit. Hours later, Murray, still muttering things I could not understand, came back in the tent and crawled into bed. I covered him up and he went to sleep. I went to sleep too, but not until I had resolved to my-self that we were not going to live at the GoodHorses' any more.

The next morning Murray was rational but very weak. As soon as there was enough light, I crawled out of bed and searched through our storage tent until I found our thermometer. His temperature was 103°. We talked about trying to get him to a doctor, but de-cided that, if his temperature continued to go down, he probably needed rest and quiet more than an antibiotic. I made him some extremely strong black tea (to drink in place of water), and I also located my bottle of sleeping pills. I gave him a pill and he slept all morning. By noon his temperature was 101°, and I could see that the worst was over. Walter and Gloria came round in the afternoon and were very much concerned. They remarked that this was indeed a bad case. I did not say much because I had resolved that, as soon as Murray could walk, we were going to move into the old school-house.

Beula must have read my mind because Walter came over the next day before breakfast and told us that his mother had seen spirits flying over our tent in the night. The spirits made whistling noises like little birds, and these whistles were very hard to under-stand. The one word that his mother had heard was Witkokia . . . Witkokia. Shortly thereafter, Beula herself walked over and gave me a more elaborate report of the spiritual visitation. Numerous spirits, glowing like fireflies, had lighted on our tent, trying to help us. We, of course, had not been able to see or hear them. But Beula had listened very hard and had heard the words, "Witkokia . . . Witkokia." Then the spirits had said, "It's the water . . . it's the water." We all stood about for some time, wondering what the spirits could have meant. Then, I said, "Maybe the spirits are trying to tell us that the water at Witkokia is polluted." Beula and Walter agreed, and Beula told me that many people had become sick from drinking the water at Witkokia. My state of mind may be inferred from the fact that I took this suggestion quite seriously. Perhaps Witkokia's water was bad, and we could have it analyzed and find out. But *move out we would,* because I realized that staying at the GoodHorses' would, in the end, drive me crazy.

Though I had said not a word about moving or staying, Beula called again that afternoon when Murray was awake but still groggy. She told us that the people who lived near the Witkokia schoolhouse were jailbirds, bootleggers, drunks, and cattle rustlers, whereas the people who lived around the GoodHorse homestead were, as we could see, quiet and well behaved. I refrained from reminding her that only the week before she had told me that the neighbors to the west of her home "stole things" and that the women who lived in the house to the south "kept having babies without a husband all the time."

It is my suspicion that I lived through the days and weeks that followed in a state of semiparanoia. It was not so much that I disliked or hated any of the GoodHorses; it was that I simply could not trust or credit anything they said. I often felt that I must be flipping my lid because Murray did not share my views. He knew, of course, that the GoodHorses were odd and unreliable and that they were putting on a front, but this did not bother him. I, on the other hand, knew that something was very wrong, but I could not be sure what. Had I been brought up in a society with a magical world view, I would have fallen into a trance and announced the presence of an evil and dangerous influence. And the sooner we removed ourselves from this evil influence, the better.

Just as Murray had recovered sufficiently to walk about a bit, Walter and Gloria informed us that the great moment was at hand: we were to be formally adopted into their family at the local Standing Man Fair on the coming weekend. Tom would make a speech to the assembled people, explaining our research project and our plans "to help the education of the Indian people." We would be given Indian names, we would dance, and we would give a gift to the singers. Beula gave me a green squaw dress (a long dress with flounces trimmed with rickrack) and teased Murray about making him a chief's war bonnet. I gave Beula a beautiful Seminole apron, with which she was very pleased. Walter hinted that, after this ceremony, we and our work would be understood and would be generally accepted by the community.

Two weeks earlier we would have been delighted by the whole affair. Now I, at least, had reached a stage where I could not care less. But to make an issue of moving away at this point seemed silly, and so I braced myself to stay at the GoodHorses' until the adoption ceremony was over. Nevertheless, most of my memories of the Standing Man Fair and the ceremony are pleasant. The dancing was fine and the rodeo interesting. When the time for our "adoption" came, Tom made a very long and relatively coherent speech, praising education and our "survey" in grandiloquent terms. The many Indians present listened with solemn attention (though much later we heard that some people had kept teasing Tom throughout his speech, about the supposed "affair" between Beula and Victor). Murray was given the name of GoodHorse and I was given the name of one of Tom's female relatives. I did not mind dancing because the women's step is easy and I had been practicing. Murray flung himself courageously into something that looked a little like a Chassidic jig. Beula laughed, but I thought Murray showed spirit, since most white men who are obliged to dance at Indian ceremonies behave as if they were stepping on their own feet. If the other Indians thought Murray looked funny, they showed great self-control. Nobody even grinned.

After our ordeal Beula gave me a package which she said was a present to me from her sister-in-law, Mrs. ChargingBear. The package contained a star-pattern quilt cover, a pretty scarf, and a patchwork pillow. I did not know what to make of this, and when I asked Beula what I should do, she shrugged her shoulders and walked away. So I walked through the encampment until I found the ChargingBear's tent, and I asked if I could come in. My new "relative" was a dumpy little lady with fine-hewn features, a strong thin nose, and an enormous dignity. I did not know it at the time, but she came from one of the great families of the reservation, and she was one of the most influential women in our local community. We both sat down on camp chairs, and she asked her son to light a kerosene stove, lest I should find the tent cold. Neither of us said much because I did not know what to say and Mrs. ChargingBear kept turning her face away to show how much she respected me. Finally, I thanked her for the presents and said I would try to be a good relative.

I can remember almost nothing about packing and moving into Witkokia. This is not surprising, because I did almost no packing. We left our things at the GoodHorses' and came back for them in installments. I went back alone to get WeaselBear, who by this time was pregnant. The poor dog had never been in a car and she nearly collapsed with fear when I pushed her in. Then, when I tried to get in myself, she rushed between my legs and made off. It took active assistance from Victor before I could catch her again and put her in the car. (Vic was planning to stay at the GoodHorses' during the winter. He said that he and Walter were good friends and that

219

Walter and Gloria would soon be building a house into which they and the baby could move. This, of course, would leave the chicken coop for Victor. The baby had arrived in about two hours, just before the adoption celebration.) When WeaselBear and I arrived at Witkokia, Murray was annoyed. He had not wanted me to take the dog along. But on this matter I was adamant. I was not going to leave my dog where Beula could get her hands on it.

18   Life at Witkokia

I began to like the old schoolhouse. It had been built around 1910 and had two major rooms; one was enormous—25 × 50 feet—with its northern side composed almost entirely of high windows. When the blizzard winds blew through these windows, it was awful, even though we improvised storm windows out of clear plastic. But when the wind did not blow, the view was a joy to the soul—a great meadow (on which one might see pheasants in the early morning) rising gradually for three or four miles to some splendid hills. The other room was a large kitchen with a big, old-fashioned sink, a gas range, and all sorts of cupboards. At first we slept on the floor in a corner of the vast classroom. But when Tom and Beula came to call and saw our bed rolls there, they were once again shocked at our unhealthy habits and insisted on relending us their hideous old bed. So we resignedly set up the bed in the kitchen, bought a bed-sized piece of plywood from the local coffin makers (a tribal enterprise), and put our bed rolls on the board. In time, we added a kitchen table with a red and white oilcloth cover and some chairs. The west side of the big schoolroom we furnished with work tables, desks, and file cases; the east side already had a big oilstove, and we added two fat, second-hand easy chairs with lamps and a second-hand refrigerator, purchased in a town about sixty miles southwest of the reservation.

Since the building had been a schoolhouse, it had two outdoor privies. Neither, however, had a complete door. But since the doorways of the privies faced only on hills and prairie, we did not mind, though in the winter we had the illusion that we would have frozen less had the privies had doors. The inside walls of these structures were decorated with grotesque pencil drawings, which suggested that the neighborhood children, who also used the privies, knew a good deal about sex. Most of the female figures were drawn with bodies like packing boxes. They looked odd to us because, as children, we had always drawn dumb-bell-shaped ladies. At first we left our rolls of toilet paper in the privies. But since they always promptly disappeared, we took to following the usual Indian custom, keeping toilet paper in the house and "taking the roll along."

Our leaving the GoodHorse household was not accompanied by any display of ill feelings on either side, and, indeed, we (and they, I think) assumed that our relationship would continue much as before. So far as our "rapport" with the community was concerned, we felt entirely dependent on them, for we had been kept so isolated that we did not know any other Indian family. Murray still was on the best of terms with them and seemed to think that Beula would shortly settle down and introduce me to the Indian women. On this point I had strong doubts, but I did not know what to do about it. I would have liked to hire some other Indians besides the GoodHorses, but Murray and I were afraid that other Indians would regard this as another example of the white man's treachery and that if we tried to break with the GoodHorses we would have no Indian contact at all. Besides, Murray had promised to employ Walter for the duration of the project, and this obligation tied up the major part of funds which we had allocated for Indian assistants.

I should point out that in this account I have probably exaggerated the conscious dislike I felt for Beula and her family. In actuality, I was more ambivalent than wise or foreknowing, swinging between fits of stifled rage, for which I would feel guilty and reproach myself, and fits of forced friendliness, in which I would remind myself of all the kind and considerate things the GoodHorses had done for us and, especially, of some of the warm and comic moments in our conversations.

Perhaps it would be well to remark here that, before a fieldworker goes into the field, he tends unconsciously to condition himself against getting angry at his hosts. After all, he does not want to be "ethnocentric" or to feel that his ways are better than theirs. But even if he and they are relatively amiable folk, he tends to get exasperated and angry with them. If he is alone, as I was at Gila, he tends to take out his anger and frustration on himself or on his superior. At Thrashing Buffalo I took it out on Murray and on Beula. This sort of thing is an inescapable part of fieldwork, and husbands and wives who go into the field together should expect to encounter marital strains far exceeding the ordinary. Later, when the fieldworker becomes somewhat involved, finds himself playing helpful roles, and begins to understand something of what is going on around him, the strains begin to ease. Now when he gets angry it will usually be for some "good reason," that is, a reason that makes sense to him and to his hosts.

It is interesting and significant that at this period in our research Murray felt quite differently about the situation than did I. Here is an excerpt from his field notes:

> Life at the GoodHorses' seemed peaceful enough. Except for my illnesses (a bad cough and intestinal flu) I enjoyed living there. Mrs. GoodHorse did the cooking for everyone, and the communal meals, out of doors, under the shade, were pleasant. But after a few weeks of this Rosalie began to get terribly upset—great outbursts of emotion. Mrs. GoodHorse was pleasant, instructing us in the language and customs. The education study seemed to be moving.
>
> In early September I rented the schoolhouse, thinking we might move into it when real cold weather came, but Rosalie propelled us into inhabiting it by mid-September, so distressed was she at life at the GoodHorses'. During the moving, Mrs. GoodHorse got the opportunity to get hold of me by myself and really propositioned me. I evaded her, though somewhat tempted. Later, she made several other plays for me, all equally unsuccessful.

Beula and Walter strove hard to keep us in a state of apprehension about our new Indian neighbors, the people who lived around Witkokia. Beula told us that the people who lived up the road were bootleggers. One of their drunken customers, she said, had recently beaten and raped the eighty-five-year-old woman who lived down the road from us. Walter warned us not to go walking at night because we might be robbed or beaten. Since we knew only the Good-Horses, and all of our neighbors kept out of sight, we did not know what to believe. When I went walking alone at night, I *was* nervous, but I walked anyway. When I went walking in daylight, with the now matronly-looking WeaselBear, I saw nothing but dogs, which barked at us, and a few cabins located quite far from the road. Sometimes, in the hills, we saw three or four wild-looking horses or some cattle. People must have taken great care to stay out of our sight, because (though we did not know it) there were at least ten or twelve families within the radius of a mile from us.

One night after we had gone to bed there was a tremendous knocking at our door. The knocker did not pause for a response but kept beating away as if to wake the dead. "This must be the drunks," we thought. Murray got out of bed, went to the door and hollered out, "Who is it?" Someone outside hollered back, "This is the police. Open up! We want Mr. BadBreathBear!" Murray opened

223

the door and a tall Indian policeman walked in, shouting loudly and, it seemed, aggressively, "Where is Mr. BadBreathBear?" We explained that we did not know Mr. BadBreathBear; indeed, we had never heard of him. Somewhat mollified, the policeman explained that Mr. BadBreathBear had telephoned him, complaining that a lot of drunks were bothering him. The policeman knew that Mr. BadBreathBear lived somewhere near Witkokia, but not exactly where. Then he went away. Many weeks later we learned that Mr. BadBreathBear, a tall and rather impressive-looking Indian elder, did live up the road a couple of miles. His two daughters lived near him, and their husbands got drunk and disorderly rather frequently. When he could reach a telephone, Mr. BadBreathBear then called the police, who would pick up his sons-in-law and lock them up for the night. We also learned that the loud talk and aggressive manner of the policeman was the usual way Indian men behaved when they were doing something bold or venturesome. Months later, when a friendly Indian neighbor came to help us start our frozen car, he talked and carried himself in the same way. So, also, did the Indian employees of the Bureau who suddenly appeared one day, announced loudly that they had come to take away our gas stove, laid hold of it, and prepared to wrench it out of the wall. My loud squawks made them hesitate long enough for Murray to explain to them that the gas had to be turned off at the main tank and the fittings unscrewed from the pipe in the wall. (The stove did belong to the BIA; so we could not complain. But we would have appreciated a little warning.)

The next indication that we had neighbors occurred when our car suddenly stalled on the highway, many miles, so to speak, from nowhere. The gas gauge stood at zero, but since Murray had had the tank filled the day before and we had driven only thirty miles, he had assumed that the gauge was broken. Fortunately we had some white gas in the car and we poured some of this into the gas tank. But the car still would not start. Then an Indian neighbor drove up, stopped, and suggested that we pour a cup of the gas into the carburetor. This did the trick, and we were able to proceed. The next day we bought a lock for our gas tank. This device seemed to impress the people who were "borrowing" our gas, because nobody ever stole anything important from us again.

The GoodHorses dropped in on us at Witkokia frequently, especially at dinnertime or just before we were about to go to bed or, worst of all, just as we were about to have a surreptitious (the reservation being dry) martini. On one occasion, Beula, Tom, and the little boys arrived at suppertime, carrying a great heap of quilts. Beula announced that they were going to stay the night with us because her son Lewis was drunk. This was Victor Hibou's fault, she said, because Vic had brought a great deal of beer to the Good-Horses, everyone was drunk, and Lewis had threatened to beat up his mother. I made a huge supper while Beula regaled Murray with tales of how she often walked in her sleep. Today, Murray enjoys telling people how, on that night, I made him sleep next to the wall and locked the door between the schoolroom, where all the Good-Horses slept, and the kitchen, where we slept. The next morning the GoodHorses left, and Gloria, Walter's wife, who was now doing some typing for us, showed up with her baby. We asked her about the drinking bout. She told us that it was Lewis who had brought the beer and that Beula had scolded him. Then Lewis had said, rather pointedly, "I don't criticize what you do, so don't criticize what I do." Thereupon Beula had gathered up Tom and the children and left.

Judging by his field diary, Murray did not feel that moving into Witkokia was much of an improvement. But I felt like a new person. The change in my field notes is striking. The notes written at the GoodHorses', while they contain many useful observations, are uneven and confused. Read as a whole they do not make much sense, and they contain a good deal of misinformation. They are the notes of an amateur who observes and records without conscious or unconscious discrimination. The notes written after we moved to Witkokia begin to make sense, by which I mean that if an outsider reads them he can begin to perceive what was happening to us, what the GoodHorses were up to, and even how other Indians were beginning to try to involve themselves in the situation, even though we ourselves were not able to perceive these phenomena at this time. What this suggests, I think, is that by this time we had learned a good deal about the basic meanings of our new situation *without being aware that we had learned.* And again, without being aware of it, we were able to express some of this understanding in our field notes and field diaries.

Again, one might say that the notes I took at the GoodHorses' read like the images of a kaleidoscope: each picture bears little or no relation to all the others. But the notes of what occurred at

Witkokia are the diachronic observations of a rapidly developing social situation in which we as would-be "participant observers" were unwittingly involved.

The first theme in the social situation consists of the GoodHorses' ominous warnings about the evil or lawless character of all of our neighbors. The first act in the development was the senior Good-Horses' suggestion that we drive them to the Trap Fair, which was to take place sometime at the end of September.[1] Trap was about sixty miles from Witkokia, and we would have to drive much of the way on dirt roads. Still, this would be our first entrance into Indian society after our formal adoption and introduction at the Standing Man Fair, and we had high hopes that *this time,* finally, we would be able to approach people and talk to them.

A few days before we were to leave for Trap, Murray went to the post office in the agency town and ran into Harold EatsThunder. Mr. EatsThunder was a lineal descendant of a great chief, and the head man of one of the more important communities on the reservation. He was generally respected and had worked as informant to a number of anthropologists and ethnohistorians. Murray had been introduced to him at the Sun Dance. While chatting with Mr. Eats-Thunder, Murray mentioned that he was going to the Trap Fair, and Mr. EatsThunder asked if Murray would drive him there also. Murray was pleased, because he wanted very much to develop a friendly relationship with some of the older Indian men.

That evening after supper Tom dropped in alone at Witkokia. He told Murray that a payment on his car had come due and that he had to raise a hundred dollars or the car would be taken from him. Would Murray lend him the money? Murray said he would think about it, and while they discussed the matter Murray asked if it would be all right if he took Mr. EatsThunder along with him when we all went to Trap. "OK," said Tom. After Tom left, Murray told me that he would probably give Tom the money since it was not an unreasonable sum to pay for his trouble and for letting us live on his land. Besides, a canceled check would be a kind of insurance. Tom could not claim that we had imposed on him.

---

1. Each *tiyospaye* or district tried to have an annual dance ceremony and celebration in the autumn which all of the members of the *tiyospaye* were expected to attend. This event lasted three or four days. Those we attended involved both ceremonial dancing in which, for example, the relatives of young men killed in the war might dance in their honor, and Pow-wow dancing, which was done for everyone's pleasure.

The following day Murray again drove to the agency town, primarily to tell Mr. EatsThunder that we would take him along. Then he stopped at the post office, where he met Beula, all dressed up and lavishly perfumed. She announced meaningfully, "Today is my day off." Murray, so he says, did not take the hint. Thereupon, Beula declared, "If that Harold EatsThunder is riding with you to Trap on Sunday, I'm not going!"

"But Tom told me last night that it was all right to take Harold along," replied Murray.

"It may be all right with Tom but it's not all right with me," said Beula.

Perplexed at this turn of events, Murray asked, "What's the matter with Mr. EatsThunder?" But Beula now became coy and would only say, "Harold is a nosy guy."

Murray was distressed. He had begun to hope that he might develop a friendly relationship with the knowledgeable Mr. Eats-Thunder and, perhaps, learn the language from him. He went back once again to Harold and talked the situation over. They agreed that Murray would pick Harold up at eight on Sunday morning. If Harold was not waiting at the town's major intersection at that time, it would mean that he had found some other means of transportation. (By this time Murray had decided to ask Victor Hibou to drive Beula and the young boys to Trap if she continued to make a fuss.)

That evening Walter dropped in at Witkokia for instructions, and Murray related the complicated series of events, asking for an explanation. But all Walter would say was "That's the way women are, always making trouble for us men." He then changed the subject and told us that we must put off our plans to talk to the people in the community for several weeks more, because his mother had just had a serious quarrel with her relatives. Murray found this pronouncement very irritating indeed. In addition, Walter told us that his father and mother had decided that if we wished to be really accepted by the people, we ought to participate in a medicine ceremony. Murray and I, of course, knew virtually nothing about the traditional ceremonies of the Thrashing Buffalo, and we were not especially interested, since they did not seem to be at all related to our study of the schools. Walter, however, seemed convinced that if "the people" knew we had been participants in a "heathen" ceremony, the kind of ceremony denounced by the Christian ministers, the fullbloods would accept us as different from other white people. I, as an anthropologist, ought to have been enthusiastic about the prospect of witnessing such a ceremony, but by this time I could not get excited about anything suggested by the GoodHorses. Murray, for his part, wished to go through with the medicine ceremony because he felt it would give us the opportunity to meet some of our Indian neighbors.

There is, I think, something admirable in Murray's determination to play fair with everybody. The next day being the day for the Trap outing, we rose at dawn and arrived at the GoodHorses' at 7:15 in the morning. Nobody was up. This was strange because Tom and Beula usually got up about six o'clock. While Beula and the children dressed and had breakfast, Tom treated Murray to a lecture about the false pretenses of the great Thrashing Buffalo chief, Mr. EatsThunder's great-grandfather. EatsThunder, Tom insisted, had had no right to be a chief at all. "I uncovered all these facts when I was working on the tribal enrollment committee, and I announced it to all the people because the people need to know these things to decide about enrollment."

But Murray was beginning to lose patience: "Do you have any criticism of Harold himself?" he asked bluntly.

"No," said Tom.

At long last, all of us—that is Murray, Mr. and Mrs. GoodHorse, the little boys, and I—were packed in the car. But by the time we reached the intersection where we were supposed to pick up Mr. EatsThunder, it was nine o'clock and nobody was there.

On the long drive to Trap, Tom and Beula held the promise of the medicine ceremony before us, much as parents might dangle candy before sullen children. This would have been shrewd if we had been ordinary anthropologists or thrill-hungry white men, because this was to be a genuine traditional ceremony with medicine man (shaman), spirits, a darkened room, and a ceremonial meal (the most important part of which is supposed to consist of a ritually strangled dog). The medicine man, we were informed, had told Tom that they had been putting off having a ceremony for too long a time. The last time Walter had put tobacco offerings on the hill, the spirits had flown at him in bird shape, and he had run back to the car. Beula had told Walter that he should stand his ground, but he was afraid. "They have little tiny voices—like little baby birds," piped Tom. Tom also explained that if you attend the ceremony as a doubter, the spirits may poke you or throw things at you. That is why objects that can be thrown must be taken from the walls and put away. "Walter could be a medicine man if he would fast four days," said his mother, "but he loves to eat." The medicine man had also told her that she could get Power if she fasted, "but I don't have the willpower." Here Tom interrupted happily, explaining that if you were on good terms with the spirits they would work for you something like a pet. But Beula's voice took on a hard ring as she rephrased her husband's words, "If you fast, you can *make* the spirits do what you want them to do."

I could not see why we had to bother the spirits about such a small matter as going around and talking to Indian mothers about how their children were doing in school. Besides, I don't like to call on the spirits unless I'm in bad trouble, and as yet we weren't in trouble with anyone except the GoodHorses.

I had made up my mind that I had had it that night when Murray became so ill; I think Murray made up his mind that he had had it because of what happened at the Trap Fair. We arrived at Trap late in the morning, and the GoodHorses immediately disappeared. For several hot and dusty hours we sat or leaned against the car. Nobody talked to us and nothing happened. Finally there was a parade of cars, in which the major attraction was a young man in chieftain's bonnet and buckskin dress, seated on top of a car and accompanied by young women, also in buckskin dress. Later, there were speeches in the Indian language, and the young man's parents gave away some truly fine beaded robes and other ornaments in the young man's honor. We asked some Indians standing near what this was all about, and learned that the young man was going away to a trade school. "What if he should flunk and have to come back?" asked Murray. "That doesn't matter," said the unknown Indian; "They honor him because he is going to try."

About one o'clock, Tom, who had been warming up with the singers, suddenly ran up to us and shouted that we should get in line for food. We went toward the chow line accompanied by Beula and the boys. Immediately many older men smilingly insinuated themselves in front of us and in front of the GoodHorses. This was, I think, the only time I saw Tom publicly outwitted. The men would stroll up, greet him in a jovial, long-time-no-see manner, and deftly squeeze in front of him. Finally, Tom grabbed the belt of the man ahead of him, but then people squeezed in front of this man. By the time we reached the food kettles there was nothing left. Beula was furious and said bitterly, "These people are real fullbloods. They step all over you." But later she told us that we had been treated in this fashion because the Indians at Trap did not like white people. By this time we were so dazed and hungry we did not care who liked us. Murray and I walked toward a settlement a mile or so from the dance ground where, from a large school building came a tempting aroma of food. But a white lady told us this luncheon was only for members of the American Legion who had come to participate in the fair. Eventually, we found a tiny store where we were able to get coffee and potato chips; neither of us cares for potato chips. Murray was becoming extremely angry. I can go without eating all day without becoming particularly upset, but Murray turns into a fiend if he misses a meal. "We've been here practically all day and we haven't talked to a single person," he kept saying. I shrugged. We watched the dull and seemingly interminable ceremonies carried on by members of the American Legion, and Murray kept biting his lips and scowling. Late in the afternoon, some very fine quilt tops were auctioned off to pay for the singers. Murray surprised me by bidding aggressively for them. Every time he bought a quilt he gave it to me, and some of the Indian ladies present began to look at him admiringly. (Later we were told that Murray's buying the quilts was considered a handsome and courteous gesture. Expert quilt makers had donated the quilts to pay the singers, and by buying them Murray was contributing to the ceremony. Perhaps he was even heaping coals of fire on the heads of the people who had been rude to us.) When the auction ended, Murray went off to find a privy and was gone so long that it began to grow dark. I went back to the car and found that Beula had disappeared too. One of the Indian ladies standing nearby giggled and said to me, "Are you looking for your husband?" I was so tickled that I laughed aloud, for if Beula could make time with Murray while he was hungry, she was way out of this world. The other Indian ladies looked at me curiously. Perhaps they thought I was showing remarkable fortitude or perhaps they thought I was crazy.

Eventually, everybody straggled back to the car, and we started for home. Ravenous Murray drove so fast that he almost ran down a cow, whose rump, suddenly appearing in the headlights, seemed to come at us like a pitched ball. We got back to Witkokia about two in the morning, and I immediately made Murray a big meal. But he was still mad at Tom and Beula.

The next day Murray tried to find Mr. EatsThunder and apologize, but EatsThunder was not to be found. Now, however, Murray was absolutely determined to establish a relationship with some respected Indian outside the GoodHorse clan. So he made an expedition into the reservation, trying to locate Judge NoBear, whom we had met at the Indian workshops held in Boulder, Colorado. But although he did find his house, the judge was not at home. On the way back, on impulse, Murray decided to stop at the homestead of Bill ChargingBear, whom he had met at the Sun Dance. Bill was Beula's half-brother and, of course, Walter's uncle, and we might have asked his advice sooner, had we not feared that this implicit criticism of Walter might be considered indelicate. Bill was also the husband of the lady who had given me the quilt and scarf at the "adoption" ceremony. But Bill was not at home either, though a young Indian woman told Murray that he would be there the next day.

Murray drove back at the appropriate hour the next day, and this time Mr. ChargingBear himself came to the door. "Can you come in?" he asked. This, incidentally, was the first time either of us had been invited into an Indian home, except for the occasions when we had eaten breakfast in the GoodHorses' kitchen. By Thrashing Buffalo standards, the house was a large and fine dwelling. The living room resembled the main room of a fairly large but unpretentious hunting cabin, with an old sofa, a wooden table, two beds covered with Indian patchwork quilts, and a small wood-burning stove in the center of the room. Seated on one of the beds was Mrs. ChargingBear. On the sofa, reading a newspaper, sat a slender, finely featured young man, who respectfully remained silent during the visit; this was Martin, one of the family's sons. Three or four other adults and children stayed in the kitchen.

After the men had seated themselves, Mr. ChargingBear commented on the weather. Murray then told the story of how we "had run out of gas." Mr. ChargingBear then remarked that he had attended the Trap Fair on the day before we went. After the fair had been discussed in detail, Murray explained what we were trying to do on the reservation and added that he felt that we had reached a point where we would very much like to talk with, and get the opinions of, parents whose children were attending the schools.

"That," said Mr. ChargingBear, loudly and decisively, "is a good idea."

Murray was so taken aback, that he did not at first know what to say, so thoroughly had he been indoctrinated with the GoodHorses' notion that talking to people was a matter calling for the utmost delicacy and discretion. But he pulled himself together and continued, "We aren't sure how we should go about this. Do you think it would be better if Walter talked to folks alone . . . or should I go along? Maybe it would be better if Walter and I went together?" Bill did not answer these questions. Instead, he sat erect and delivered a lecture on the difficulties of Indian schoolchildren as he saw them. During the speech, Mrs. ChargingBear, with her face carefully turned away, made occasional remarks in the Indian language, which her husband sometimes translated. Just as Murray was about to leave, Mrs. ChargingBear said in excellent, if strangely musical and accented English, "Your wife's name is Rosalie, isn't it. I have a daughter who has the same name like your wife. She can talk good English and Indian. I'll ask if she would care to go with your wife to talk to people." Thus Murray had his answer to the question who should make visits and talk to people.

In appearance, Rose WhiteElk was a younger edition of her mother, which is to say that she was a short, delicately boned woman in her early thirties, with tiny hands and feet, a plump torso, elegant, aquiline features, and sharp, bright eyes. She did not know what anthropology or social science was but, as we became acquainted, she revealed herself as a person of fine sensibility and intelligence, agreeable, entertaining, and compassionate. She had been married twice and had four children. She, her husband, and her four children, lived with her parents, because her husband, like most men on the reservation, could get only occasional employment.

I explained what I hoped to do and told her that I would pay her for her time and pay extra for each interview we completed. I showed her the list of questions Murray and I had composed, and suggested that we test them by my asking her the questions. In this way we could spot any poorly phrased or impolite queries. We did this and improved several misleading items. I then asked her to translate the questions into the Indian language, for most of the ladies we would be interviewing did not speak English fluently. I also had her ask her father whether the questions were proper and the translation accurate, not because I mistrusted Mrs. WhiteElk's ability as an interpreter, but because I wanted her father, one of the most important men in the community, to know precisely what we were doing. Then, with our amended interview written out in English and Lakota, we two ladies sallied forth, driving many miles every day over the sometimes incredible reservation roads.

Mrs. WhiteElk worked me to the point of exhaustion. Day after day she conscientiously took me to call on the families with children of school age, making, so far as I could see, no distinctions or discriminations whatever. This meant that we talked to the poor, the very poor, and the incredibly poor; to married mothers, unmarried mothers, grandmothers and grandfathers; to people whose children had "perfect attendance certificates" and to people whose children "fooled around and played hooky all the time." We visited families that Mrs. WhiteElk considered very well off, which meant that the father or mother had a steady job with the Bureau (like janitor or bus driver), that people had enough to eat, and that they lived in a cabin with three or four rooms. We visited families on ADC (Aid to Dependent Children), where the children usually had something to eat but the adults had to scrounge to get clothing or buy gasoline. We visited in homes where people "were really having a hard time," where even Mrs. WhiteElk's sharp eye could spy "no groceries anywhere," where an aged or ill grandmother might be caring for three or four toddlers whose mother had run off, or where the mother had sent her children to the boarding school so that they would not be hungry. Once in a while we visited in houses where we saw things so dreadful that I would just as soon not speak of them.

I cannot adequately describe what these visits meant to me as a human being. Some ethnographers and historians have said that the Thrashing Buffalo were once a great people. I would say that they still are a great people.

In my account of working at Gila, I pointed out that, after months of confusion and misery, I suddenly became aware that I had reached a place in my investigations where most of what happened made sense. I felt as if I had entered another dimension and "could proceed boldly where previously I had crept step by step" (Wax, 1957). In our work at Thrashing Buffalo this turning point came when Mrs. ChargingBear delegated her daughter to be my guide and interpreter. All manner of encouraging and illuminating things seemed to happen at once. Murray drove boldly around the community and talked with a number of the respected older men, making plans for interviewing young men of high school age. I, through my talks with Mrs. WhiteElk and the other Indian ladies, began to see that many of the things that had befuddled or frightened us either made good sense, or did not exist, or were inventions of the Good-Horses. Simultaneously, I began to learn a great deal about things as they really were—and I confess that I rather enjoyed this gradual revelation of the extent to which our ex-hosts had been pulling the wool over our eyes.

While all of this was going on, the GoodHorses were feverishly preparing for the *yuwipe* ceremony, which was supposed to make people willing to talk to us. I do not think they were fully aware of our sudden emancipation, and they certainly did not realize that we had changed almost overnight from timid dupes to disenchanted employers. Walter dropped in one evening to tell us that the medicine ceremony would be held in the old schoolhouse where we were living and that it would be paid for by a white friend of his who taught anthropology at Plains State University. To this, Murray replied that it would be all right to use the schoolhouse, provided that some of our immediate Indian neighbors were invited. The next day Murray tried to make sure that some of our neighbors would come: when two strange old men drove by in their horse and wagon, he stopped them and invited them to the ceremony. These old men did not say they would come. Instead, like two elderly professors, they told him that the ceremony he was referring to was called *wanblee* and not *yuwipe*. Murray did not know what to make of this, but later found that the old men were correct and the GoodHorses had misinformed us.

Many of the ceremonies of the Thrashing Buffalo have been described by competent observers. But in this ceremony we were not only observers but curiously involved participants. Mrs. GoodHorse was going to prepare all the food, including obtaining, strangling, and cooking the unfortunate dog which was to constitute the pièce de résistance for the spirits. I contributed the dishes, some coffee and sugar, and the time needed to sweep the floor of the large old schoolroom. Murray took the business more seriously than I did because, I think, he expected that some of our Indian neighbors would come and because the anthropologist in question had told him that the ceremony would help us in establishing ourselves on the reservation. So he brought some Bull Durham and cloth, and I prepared a tobacco offering. As I worked, I thought I might as well make a bit of medicine on my own. So, since 4 is the holy Indian number, I carefully prepared strings of sixteen (4 × 4) tiny bags of tobacco, and tied the neck of each bag with four turns of the string and four knots. I figured that this tremendous multiplicity of fours would contribute to a wholesome spiritual atmosphere. Since all the bags were tied with the same string, the end product looked rather like a necklace with the bags forming the beads. Meanwhile, Mrs. GoodHorse was strangling and cooking the dog. This preparation, fortunately, I did not observe. But Victor Hibou saw it and put it in his field notes:

> The dog was brought in the car. Mrs. GoodHorse sat with the dog until her husband gathered the necessary ropes for the strangling. Then she got out and said: "Gloria, get me the lipstick." She then marked the dog's head red and then walked over to the two posts between which a rope was being strung. It was attached around the dog's neck and then tied to the next [post]. She let go of the dog. The rope tightened and the dog's legs barely touched the ground. There came a sound, undefineable for only a second and then out. The dog still moved and they pulled down on the ropes, tightening the rope around the neck. One more weird sound was squeezed out. Gloria stood away watching, with her arms clutched to her. I could feel the nausea building inside of her but she stood watching, saying nothing until it was over. The dog was finally taken down and lain on the grate over the open fire. It faced east while it was singed.

Sometime after dark, Walter and his brother arrived and set to work putting blankets and sheets of newspaper over the windows. Soon we heard several cars driving up, and the elder GoodHorses came in carrying large bundles of sage (which supernatural beings like to smell). With them came the ancient but spry medicine man. He wore his hair in the twin braids of old but was dressed in a handsome, fur-trimmed overcoat which looked as if it had been designed in 1900. Ray, the young anthropologist from Plains State University, entered carrying a brightly colored, gift-wrapped blanket, which was to be one of his presents to the medicine man. He was followed by seven Indians, none of whom lived in our community. These carried ritual paraphernalia such as pans of earth, hot stones, and the pots full of food. There were three fine male singers from a small settlement about fifteen miles distant, an old blind lady who had come with the medicine man, and three other Indians from a long way off. There were also the GoodHorses' daughters-in-law with their babies, Walter's little brothers, and finally Vic Hibou, who seemed reluctant to come to the ceremony.

Everyone bustled about with the infectious mixture of gaiety and

235

efficiency that Indians display when they know exactly what they are doing and are eager to get a show on the road. We were introduced to the medicine man and we shook hands with the singers, who rapidly set up the objects that constitute the altar. Walter's father ran about giving everyone sprays of sage to put in their hair or clothing so that the spirits would not bother them. Beula, arrayed in a blood red woolen shirt (which I had given her), looked handsome and vivacious; obviously she enjoyed the ceremony a great deal and she behaved like a wise and happy little girl at a party, carefully seating herself on the floor close to Ray. The few objects which mischievious spirits might throw at people were taken from the walls and put away; Murray and I were cautioned to take off our glasses, and all of us sat down on the floor with our backs to the wall; then the lights were turned off, and, since all the windows had been covered, we sat in complete, disorienting darkness.

I did not make a conscious effort to record the ceremony in my mind, and there may be errors or omissions in the following account.

Things started off with some hair-raising songs. The singers sang in as high and intense a range as possible, beating the drum with a force that made the walls of the room vibrate. Even higher was the piercing song of the old blind woman: for sheer carrying power I have never heard a human sound like it. But the sound was as nothing compared to the emotion expressed by the singers. All my life I have heard people pray in church or sing songs in which, ostensibly, they are addressing themselves to God. These Indian songs were different. The best I can say is that the church prayers and songs usually sound like people rehearsing a speech to themselves. The Thrashing Buffalo songs sounded as if the singers knew for a fact that some powerful being was within hailing distance. When they really got warmed up, it was almost more than one could endure. They yelled like people calling for help from inside a burning building. Someone began to dance with an occasional stamp that felt as if a two-hundred-pound weight had been dropped to the floor. Then every sound stopped, and the silence was like diving under water. Everybody listened. Not a sound. There were more songs and more ear-cracking silences. Then at last a tiny piping began, just as Tom had said, like baby birds, and one could hear in response the voice of the medicine man, speaking in the gentle tone a man might use to coax a nervous pet to settle down. The piping grew louder and one could hear the wing beats of very large birds.

Now that the spirits had arrived, questions were put to them. Ray addressed the spirits properly as "Grandfathers" and thanked them for past assistance. He also asked about some problem associated with his academic career and was advised to pursue his plan. Then, however, the spirits gratuitously warned him "to watch out because he could get into trouble going around with that married woman." (Later Ray laughed about the married woman business and told us that it was the only point on which the medicine man had slipped up. His current girlfriend was not married. Poor Ray—he did not realize that the bird spirits were referring to Beula.) Mr. GoodHorse served as interpreter between the medicine man and Ray, while the medicine man, of course, interpreted the remarks of the spirits. After each request or remark the Indians present said "Hau." Other Indian participants put questions in the Indian language, most of which I did not understand. Everyone made his request in a humble and respectful tone except Beula, who talked to the spirits in the tone of an aggressive graduate student picking the brains of a brilliant but easygoing peer. But she did get the information she wanted and she took great pains to get it straight.

When Murray's turn came, he went out and stood in the small ceremonial area as the other men had done (women, apparently, were not supposed to come too close to the sacred objects). I wondered how Murray would phrase his request for spiritual assistance for our research. But Murray had been touched by the terrible poverty and by the courtesy of the people he and I had visited that week, and he knew that the community from which the singers came was one of the poorest. So he surprised even me by saying, "Grandfathers: there are many poor Indians on the reservation. I would like to ask you to help these poor people." This request was echoed by remarkably loud and enthusiastic Hau's from that side of the room where the singers and the other Indian guests were seated. From the side of the room where the GoodHorses sat there came no sound. The spirits seemed surprised, because they took an unusually long time to frame a reply. But being Indian spirits they replied with style: "We see," interpreted the medicine man, "that you are a White man who has sympathy for *all* the Indian Peoples. We thank you." This time the *Hau Hau* from the Indian visitors was even louder. But the GoodHorses didn't *Hau* very loud. I felt happy because I thought that Murray had spoken well.

The lights were now turned on. The singers, who also served as the medicine man's assistants, took a large cooking pot filled with stones upon which water had been poured. They held this before every participant so that he might put his hands over the steam and purify them. Then the medicine pipe was passed around the circle clockwise, and everyone took a puff, even the women. It was strong. After each person smoked, he said in Indian or in English, "All my relatives," which meant that all present, including the spirits, were thenceforth related; and, of course, if they were related they were expected to help each other. Then followed the feast.

Neither Murray nor I ever developed a taste for the kind of food served at Indian banquets. Young dog is mostly fat, and if you do strike a piece of meat it tastes like boiled veal. The store-bought sweet rolls, doughnuts, soda crackers, canned peaches, and heavily sugared coffee gave us indigestion. But I noted that the old blind lady was skillfully filling a quart jar with extra peaches and a large bag with extra rolls and crackers, and this made me feel good. I saved a couple of rolls and some crackers for WeaselBear (who was now eating for nine), for though she often turned up her nose at canned dog food, she doted on the crackers and sweets of a ceremonial meal. I thought there was an eerie kind of justice in this.

The next morning Ray dropped in on his way to the university. He told us that he had lectured Walter sternly and impressed him with the fact that what we were asking of him as a research assistant was reasonable and proper. Walter (said Ray) was now all set to work. We were much cheered by this news. Ray then explained that the GoodHorses had told him that the major source of trouble was Vic Hibou. Mrs. GoodHorse was distressed because Vic was taking field notes in which he mentioned her name. Ray was convinced that everything would straighten out if we ordered Vic to stop this. We promised to do this, although the whole business made little sense to us. Beula had known for a long time how we took our notes. As Ray was leaving, I remarked that I thought Beula was making a mountain out of a molehill. "Don't underestimate that lady," said he; "in this community she can make or break you."

"Hah!" I snorted, sounding more like an Indian woman than I realized at the time.

19   The Scandal

For two weeks following the medicine ceremony everything suddenly went very well. Walter began to work in earnest and produced some really good interviews. Vic Hibou, who had been working hard all along, began to turn in some splendid interviews and some excellent classroom observations. Mrs. WhiteElk and I continued to visit Indian mothers in their homes, and, since we were now for the first time communicating with the Indians, we kept getting new insights and accurate information every day. Murray felt so good that he lent Mr. GoodHorse the hundred dollars he had asked for. He also helped Walter obtain a bank loan so that he could begin construction on the house that Gloria wanted so much. On one particularly happy day I remarked to Murray that maybe we ought to hold medicine ceremonies more often if they resulted in so much good feeling and good work.

Meanwhile, I was gradually learning how to behave toward Indian ladies. After the ladies had answered my questions about the school and the children, we all relaxed and exchanged news about current events, accidents, assaults, illnesses, births, quarrels, relatives, losing or getting jobs, wife-beatings—in short, all manner of notable, deplorable, tragic, or comic community activities. Any lady who had seen something interesting or had talked to an eyewitness held the floor. I began to see that this "gossip" was really an exchange of news and constituted an essential part of reservation life. Ignorance of "what was going on" would inevitably lead to painful or embarrassing social errors. For example, one might ask a woman whose child had died how her baby was getting along. Or one might address a man as Mr. SourWeed because he was living with a woman called Mrs. SourWeed, if one did not know that the genuine Mr. SourWeed had run off two months before. By means of this gossip I soon learned that most of the women in our community did not approve of Mrs. GoodHorse. I had previously noticed that Mrs. GoodHorse had never once said a kindly thing about any person but her sons. Now I found that no Indian woman had a good word to say for her. Since it was known that we had been living with the

GoodHorses, the ladies at first would express their views delicately. One might ask me politely, "How did the *yuwipe* go?" I would relate what happened in some detail, having learned that this was what was expected of me. Then the lady might say, with a little laugh, "My goodness, but Beula sure made a *secret* out of it." "Yes," I would say, with another little laugh; "my husband asked her to invite other people from around here but I guess she didn't." At this point, an older woman might remark bluntly, "Beula has really been acting crazy again." Then everybody but me would begin to talk animatedly in the Indian language. Driving home, Mrs. White-Elk would tell me that "people were saying" that Beula was going around telling everybody that she was going to leave Tom. "My goodness!" I would say, for I had learned that this was the proper way for a woman to express astonishment.

On the fifth of October, Walter came over looking upset, and told Murray that his parents were quarreling so much that they might separate. The trouble, Walter said, was caused by distant kin who were making unreasonable financial demands on Beula and Tom. When Murray and I were alone, we wondered whether Tom had been bragging about the hundred dollars Murray had given him and had thus brought down his impoverished kin on his neck. According to traditional custom, a man who has had a windfall ought to share his good fortune with his relatives. I suggested that Beula wanted some of the money and was raising hell because Tom wouldn't give it to her. In any case, we felt that it was no skin off our noses. So we kept on working and I even began an article— which I was never to finish.

On 14 October, Sunday, Tom drove up very early in the morning and pounded on our door. We gave him some breakfast, and, after a few polite preliminary remarks, he told us that he and Beula would like to use the little shack in which Vic Hibou was living. Would we ask Vic to move out? Murray said that he would tell Vic to move immediately. Neither of us spent much time speculating about why Tom had made this rather ungracious request. We had guessed wrong about the GoodHorses so many times that we had lost the impulse to wonder overmuch about people's motivations or intentions.

In my case this repression of speculation was a conscious defense. Soon after our arrival on the reservation we were forced to make many apparently crucial decisions without adequate knowledge of what we were doing. In our anxiety we sometimes talked ourselves into mental exhaustion, considering and discarding tactic after tactic. When we moved to Witkokia, matters grew even worse, because many Indians began to tell us all manner of things about the other Indians who lived nearby. As we tried to make sense of these various (and sometimes frightening) stories and decide on a possible course of action, I became so confused and nervous that I sometimes lay awake all night, trying to sort things out. But as soon as I began to visit and talk to the Indian women, I saw that most of the people who told these stories were merely relating what they considered an interesting yarn or item of gossip. They themselves never seemed to give a thought to how a situation might be resolved, and they never (unlike Murray and me) seemed to spend time wondering what people *might* be up to or what people *might* do. Instead, they waited until somebody *did* something and then they did what seemed best.

I found myself developing a similar attitude toward crises. No matter what people *said,* no matter what people *said* had been said or done, I refused to let myself get upset or worry about what might happen. Only when something upsetting really happened, did I get stirred up, and then, of course, I did what I could.

On Tuesday, just as we were sitting down to supper, Beula called on us, bringing her two little boys with her. Her face was a shocking mess—so swollen with weeping that she looked as if she had been beaten. Almost hysterical, she pleaded with Murray not to make Victor move away. Tom, she explained, earned nothing, and she and the twins had been kept from starvation only by the rent and food money furnished by Victor. If Victor left, they would be destitute. Tom, she added, had no right to order anyone away, because the land on which they were living was hers. She looked so desperate and stricken that even I pitied her—a little. I felt sorrier for the little boys, who stood around looking wild and sad.

By this time Murray had been faced by a number of excited Indians and he had developed what might be called "a structural pose." This consisted of sitting down, looking very solemn, listening, nodding, and saying little. To me, he looked like a Jewish intellectual trying to give an imitation of Sitting Bull, but I never told him this because it would have embarrassed him. Besides, all the Indians seemed to find his pose impressive and reassuring. After Beula had told her story at least three times—each time with additional pitiful details—Murray nodded his head and said slowly and impressively that he was sorry and that he would tell Victor to do as he saw fit.

When Beula left we shook our heads. We were paying both Walter and his wife very good salaries, and since Walter's brother and his wife also had fairly good jobs, and we had just given Tom a hundred dollars, we could only conclude (1) that Beula was telling us what Indians call "a real good hard-luck story" or (2) that her sons and husband must be the stingiest men on the reservation. With four salaries coming in, the GoodHorses were a particularly flush family within the community. Besides, all Indians, we had been told a hundred times, were supposed to share what they had with their relatives.

Victor Hibou moved away from the GoodHorses on Wednesday afternoon. He took a room in the motel in the agency town.

Wednesday night, just as we were preparing for bed, Tom rushed precipitously into our house, yelling dramatically: "My wife has kicked me out! My wife has kicked me out!" We put on our woolen bathrobes, turned up the oil stove again, and sat down to hear about this. Tom said that Beula had accused him of driving Victor away. Even worse, she had accused Tom of accomplishing this by telling us that Victor was sleeping with Beula. Astonished and bewildered, Murray and I did not at first know what to say. Finally I tried to reassure Tom by saying that he had never made any such ridiculous statement. But the implication that this romance was ridiculous and fantastic seemed only to increase Tom's distress, for he now embarked on an agonizing chronicle of sorrow and dishonor. He insisted that Beula and Victor had been having an affair since the Sun Dance. Everybody knew about it. Why, Mrs. ChargingBear and some of the other ladies of the community had even once caught Vic and Beula in the act! All of the decent people in the community were so disgusted over this hitherto unheard-of immorality that the Indian Ladies' Auxiliary had been planning to call on us in a body and remonstrate with us. (I had a sudden crazy vision of a great array of stalwart Indian matrons wearing full dance regalia and expressions of moral indignation, bearing down on Witkokia to tell us that Victor would have to stop sleeping with Beula.) Some people, Tom continued, were already preparing a petition to the Commissioner of Indian Affairs, requesting that our project be removed from the reservation. Beula had told Tom, and was telling everyone else, that she was going to divorce Tom and run off with Victor. Dreadful things were going to happen. The medicine man had been consulted and had prophesied that there would be bloodshed. Then he had told Tom to go home and be quiet.

This oration was marvelously well delivered, and, had we heard it several weeks before, we might have believed at least a part of it. Now, however, we were inclined to believe only that the medicine man had told Tom to go home and be quiet. Anyway, Murray braced himself, assumed his Indian elder pose, and calmly said, "If Beula starts divorce proceedings, she will probably hurt only herself."

Tom had not expected this response, and he repeated and elaborated his warnings that we might be expelled from the reservation and our research stopped. But Murray kept as straight and unconcerned a face as an Indian, and after a while, looking rather disappointed, Tom took himself off, stopping at the door to say in a broken voice that he was going to spend the night with the old people who had reared him as an orphan.

We, of course, were too amazed to go to bed. Under different circumstances we might have been angry, frightened, or both, but, as it was, we paced up and down the school room remarking, "So this is what Bill meant" (Bill being the friend who, months ago, had warned us not to get involved with the GoodHorses). After a while this remark became monotonous. So Murray sat down at the typewriter and wrote a detailed chronological account of our doings with the GoodHorses. As the additional details of how we had been hoodwinked dawned upon us, we laughed until we almost cried. In consequence, it took some time to write the account. Perhaps I should add that we did not laugh because we felt safe or secure or because we enjoyed the prospect of trying to continue our work in the face of a scandal as lurid and ludicrous as this one. Rather, our laughter was an appreciation of the conspiratorial work of art to which we had been subjected. We had been fooled before in our lives but never with such drama and finesse.

The morning after Tom's revelation, Beula arrived carrying Gloria's six-week-old infant, tightly swaddled in a patchwork blanket. She began a piteous denunciation of the evil and stingy behavior of Tom. Gloria's little daughter seemed to sense her grandmother's inner fury, for she began to howl at the top of her lungs. Beula jounced the baby with ferocious energy, and though Indian infants are usually soothed by a rhythmic bouncing, this one fell into a paroxysm of squealing. Through this noise Beula kept demanding that Murray lend her thirty dollars to start divorce proceedings, promising to pay it back when her lease money came through. But Murray would not give Beula the money for a divorce. "I think you and Tom ought to patch things up," said he. Beula argued for a long time saying, "But Mr. Wax—you don't understand," and then she would tell her story all over again. Murray always replied in the same way. Finally, looking very angry indeed, Beula rushed away, still clutching the screaming baby. We went back to work, unaware that Beula had walked to the highway, hitched a ride to the agency town, and called on Vic Hibou in his motel room.

We had told Vic nothing about the GoodHorse uproar and nothing about his alleged role as the seducer of Walter's mother. In consequence, he interpreted Beula's visit as a motherly gesture and took the opportunity to interview her on child-rearing practices. His field notes indicate that she answered his questions carefully and conscientiously. Then she told him that her little boys needed clothes, and he gave her thirty dollars. She went immediately to the courthouse, and with the thirty dollars instituted divorce proceedings against Tom.

We knew nothing of this visit, and we saw no reason to bother Vic with any of the wild and farcical accusations of the elder Good-Horses. So that afternoon Murray went to the agency town to pick up his mail, and I went out with Mrs. WhiteElk to do a stint of interviewing. At the agency town, Beula again picked up Murray at the Post Office and demanded a ride home. She made no reference to Vic or to the divorce. Instead, she told Murray that many Indian people were saying that Mrs. WhiteElk and I were FBI investigators who were visiting people so that we might discover and prosecute families who were illegally obtaining welfare monies. Murray, who by this time was feeling a bit reckless, responded gaily that we really were investigators but that we had been hired to find and expose those Indians who were crocodiles. That it was Beula who had been going about telling people that Mrs. WhiteElk and I were in the pay of the FBI, and were looking for people who were cheating on their welfare checks, did not occur to him.

The next day Mrs. WhiteElk and I called on a number of Indian ladies to administer our interview on education. The ladies answered our questions with businesslike speed and then plunged eagerly into an exchange of stories about what was going on at the GoodHorses'. One story, told with particular relish, concerned a knockdown, drag-out battle in which Tom and Beula had engaged on the highway. Beula, the story went, had tried to walk to the agency town to find Vic Hibou and elope with him. Tom had gone after her in his car and tried to stop her. Later, Mrs. WhiteElk told me that her father was teasing Tom about this, asking whether he and Beula intended going on TV as professional wrestlers. Another story concerned Irene, Walter's brother's wife, who had fled from the uproar at GoodHorses' and gone to her folks. One elderly lady made the rather horrid suggestion that Beula had offered one of her little boys to the spirits "so as to get Victor." When current gossip lagged, the ladies began to recount other scandals in which Beula had been involved. Older women asserted that she had begun to run off with men at the age of fifteen. Then she had had an affair with a man from another tribe, which was still going on. She also (they said) had had an affair with Tom's brother, an affair with the young man who had helped us build our shade, an affair with a young missionary (whose career she had ruined by accusing him to his superiors), an affair with Ray, the young anthropologist, and finally this present romance with handsome young Victor. As an involved "participant" I found this gossip highly interesting. But as an "observer" I could not help but notice that many of the stories were told as interesting and amusing yarns and did not seem to carry a connotation of reproof or criticism. Indeed, when I ventured to suggest that Beula and Ray, or Beula and Victor, had not *really* "carried on" (which is what I personally believed), the ladies behaved as if they had not heard me, and I felt like an amateur who has made an error that the professionals are too polite to notice.

When I came home that Friday evening and told Murray "what everybody was saying," he suggested that the time had come to take a day off. So early the next morning we drove to a small college town about sixty miles from the reservation, where I indulged in the great treat of shopping at a supermarket. Then we walked about all morning in a handsome state park. We decided, as we walked, that we would send Victor away from the reservation and tell no one where he had gone. With Victor gone, Beula might' quiet down (we hoped), and Mr. GoodHorse would be less likely to bring suit for alienation of affection.

When Victor arrived at Witkokia in response to our summons, we told him all of the story known to us, and, with each incredible detail, he looked more and more aghast. In the middle of the story (narrated by Murray) I wondered aloud who in the world had lent Beula the thirty dollars to start divorce proceedings. When Victor admitted that he had given Beula the money, I laughed so loudly that I almost drowned out his honorable offer to resign from the project. Beula, I admitted, was truly an outstanding adversary.

But Murray explained to Victor that we simply wanted him to disappear until the noise died down. Between them, they figured out a plan whereby Vic would leave Thrashing Buffalo immediately, go to another reservation, and continue his study of schools.

So far as we and Victor were concerned, this device worked beautifully. When Walter, Gloria, and Mrs. WhiteElk asked where Victor had gone, Murray told them only that he had sent Victor away. Many of our Indian neighbors also tried to find out what had happened, but to no avail. Beula, I suspected, must have been really furious.

From this point on, the scandal faded rapidly away. When Beula's suit for divorce was heard in tribal court, the Indian judge admonished her and Tom for setting a poor example before the young people. He also instructed them to resume their marital existence. After a few weeks Victor returned to the reservation. He continued to do fine fieldwork, but he and Beula no longer spoke to each other. Beula, however, applied herself assiduously to making trouble for us and for our project. She tried particularly hard to turn the Indian ladies in the community against Mrs. WhiteElk and myself. When the rumor that we were working for the FBI did us no harm, she began to tell people that we were working for the communists. When this tale was brought to Mrs. WhiteElk's father, he remarked jokingly that he was planning to ship his daughter and me off to Russia. The Indian listeners laughed and no one seemed to object to being interviewed by the "lady communists." Then Beula spread the rumor that Mrs. WhiteElk and I were secret recruiting agents for the WAVES. This tale gained some credence, because, for several weeks, young unmarried women were reluctant to talk to us. Next Beula told people that Mrs. WhiteElk and I were laughing or "poking fun" at the poor people whose houses we visited because their houses had dirt floors or because they had illegitimate children. Mrs. WhiteElk was particularly distressed by this story, for to make fun of the poor is one of the most indecent things a Thrashing Buffalo can do. Then Beula struck directly at Mrs. WhiteElk. Apparently, she encountered Mrs. WhiteElk's husband in a bar in one of the small towns near the reservation. Before many people she informed him that his wife "was telling people" that she now had a fine job and was making a great deal of money and no longer needed her worthless, unemployed husband. Mr. WhiteElk, greatly embarrassed, left his wife and went home to his folks. When I heard about this I was dismayed, and I suggested to my friend that she might want to stop work until this misunderstanding had been cleared up. But Mrs. WhiteElk calmly asserted that this would not be necessary. Her mother would see that someone would "go and talk to" her husband. Perhaps this is what happened, for the husband soon returned.

As we continued our work in the face of this continuous harassment, I began to feel quite guilty about being the cause of so much discord and conflict among the people I was supposed to be studying. But as time passed and I learned more about the situation, I perceived that this present squabble was only the most recent episode in an ancient feud between the ChargingBears and the Good-Horses. The battle had been joined for decades before we arrived on the reservation and it would probably continue for decades after we left. When Beula lost us to the ChargingBears, she had suffered a severe tactical defeat—a fact thoroughly appreciated by all the members of the community. Her attempts to even the score were quite understandable.

After about six weeks the spate of rumors abated, and our work went marvelously well. Murray interviewed principals and teachers and older Indian men. Victor did excellent classroom observations and obtained many illuminating interviews with young people, day and high school dropouts, and children. Mrs. WhiteElk and I visited women. We encouraged Mrs. WhiteElk to try interviewing and class observation on her own. She became very skillful at both, and her class observations were particularly helpful because she saw and understood so much more of what was going on among the children than we did.

No Indian woman ever refused to talk to us, and, once the bitterly cold weather had set in, no Indian woman ever refused to invite us into her house. Some ladies told us a great deal more than others about their children and the schools, sometimes because they had more to tell and sometimes because they had a particularly close relationship with the ChargingBears. Usually I could do little to influence the quality of an interview—except to behave like a sympathetic and interested woman—because Mrs. WhiteElk knew so much more about the ladies and their problems than I did. I participated actively in conversations and asked pertinent questions, but I often felt that the degree to which respondents talked frankly and at length depended primarily on their rapport with the Charging-Bear family and, only secondarily on their interest in reporting their situation to a strange white woman. In many of the more remote homes I was probably the first white woman visitor these ladies had ever received. Some were shy and embarrassed, because they felt that I would find their homes poor and bare. But most were pleased that they had been visited, and I felt that if I ever returned I would be received with courtesy and cordiality.

I came to enjoy these visits so much that in January I urged Murray to extend our stay in the field by another month. So we spent seven instead of our scheduled six months among the Thrashing Buffalo. When we left, I was almost as shaken as I had been when I left Tule Lake. But perhaps Murray and I will return some day, since Mrs. WhiteElk writes and tells us that some of the Indians who have read our book on the Indian schools have told her, "If we had known that this was the kind of book those white people were going to write, we would *really* have talked to them."

248

20   How Does One Find and Work on a Problem?

There are many works which discuss the definition, framing, and solution of problems in the social sciences in general and abstract terms. So far as I know, none discuss what this process is like in specific and intimate detail. Here, then, is an account of how Murray and I went about finding, defining, solving, and testing one of the major problems relating to our research on the Thrashing Buffalo reservation.

To begin with, Murray and I did not invent, search for, or discover our problem: it forced itself upon us. For two summers, in 1959 and 1960, we directed a college workshop for American Indian students. Repeatedly we were made aware that these students —most of whom had been admitted to or had attended colleges or universities—simply did not have the scholastic background to cope with the curriculum of a progressive high school, much less a college or university. Some of them could not speak English fluently. Most could not understand or apply the simplest of new concepts. If we tried to start a discussion, they looked down. If we asked their opinion about anything, they looked astonished. If we gave them an assignment, they were disconcertingly obedient and unimaginative. Most moving of all to us as teachers was the fact that, with all these handicaps, they tried so doggedly "to learn."

Most of these students had received their elementary and high school education in schools operated by the Bureau of Indian Affairs, and we were told by well-informed persons that these schools were well equipped and staffed by qualified teachers. Why then, we asked ourselves, should even the brightest and most conscientious of the students be so ignorant and ill trained?

Nothing that we could learn from the students or from the few people we met who knew anything about Indian education threw much light on this question. The students naïvely believed that they were well educated; the other people had never been inside the Indian schools and could only speak from hearsay. Thus, the question continued to vex us, and in 1961, when I conducted a mailed ques-

tionnaire of young Indians who had attended workshops, I referred
to it in my report:

> Although the participants were among the best Indian college students
> in the nation, a fair number were not fluent in English and a large
> number were inhibited about participating in class discussion; despite
> their intelligence and originality, many were shockingly provincial
> and miseducated, as compared to college students at any major
> university. Even their knowledge of American and Indian history,
> which one might have expected to have some depth, was of the level
> of American popular culture. [R. Wax 1961]

Meanwhile, Murray had heard that the U.S. Office of Education
had funds for sociological and anthropological studies of education.
He forthwith conceived the notion of doing a comparative study of
education on several Indian reservations, with the basic aim of finding out how it was that even the most able of the Indian youth were
learning so little in their schools. He prepared and submitted a relatively simple, straightforward research proposal, conforming to all
of the directives on the form. This proposal was turned down. Being advised by members of the research staff of the Office of Education that he should express himself in more formal and elaborate
terms—show more familiarity with previous research, describe his
objectives and procedure in detail, in short, demonstrate his competence to study Indian education—he prepared a proposal of
twenty-one, single-spaced, typewritten pages and a nine-page ap-
pendix. This proposal was accepted.

In describing our procedure we pointed out that previous research
had yielded little useful information and that it had all been done
through the media of structured questionnaires and statistical studies
of scholastic achievement. We therefore proposed to follow the pattern of the ethnographic community study, to live as close to the
people we were studying as conveniently possible, to attend community functions, to talk informally with and interview parents,
teen-agers, and children, and to observe classroom interaction in
the elementary and high schools. On the basis of what we had read
and heard about the Thrashing Buffalo, we formulated several theories which might help to explain why Indian children did so poorly
in school and why so many dropped out. We suggested a theory of
"cultural disharmony," by which we meant that children reared in
conservative Indian fashion might find the atmosphere of a conventional American school painful, incomprehensible, or even im-

250

moral and that, conversely, middle-class American teachers might see the Indian children as undisciplined, apathetic, or immoral. We also had a theory about the "preservation of identity." By this we meant that Indian parents might see formal education as a technique of turning their children into white people, and, in consequence, as a threat to their identity as Thrashing Buffalo and to their existence as a people.

Working on the Problem in the Field

Once formulated and written down, these theories stayed stubbornly with us. Even in the turmoil and anxiety of our first weeks at Thrashing Buffalo, we saw and heard many things which we thought might help to explain why the Indian children did poorly in school. But whenever we tried to relate these initial observations to our stated theories or to whatever else we saw going on around us, we found that the faint gleam of understanding had vanished. Indeed, very little that we heard or saw during our first weeks on the reservation could logically be related to any of the theories or ideas so explicitly stated in our research proposal. For, what people were telling us was how *they* saw things, just as what we were seeing was things as they were. And we had not yet been around long enough to realize that the way the Indians saw things and the way things really were, bore very little relationship to the basic theories constructed by previous researchers.

For example, on 13 August I tried to ask Mrs. GoodHorse questions which I hoped would help me understand what she thought the schools were doing to her children or how she defined education. But she told me only that she had recently decided to send her twin sons to the Methodist rather than the Episcopal boarding school. When I asked why she preferred the Methodist school, she replied in a calm, aristocratic tone that the boys would learn to read the Bible there and obtain, on the whole, a better religious education. This response baffled me; so two days later I tried again. This time she told me: "They have PTA meetings [at the school] but we won't go. You have to pay money to belong, but we know that if we go, it will be run by white people. So we won't go."

I concluded that Mrs. GoodHorse did not want to talk about the day school (indeed, like most mothers, Indian or white, she had no idea of what went on there). So I asked her what she herself taught her children. Now she replied with authority: "I teach them self-

respect, which is most important; obedience, which is second, and
[here she paused and thought, like a person who had forgotten the
exact wording of a poem] . . . and cleanliness. If you teach these
at a young age, all the rest will follow." I did not know whether
these were old Indian virtues or whether Mrs. GoodHorse had
picked them up from some missionary or extension agent (and since
she would not let me talk to any of the other Indian women I was
in no position to find out). So I asked her how she would say in the
Indian language: "I teach my children" and how she would say:
"The schoolteacher teaches my children." The verbs she used were
quite different, and I gathered that one meant teaching "one of us"
and the other meant teaching "one of them." I thought I had hit on
something here—and I still do. But at this point I was obliged to
begin my observations of the orientation meetings held for the teaching and administrative staff of the reservation and I had few opportunities to pursue this linguistic lead.

The orientation meetings gave us a great deal of material supporting one part of the theory of cultural disharmony: namely, that
lower-middle-class teachers perceive the behavior of Indian children
as undisciplined, lacking in initiative, and even as immoral. For days
we listened to the educational specialists and the teachers telling each
other that the home background of Indian children was empty or
"lacking," that Indian children needed to be taught courtesy, that
their parents did not tell them stories, that they lacked musical experience, and even that their parents taught them obscenities. While
nobody said so outright, it was clear that some teachers believed
that the adult Indians who "lived out on the reservation" were a
backward, dirty, and immoral folk. We felt it reasonable to assume
that children would feel ill at ease with teachers who regarded them
and their parents in this fashion. Still, we did not, as yet, have any
evidence that the Indian children or their parents were aware of this
derogatory image and that this awareness caused them to do poorly
in school.

A week later school opened, and we had our long-awaited opportunity to see what was going on in the classrooms. I was taken
completely aback, for almost everything I saw in the early elementary grades suggested that the little children were enjoying themselves. They were attentive and obedient, and some even seemed to
delight in the drill routines by which the teacher tried to teach them
to read and write English and learn arithmetic. I was so impressed

that I commented, "These beginners are phenomenally quiet. They sit like little birds, ever alert for a guiding cue from the teacher. They do not seem even to be conscious of potential distractions like adult visitors (ourselves) or noisy and aggressive schoolmates."

On the negative side I often doubted the value of what the children were being taught, but then I told myself that I was, after all, a snobbish, liberal intellectual. Further, having had some good training in linguistics, I noticed almost immediately that the children were not learning to *speak* English with anything like ease or fluency, despite the great amount of time spent in phonics, reading, writing, and spelling. When the teacher spoke to them in English they responded with a few English words. But when they talked or whispered to each other they spoke in their native tongue. Here, then, was one explanation of the phenomenon we had noticed in the workshop, namely that the college students would rather write essays for us than answer a question verbally. Nevertheless, my general impression of these classrooms was positive. The atmosphere was one of orderly bustle and well-being. Many of the beginners who in the first days of school had been too shy to say even a word soon became alert, willing, and sometimes, even enthusiastic pupils.

When, however, I systematically proceeded to visit and observe the intermediate grades, I felt at first as if I had been thrust into some scene from *Alice in Wonderland*. Never in my most anxiety-ridden professional nightmares had I imagined that a schoolroom could be like this one:

I enter at 10:30, after recess. The pupils are beginning an arithmetic lesson taken from a book with large and highly colored illustrations representing a circus ring, with clown, horses, and acrobats.

Mrs. Walker asks, "How many have ever been to a circus?" There is absolutely no visible or audible response. It would be inaccurate to say that there is silence, because there is enough squirming, whispering, page ruffling, and desk creaking to make the room quite animated.

Mrs. Walker waits a moment and then asks, "How many have been on a trampoline?" Again, there is no visible or audible response. It is as if Mrs. Walker were not there. . . . Mrs. Walker now calls on a pupil to read a problem aloud and answer it. Immediately two children and then a third get up and go to the back of the room to sharpen pencils. I cannot hear whether the pupil called on answers or not. Singly and in twos, more children go to the pencil sharpener. As they pass me, two of the boys grin at me knowingly. For ten minutes there is bedlam—a rising and falling grind-grind-grind—and sound of moving children. During the less intense grinding periods

253

Mrs. Walker's voice could be heard but not intelligibly. By listening very carefully I at length make out that she is calling for somebody to go to the board and write out a problem. Nobody pays any attention to her, and as soon as it looks as if the noise might stop, another cluster of kids walks to the pencil sharpener. Still, she keeps trying to make herself heard, and when relative quiet descends it is because the pupils grow tired of their game. [R. Wax 1962:28 Aug.]

At the end of this observation period I was exhausted and dazed. Nevertheless, I managed to write the following comments:

It would look as if the disintegration of the Indian child as student is beginning right here in the fourth grade, age about ten. This is something to check, as are also the contributing factors. Is this because the teacher doesn't "keep things running" and thus permits the children to become disruptive? Or is it because the children have reached an age where they may choose for themselves whether or not they want to pay attention. This latter I really doubt.

As it turned out, the latter guess was closer to the mark. But the idea that a class of nine- and ten-year-old children could take the classroom situation away from a teacher and run it as they chose was too bizarre or, perhaps (to a professional teacher like me), too threatening to be considered. But though my analytical powers were not functioning very well, my social sensitivity had not deserted me. I noticed that many of the Indian children in this uncanny classroom behaved toward me in a way that Indian adults would have considered very rude. They turned in their seats and goggled at me as if I were some kind of a freak.

That evening I compared my observations with those which Murray had made of the combined seventh and eighth grades, and found that he had been just as amazed as I had. But whereas I had found the fourth and fifth grades whirling in noisy disorder, he had found the seventh and eighth grade room enveloped in an eerie silence. Nothing could be heard for long periods of time but the voice of the teacher.

Teacher: "What do we do while we are in line?
(Silence)
Teacher: Do we push; do we try to trip somebody?
(Silence to my ears, but visibly to her some of the pupils must have indicated the sought-for negative.)
Teacher: "No, we don't push. . . . If you spill something [on cafeteria floor] what do you do? Do you just leave it there? . . .
(Again, silence to my ears, but teacher carries on:)

"No, you are responsible for cleaning up what you spill. So we write: 'Carry trays carefully.'"

She now asked for a volunteer to write the rules on the board and stood there at the front of the room with chalk in hand, pleading for one. Half the boys at the rear of the room raised the tops of their desks, some making a pretense of looking for materials, others just plain hiding behind them, while other boys tried to make themselves invisible. . . . [I felt that the absence of the kind of response white kids would have given, must have been a great irritation to the teacher]. [M. Wax 1962: 28 Aug.]

Murray's comments on these observations were more practical than mine, but it is interesting that he, too, identified with the teacher.

Murray and I had no doubt that what we had observed in these classes was extremely significant. But try as we might—and we discussed the "problem" almost every day—we could neither understand nor explain it. Why should eager, industrious litle children, who hung on every word their teacher said, turn suddenly into little imps who seemed deliberately to frustrate everything the teacher tried to do? And why, again, should these imps, at age thirteen to fifteen, turn into young people who behaved as if they were deaf and dumb?

While I myself sat in the silent seventh and eighth grade classroom, pondering these questions, I remembered certain things I had seen at the GoodHorses', which, I felt, were somehow related to what we had seen in the schools. I did not at this time realize how close I had come to an understanding of what was going on:

Since so much of the time I observed in this class was taken up by silence—as students worked or went through the motions of working on their assignments—I had nothing better to do than think up ideas. Here is one of them. We have noticed that Indian infants or babies are given a great deal of attention. In fact, even as quite young children, somebody is watching them or holding them every waking minute. Again, we have seen that, at about age ten, the attitude of elders [toward children] seems to be entirely different. Nobody hovers over the GoodHorse boys, talks to them, remarks how cute they are—they seem to live in a world apart from adults. . . . It would be almost impossible, I would guess, to find any white children who are left so much "to their own devices" as are these boys. They really seem to live a life apart, and nobody ever dreams of "trying to understand them." So far as I have observed, adults rarely address them, except to tell them to fetch something or to run an errand, or to tease them, but pleasantly, or to tell them to go off and play. The last happens not when they stand around and watch but when they interfere in the

255

doings of adults in a fashion which is thought not correct. No Indian adult in my hearing has ever tried to start a conversation with the boys.

After typing these notes I drove into town to wash our clothes at the laundromat. Here I asked the mixedblood Indian lady in charge why the Indian children seemed to do so well in the elementary grades and then—at about age ten—began to do so badly.

She explained that the trouble was that the Bureau teachers did not teach the Indian children to "be competitive." When I asked how a teacher could do this, she said, "The teacher urges each to do better than the others and that's the way they learn—the Bureau teachers don't do that." This explanation was not consistent with the fact that the Indian children in the elementary grades were doing so well with teachers who, so far as I could see, were not making a big thing out of competition.[1]

That evening, while Murray and I were sitting at supper with the GoodHorses, I tried to talk to the boys about how they liked school and their teacher. They were both members of the intermediate (fourth and fifth) grade class which I had found so appalling. One boy admitted shyly that he liked Mrs. Walker, his teacher, but after this remark they both shut up like little clams. While I wondered why the boys treated Mrs. Walker so disrespectfully if they liked her so much, Mrs. GoodHorse broke in with the authoritative statement that both of the boys liked Mrs. Walker but they did not like Mrs. Gruber, who, I had noticed, kept a much more orderly classroom. (Murray and I always conversed with the Indian children in English.)

Five days later I tried to talk over these puzzling phenomena with Walter GoodHorse, our research assistant. But Walter was going through a stage of "explaining" everything by making distinctions between fullbloods and mixedbloods. He told me that fullbloods are suspicious and afraid of white men, that they will not react to anything with which they cannot associate themselves, whereas mixedbloods "go to extremes." Though these statements were made in an impressive tone, they did not clear up anything.

1. The notion of a socially sanctioned but invidious competition *between* members of a group is alien to Indian notions of propriety. But Indians acting as a group enjoy competing with *other* groups. This, however, is another story—though it does have an important bearing on the philosophy of classroom instruction and interaction.

Since talking to people was not proving helpful, I decided to observe more classrooms. Accordingly I went to the Catholic boarding school and to the large elementary day and boarding school that served the town of Thrashing Buffalo. The Catholic school did not seem to suffer at all from a breakdown of communication between students and teacher. But in the town day and boarding school I observed much the same pattern as at the small school at Standing Man. In the elementary class the children were eager and obedient, in the middle grades they tended to be hard to handle, and in the upper grades they tended to be reserved and "withdrawn." But in most classes there were a fair number of white and mixedblood students present, and these responded to the teacher. The result was that most classes did not look too bad. In a few classes taught by skillful teachers even the shyer of the fullblood children seemed to be learning and enjoying it.

These observations and my interviews with the teachers were to prove useful later in the study. But they did not at this time help me to understand what was going on in the classroom at Standing Man.

Next I tried to get some enlightenment from Mr. Anthony, the adult education specialist. Anthony was a trained ethnographer who had lived at Thrashing Buffalo for many years. He spoke the Indian language fluently and he knew more about the Thrashing Buffalo than I could ever hope to learn. When I asked him why the Indian children began to "withdraw from the teachers" in the fourth or fifth grades, he replied, "It's because by then they're beginning to realize that to be an Indian is to be lousy, filthy, and poor. They're beginning to think, 'What the hell!' They see that their teachers are fools." I then asked him why the children in the Catholic mission school did not withdraw in like manner, and he responded, "They discipline them there. If kids don't speak up loud and clear they are punished. They're also given assignments, made to do them, and get a sense of accomplishment. From the earliest grades their education is strictly supervised, with the intent that they will produce."

Mr. Anthony's comments could be seen as a kind of variation on the theme of cultural disharmony: that is, the teachers held a low opinion of the Indian children and the Indian parents' way of life; the children, by age nine or ten, began to sense this, resented it, and withdrew. So I carefully reread my notes and I carefully observed more classes. But try as I might, I could not discover a single instance which showed that the Indian children were aware that their teachers thought poorly of them.

After we had moved away from the GoodHorses into the condemned schoolhouse, we had many more and better opportunities to talk to the schoolchildren. They waited inside our dwelling for the morning school bus and they "visited" us in the afternoon, after the bus had brought them home. At first the children were shy and did not talk much, preferring to play with our typewriters or look through our mail order catalogues. But when Murray asked them how they were getting along in school, almost all replied without hesitation that they liked school, and many said that they liked their teacher. At first we thought they were telling us what they thought we wanted to hear. But the better we came to know them, the more it seemed to us that, insofar as the children talked to us at all, they did so with candor. Then we began to ask them, "Why is it that some kids won't answer the teacher?" and "Why do some kids just go mumble-mumble when the teacher calls on them to read aloud?" and "Why do some kids write such tiny numbers on the blackboard?" Shyly, and with giggles, the children would reply, "They're afraid."

In the manner of people obsessed with a problem, Murray and I discussed this meager response at length. Following the hypothesis about cultural disharmony, we at first tended to assume that when the children said they were afraid, they meant they were afraid of the teacher. But this assumption, we were forced to admit, was not consistent with the fact that so many of the children insisted that they liked the school and that they even liked their teachers. In addition, it did not explain why obedient and unafraid tots of 6, 7, and 8 years of age should turn, at age 9 or 10, into noisy little demons who suddenly became tongue-tied when the teacher asked them to read.

Then Murray and I began to ask the children, "Why are the other kids afraid?" or "What are they afraid of?" Sometimes a particularly bold or friendly child would answer, "They are afraid the other kids will laugh at them," or "They are afraid if they make a mistake they will be teased."

Now we felt we were really getting somewhere. The children were afraid of the other children. But why?

For several weeks we entertained the notion that the children were ashamed of their incompetence in the English language. We knew that adult Indians will not attempt anything unless they are competent, for if they perform clumsily they will be teased mercilessly. Could it be that the children were teasing—and silencing—

each other because they made mistakes in English? Interestingly, we were encouraged in this hypothesis by the most able and intelligent of our Indian research assistants. Mrs. WhiteElk, my interpreter, told me that many adult Indians were "bashful" because their English was so poor. And her brother, Mr. Martin ChargingBear, also emphasized the language difficulty. Here is our discussion as recorded in our notes for early November:

> Martin: Lots of children talk Indian most of the time. The teachers don't understand. They get mad at the kid. The kids in school talk Indian all the time. Sometimes they want to do something and they don't know how to ask. The little kid just knows a few words. He tells the teacher his way and the teacher doesn't understand.
>
> Murray: At Standing Man [day school] I noticed in classes in some of the younger grades that the children stand up and speak out. But when you get to the fifth or sixth grades, the teacher calls on them and they don't want to stand up and speak.
>
> Martin: They're probably afraid to make mistakes. So they don't speak out loud enough. They're afraid to get up, because they're afraid the other kids will laugh at them.
>
> Murray: You mean, if the kids don't know the right answer, the other kids will ridicule them?
>
> Martin: Most of the kids tease each other.
>
> Rosalie: Why do the little kids in the early grades speak up so well?
>
> Martin: They're just noisy. They get that way [quiet and shy] later on. . . . Sometimes kids aren't too good in the English language. He can't put his thoughts down in English. To the little kids it doesn't make any difference who's in the class.
>
> Murray: So it's not so much the whites that look down at him. It's the Indian fullblood children.

I cannot read these notes today without feeling chagrined because I did not recognize that Mr. ChargingBear had given us the answer to our problem when he said: "To the little kids it doesn't make any difference who's in class." If I had been alert I would have asked, "Well, just why does it make so much difference to the bigger ones? After all, the little kids make many mistakes in English too."

During November Mrs. WhiteElk and I worked very hard. We drove long distances every day, interviewing the mothers or grandparents of the children we were observing in class. In my spare time I tried to train Mrs. WhiteElk and several other young Indian matrons to do interviewing on their own.[2] I did not think very much

---

2. The only one of my Thrashing Buffalo trainees to become a really good interviewer was Mrs. Rose WhiteElk. Part of her skill rested on her social sensitivity and conscientiousness. But also important, in my opinion, was the

about the Indian children in the classrooms, especially since most of the Indian women to whom Mrs. WhiteElk and I were talking had never seen their children in class. But the "problem" remained on my mind, for on 26 November I recorded in my notes that Walter had said that he had been talking to a friend of his and that the friend had told him that many Indian pupils lost heart and stopped being interested in school at the moment when they first realized that they did not know English.[3] But I did not think this explanation applied to the children in the elementary schools. They were not learning to speak English, and this fact was both important and disturbing to me. But I could not find the evidence to convince myself or anyone else that the children's realization that they did not now know English was responsible for the dramatic change between the third and the fifth grades.

Sometime in late November, Murray and I left the reservation for a few days to attend the meetings of the American Anthropological Association in Denver. We told several of our colleagues—anthropologists, sociologists, social psychologists, men of great experience and repute—about some of our more striking experiences and observations. Several times I described the bizarre behavior of the children in the classrooms. But our colleagues only shook their heads in amused bewilderment. One man who had worked with Indians said, "Those children must be terribly ashamed."

Then, on 2 December, Mrs. WhiteElk and I made a long trip into a remote district—forty miles on dirt roads, often not more than trails—and found almost nobody at home. Only then did it occur to us that this was tribal business day and that almost everybody in the district had gone to the agency town. One old man, however, told us that one of the local ladies had recently moved into our district and was living in a tent near the Standing Man school. This was Mrs.

---

fact that she was the only one of my trainees who accompanied me on my visits and thus had the opportunity to observe what I said and did. I literally though quite unconsciously *showed* her how to interview. To the other Indian ladies I merely gave careful verbal instructions, and none of them became good interviewers. I do not, however, wish to make too much of this point, because later, when we worked in Ottawa, we found two Indian women who, with only verbal instructions, became excellent interviewers.

3. The friend was right. But this particular awareness, as we were later to learn, did not come until the students left the rural elementary school and entered the high school in the agency town.

Fire, a woman who was rearing and sending through school six orphaned nieces and nephews. So we drove back to Standing Man and, after crawling under several barbed wire fences, we found Mrs. Fire's tent just as she herself was emerging from the nearby outhouse. With an apologetic smile, she asked us to enter her "poor Indian tent." We entered and sat down on blankets folded on the canvas floor.

The inside of the tent was a marvel of organization and order. Along the side, there were narrow mattresses neatly covered by Indian blankets; and in the center there was a polished Franklin stove with a fire inside; and in the corners were trunks and heavy suitcases skillfully stacked. What looked like a change of clothes for three children hung from a clothesline. There was an alarm clock—the first I had seen in any Indian home—a big blue stuffed toy, and even a child's storybook on which stood a worn pair of children's shoes. Only someone who has tried to live in a tent can appreciate the art and skill that had been expended in making this dwelling so pleasant and comfortable.

Mrs. Fire looked like the Indian women in the oldest photographs —gaunt, large boned, broad-faced, and very powerful. As we conversed, Mrs. WhiteElk interpreting, I noticed that she understood English very well but preferred to talk to me in the Indian language. She told me that she had once worked as a cook's helper in the day school and she was now living near the school and helping a relative currently employed as cook.

The interview began well, with Mrs. Fire telling me, in a long and detailed monologue, how well all of her nieces and nephews were doing in school. When she paused for breath, I asked her the first question on our schedule, "Do your nieces and nephews ever learn things at school that make them be disrespectful or mean to you? Do they ever learn things that make you feel sad?" Mrs. Fire took a deep breath, ignored my question, and proceeded with her speech. She told me how her niece, Sally, after having "really liked school" and after having "a perfect attendance record," had unexpectedly been failed by her teacher in the seventh grade. She explained the reasons for Sally's failure in detail. Sally, she said, was a quiet girl, that is, shy and reserved, and "if they get her mad she doesn't talk." Sally was, moreover, very good in arithmetic, and when the pupils exchanged their papers to correct them, the other girls erased their incorrect answers, wrote in Sally's, and took the credit. This,

261

apparently, led to some kind of quarrel or confrontation (which Mrs. Fire did not explain), and the upshot was that Sally's teacher made her repeat the seventh grade and the other girls picked on her. "They pick on her so much that she doesn't want to go to school."

Mrs. Fire continued to turn all my subsequent questions into opportunities to tell me how talented Sally was and how much she wished to learn. Sally, I was told, was learning beadwork, and she loved to bring her books home and study after school. But now their teacher had forbidden the pupils to take their books home (a BIA policy to preserve books and keep them from getting lost).

Now it happened that I had looked at the intelligence and achievement scores of the seventh and eighth grade girls, and I had noticed that Sally possessed a phenomenal ability in arithmetic and mathematics. I could therefore in good conscience tell Mrs. Fire that I was certain that Sally was a very bright girl, and that when I had sat in the class, she had been one of the pupils who genuinely tried to learn. This seemed to reassure Sally's aunt, and since she had talked so much and so fluently about the school, it occurred to me to ask her what it was that made some of the children act so ashamed in class.

She told me in a matter-of-fact way that when she had worked as a cook, she had sometimes gone into the classrooms to watch. At this I really pricked up my ears, for here before me sat the first Indian parent or guardian who had actually watched what went on in a classroom.

> Those children! They didn't have respect for other people or for their teachers! When the other kids tried to read or study, they really made fun of them. . . . It is the other kids that are making fun. They even make fun of the writing. If they make one little mistake in writing, the other kids make fun of them.

Then I asked the question to which no one up to now had been able to give me an answer I found both comprehensible and valid: "Why is it that the fifth, sixth, seventh, and eighth graders are so much more bashful than the little kids in the first, second, and third grades. The little kids aren't afraid to speak out loud." Mrs. Fire smiled and explained how the little children differed from the juveniles:

> The little ones. They're still small. They don't know anything. They don't mind about the other kids making fun. They don't care. But the

other ones in the fifth, sixth, seventh and eighth grades—they are always teasing each other about boyfriends and girlfriends and they make fun of each other. They tease each other and they get more and more bashful. There is too much romancing with them. If a kid is very quiet and likes to study, then they tease him about some girl that he doesn't like. They tease him all the time. Then when the teacher calls on him, he hates to talk because they will make remarks to him. . . . They tease the little ones like this too, but the little ones don't care.

I wish that I could say that, on hearing this straightforward spelling out of the essential data needed for the solution of our problem, I immediately perceived the significance of what was going on in the country day schools. But this was not the case. When I typed up my notes that evening, I did not conclude with an ecstatic "Eureka!" Instead, I put down several very unpleasant and disturbing incidents I had observed of Indian children teasing each other, incidents which, up to that time, I had not had the moral courage to insert in my notes. I suppose that before I could think clearly about what I learned, I had to accept it—that is, accept the fact that Indian children were sometimes very "mean" to each other and that sometimes they were downright cruel. Further, I had to accept the novel fact that, as the situation now stood, it was the children who were successfully sabotaging the process of learning, not because they disliked learning, the school, or the teacher, but as part of the development of their own group discipline.

On the other hand, I realized that what Mrs. Fire had told me was very important, and when, after supper, I told Murray about it and read her words to him, we both began all at once to see that hers was the only explanation that fitted with all we had seen and with all we had been told by the Indians, old or young. As we began to appreciate how "simple" and "clear" the explanation was, and how we had misinterpreted the remarks made by our respondents, we became progressively more euphoric and excited. Had it not been so late at night we might have run round and round the long tables in the old schoolhouse, shouting "We've got it! We've got it!"

Reduced to its bare essentials, the "solution" was that the little Indians, like all little children, were oriented to adults, parents, grandparents, teachers, or older siblings. Thus, when their parents told them to learn, they tried very hard to do what their parents and the teacher told them to do—and during their first years at school they tried so hard that by the fourth grade many were doing better than the white children. When other children tried to tease, interrupt, or "bother" them, they paid no heed. As Mrs. Fire put it, they didn't "care" what the other children did or said. But by the time they reached the age of nine or ten, the "agent of socialization" had shifted from the older person, parent, teacher, or older sibling, to the peer group. Now when the children were teased, especially by their peers, they "cared" very much indeed.[4] The teachers, not understanding the native language, never seemed to catch on to what was going on, and the parents never saw what was going on in the classroom (except in the rare case of Mrs. Fire). In consequence, the peers in the classroom were able, from about the fifth grade on, to do just about as they pleased. And usually, at this age, the suggestions made by the teacher did not please them. By the seventh or eighth grade—without a significant interference or influence from an external authority—the power of the peer group had become almost absolute. Thus, the uncanny and interminable silences to which the students in the upper elementary grades subjected their teachers did not spring from individual "withdrawal," stupidity, shyness, or from a reluctance to study, or from what some investigators have called "hostile dependence" on the white man. They sprang from the extraordinary discipline which the members of the peer group were enforcing on themselves.

Now, for Murray and myself, the Indian parents' insistence that they wanted their children to learn and that they told them to learn, and the Indian children's insistence that they liked school but could not "speak up" because they "were afraid," began to make a kind of glorious sense. As peers, they did like school—for the excellent reason that as peers they could go there, associate with each other, and enjoy themselves.

Murray and I next began to tell each other that what was going on in the day school classrooms was an interesting and extreme variant of what goes on in virtually all classrooms with children of this age. Most children, if permitted to associate with each other, develop peer groups, and all peer groups tend to subvert or get around the authorities placed over them. But no peer group that we had ever seen before was so isolated from meaningful contact

4. Later I learned that "care" has a special connotation in the English dialect spoken on the reservation. It means something like being sensitive and responsive to the feelings and sensitivities of other human beings. Thus, a mother complaining to me about a wild daughter, might say, "I talk to her and I talk to her, but she doesn't even care!"

with adults as were the Indian children in the Standing Man classrooms.

As we proceeded in our discussion, we saw that this explanation was related to the theories of Piaget (though Piaget probably never had to contend with anything as self-contained as the Indian peer group), and we also recalled that the ethnographers who had had the opportunity to study the Plains people had emphasized the importance of the age-grade societies. For centuries the peer group had been the major Plains Indian "agent of socialization," and individuals who did not conform to peer standards were teased or "made fun of." Certainly, as far as behavior in school was concerned, it was from his peers that the young Thrashing Buffalo learned how to behave like an Indian rather than an outsider.

Finally, as sociologists we began to suspect that the phenomena going on in these day schools were very much like those that had been observed in factories and in armies and, subsequently, in urban schools. Wherever an organizational structure imposes one group over another, there is a strong tendency for the subordinate group to develop a private set of understandings concerning the tasks they are supposed to perform and the deference they are supposed to display. In the case of the Indian peer groups, individuals who tried to work too hard or tried to perform their tasks correctly or excellently by the teacher's standards were usually seen as making life hard for their peers.

Working together, we then wrote a rough draft, outlining our interpretation of what we had seen and were continuing to see in the day schools. Week by week we perceived new relationships or hit upon more accurate or vivid ways of expressing what we were observing and coming to understand. We also asked Mrs. WhiteElk to visit the schools, sit in the classrooms, and observe the children in the hallways and on the playground. Mrs. WhiteElk, of course, could not take notes or write English with ease. But she had a superb memory and could give detailed and accurate accounts of what she had seen and what people had said. At first, she dictated as I typed. Then one day I asked her to talk into the dictating machine, and after a few sessions she was able to operate the machine more skillfully than I and could record her observations without my being there. Her observations of the children were in many ways more precise and illuminating than ours, for she understood the children's verbal language and their language of gestures. Moreover, the children, having learned very early that an Indian matron had no authority in the schools, often behaved as if she were not there. Everything she reported tended to support and enlarge our newfound explanation and understanding. The effortless ease with which she perceived the significance of "social actions" among the pupils and the teacher, and the clarity with which she reported it, continue to excite my admiration:

[When the] fourth grade . . . took up reading . . . you can't even hear what they are saying. They held their books right in front of their faces. Mrs. Forrester said [to them], "Put the book down." But they'll be ba-a-a-rely talking! [The] next one gets up and does the same thing. . . . I don't know what's wrong with them. [Listening to them read] I felt like I was deaf. . . . When the fourth grade kids do arithmetic they just *act* dumb. All they do is copy it off from each other. One gets it wrong and then the whole aisle gets it wrong. The teacher gets mad. . . .

In the seventh and eighth grades they were having Reading Skills when I went in—they were reading something called "Atomic Submarines." When she asks them questions about it, I don't see none of them answer. But she says they answer . . . maybe she's a lip reader. Out of the whole room no one made a sound except one boy. He barely whispers to her. He sits in the back of the room. But she says, "That's right. That's right." But I can't hear what they're saying . . . maybe he whispers. . . . When I couldn't see who was answering, I moved to the other side of the room to watch. But even then I couldn't see anybody's lips move. I even watched here (pointing to juncture of jaw bone and skull) because that way you can see if somebody is talking— but nobody moved there. . . . It was just awful. . . . It reminded me of when I went to visit Watson and there were some blind and deaf there. They were quiet but they made signs, and at least you could see them make signs. But in this class they didn't even make signs. . . . It was like she had a room full of dead people and she was trying to talk to them.

At about 11:00 she gave them a three-minute recess. I went and watched them and, boy!—they were really teasing each other. Noisy —like other kids. Three girls had one of the boys down and they were beating him up and he was hollering. They really act different out of the classroom. But when they went back in the room they didn't make no sound.

Do Not Make or Let Other People
Do Your Fieldwork

The astute student will not need to have the more obvious implications of this narrative spelled out for him. Nevertheless, there is one important "moral" which may not be immediately apparent. No matter how many research assistants are available, the head researcher, the person who is going to analyze the material and write the major report, should himself do as much of the interviewing and observation as he possibly can. There were many times when I found sitting in the classrooms or driving many miles to call on Indian mothers so tiring and time-consuming that I was tempted to stay home and busy myself with "analyzing my materials" and letting the younger research assistants do the hard, dirty, and sometimes very depressing legwork. But circumstances forced me to do much of the observation and quasi participation myself. When the time came to write our report, I was intensely grateful that I had done this, for there were all manner of statements and remarks in our field notes (and the fill-in interviews) that we would otherwise have been unable to understand. Somehow, by sitting in so many Indian homes, by talking to so many people in so many different circumstances, Murray and I, consciously and unconsciously, had picked up the cues that helped us to "understand." And we picked up these cues, not through introspection or by extrapolation from someone else's notes, but by remembering what we saw and listening to what we heard.

21 Good Fieldworkers and Good Respondents

Better burden bearest thou nowise
than shrewd head on thy shoulders;
in good stead will it stand among stranger folk,
and shield when unsheltered thou art.
—Old Norse proverb

A number of fieldworkers (Radin, Berreman, Cicourel, Evans-Pritchard) have listed the attributes which, for them, contribute to the making of a good ethnographer: humility, empathy, maturity, energy, determination, fundamental creativity, and so forth. Some students may be encouraged (or discouraged) as they read of these attributes and consider themselves. But to me they communicate very little of the reality of field experience.

In point of fact, the most valuable thing any fieldworker can take with him into the field is good luck. But luck is a gift of the Powers and cannot be acquired by determination or study. The next most useful thing to take into the field is the attribute which the Old Scandinavians called *manvit,* that is, intelligence manifested in common sense, shrewdness, and flexibility—the property called "having one's wits about one."

I cannot tell a student how to acquire or develop wits, but I can tell him this: that if he does not have his wits about him while he is in the field, the chances are that he will not be given the opportunity to exercise any of his other attributes or virtues. To begin with, he will often need better than average wits to get into the area he wishes to study. And he will need even more wits if he finds that he cannot get in. Thus, he may spend months or even years preparing for a particular undertaking, learn a new language, buy equipment, travel halfway around the world, and then find that the authorities will not permit him to enter the area where "his people" are. This happened to Powdermaker in 1929 on her first field trip to New Guinea: she went to study the Mafalu and ended up studying the Lesu. It happened again in 1953 when she prepared to go to Uganda—even learning Swahili—but was detoured to Northern

Rhodesia and ended studying a different people speaking a different vernacular. Equally challenging was the fate of Cornelius Osgood, who, after a long and arduous journey into the Canadian backwoods, found that "his people" had departed on a trek to parts unknown and were not expected back until the end of winter. But perhaps the prize for flexibility should be given to an anthropological colleague who was assured of a grant to study Africa, only to find, at the last moment, that because of a misunderstanding between fund granting foundations no funds at all had been set aside for African studies. Overnight he prepared an application to conduct a study in Rarotonga, and he was given a grant. But when he got to Rarotonga, the authorities refused to admit him, and he was obliged once again to shift the location of his study—this time to Samoa.

If the student manages to arrive somewhere "in the field," he will immediately be obliged to exercise his wits in finding suitable living and working quarters. In most field situations this will take far more time and ingenuity than he has allowed for. It is also likely to involve some very significant compromises. Ideally, of course, the nature of the fieldworker's research problem ought to determine where and with whom he eats, sleeps and works. If he plans to observe child-rearing practices, he must live with the people or, at least, do a great deal of informal home visiting. If he plans only to collect folktales or distribute fill-in questionnaires, he may prefer to live outside the community. In reality, however, his living quarters are often determined by all manner of conditions or powers over which he has little control. The mine officials in Northern Rhodesia would not hear of Powdermaker's residing in the African miners' compound. Similarly, in the Tule Lake center the authorities permitted no one but "disloyal" Japanese Americans to live in the evacuee quarters. Powdermaker tells us that in her study of a Mississippi town she was almost stopped before she started, because the boarding houses for whites asserted that they had no room for her and she knew that the whites would not allow her to live in a Negro home.[1] Evans-Pritchard reports that the Azande would not think of letting him live with them, whereas the Nuer would tolerate him only if he did what amounted to letting them live with him. In many very poor rural and urban areas a fieldworker will have to cope with a differ-

---

1. Powdermaker's (1966:138–42.) account of her first day in Indianola is a fine description of a fieldworker using his wits.

ent type of problem. Nobody may care very much where he lives, but the poverty is so great and housing so hard to come by that every possible space is occupied. Even thirty years ago, when Whyte did his study of a Boston slum, the district was so overcrowded "that a spare room was practically nonexistent" ([1943] 1955:294). We could not at first find so much as an unoccupied chicken coop on the Thrashing Buffalo reservation (except in the agency town, where we did not wish to reside). Having anticipated this, we brought tenting equipment with us. Nonetheless, finding and establishing a suitable relationship with a congenial Indian landlord in a suitable location consumed weeks of time and energy—a contingency for which we were not prepared. We would have encountered a similar problem—complete absence of vacant housing—among the poor rural Indians of Ottawa. Indeed, I would wager that it is almost always harder to find living space among the poor than among the well-to-do. The exasperating, depressing, and exhausting experiences that await the fieldworker who tries to "live with" a nomadic people have been superlatively described by Doughty. These difficulties are compounded when a nomadic or nomadic-hunting people have been deprived of most of their economic subsistence and are faced with the total obliteration of their society. Fieldwork under these latter conditions can be one of the most desperate and heartbreaking experiences in which a human being can involve himself.[2]

A good store of solid common sense also provides an antidote to the excess ideological baggage which some students carry with them into the field. For example, some fieldworkers seem to believe that there is something peculiarly professional in living under the most harsh or the most difficult conditions, something innately admirable in being able to "take it." Young people with this disposition might remind themselves that they may be indulging their masochistic or pseudoheroic tendencies at the expense of their professional obligations. They are in the field to get a piece of work done and develop an understanding of their hosts, not to establish a record of personal suffering or determine the limits of their endurance. Besides, most field trips provide many unanticipated tests of character and fortitude, even when the fieldworker tries to lives as comfortably as possible.

In my first field trip to the Gila center I deliberately subjected

2. See, for example, Maybury-Lewis's account of his fieldwork among the Sherente and Shavante of Brazil.

myself to a great deal of gratuitous suffering, and for several months I lived in a physical situation considerably more uncomfortable than that of most of the evacuees. This self-torment may have been my way of forcing myself into the shifting of mental gears necessary to see the people and their situation as they really were. But it was also based on the childish and patronizing delusion that the Japanese Americans ought to trust me because I was living under conditions as uncomfortable as theirs. I would have done better to live in the tolerable discomfort of the WRA women's barracks—which, God knows, were bad enough—while reminding myself every day that I was there of my own free will and that the Japanese Americans were not.

Another common impulse for which the fieldworker might well substitute good horse sense is the disposition of male fieldworkers to prove their manhood before the men of the host society. I stress this point at the specific request of my husband. Like many other in-experienced fieldworkers he assumed that any man in good physical condition ought to be able to participate in at least some of the men's activities. Indeed, this is what the unreflective advocates of "participant observation" assert that a fieldworker ought to do. But Murray found that such seemingly simple tasks as digging a post hole required some know-how, special muscles, and much practice. Urbanite that he was, he also found that Indian boys, six or seven years old, rode spirited horses with ease, but that he could not even get a gentle horse to start walking. And though he had done modern dance exercises regularly for years, he found the Indian style of dancing taxing of his endurance. Fate finally gave him the oppor-tunity to display his physical prowess when we went swimming in the local reservoir with some Indian friends. The Indians, male and female, paddled about modestly, admiring Murray's spectacular aquatic feats. Alas, no one told him that all the outhouses for miles around drained into this reservoir; and, within a few days he came down with fever and dysentery which robbed him of weeks of work-ing time. I suspect that it was the same impulse that led Maybury-Lewis (1965:85–88) to participate in the Sherente log racing, even though he might easily have fallen and broken a limb, and, as he remarks, "a broken limb on the Gurgilho . . . well, it did not bear thinking about."

After several disconcerting experiences, Murray learned that most of the Indians had defined him as a middle-aged man of wealth and substance, a "teacher," and in any case, a white man. Nobody expected that he be skillful in any of the activities of the local menfolk. It was enough that he show respect for these activities, be reasonably friendly, unpretentious, and courteous, and perform such neighborly acts as letting Indian neighbors use the telephone or helping them to go to town or to the hospital when their cars had broken down. This was how "a man of his age" was supposed to behave. So long as he paid for any services he asked, most adults were willing to consider him an asset to the community rather than a liability, and most of the older men were pleased to engage in long and solemn discussions of the plight of the Indians and of what they thought of education. With the young men, the "warriors," Murray was rarely able to talk openly, because they "respected" him, which meant that in his presence they were supposed to listen rather than speak. Besides, school and education were not popular topics of discussion among young or active Indian men. They belonged to the realm of children, and only women or aged and responsible men talked much about the children.

When I suggest that a fieldworker should not seek out ways to make himself uncomfortable and that he should have the common sense to realize that he (or she) cannot be anything but a clumsy and doltish participant in most of the traditional activities of his hosts, I am not suggesting that he should not try to live as closely and intimately with the people he is studying as he can stand and they will permit. Trying to live with the GoodHorses was one of the most enlightening experiences of our lives. Had we not made the attempt to participate in country Indian life, we would never have come to appreciate the cultural and social skills necessary to live it or, more concretely, to appreciate that singing Indian-style, making frybread, or washing clothes over an open fire may require as much practice and experience as writing a journal article or playing a good game of bridge.

How Do I Get My Respondents?

The inclination to talk and listen to as many different people as he can is one of the essential traits of the really good fieldworker. Indeed, the scrupulous fieldworker makes a conscious effort and, if need be, forces himself to talk to the people whom he dislikes, mistrusts, or despises (or who dislike, mistrust, or despise him) and, in like manner, he listens to and tries to understand the things he does not want to hear. He does this because, the more numerous and varied are the people with whom he talks, the greater is the possibility that he will learn to understand the whole situation thoroughly and accurately and the better will be his final analysis and report. In my own fieldwork I sometimes fell short of this goal, and my work suffered. For example, at the Gila center I might have saved myself weeks of blundering, had I listened to and pondered the words of a paunchy and coarse-spoken policeman, who, I privately decided, could not possibly understand the Japanese because he was an uneducated man (see chap. 5). I did considerably better at Thrashing Buffalo, and the reader will note (chap. 20) that it was from an unemployed cook's helper that I finally learned to understand the classroom behavior of the Indian juveniles.

When all is said and done, a fieldworker is usually obliged to talk to all manner and variety of people. There are administrators, teachers, missionaries, the police, storekeepers, people who want jobs, local sharpies, and inside dopesters. Any and all of these have developed devices for dealing with or exploiting fieldworkers and other visitors. The fieldworker can learn from all of these folk once he has come to understand their vested interests and the roles they play in the community. He should resist the temptation to tune them out because they do not conform to his prejudged notion of the genuine or the typical "native."

In the course of his career a fieldworker is likely to meet some respondents with whom he can develop a profound relationship of mutual assistance and trust. This relationship is one that the fieldworker never forgets and, in my experience, the respondent does not forget either. In the Japanese centers I was helped by several such respondents, and we continue to correspond to this day. Without the assistance of Rose WhiteElk, my work at Thrashing Buffalo would have been meager and superficial. She guided me to every home in the district where children of school age lived—and her guidance was essential since many homesteads could be reached only by wagon trail. She knew the etiquette which would get us both admitted to the house, and she soon learned to interpret or rephrase my questions with skill and tact. When we met responses or phenomena which neither of us could understand or explain, she would find some informed or experienced person to help us. She did all she could to further our study, without offending any member of her community or injuring her own status in it.

273

But to apostrophize a superb helper and friend is one thing: to tell a student where and how to find one is another. These relationships, like genuine friendships, are unpredictable and cannot be created or "developed" by effort or intellect. On the other hand, the fieldworker, like any other human being, can increase his chances of finding a great respondent by making himself available. And he does this by trying all manner of avenues and talking to all manner of people.

How Can I Do Fieldwork without Hurting People?

The problem of how to live without hurting other people or other living beings has moral complications and profundities which, so far as I know, no one has been able to resolve. Personally, I cannot even say with Powdermaker or Hughes that I tried never to hurt anyone while I was in the field, for at Tule Lake I deliberately and successfully tried to injure the man who had beaten my friend. But on a more practical level I may point out that the fieldworker's concern over hurting his respondents is sometimes a device for concealing his own embarrassment or shyness. He may be genuinely afraid of hurting the strangers he is going to approach, but he is also afraid (and this is something he is less inclined to admit to himself) that they will hurt him—by rebuffing him or telling him to peddle his papers elsewhere. Indeed, I have in recent years been amazed and amused by the resistance which some graduate students in sociology and anthropology offer to the suggestion that they try to conduct a formal or an informal interview. Three students known to me became so nervous at the prospect of approaching the residents of an old people's home that they spent their first "interviewing session" driving around the home observing it through binoculars.

There are certain periods, particularly in the first and most difficult stage of fieldwork, when a fieldworker's overblown sense of his ability to offend or injure his hosts may so paralyze him that he cannot carry on with his work. This is especially likely to happen if he has been led to expect that everything will go well and finds, instead, that everything is going very badly.

In Gila, for example, my first attempts to approach and talk to people were so fruitless and depressing that I found myself wincing inwardly whenever I tried to initiate a conversation. At Thrashing Buffalo, after Murray and I had fled the GoodHorse abode, we were so shaken in our confidence in the Indians (and in ourselves) that we spent about two weeks doing little but debate whether or not we ought to ask some Indian elder for advice. In this case we were not afraid of hurting the Indians but afraid of hurting ourselves, for what we feared was that our overtures to Indian elders or other Indian families would be interpreted by the Indian community as white man's treachery toward the GoodHorses. In our innocence we did not realize that most of the Indians would interpret our leaving the GoodHorses as a sign that we were beginning to get some sense.

In each case, the cure for the paralysis lay in hitting upon and trying a radically new tactic, or, in realizing, as Pauline Kael puts it ([1965]1966:22) that a mistake in judgment is not necessarily fatal but that too much anxiety about judgment is. In Gila I gave up trying to follow my employer's instructions to behave like a participant observer and began, instead, to initiate a number of formal-looking investigations. Gradually some people accepted me as a person, and I was able to become a quasi participant (see chap. 5). At Thrashing Buffalo, it was Murray who shook us out of our paralysis by risking everything (as we saw it) on a visit to Mr. ChargingBear.

At Thrashing Buffalo we were also helped a great deal by discussing our fears or anxieties with outsiders: in one case, with a young anthropologist who knew something of the district; in another, with an experienced police officer. The advice we received was sometimes excellent (as when the police officer suggested that we talk over our problems with the local Indian police), and sometimes it was only fair. But the opportunity to express our fears—to bring them into the air—was enough to show us that most of them were baseless and to raise our morale to the point where we regained something like our normal initiative and judgment.

PART FOUR

Fieldwork among the Six Friendly Tribes, 1966-1967

22   A Difficult Beginning

Very few fieldworkers have written detailed accounts of field experiences which turned out so badly that they could be called total or partial "failures." Offhand, I can recall only the accounts by Diamond of how he was forced to leave Nigeria and by Powdermaker of her difficulties in studying the motion picture industry. (I do not count Evans-Pritchard's tribulations among the Nuer, because I would judge this an extremely difficult rather than an abortive or unlucky situation.) Practically and theoretically, the disinclination to discuss failures is unfortunate, because it would be useful to know how and why a particular community or group rejected a particular researcher. It would also be useful to know under what conditions a researcher was not able to accomplish his proposed aims and objectives, how he found himself blocked; whether he had to give up completely, or whether he found some way to circumvent his difficulties. And finally, it might strengthen the morale of inexperienced fieldworkers to know that many attempts at research turn out badly and some turn into total flops. Perhaps the true professional is characterized, not by his one grand success but by his ability to transcend a resounding failure and keep on with his work.

It is, then, as something of a pioneer that I begin the account of our research on American Indians in the public schools. During the course of this project almost everything went wrong: the institutions that funded and sponsored us made errors; the power groups that feared our project and tried to eject us made errors; our research assistants made errors; and we made errors. Worst of all, none of these errors turned out to be "lucky mistakes" in the sense that they forwarded or improved the nature of the research. After seven or eight months the situation was so messy and looked so hopeless that Murray and I were ready to drop the whole business and move our research project to another location. The major reason we stayed and stuck it out to the end was that we were asked to do so by two of our Indian assistants.

Why We Undertook the Research
One of the results of our field experience at Thrashing Buffalo was a strong determination to undertake another field trip. For

279

though I had complained loudly and even profanely while we lived on the reservation, I had enjoyed myself and was quite ready to repeat the experience. During 1963 and the spring of 1964 we seriously considered going to Africa. But since foundations and government agencies were cutting back their appropriations for research in the areas that interested us most, we received little encouragement. In August of 1964 we moved to Midwest University, and, as we took up our teaching duties, we continued to scout about for an interesting research project. Indeed, Murray felt that it would be useful to his department (sociology) and to the university if he were able to launch a fair-sized research program as soon as possible.

We had, in part, been drawn to Midwest by the fact that one of our best and oldest friends, Bill James, was working in a town only a half-day's drive from the university. Murray and I had moved our base of operations four times in three years, and that kind of life is hard on friendships. The prospect of living within driving distance of someone who talked the same academic dialect and with whom we had shared many experiences was very attractive. After we moved to Midwest, we visited Bill and his family several times, talked over the old days, played records, watched TV with his children, read each other's current manuscripts, and discussed the ins and outs of social science as we saw them.

Bill at this time was working as field director of the Lincoln Cross-cultural Project, sponsored by the Metropolis University. A major aim of the project (according to Bill) was to help the ten thousand or so Indians who spoke Gokachi to become literate in their own language. At the time these people were literate neither in English nor Gokachi, and their economic situation was one of extreme depression. If they became literate in Gokachi, the project sponsors argued, this might serve as a stimulus to increase their knowledge of the larger world and give them the impetus to try to cope with it. In any case, the project seemed to be going pretty well: its offices were located at a state teachers' college; its staff included a specialist in American Indian languages who was engaged in the preparation of a Gokachi primer; and it had begun to conduct a radio program in Gokachi directed at the local community.

Some time during the fall of 1964, Murray and I decided that if nothing more interesting offered itself, we could do worse than study the Indians in the area where Bill was working. We surmised that we could easily get such a project funded, and we anticipated that the situation would be interesting and the living conditions reasonably comfortable. I liked the idea of living in a college town, close both to open country and to lakes with plenty of fish. Both of us felt that since we had made one intensive study of Indians in Bureau and boarding schools, we were now in a good position to make a comparative study of Indians in public schools. Moreover, in this particular area, with a reasonably competent staff, we could study and compare the Indians' situation in school in rural areas, in small towns, and in an urban center.

We were less sanguine about coping with the political power structures of the area, for we had lived for six years in the South (four in Florida and two in Georgia) and we knew that the organizations that control these regions do not welcome any but establishment-oriented or -directed research. Still, we had managed to live in the South for a long time as teachers and observers, and we knew a great deal more about the people and the general social structure than do most Northerners.

In earlier years we had seen and heard just enough about the Indian power structure to baffle and confuse us. We knew that among the most powerful of the Indian politicians were the chiefs of the Six Friendly Tribes, who, we had been told, were appointed by the president of the United States. The most influential of these appointed chiefs was Bayard Mayard, who in 1964 was chief of the Gokachi tribe and a major executive of one of the nation's great industrial corporations. We had first met Mayard in the summer of 1959, when Murray and I were directing a workshop for American Indian college students. I had invited Mayard to lecture to the students (he being at that time a member of a prominent national commission reviewing Indian affairs). Mayard complied with polished grace and modesty, addressing the Indian students as if they, as Indians, were worthy of regard and respect. I remember thinking that if many of the wealthy and powerful men in our country were as decent and intelligent as Mayard, and so willing to devote their time to helping the abused and underprivileged, the U.S.A. must be in pretty good shape. The next summer, however, when we encountered Mayard at the American Indian conference in Metropolis, his role as Principal Chief of the Gokachi tribe began to puzzle us. At this conference Mayard kept in the background, taking no part in the discussions and behaving as if he were not a delegate (as was proper, since he had chosen not to be). But those who were the delegates of the Gokachis and who were therefore Mayard's colleagues (or subordinates) grabbed the rostrum as soon as the conference opened. Looking and speaking like something out of the more outlandish pages of Mark Twain, they then proceeded to use their skill at parliamentary procedure to bully and befuddle the other less-experienced Indian delegates. Whenever a delegate proposed a recommendation that was the least bit radical, a member of the Gokachi delegation would rephrase the motion, so that the people who did not know English well would find themselves voting for the alternative they wished really to vote against. When this device did not work, the Gokachi delegates insisted loudly that "we Indians don't have the right to make that kind of a recommendation." Finally, some young Indians did venture to stand up and assert that Indians were being treated very badly in many areas of the United States and that the federal government should be told about this. For a moment I thought that these young folk, because they understood parliamentary procedure and the English language, would be able to cope with the experienced politicians on the rostrum. But Lloyd Spear, one of the Gokachi delegates, managed to put through a motion that the young people would not be permitted to speak until the last day. Finally, when the young people did speak, the Gokachi delegates, who were still dominating the rostrum, assumed expressions of horror and disgust. Lloyd Spear implied that the young people were communists, and he hinted broadly that dire punishment would fall on people who thought and spoke as they did. In embarrassed bewilderment most of the older Indians turned their eyes away from the scene. The conference ended in pitiful fashion, with the assembled body sending the usual inoffensive and ingratiating suggestions to the president of the United States.

I became very angry watching this drama, and at one point I went up to Mayard and asked him just what these jackasses from his neck of the woods were up to. But he only looked pained and implied, in an urbane and courteous way, that he was not responsible. (Subsequently we were told that Spear and the other Gokachi delegates were not elected by the Gokachi but were appointed by Mr. Mayard. Thus, it could have been argued that as nonrepresentatives they had no right even to participate in the conference, much less dominate it.)

I suppose that if we had realized that this Gokachi "Establish-ment" would immediately define us as enemies and that they were prepared to do everything in their power to keep us (or any other researchers whom they could not control) out of the areas for which they saw themselves responsible, we would not have under-taken the study—at least not in the open, naïve fashion we did. But we did not know this.

We visited Bill again during the Christmas holidays of 1964, and he was as cordial and helpful as ever. While he did warn us that Lloyd Spear and other members of the Six Friendly Tribes Estab-lishment had tried to make trouble for the Lincoln Project, he also implied that he himself had the situation well in hand. At the same time he warned use emphatically that, in the event of our getting the grant, we should be very careful to notify Mayard and the various political and educational authorities, telling them who we were, who was sponsoring and funding the project, and what type of research we intended to do. Otherwise, he told us, these officials would re-gard us with a great deal of fear and suspicion. Accordingly, Murray went diligently to work, framed a proposal calling for three years of research, and on 22 February 1965 he submitted it to the Office of Education. If funded, we anticipated beginning our fieldwork about the beginning of February 1966.

Meanwhile, our implication in and commitment to Indian educa-tion continued to grow. In March, Murray participated in a Wen-ner-Gren-sponsored conference on the Sioux held at the University of Chicago. Subsequently, he delivered a lecture on Indian educa-tion in a sequence of taped presentations assembled by one of the centers associated with the University of Minnesota. We were also invited by the Head Start program of the Office of Economic Op-portunity to serve as consultants in regard to programs and research proposals on Indian education.

THE FUN BEGINS

On 26 June 1965 we received informal notification from the Office of Education that our research proposal had been accepted. This was the first step in an elaborate bureaucratic song and dance that would have been comic—had it not been happening to us. For the telegram specifically stated, "Please do not release any informa-tion till a contract has been signed." This tied our hands so far as

283

publicizing the nature of our research and its sponsorship, whereas the one thing Bill James had specifically warned us about was not to try to begin this research without thoroughly publicizing its nature and the institutions that sponsored it. Month followed month and the contract was not negotiated. Now we began to worry not only about our inability to publicize the project but because—if we were to begin work on 1 February—we had to hire personnel, and we could not honorably hire personnel until the contract had been negotiated.

In the fall Murray went to Washington on other business and tried to arrange a negotiation, but he was told that, since such negotiations had been transferred to a special division of the Office of Education, the arrangements could not be carried out at that time. He was also told to relax and wait for Washington to contact him. More time passed, and we became more and more concerned, because, in anticipation of the research, Murray was not scheduled to teach during the coming year, and if the contract were not negotiated, we would be in a very awkward economic situation.

The one encouraging happening of this period was that Dr. Elsie Reed, who at that time was an assistant professor in the department of Anthropology at Midwest, consented to work on the project with us. Dr. Reed had done field work in Africa and had also done some research in education. To obtain a professional assistant of this caliber and experience was most reassuring. We tentatively decided that Dr. Reed would observe a hill-country or rural Indian day school and interview the parents in the area, whereas Murray and I would live in a town, study both day and high schools, and talk to the Indian pupils, their parents, and their teachers. We also, of course, hoped to hire a number of Indian research assistants, and we reasoned that Bill James, who had been working in the area for several years, would be able to recommend some competent young people.

Finally, late in November, Murray prevailed upon the dean of research administration at Midwest University to correspond with high officials in the Department of Health, Education, and Welfare. This brought a response instructing Murray that the Contracts and Construction Division, under a new ruling, now required a budget itemized in more detail than that already submitted for the next fiscal year, together with a parallel description of proposed project activities. After our research experience at Thrashing Buffalo, this request had something of the flavor of *Catch 22*. We knew all too well that no honest person could contract to do any specific kind of research in an alien community. Or, as Murray put it, "To prepare a detailed and itemized budget requires that one envisage a precise and predictable future, whereas the essence of good and honest ethnographic research is flexibility." In order then to prepare an itemized budget Murray was forced to project a fantasy of what would be practicable and useful to be doing with an idealized staff, and then to estimate what this would cost, month by month, when, in fact, he knew all the time that in all probability most of this elaborate structure was a delusion. The situation would not be what he expected it to be; the staff would have talents different from those he had anticipated; the subjects would have strong ideas of their own; and the research would inevitably be led into channels which neither he nor anyone else could foresee. Nevertheless, Murray went manfully to work and complied with every detail, struggling with the calendar year (which determines OASI payments), the university calendar year (which determines salary rates and the most convenient times for personnel to enter or leave the project activity), and the federal fiscal year (by which totals must be computed in order to be fitted to federal accounting systems). Since he was teaching full time, he was obliged to work on the budget at night and on weekends, and it was not until 23 December that the exasperating and somewhat degrading documents were completed and mailed to Washington.

During the Christmas vacation of December 1965, Murray and I once again visited Bill, this time with the intention of picking locations for the project research and finding a dwelling for ourselves. We had specified in our research proposal that we would work at three locations: a rural, Gokachi-speaking community; an urban metropolitan area which contained an Indian enclave; and finally some point demographically in between.

But on this trip we found Bill James much changed in mood. His project, as he told us, was being vigorously attacked by Lloyd Spear and other members of the Six Friendly Tribes Establishment, who were calling Bill and his employees radicals, troublemakers, and communists.

Bill did, however, recommend that we hire two of his Indian assistants, Arthur Braveheart and Soobey Fields, both of whom had worked on Bill's project. Arthur was a college graduate and had written some brilliant essays on the situation and plight of American Indian youth. For the past semester he had been teaching American history at an Indian boarding school. He was, moreover, passionately devoted to improving the situation of the Indians. As a youth he had been one of the finest Indian dancers in the United States. With this background we thought that he would be able to do fine work interviewing Indian high school students and that he would make an excellent classroom observer. Arthur, on the other hand, seemed hesitant about working for us, and Bill explained that he probably felt that he could not perform the kind of work we would require. Murray, however, laid this to Indian modesty, and when Arthur later wrote Murray a letter accepting the position, we were very happy about it.

Murray hired Soobey Fields because Bill recommended him as one of the few Gokachi who could serve as a competent interpreter —from English to Gokachi and from Gokachi to English. Soobey, Bill told us, was the ceremonial leader of one of the pagan congregations that held their ancient rites at nighttime on "stomp-grounds" deep in the forested hills. Soobey was also serving as radio announcer on the Gokachi-language program sponsored by Lincoln Project. At first meeting, Soobey impressed us as a reserved and intelligent man, considerably more mature than Arthur.

We also at this visit decided on the Sherwood district as the one in which it might be best for Dr. Reed to work, for Bill indicated that it would probably be the least difficult rural area for a strange researcher. First of all, the school principal, Verne Waters, seemed to be a man of distinctly more liberal outlook than the usual rural school principal. Waters had, in recent years, fought hard to maintain the independent rural school systems in the face of pressures coming from the state education establishment to consolidate all schools. Murray was heartily in favor of picking a school with a good principal, since he felt that it would be easy to find a rural school where the principal was both ignorant and authoritarian and where nothing educational was being accomplished. What Murray wanted to find out was not how bad a school could be but what could be done for Indian children in a classroom under relatively normal circumstances. The second reason we chose the Sherwood district was that it was an area in which Soobey Fields had a great deal of influence. Soobey, we anticipated, would be able to help Dr. Reed become acquainted with the parents of the school children.

Nonetheless, we continued to feel uncomfortable because we knew that we should inform the various local tribal and educational administrators that we planned to do a particular type of educational study funded by the Office of Education through Midwest University. We knew that it would make a very bad impression if we appeared unheralded and announced that we were going to study the schools. But we had been told by the Office of Education that we were not to announce our study *until* the contract was negotiated, and the contract was still not negotiated. Accordingly, in late December of 1965 Murray wrote to Bayard Mayard, conveying the news of our forthcoming research. At the same time he asked the dean of the School of Education at Midwest University to send parallel notices to high-ranking educational officials in the area and, particularly, to the state superintendent of education. Mayard's response was dated 6 January, and was brief but cordial. He expressed willingness to talk to us about the project and to recommend others with whom we might meet. Murray did not accept this invitation, and this may have been his first major error. He underestimated the degree of Mayard's interest and interpreted the note as a formal gesture rather than an insistent invitation; also, he reasoned that he would be able to talk to Mayard more sensibly and knowledgeably after he had done some preliminary fieldwork. Mayard probably wanted to find out what Murray expected to do, and he probably wanted to let Murray know what was expected of him. Mayard's suggestions would have provided valuable information, and Murray might also have come away from such a talk with a reasonably accurate picture of what we were up against.

We passed the month of January in a state of acute discomfort. Week followed week, and we heard nothing from Washington. Whenever we went to a faculty meeting or social gathering, we were asked whether we had heard anything. Sometimes Murray answered these questions with jokes, and he gave even me the impression that he was not worried. Whatever happened, he implied, he would be able to cope with it.

In January of 1966 the university received a telegram that constituted an official acceptance of the research proposal. However, it authorized Murray to proceed for not more than forty-five days and spend not more than four thousand dollars. Murray coped with this new development by writing an irate letter to the Deputy Associate Commissioner for Research in Education. This letter brought some action, for on 4 February the university received the draft of a year's contract, with instructions to review and execute. Thus encouraged, Murray arranged to have our staff of three research assistants begin work, figuring that, if everything fell through, we could still pay their back salaries out of our own pockets. We ourselves, at this time, planned to move to Ottawa about mid-February, as soon as the contract was settled. However, the draft of the contract received by the university proved to be incorrect, for though it authorized the project to continue for a full year—till January of 1967—it authorized funds only for five months—till June of 1966. The Dean of Research caught the error, and a lengthy process of correction began. It was not until 15 April, two and a half months after the project had begun, that we received what we took to be a correct year's contract, and heaved sighs of relief. By this time, of course, we were in the thick of our field activities.

As it turned out, Murray and I did not move to Ottawa until 4 March. This delay occured because we received a second offer to participate in an assessment of Head Start programs on the Thrashing Buffalo reservation. I spoke against our accepting this assignment (and delaying the Gokachi project) because we still had ahead of us the unpleasant job of packing, renting our house in Midwest, moving, and finding a house in Ottawa. Besides, I was worried about leaving three research assistants—two of them with no experience in interviewing—to work for so long without advice and support. So I suggested that Murray consult Bill James about the matter, anticipating that Bill would tell us to come to Ottawa immediately. But Bill suggested that Murray go to Thrashing Buffalo, pointing out that a clear connection with Head Start or OEO would make a favorable impression on the local politicians. Bill also said that he would keep an eye on Arthur and Soobey and that Elsie Reed was getting along very well. The upshot was that Murray and Bill's assistant, Rudy Nimmermehr, went to Thrashing Buffalo while I stayed in Midwest, packing and making moving arrangements. This final delay left us with no time at all to find a place to live, and since Ottawa is a college town and we arrived after the start of the semester, housing space was almost nonexistent. We ended up in a vast, ancient dwelling from which the furnace and all the gas heaters had been removed and in which the water pipes had been permitted to freeze (and break) in the previous winter. We had the pipes repaired at least six times and, after each repair, we would once again hear the ominous trickles from beneath the floor. After about six weeks this subterranean sound of water got on my nerves, and I began to feel as if I were living in the House of Usher. One day the electric wiring acted up, and vast blue sparks flew out of the refrigerator. On another day, after a storm, half the plaster in our bedroom and the upstairs hall fell down. Moreover, all the screens and several of the windows were broken, and the roof leaked badly in half a dozen places. But in time we got everything essential repaired, and after we had put a great deal of money into stoves, screens, and plumbing, our landlady (the town banker's wife), put on a new roof. After this we lived in reasonable comfort, though Arthur and Soobey were clearly puzzled that people of our status and income would be willing to live in so ancient a dump, use shabby second-hand furniture, and drive about in a modest car.

23   The First Six Weeks

For all our trials about the contract, the first six weeks we spent in Ottawa were the happiest that we have ever spent in the field. While Arthur and Soobey had not worked particularly well in our absence, they were obviously intelligent and able men, and we felt that they would be able to do very good work if they set their minds to it. Elsie Reed was comfortably settled in the Sherwood community (having rented a small farmhouse belonging to the school principal) and was making daily observations of the local rural school.

Murray and I spent a great deal of time explaining the practical aspects of research to Arthur and Soobey, instructing and advising them how to proceed with their interviewing and, in Arthur's case, with classroom observation. Murray went with Arthur to talk with the school principals, and we both did our best to encourage him to talk to the high school and junior high school students, to observe what went on in the schools, and to write up his observations in detail. Arthur went to the classrooms and he talked to some of the teachers, but his reports were more like poems than like field data. They provided us with a poignant picture of how he felt, and how he was repelled by what he saw and heard, but they rarely provided us with a quotable or insightful picture of what anybody else had said or done. Indeed, Arthur seemed to have difficulty in "taking the role of the other," and within a few weeks I began to suspect that, though he was an Indian, born and bred in the state, he really knew less about how to talk to the local teachers and the Gokachi high school students than I did.

During these months Arthur produced about one-third or one-fourth of the amount of written reports we had expected of him. Yet some of his remarks and observations were so shrewd and so eloquent that I tried, week after week, to think of some way to make clearer and more comprehensible my instructions about interviewing and class observation. I could not understand why a man who had so much charisma and political astuteness—and could express himself so well—could not learn how to conduct a better-than-average interview. In all I spent about three months on this task. I even observed classes myself and showed him how it was done and what I had written. Then one day I gave his wife—a quiet young woman who had sometimes sat by with her child while Arthur and I talked—an interview schedule and a few words of advice. Forthwith she brought me several interviews that were better than any Arthur had done.

In a number of other respects Arthur was an asset to the project. He knew a great deal about local Indian politics, and on a number of occasions he gave us excellent advice. He was, in addition, intelligent and witty, and his written work—what he did of it—was vivid, expressive, and moving.

I did no better when I tried to help Elsie Reed with her interviewing of Indian mothers. I discussed problems, approaches, and techniques, gave her the schedules I was using in Ottawa, and asked her to read the interviews I had conducted with the schedules. The interviews she produced were fairly good, but, like Arthur and like Walter GoodHorse at Thrashing Buffalo, she seemed to find it very difficult to approach and converse with the people we wanted her to talk to—in this case, the mothers of the Gokachi school children. After a few weeks of trying, she confessed that she hated to do interviewing of any kind and that she could not stomach approaching strangers and asking them questions. Eventually Dr. Reed hired a Gokachi matron as an interviewer, and the Indian lady obtained numerous excellent interviews, though she had no formal training in the social sciences. Unfortunately, Dr. Reed did not accompany the Gokachi matron and participate in the interviews, again, I suspect, because she felt that she would be intruding. This made it difficult for her to develop the depth of "understanding" which, when all is said and done, is the primary reason for doing fieldwork.

Soobey Fields proved to be a total washout. I have remarked that we had hired him because he was a ceremonial (or stomp dance) leader and had considerable following in the community in which Dr. Reed intended to work; we assumed that he could help (or harm) her efforts a good deal. We had also hired him because, according to Bill James, he was one of the very few first-rate Gokachi interpreters. We anticipated that he would teach us Gokachi and that each week he would himself interview a few of the poor Gokachi families.

For about two weeks Soobey gave us lessons in Gokachi, and he seemed genuinely surprised at how fast and how well we learned.

Then he began to cancel appointments and after a few weeks he did not even bother to cancel them. His interviewing was equally unimpressive. He blithely ignored Murray's repeated instructions that he write down his respondent's answers. Once a week or so, he would turn up and give us verbally two or three tantalizing vignettes about things that the Gokachi speakers had told him. Murray then provided Soobey with a tape recorder so that he could at least dictate the responses. But though he assured us that he was working hard, he never gave us any tapes. (Indeed, I think we never got the recorder back.) We sent Arthur out to interview with him, but Arthur reported that Soobey deliberately kept the entire conversation in Gokachi, so that Arthur felt very uncomfortable. Then we ourselves went out to call on Gokachi families with Soobey, but he refused to function as an interpreter and tried to keep all of the conversation in Gokachi. Finally, Murray and I began to ask the Gokachi respondents questions in English and found that some of the younger people present spoke English moderately well and were quite willing to answer our questions. We also felt that the older people present would not have minded at all, had Soobey translated their remarks for us.

When Murray told Bill James that Soobey was not doing any work, Bill did not appear surprised. "What do you expect?" he said, "This is the South." Bill then explained that Soobey was a kind of war chief with a great deal of charisma and very little common sense. According to Bill, the best thing that Murray could do for the poor Gokachi was to keep Soobey extremely busy—so busy, in fact, that he would not have the free time to get himself into trouble. Murray (Bill suggested) ought to insist that Soobey be present at our house whenever he was not otherwise occupied. This idea did not sit well with Murray, who felt that with Soobey around all the time we would never get any work done. Murray then asked Bill to recommend someone who would at least teach us the Gokachi language. But Bill said there was no one whom he could really recommend. Shortly thereafter Soobey asked for a raise, which Murray did not give him. After four months, during which Soobey did progressively less and less work, Murray dropped him from the payroll.

On Hiring Field Assistants

On two different occasions Murray and I have worked with research assistants whom we hired before or very soon after we began our fieldwork. With one notable exception, all of these assistants did inadequate or unsatisfactory work, despite the fact that we gave them a great deal of instruction and support. The people who worked really well, who provided us with, or helped us get, our most useful data and insights, were genuine natives of the community, whom we had met, hired, and instructed after our research was well underway. On the basis of these experiences I do not wish to make any dogmatic assertions or recommendations. But if anyone were to ask me for advice, I would say the following. Go into the field alone or, if you must have company, with a companion who is not your employer or your employee. Make no long-term financial commitments to anyone. If you are required to hire research assistants before you enter the field, select those who, to your certain knowledge, like to talk to strangers and observe them, and *like to write,* accurately and vividly, about what they have heard and seen. People who are good mixers often make poor fieldworkers: they are so busy "presenting themselves" that they do not notice what anyone else is doing. Again, people who write splendid polemics may be poor fieldworkers, for they have little interest in trying to understand anyone who does not agree with them.

Be prepared to wait weeks or, if need be, months to meet the person or persons who will be your most helpful assistants. Such a person need not be a "native," but he or she should be a functioning member of the community you wish to study, a person who has *lived in and with the community for at least three years immediately preceding your arrival.* Only such a person is well informed about recent events and developments, politics, feuds, marital difficulties, scandals, and the like. He knows who is running the show now, whom to approach, and whom to avoid. Judging by our experience, it is easy to fool oneself into thinking that one is hiring such a person. For example, we were very happy when we were able to hire Walter GoodHorse because he was a fullblood member of the Standing Man community and we assumed that his being a fullblood would put him on easy and cordial terms with all the other members of his community. What we did not realize was that Walter belonged to a family unpopular with the other members of the community. Nor were we aware that Walter's having lived away from the reservation for five or six years, attending colleges and universities, meant that he had lost touch with what was going on at Thrashing Buffalo. Nor did we realize that his education, which by reservation standards was excessive, alienated him from most of the young men of his age. When we hired Soobey Fields as our assistant in Ottawa, we were taken in on another level, for Mr. Fields could have done first-rate interviewing for us had he chosen to do so.

The age and sex of such local assistants will vary with the kind of data required by the research. When we wanted to interview Indian parents on their attitudes toward education and the schools, we found our most able assistants to be Indian matrons in their thirties and forties. These women, though they had little formal education, were very concerned with what happened to the children, and they picked up the basic skills of interviewing in no time at all.

I am convinced that the ability to conduct a good interview involves a particular kind of adeptness at relating to other human beings—to the respondent and to the person for whom the interview is being done. It has very little to do with formal education or even with instruction and training. Moreover, to be a good interviewer, a person must get a personal satisfaction out of finding out "how people feel," of understanding their point of view. And, if he expects to use his interview to make a contribution to the social sciences, he must be able to derive satisfaction out of recording and writing down what he has learned in a form that will be useful for his own study or analysis, or for the study and analysis of someone else.

Researchers who must hire interviewing assistants face many difficulties and disappointments. Ideally, they ought to hire both interviewers from outside the culture and community being studied and interviewers who are active and involved members, for the depth and richness of perspective that one gets from comparing the views of an outsider and an insider are of enormous help in understanding the situation. But there is, so far as I know, no simple way to tell whether a prospective employee will make a good interviewer. A graduate student may be intelligent, conscientious, and fluent in speech, and he may appear to be socially sensitive and perceptive, but he may be a very poor and, what is worse, a virtually untrainable interviewer. Similarly, a native resident of a community may be friendly, vocal, and likable, and he may carry many recommendations, but he may turn out to be a domineering and opinionated interviewer, a lazy and slipshod worker, or a faker. With interviewing, the proof of the pudding is only in the eating. And this is unfortunate, because most researchers are obliged to hire their major or permanent staff *before* they go into the field.

Still, when we recalled our initial difficulties at Thrashing Buffalo, we felt that our troubles were minor. Dr. Reed was producing voluminous pages on classroom observation. Arthur was turning in at least some interesting material. Murray and I were beginning to interview principals, officials, and Gokachi parents. The water pipes in our combination house-and-office did not leak any more. On the whole, the project was proceeding as well as could be expected, and, judging by previous experience, we anticipated that most aspects of the situation would improve as we learned more and met more people.

INTERVIEWING INDIAN PARENTS IN OTTAWA

For more than ten years Bill James had been telling us—and, I surmise, all his other friends and students—that the Gokachi were among the most retiring and shy of the American Indians. On our visits to Ottawa, he and his assistant Rudy Nimmermehr repeated and enlarged on this depiction, regaling us with anecdotes illustrating how efficiently and ruthlessly the Gokachi shut out all intruders.

Because of these stories I assumed that interviewing the poor Indians of Ottawa would be extraordinarily difficult. Accordingly, soon after we arrived, I asked that Bill select among the Gokachi-speaking women of his acquaintance one who might be willing to work as a guide and interpreter. But Bill said there was no one he could recommend, because there were very few people, male or female, who were competent interpreters. Strictly speaking, he was right; scrupulous and fluent interpreters, who could put English into Gokachi and Gokachi into English with a minimum of distortion, were almost impossible to find. But I did not need a linguistically perfect interpreter so much as a tactful, friendly, and honest woman who spoke both languages reasonably well and would accompany me on my visits. I tried to explain this to Bill, pointing out that, in talking to mothers about their children and the schools, a socially sensitive interpreter who can reassure respondents and get them to talk easily and naturally about the school situation—as they see it —is much to be preferred to a socially inept linguistic genius. Finally I became so impatient that I decided to try interviewing the Indian mothers in Ottawa without the aid of an interpreter. I was champing at the bit to do some tangible work—to talk to somebody besides our research assistants and school principals. I told myself that it would be a useful datum to find out just how "absolutely unapproachable" were the Gokachi who lived in Ottawa.

Accordingly, I walked to one of the poorest sections of town and began to knock on doors. In three successive houses, I encountered an elderly white lady whose husband taught school, a very old but quite deaf Indian lady, and an emaciated, tired-looking woman about thirty-five, who bravely looked me in the eye, told me that she had a man in the house, and asked me to come back the next day. The fourth door was opened by a little Indian boy, who, unlike most of the Indian children I had met, was not shy, and when I asked him if his mother was home, he told me to come in and sit down. His mother was a plump, pleasant-looking woman of mixed Indian and white ancestry. She was very amiable and answered all of my questions as best she could, adding a good deal of helpful detail. She explained, for example, that it was an advantage to be of Indian descent because this made it possible to obtain many free services, hospital attention, and scholarships for the children. Her oldest son, whose father had been a white man, was not eligible for these benefits (she herself being only one-fourth Indian), but her younger children would profit by them because her present husband was an Indian. When I began to gather up my writing materials and purse, she did her best to think of more things to tell me, and I suspected that like so many American women (who have no one to talk to all day but their little children) she was lonely and enjoyed talking to any interested stranger.

I knocked on four more doors and encountered more white people, an elderly couple who insisted that I come in and sit down and showed me many pictures of their children, grandchildren, and great grandchildren, the wife of a university student, an empty house, and a young man watching television. The door of the next house was opened by a naked little Indian boy who was brandishing a commode brush smeared with what could only have been human excrement. Immediately behind him came another Indian boy of about thirteen, who, with a shocked and apologetic glance at me, grabbed the little boy and pulled him away from the door. This youth told me that his mother was not at home but his grandmother was. While he was telling me this, two Indian men, one of whom had been reclining on the sofa, got up and, without looking at me, silently drifted out of the room.[1] The youth followed, shooing his dangerously armed little brother before him. I noticed that the house furnishings were not the worn, secondhand articles that most poor people make do with. Rather, most of them were well made, extremely old, and well cared-for. Some looked like the pieces one occasionally finds in a good antique shop. On the wall hung a large, framed photograph of soldiers in World War I uniform, ranged in ascending rows like the members of a graduating class.

With the entry of the grandmother, I had my first meeting with a Gokachi matriarch. She was a small, strong woman with the features of a sober doll. I had never before met a woman who was so naturally and unequivocally the head of her house. She graciously indicated that I should seat myself in the most comfortable chair in the room, and, seating herself erectly on the edge of a nearby chair, she folded her hands in her lap and waited for me to begin. I began to explain what I was trying to do, but I sensed from the lady's expression that she did not understand me very well.

After a few questions it was clear that the lady knew very little English but was making a gallant effort to convince me that she understood everything I said. She did this with such polite anxiety that I did not have the heart to do anything but play the game and pretend that all of her answers made sense. I did not learn very

---

1. When I entered a Gokachi house and asked to speak to the mother or grandmother, the men present left the room. But if I said I was interested in the children and the schools, the entire family—men, women, and children— might gather round and participate in the interview. (Men, of course, were often at home because they found it hard to find employment.) It was most instructive to see which questions or points of discussion were automatically referred to the men, which to the women, and which to the children. Questions about what went on in the school and what they liked or disliked about school were always turned over to the children, who spoke up with an unhesitating frankness and self-possession that surprised me, since I was accustomed to the shy and diffident Plains Indian youngsters. On one occasion I began an interview by remarking that I was also interested in higher education. This time the man of the house took charge and gave me an informative lecture on the problems his children had encountered in high school and vocational schools. But when my questions concerned the younger children, he consulted his wife, who came out of the kitchen and voiced her views. This pattern of response was different from that on Thrashing Buffalo, where an older man, if he were present, usually monopolized an interview, even if he did not know what he was talking about. Having had his say, he might leave, and the ladies would tell their side of the story.

much about what the children were doing in school, but I did learn that seven or eight people lived in this tiny, three-room house, that the mother worked, that the father and brother could not find work, and that the grandmother kept it very clean. Whenever she could do so, the grandmother answered my questions so as to let me know, directly or indirectly, that she was taking very good care of the children and that they were doing very well in school. I also learned that the three children of school age did not go to school in Ottawa but were bussed out to a rural schoolhouse. The grandmother told me about this as if it were a matter of course. The teacher came for the children in her car, they went with her, and they liked school. Just before I left, the older boy ushered his little brother back into the room. The child had been thoroughly scrubbed and dressed in a spectacularly neat outfit.

I walked home feeling tired and sad. I had interviewed in many different situations and sections in the United States and I had tried to interview many different kinds of people. But I had never been received with such consistent courtesy and consideration as by the people, white or Indian, who lived in this decrepit section of Ottawa. Clearly, if I had the stomach for it, I could do scores of interviews, even among the shyest of the town Indians. I would, however, have to find an interpreter.

I wondered why the Gokachi grandmother had tried so hard to talk to me in English. Later, when I had talked to a considerable number of the poor Gokachi women who were bringing up their children "on welfare," I found that most of them lived in fear that their children might be taken from them by the department of social welfare and sent to boarding school, if the welfare worker found the "home environment" unsuitable. Since I was sometimes taken for a new kind of social worker, many of the Gokachi women's responses, and, I suspect, their pretended facility in English, were directed at convincing me that they were bringing up their children in the kind of environment which, they thought, would meet with the approval of the welfare worker.

I GET AN INTERPRETER

It was on my third day of knocking on doors that I met Mrs. Hobson, the woman who was to become my interpreter. After several fruitless approaches, I was directed to a shack at the rear of a lot where, I was told, there were children of school age. A stocky

Indian woman opened the door and, though she could barely find the English words to do so, she invited me in. She led me through a small parlor crowded with fine, old furniture into a kitchen, equally crowded by an open ironing board and two other Indian women. One of the women sitting in the kitchen was the owner of the house. The woman who had answered the door was her sister, and it was she who had a child at school. The third woman, who was tall and thin and wore glasses, was Mrs. Hobson, a neighbor who had dropped in for a chat.

The women insisted that I take the most comfortable chair, and the sister then resumed her ironing. I explained my errand and began to address my questions to the sister, since it was she who had a child in school. But the sister soon began to throw embarrassed and beseeching glances at Mrs. Hobson. With some diffidence Mrs. Hobson responded by putting my questions into Gokachi and the sister's answers into English. But no sooner had she begun to do this than the house owner began to interrogate me in Gokachi, asking all manner of questions about our study and my job. She asked what we planned to do, where we had procured our funds, whether we were working for the government, whether we were going to study everybody in Ottawa or just the Indians, and so forth. I answered as accurately and honestly as I could, and while I was struggling to make myself clear I noticed that poor Mrs. Hobson, who was interpreting like a house afire, was being worked even harder than I. Finally the women were satisfied, and they all sat back and smiled at me. One explained that "there had been other people interviewing downtown" and that a Gokachi man, when asked how far he had gone in school, had replied, "three miles." When the interviewer had asked what his personality was, the Gokachi man had replied, "Baptist." "Of course he was just joking him," the women explained.

I smiled, and Mrs. Hobson indicated that I might now ask *my* questions. I did so, and all three of the women did their cooperative best to answer me. I continued to be impressed by the way in which the two sisters used Mrs. Hobson and by her courtesy toward them. Once, while I was writing down responses in the extremely rapid longhand which I taught myself at Tule Lake, one of the sisters looked at Mrs. Hobson and, with her head, pointed to my scrabbling fingers. "That's shorthand," Mrs. Hobson told her; "That's how she does it." Later, when I asked the sisters in what way they thought things had improved for the Indians, they told me that things were a little better now because "the government is really trying to help the Indians . . . with grants to the schools." But then Mrs. Hobson added:

> I remember what our preacher used to say. As long as the world stands, he'd say, as long as the world stands, a hog is a hog. You can take him and wash him and scrub him and rinse (pronounced "rench" in her dialect) him, and then you put him back in his pen and he'll just wallow around again. Now that's how the Indians are—you can't turn them—you just can't turn them.

The two other Indian ladies nodded their heads in calm, judicial agreement.

When this interview was over, I asked Mrs. Hobson if she would care to work for me as interpreter. She indicated that she would be glad to have the employment, and from that day on we went out visiting together.

I was very happy to get the assistance of Mrs. Hobson and we learned a great deal on our visits. Though she was not always the best of interpreters, she was adequate and she had a great deal of integrity and spunk. Ideally, I would have preferred to work with a younger matron who herself had children of school age (Mrs. Hobson was fifty-eight and childless). But mothers who live in a town or city are more housebound than are mothers on the reservation. The latter, if they find work, leave their children with aunts or grandmothers as a matter of course. The former must find baby-sitters, whose pay may amount to almost as much as the working mother's.

24 Distressing and Confusing Developments

By the end of April we were obliged to face the fact that Arthur was an alcoholic. Not only was he an alcoholic but he had been an alcoholic for many years, and, it seemed, everyone in Indian affairs knew this but ourselves. As soon as we arrived in Ottawa and began to work with Arthur every day, we noticed that he drank a great deal. But he never appeared intoxicated or stupid, and his work, for a beginner, was of reasonably high quality. Indeed, some of it was very fine. So we reasoned that what he ate or drank was his own affair.

During the spring recess, Arthur threw a grand party. Friends came from all over the country, and many of them got drunk. Some drank much, but none got as drunk as Arthur. After four or five days (that included the Easter weekend), Murray decided that it would be wise for Arthur to get back to work. Arthur agreed, although his friends thought Murray a spoilsport, but the next day Arthur became very ill indeed. After three or four days during which he could not keep any food on his stomach, he managed to find a doctor who gave him a powerful sedative. But by this time he looked like a walking dead man.

We were also distressed because our relations with Bill James and Rudy Nimmermehr were becoming touchy and ambiguous. Bill and Rudy often behaved as if things were going on that they did not want us to know about, and we could not help but feel that they would have been happier if we had stayed away from Ottawa. Sometimes we were made to feel like spies or, as they put it, finks. They frequently talked about a recent case at law in which a Gokachi Indian had been arrested for killing a deer out of season. We gathered that Soobey Fields and the group of poor Gokachi who met with Soobey in the hills were somehow involved in this "deerslayer" case, but precisely who these people were, what they planned to do, or how Bill and Rudy were related to them was never made clear.

Murray listened to Bill and Rudy's complaints about how the Establishment was harassing them, and he sometimes gave them advice. But he told me later that he felt that they were concealing important aspects of the situation, which, he added, was their business. I was inclined to be less charitable. As an old, hard-nosed fieldworker, I thought they talked too much and worked too little.

Though Elsie Reed was not an outstanding interviewer, she produced a great many useful pages of recorded classroom observations. She also maintained a dialogue with the school principal, Mr. Waters, in which she expounded her liberal views to him and he told her about his boyhood and his amateur chicken and hog raising. Waters also told Elsie that he was reporting what she said to Chief Mayard. At the time, this remark did not seem to be particularly threatening to her or to us. If Mr. Waters wanted to report Elsie's liberal views to Mayard, that was his affair and no skin off anyone's nose. On the other hand, her conversations with Mr. Waters were not providing us with the kind of data we had hoped she would get—namely, how Gokachi parents felt about the schools —and when she reported that Mrs. Waters was becoming very cool toward her, I was amused. Elsie and Waters appeared to have no romantic interest in each other, but that Mrs. Waters should resent the fact that her husband spent so much time talking to another woman was natural. We did suggest, as the weeks passed, that Elsie make more energetic efforts to find an interpreter guide (as I had done on Thrashing Buffalo) and begin to get acquainted with some of the parents whose children attended the school in which she was making her observations. With our vigorous encouragement. Elsie found herself a Gokachi teacher and began to develop friendly relations with one or two Gokachi families.

Elsie's scrupulously recorded talks with Waters furnished us with some information about the operation of the Friendly Tribal Establishment, at least in the district where Waters and Elsie were working. Thus, soon after Elsie arrived in Sherwood, Waters boasted that he had succeeded in persuading Mayard to donate Gokachi funds for the construction of a ball park in the Sherwood community. Waters also reported that Mayard had appointed him to an important position in the council of the Six Friendly Tribes.

Elsie also heard occasional reports that another member of the tribal council was telling the Gokachi people in the Sherwood district that Elsie was a communist and possibly even a civil rights worker, the implication being that people who were friendly to

Elsie would have reason to regret it. This news did not particularly alarm us, since Beula GoodHorse had tried the same ploy at Thrashing Buffalo without doing us any harm. (After our experience at Thrashing Buffalo and elsewhere we had begun to suspect that gossip is ubiquitous in a folk or tribal community. People who do not like other people say bad things about them—and everybody expects them to do this. The important thing to know—if one is on the receiving end of malicious gossip—is whether the person who is spreading the rumors has power or access to power.)

APPROACHING THE SCHOOL OFFICIALS

It was becoming increasingly clear that, in order to be allowed to conduct our project in relative tranquility, we needed either to establish our credentials with the administrators and officials of the area or otherwise to reach some sort of agreement with them. Murray felt that by visiting these men, explaining who we were and why we were there, and requesting advice and suggestions, we might reduce some of the hostility that our staff was beginning to perceive in certain areas. He also hoped that he would encounter some congenial and thoughtful men (as we had done at Thrashing Buffalo) with whom we could explore some issues relatively honestly; and he hoped as well that in conversation with some officials we could define subprojects which would be of mutual interest, so that their staffs and ours could cooperatively assemble data on the matter. He had little hopes of convincing people to tolerate our project by a process of verbal explanations, but he thought that a series of visits and informal discussions would serve to relax things and open up possibilities. Instead, we met a wall, which varied from indifference and ignorance to open hostility. We never met any official who was genuinely interested in Indian education or in Indian life, or who was prepared to treat us as what we were—academic researchers—and we found the whole phenomenon greatly puzzling until, much later, we realized that we had been the targets of a well-organized plot to thwart our activities.

A few weeks after our arrival, Murray, sometimes accompanied by Arthur and sometimes by me, called on the principals of the schools located in or very near Ottawa. (These included a consolidated high school and a junior high school, two day schools, and an Indian boarding school.) Before Murray could even begin to explain who we were and what he hoped eventually to do, the principals of the high and junior high schools said, "We do not practice any discrimination in our schools." Before he could explain that we were not federal agents looking for "discrimination," they added, "And besides, we have scarcely any Indians in this school." Some of the principals and teachers said, "Most of us are Indian," and they assured us that almost every person in Ottawa has some Indian blood. "Why don't you go to Powhatan?" (the Indian boarding school run by the Indian bureau) they asked; "There are plenty of Indians there." After we had visited several classrooms, we concluded that the principals and teachers were right. There were very few pupils in the high school and the upper grades of the junior high who looked and behaved like Indians. (One reason was that many of the poor or rural Gokachi, after finishing day school, did not attempt to enter the consolidated junior high in Ottawa, and many of those who did enter dropped out very shortly.)

The principals of the town elementary schools received us with less suspicion. They, too, told us that they had relatively few Indian pupils, but they explained that a large proportion of the children of the Indians who had migrated to Ottawa from the rural regions were bussed out to the rural elementary schools by the rural schoolteachers. This, they explained, was one of the ways in which rural schoolteachers maintained sufficient attendance to keep their schools open and their jobs in existence. (When I began to interview the Indian parents living in Ottawa, I found that they and their children preferred this system. The Indian children found the small rural schools more congenial than the crowded town schools with their population of white pupils.)

Next, Murray and I visited a high school some twenty miles out of Ottawa in a community called Philbert. Here the local superintendent and other officials told us that our research project was pointless because most people were part Indian. There was no line between Indian and white, and there were no specifically Indian problems. If there was a problem, the superintendent insisted, it was one of rural poverty. All students from rural areas, white or Indian, did poorly in school and dropped out at equally high rates. There was no language problem, because most Indians spoke English quite well, though they often pretended that they could not understand. Another school official kept asking us what it was that we were really trying to prove—What was our angle? Another told us anecdotes about one or two Indian pupils who did amazingly well in school.

We found these remarks interesting because several people had told us that the district served by the Philbert high school contained a strong concentration of very impoverished Indian families and that the relations between these Indians and the whites were particularly strained. Several months later, when our Indian research assistast Victor Hibou asked for permission to observe classes in Philbert, he was curtly refused.

We came away from these encounters with the impression that the school officials were frightened by the idea that their communities contained any people that could truly be called Indians. They unequivocally believed that the communities in which they lived were inhabited only by people like themselves—respectable, cultivated, with steady jobs—and by poor trashy "rural" people who lacked will and initiative. The notion that anyone qualified as more Indian than anyone else in a positive sense struck them as heretical and subversive, and they reacted with anger and fear. People like us, who suggested that there might be special problems of, and therefore special treatment for, Indians (other than the general treatment given to poor, ignorant, lazy, or backward citizens) were rocking the boat.

Murray also tried very hard to explain our project interests to other local officials whose professional or political activity depended on the presence of "Indians." He felt that the making of such explanations was particularly urgent, since most of the local newspapers had ignored the announcements we had sent them, and, so far as we knew, nobody in Ottawa knew who we were or what we were up to except our staff members and the members of the project headed by Bill James.[1] Accordingly, Murray tried to make an appointment to call on the ranking local member of the executive committee of the Gokachi nation, an elderly gentleman called P. P. Disaster. Mr. Disaster insisted that he would call on Murray, and he arrived at our house-office in the company of another gentleman whom he introduced as Major Stumpfegger, the director of the Gokachi Cultural Center. Disaster and Stumpfegger announced that they had come to take Murray on a tour of the proposed center, and, en route, Major Stumpfegger explained the elaborate plans for

1. Murray and Arthur had made brief explanatory statements on the Gokachi radio program managed by Soobey, but in all the time we worked in the area we found only one individual who had heard this particular broadcast—a white man who ran a secondhand furniture store.

it. There was to be a museum, a pageant based on dramatic incidents from Gokachi history, a typical Gokachi village, and other edifying exhibits. Stumpfegger also explained the multiple and varied sources of funding, including monies from the state and federal governments and from the Gokachi tribe. Both Stumpfegger and Disaster told Murray that the major problem of the poor Gokachi—the people who had retired into the hills and lived in shacks without modern conveniences—was that they had no pride. If they could be made aware of their past and take pride in it, this would give them the self-respect to make something of themselves. This proposed cultural project would make these backward people become aware of their past and give them a needed sense of pride. It would also, Stumpfegger pointed out, bring tourists and their money into the area.

During this drive, of course, Murray was hoping to be given the opportunity to discuss what *his* project was all about. But he was unable to get a word in edgewise.

When the party arrived on the grounds of the proposed cultural center, Murray's guides took him on a long walking tour, pointing out the places where various exhibits and buildings were to be constructed. They also explained that there was some disagreement among the Gokachi people as to the value of the project. This disagreement, however, was the result of ignorance and lack of understanding and was related to a "divisiveness" among the Gokachi. Murray inquired about the causes of this divisiveness, but Stumpfegger and Disaster did not answer him.

On the drive back to Ottawa, Murray made a determined effort to discuss the nature and aims of our research project. Mr. Disaster interrupted him by inquiring how I had come to write an article with Bill James. Murray explained that in 1959 I had directed the workshop on American Indian affairs and that Bill had been my assistant director. He added that I had invited Mr. Mayard to speak to this workshop and that we had met and established cordial relations with him. Disaster and Stumpfegger said nothing, but, according to Murray, they looked at him as if they thought he was not telling the truth. And when he once again tried to tell them about our project, they listened inattentively, made no comments, and, on the whole, behaved as if he could not really be serious about the research.

After this baffling experience with the local tribal officials, Murray tried to discuss our project with the local officials of the Bureau of Indian Affairs. Here he was somewhat more successful, but not much. Mr. Hiliver, the local education specialist of the Bureau, listened courteously to what Murray had to say and agreed with a number of Murray's hypotheses. He particularly emphasized that most of the rural Gokachi could not speak English except in a most rudimentary way. He also gave Murray helpful information about the local Indian boarding school and about his own adult education program. But Mr. Hiliver's superior, Mr. Bryan, having told Murray that he "thought his project was a good thing," delivered a long monologue in which he explained why our project would not accomplish anything. Success in school, as in life, he explained, is a purely individual matter. Either one has the will to succeed—which is what Mr. Bryan and all of his brothers and sisters had had—or one has not. The crux of the problem was that most of the Indians simply did not have this will to succeed.

These encounters with the local school, tribal, and BIA employees or officials left us feeling uneasy. While the atmosphere could not be described as very bad, it was by no means good. Some teachers, principals, and educators, like Mr. Hiliver and the principals of the day schools, did not seem threatened and spoke to us with helpful courtesy. But people who were a little higher up in the system clearly wished that we would give up and go away. We were also not reassured by the indications that such members of the tribal Establishment as Mr. Disaster and Mr. Stumpfegger seemed to take it for granted that our project must be intimately related to the Lincoln Project headed by Bill James—which, though they did not come right out and say so, they seemed to have defined as a bunch of kooky social activists and communists posing as a research group. Murray figured that the best way to dissipate this unfriendly atmosphere was to talk to the high-ranking bureau and tribal officials and demonstrate his credentials, competence, and good faith.

MURRAY MEETS THE TRIBAL ESTABLISHMENT

Murray's attempt to develop reasonably cordial relationships with the ranking officials of the BIA was delayed because Mr. Waters (the principal of the Sherwood school—and newly appointed member of the education section of the intertribal council's committee on health, education, and welfare) suddenly told Elsie Reed that a number of reliable witnesses had heard her assert that Bayard

Mayard was an incompetent and would be ousted from his chieftainship in a few years. Elsie, who had not had much experience with
people like Mr. Waters, was completely taken aback. Her first concern was that we would believe she had actually made such a statement and had jeopardized our project. Much upset, she urged Murray to talk with Mayard, clarify the nature of our project, and
generally set things straight.

Murray, of course, had tried several times to make an appointment
to see Mayard, but each time he had been told that Mayard was
abroad or out of the state. With Mayard unavailable, the only tribal
officers or commitee members who could be reached and (hopefully) conciliated, were the few minor personages who lived in or
near Ottawa. Some of these were members of a local philanthropic
and improvement association called the Natoma Society. Murray
discussed the question of addressing the Natomas with Bill James,
and Bill seemed to think that it would do no harm and might do
some good. However, Bill advised Murray to take a positive and aggressive stance, to emphasize his academic affiliations and his publications on Indian education, and to point out that our project was
funded by the Office of Education. He also advised Murray to make
it clear that our project was in no way related to the Lincoln Project,
the one which Bill was directing. Accordingly, Murray telephoned
the vice-chief of the Natoma Society (whom he had met previously
and whom he rather liked) and arranged to address a meeting held
the following night.

When Murray arrived at the meeting place (the offices of the
local BIA), he found a number of men standing around at the door-
way. One of these was Mudwall Dobie, the man who (we had been
told) was particularly active in spreading invidious rumors about
Dr. Reed. Murray wondered why Dobie, who lived many miles
away, should bother to come to a minor meeting in Ottawa, and he
began to feel a little apprehensive. When Murray tried to greet some
of the other men standing about, they were pointedly cool and
formal, and he felt more apprehensive. Then everyone went into the
building and clustered in the side offices, while Dobie went from office to office talking a great deal. Murray was left standing alone in
the hallway.

When the meeting was called to order, the members proceeded
to a straightforward discussion of current and proposed community
action projects. Murray relaxed and told himself that he had been

nervous and foolish. For about half an hour the meeting proceeded serenely. Then the door burst open, and Mr. Lloyd Spear, attorney for the Gokachi tribe, strode hastily in. (Murray had not seen the formidable Mr. Spear since the Metropolis Indian conference, which Spear and other delegates from the Six Friendly Tribes had done their best to abort.) Mr. Spear immediately and very high-handedly took over the direction of the meeting. First he denounced Bill James, asserting that James was responsible for the fact that local community organizations (like the Natomas) had been unable to secure funds from the Office of Economic Opportunity. Further, he said that he had in his possession a letter written by James "to Washington" in which "James confessed that he had been causing trouble in the state." Then Mr. Spear told the Natoma Society that he had thought of a community action project for which they would be able to obtain a million dollars worth of funds. This project would consist of stamping out ticks. Ticks, Mr. Spear explained, damaged cattle and horses and frightened tourists. But modern discoveries had made it possible to eliminate them completely. Besides, once this million-dollar tick elimination project was started, many responsible people would be needed to direct it, and it would also put many men to work. He interlarded this discourse with references to himself as founder of the Natoma Society and reminded those present that he had written the society's constitution.

The Natomas listened politely to Mr. Spear, but they did not react with enthusiasm to his tick elimination project. The vice-chief pointed out that there was no quorum present and that no motion could be passed, and, besides, the members wanted to get on with questioning Dr. Wax. Someone else remarked that the rural development authority was already active and authorized to control ticks and that a tick control program had been organized. Then Murray was asked to make his statement. He sketched his academic affiliations, referred to his publications, and stressed that his research was entirely open and public. He explained how our project had been funded and he also referred to our previous study of the schools at Thrashing Buffalo. Then he handed around copies of our monograph on Thrashing Buffalo and several articles we had written on Indian education. One man asked Murray what difference it made whether Indians went to public schools or bureau schools so long as the curriculum was the same. Murray said that he did not know, and that this was one of the things our project hoped to find out.

The vice-chief remarked that the Natomas had received many complaints from Indian parents about members of our project interviewing their children. Murray replied that this was strange because we had as yet not interviewed any children. Mr. Spear then once again took charge of the meeting and, opening the copy of a sociological journal which Murray had passed around, he stated, "I notice here that William James has an article on Pan-Indianism and that in your article you also use the word Pan-Indianism. Now what does that word mean?" Murray used this opening to explain that Bill James and I were old friends and classmates. He also explained that our project was different from Bill's in almost all respects and added that we particularly wanted nothing to do with involvement in political issues. This statement did not mollify Mr. Spear. Assuming the tone of a cross-examiner, he demanded: "Do you or do you not have a lady working for you in Mohican County?" Murray replied that he did. "What is her name?" asked Spear. Murray told him. "It has been reliably reported to me," said Mr. Spear, "that Elsie Reed has denounced our chief, Bayard Mayard, as an incompetent and predicted that he would be ousted from his position as chief within a few years." By this time Murray was getting angry, but he answered quietly that Dr. Reed was a responsible professional person and that her assignment was to study the Sherwood school and other matters relating to education. As a citizen, he added, she had the right to express her views on political issues. Mr. Spear then began to rephrase what Murray had said, interposing words so as to make it appear that Murray was asserting that Dr. Reed had the right to make libelous remarks not only about Mr. Mayard but about other members of the Natoma Society. At this, Murray said that Dr. Reed was his employee and that he would defend her against any such fabricated accusations. Mr. Spear then drew from his pocket a typed list of all the alleged misdeeds of the project headed by Bill. He read this long denunciation aloud and then asked Murray if he agreed. Murray said that he was not in a position to know what the employees of Bill's project had done or had not done.

After this, the atmosphere of the meeting became somewhat more conciliatory. Murray was asked how he had obtained his grant and he explained exactly how this was done. He was then asked if he would help the Natomas write the tick-extermination proposal, and he said that he would be glad to do so but that since he knew nothing about ticks he could probably help only with the grammar. Mrs.

Dobie even invited Murray to visit the Head Start project in Mohican County.

Murray did not feel that this meeting represented a triumph in the establishment of good public relations. Still, he was baffled and exasperated rather than alarmed, for he believed that if most of the meeting had not been taken up with Spear's attempts to link our project to Bill's, he might have obtained the toleration and, perhaps, even the support of some of these local people. They represented, he believed, an organization of impecunious people from old mixedblood families, who hoped, somehow, to get hold of federal funds which they could control and dispense to "improve the lot of 'the poor Indians.'" One member, the vice-chief, seemed to have at least some contact with the rural Gokachi and with some of the very poor Indians living in Ottawa. Another member, Lloyd Spear, had "made it," in that he had become an important figure in the powerful Mr. Mayard's establishment. Many of the Natomas (Murray felt) regarded Spear with fear and envy. Later we were to learn that some, who excelled Spear in lineage and manners, regarded him with disdain and embarrassment.

After his inconclusive meeting with the Natoma Society, Murray was invited to attend and address a meeting of the public relations committee of the Gokachi tribe, held in the hall of the Indian Baptist church in Ottawa. All those present were local folk, and most of the evening was taken up by reports about funded or not-yet-funded projects such as Head Start and nurse's aide programs. A letter from Chief Mayard was read, in which Mayard stated that he had talked with an OEO official in Washington and had been told that cutbacks suffered by local projects were due to lack of funds and not to accusations. Nevertheless, several persons present at the meeting insisted that they had seen lengthy written accusations by William James. A Gokachi minister also spoke—he sounded to Murray like a good and honest man—and he remarked that he too had been accused of "testifying against the local OEO projects."

Next it was Murray's turn to speak. He described the documented facts about lack of educational achievement and poverty in the area, outlined the proposed design of our research, named the staff members, and gave something of their background. He was then asked why he had hired Soobey Fields and Arthur Braveheart. Murray explained that Soobey and Arthur had been recommended to him by Bill James, who was an old friend of ours and who, as they

311

knew, had been interested in Indian affairs for a long time. Murray also told how we had attended the American Indian conference at Metropolis University. (Murray at this time did not know that Lloyd Spear and several other high-ranking members of the tribal Establishment asserted and, perhaps, believed that this conference had been arranged by communists. Thus, Murray was openly presenting as a personal recommendation the association for which his opponents had expected to accuse and denounce him.) Thereupon a man named Dan Muffin (who, we later learned, was an impecunious hanger-on of Lloyd Spear) began to attack Murray vigorously for "worrying the people with surveys prying into their personal lives, and disturbing classrooms by entering them for observation." His tone was so abusive and he refused so pointedly to listen to anything Murray had to say that Murray finally told him there was no point to trying to answer his questions since he clearly did not wish to hear the answers. This remark seemed to startle many of those present, and the chairman closed the discussion.

Coffee was served, and most people present tried to be cordial to Murray—except for Mr. Muffin, who went into the kitchen and stayed there. Major Stumpfegger, Mr. Disaster, and Mr. Hiliver (the BIA education specialist) joined Murray. Hiliver, who spoke Gokachi, told Murray that Soobey Fields was an unreliable interpreter and deliberately mistranslated speeches if this suited his purpose. Hiliver also said that he had heard Soobey speak to the poor Gokachi and paint fantastic and misleading pictures of all that he could and would do for them; for example, he would regain all the tribal lands. To this Murray responded that he wanted very much to get another interpreter and he reminded Mr. Hiliver that he had asked him for a recommendation several weeks previously.

Murray found this meeting with the public relations committee less bewildering than his encounter with the Natomas. The committee was composed of people who represented many different factions and views. Many talked as if they genuinely wanted to help the poor Gokachi, though they often had naïve or impractical notions about how they might do this. Others had found out that "helping the poor" held the promise of good jobs and political influence. A few, like Mr. Muffin, were bent on smearing the Lincoln Project and our project, because they were convinced that we represented the same "divisive outside interests" and that we were obtaining the federal funds which rightly should have been given to them. Others were not sure whether we were troublemakers or not, and might have been willing to tolerate or even approve our study, provided that we helped them in some way. Still others, as we were to find out shortly, covertly hoped that we were troublemakers who would have sufficient power and influence to shake down the great tribal Establishment, to which they were bitterly hostile. Indeed, after Murray returned home from the meeting, one of the ladies who had been present phoned him and apologized for the discourteous treatment he had been given. "We usually crucify people here only once a year," she added, laughing. As he sat down to write up his field notes that night, Murray ruefully shook his head and remarked that he felt like a character in a detective thriller whose plot is composed of an overwhelming multitude of inexplicable crises; one could only pretend that, like Sherlock Holmes, one was not really baffled. On the other hand, some things were beginning to make sense. For if Hiliver was right in his accusations about Soobey Fields, this would help to explain why Soobey would not interpret for us or teach us Gokachi. It would also help to explain some of the confusion implicit in the tactics of the Lincoln Project. Moreover, there was the real possibility that what Soobey was preaching to his Gokachi audience was a Gokachi "Ghost Dance," that is, a nativistic and millennial vision of a reconstructed Gokachi nation in mythic autonomy.

25 The Opening of the Ball Park

We learned much more about the social and political complexities of the situation by attending the opening of the Bayard Mayard Ball Park in the Sherwood community. Socially, this affair was extraordinarily pretentious, and those attending included officers of the Gokachi tribe and important officials of the BIA, as well as other people holding political office or engaged in welfare occupations; most of them were clad in formal Sunday afternoon attire. And all this fuss to open one little ball park in a community of a few hundred people!

Considering the rural locale, the ball park itself looked impressive, with well-built backstops and fence, brand new scoreboard, and well cleared ground. (The work of clearing the ground and erecting the fence had been done by the local Gokachi men after their working hours.)

The opening ceremony was held before several large trucks which served as backdrop. In front of the trucks were ranged several rows of long, narrow, wooden benches.

The way in which the audience arranged itself would have confirmed sociometric enthusiasts in their most extreme claims. To begin with, there were the three-score or so tribal officers and Indian and welfare bureau employees. While most of these, I suspect, were of Gokachi (or other Indian) descent, they did not look or behave like Indians. All of them probably saw themselves as uplifting or working for the good of the poor people, "the Indians," for whom the ball park had been built. They also, as Murray had observed in meetings, saw themselves as protectors of the Indians and as mediators between the Indians and the "white outsiders." The fact that most of them really knew very little about the poor Gokachi and could not have carried on anything but a brief or casual conversation with them was as carefully ignored as the nakedness of the legendary emperor. These well-dressed people, along with a handful of outsiders like ourselves, seated themselves on the hard and narrow benches facing the speaker's rostrum and the hot sun. A few very important men, like Lloyd Spear, stood behind the "stage" leaning against the trucks.

Then there were the inhabitants of the Sherwood community—the people for whom the ball park had been built. These were dark, solemn, quiet folk, and poorly or plainly dressed, the men in cheap suits and work shirts, the women in cheap cotton print dresses. They arrived in old, battered cars, which they parked in a rough semi-circle around the bench area. Later arrivals parked their cars in a much larger semicircle at the extreme edge of the cleared area, so that they looked as if at any moment they might fall back into the woods. These people kept arriving throughout the long series of speeches until there must have been several hundred present. But most of them stayed in their cars, and the few who got out of the cars remained standing at the edge of the woods.

Then there were about a dozen men who looked and acted like Indians (except that they were somewhat better dressed), and who did not seem to be on terms of parity either with the well-dressed visitors or with the local Indians who stayed in their cars. Some of these men seated themselves diffidently on the benches in areas that the better-dressed people had left vacant. Others stood around the seating section or leaned against the trucks that formed the back-stop. When they exchanged a few words with the visiting dignitaries, their tone and posture were humble and respectful and they did not look particularly comfortable. They reminded me of the people who had served as bus drivers and cooks in the Bureau day schools of Thrashing Buffalo; that is, they were Indians who spoke the native language and lived in the native community, whose salary, small as it was, made them seem affluent or well-to-do to the rest of the Indian community. Later, I learned that one of them had helped to organize the group of Gokachi men volunteers who cleared the ground for the ball park.

The ceremony was very long. First came a prayer in the Gokachi language delivered by a local Christian minister. Next, Mr. Waters, the man who was really responsible for the ball park, gave a long and well-organized account of how and why the park had been built. He told how he had approached Chief Mayard, a great and good man, and how Mayard had agreed with him that a ball park in Sherwood would be a good thing. He named a number of other people and groups who had helped, ending with the Pepsi-Cola Company, which had "donated" a scoreboard for which the Sherwood community would pay by having the children sell several thousand cases of Pepsi-Cola. (Since the scoreboard consisted of a large central panel advertising Pepsi-Cola and two small side panels for scorekeeping, I thought that Waters had made a poor bargain for the Gokachi ball players. Indeed, Waters told Dr. Reed that all of the cases could be sold only if the children sold Pepsi-Cola for two summers.) After Mr. Waters had introduced thirteen or fourteen notables, each of whom stood up for applause, the speeches began.

The opening speech was to have been delivered by Mr. Mayard, but Mayard sent his regrets, and his place was taken by Mr. Shrew, Permanent Proxy for Chief Mayard and also an employee of the same corporation. Shrew was a very tall, angular, Texan-looking man, wearing the kind of beaded, pseudo-Indian tie clasp which is affected by the important officers of the Six Friendly Tribes. Addressing the well-dressed folk rather than the Indians, he explained how he and Mayard "had decided that those people out in Sherwood really needed a ball park. It will give the younger people some wholesome recreation and it will keep the older people out of the taverns." Since many of the rural Gokachi are sober people and do not hold with drinking, I glanced around to see what effect these inaccurate and uncalled-for words were having. But the faces of the Indians sitting in their cars remained expressionless. Indeed, though I watched closely throughout this speech and the subsequent address by Lloyd Spear, I saw no evidence that any of the people sitting in the cars or standing at the edge of the woods heard or understood a single word. Men, women, or children, their faces remained expressionless. Occasionally they spoke a few inaudible words to each other.

Mr. Spear began his address with the coming of the white man and presented a long and detailed historical account of the abuses suffered by the Gokachi over the centuries. He told how the government had forced them to leave their homeland and how, during the Civil War, their homes had been burned and their gardens ruined. Then he told how the government had broken the treaty and sent all manner of "wild Indians" into the Gokachi lands. At this point I blanked out—for I had been listening to several consecutive hours of speeches—and I was unable to remember what he said about the additional hardships and abuses that the Gokachi suffered in the late nineteenth and early twentieth century. But I became fully conscious again when Mr. Spear's voice changed to a great shout of joy. For he had come to the year when the government of the United States had turned from a punitive and abusive to a fair and charitable power. The first sign of the great change of heart was the appointment of Bayard Mayard as chief. From this point on, one gathered, all had gone well for the Gokachi—just as everything had gone badly in the prior period. The greatest stroke of good fortune had been the winning of a multimillion dollar claims case against the United States government. Mr. Spear, who had served as one of the attorneys for the Gokachi, gave a detailed account of what had gone on in Washington at this time. The federal government, he said, had tried to reduce the Gokachi claims by $500,000 for varying services that the government had rendered the Gokachi, and by $15,000 for burying pauper Gokachi. Spear's description of how he and Chief Mayard had stood up to the government and fought for payment in full made both of them sound like heroic and able champions of the poor. Since even I found this account somewhat stirring, I glanced covertly at the Indians still sitting patiently in their cars. But every face looked as blank as if Spear were talking in a foreign language, which, perhaps, he was. (Later, I learned that he gave much the same speech at every formal occasion.) Spear then asked Mr. Shrew to distribute a fact sheet prepared by the tribal executive, which, he said, gave all the information on what had been done with the millions of dollars of claims money. Copies were given to all the people sitting on the benches, but none were offered to the Indians.

Next, two men and a woman who looked like white people but were dressed as unpretentiously as the Indians came forward with a violin and a guitar and began a performance of country music. At once a magical change came over the gathering. The Indians smiled, looked friendly and happy, and after each song they applauded loudly and enthusiastically.

Then came the final ceremonial act, the presentation of a baseball bat by Mrs. Dobie to the captain of the Sherwood team. Mrs. Dobie, a very thin woman in a pink and white suit and a large pink crystal necklace, came to the rostrum and, in a trembling voice, made a brief and only partially audible speech of presentation. Then she presented the bat to a very embarrassed Gokachi youth. The young man took the bat, turned on his heel, and walked off the stage. But Mr. Waters recalled him and told him that he must make an acceptance speech. The youth blushed, looked to the ground, turned his head away, and said nothing. Finally Mr. Waters prompted him like a preacher prompting a bridegroom, the young man responding in almost inaudible tones.

> Mr. Waters: I thank you . . .
> Youth: I thank you.
> Mr. Waters: For the fine bat . . .
> Youth: . . . for the fine bat . . .
> Mr. Waters: (pausing and looking expectant)
> Youth: (makes no response to Waters' urging look)
> Mr. Waters: (resignedly) . . . Mrs. Dobie..
> Youth: Mrs. Dobie. (Walks rapidly away)

This ended the ceremony. The participants stood up, moved about, and began to help themselves to the appetizing and ample picnic refreshments, spread on large tables at one end of the clearing. We left at this point, but we were told that many more people came to see the ball game.

I left, marveling at how much one could learn about a social situation and social distance by attending a ceremony.

26 The Poor Man and the Aristocrat

After my interpreter and I had visited a number of very poor Go-kachi homes, I noticed that Mrs. Hobson was becoming worried that I might think that all the Gokachi were abysmally poor, wretched, and ignorant. So I decided to ask her to take me to see some of the Indian ministers, as I was, of course, very interested in hearing what these men had to say about Indian education. We set out, by chance, two days after Murray had had his uncomfortable encounter with the executive committee of the Gokachi tribe.

Mrs. Hobson took me to the homes of two ministers, but neither was at home. One minister's wife, however, remarked that Mr. Muffin was working over at the church. "Well then," suggested Mrs. Hobson to me, "let's go talk to Mr. Muffin." I broke into a cold sweat, for Muffin, two nights before, had given Murray a very rough time at the tribal executive committee meeting. Since I could not very well tell Mrs. Hobson that I did not want to talk to Mr. Muffin, I comforted myself with the thought that fate plays curious tricks on people and I might as well see this trick through as best I could.

Mr. Muffin was a short, bald, small-featured man, who looked as if he might be one-third or one-half Gokachi. Using a very small and old hand mower, he was mowing the sparse lawn in front of the modest wooden Indian Baptist Church. Mrs. Hobson introduced me and herself and explained the kind of study we were making. Then Mr. Muffin addressed me as if he were beginning a political campaign speech. He asserted that the Indians' problems with education were the same as those of the white people, for both Indians and white people pay taxes, support their schools, and buy school bonds. But there are some people (he said) who are going about investigating the schools, and "I have no qualms about telling them that the Indian people do not approve of this interference and of the way they are disturbing the children in the classrooms." "Who is doing this?" I asked, in a tone which implied that I thought such interference and disturbance very reprehensible. Mr. Muffin looked somewhat taken aback. After a moment he said in a soft and deferential voice, "Your group." Then he shifted back to his denunciatory tone

319

and announced that many students had complained to their teachers about our activities and that the teachers were helpless against us because they were government employees. Therefore it was the duty of the tribal executive committee to report these abuses to Chief Mayard. Without pause, he angrily asserted that our project was connected with Bill James's project and that both projects were run by Sam Grossdenk at Washington. Who *was* paying us, if not Sam Grossdenk? All these questions were rhetorical, and he gave me no opportunity to answer. When he paused for breath, I was moved to say that I had noticed that Indians judged people not by what they said but by what they did. Therefore, if he and the other concerned people *really* watched us carefully, they would see us for what we were and they would see that we were not members of Bill James's study. To this, however, Mr. Muffin replied quite shrewdly that they had been watching us and they knew that Mr. James and his employees came from Metropolis and that we too had gone to school in Metropolis. "People are judged by the company they keep," he concluded. I conceded that he had made a point and said that I now could understand why he and a few other people felt concerned about our presence in Ottawa. Indeed, it was at this moment that I perceived that Mr. Muffin and probably other members of the tribal Establishment really believed that Metropolis University was a center of radicalism and communism. It was here—as they saw it—that the American Indian conference had been held to organize the American Indians to agitate and make trouble for the government of the United States. From this breeding ground of radicals issued people who posed as researchers but who, in actuality, were agitators trying to incite the "ignorant" and "backward" Indians to sign petitions, initiate lawsuits, and participate in demonstrations and in other forms of disturbing and ill-advised social action. From this danger, it was the obligation and duty of the sophisticated and educated "Indians" (among whom Mr. Muffin saw himself) to save their innocent brothers.

When I pointed out that information about the schools and the parents' attitude toward education might be helpful to the Indians, Mr. Muffin retorted that all this information was now available at the office of the county superintendent of schools; so why didn't we go there? I replied that we were obtaining this kind of material from the superintendent but that this would not help us find out why so many of the young people, and especially the Indians, dropped out of high school. He retorted that this was all well and good—perhaps we might do a study and find out why the young people dropped out. But then it would take us several years to write our report and publish it, and by this time his daughter might have dropped out of high school. She would have received no help from our study, so it was a waste of time. To this argument I had no adequate reply.

He then asked me where I was from. I told him, Midwest University. Assuming an expression of extreme sharpness, he said that, since the Fraser Indian Institute was in Midwest, why didn't we stay in Midwest and study the Indians there? To this I was able to reply that we had looked into the possibility of studying Fraser, but had been told by the superintendent that an entirely adequate study had recently been made and that our efforts would be redundant.

He then asked why we hired Indians from other tribes—for example, that Yuki, Arthur BraveHeart. I replied (rather inaccurately) that we hired people because they were competent for particular jobs. For example, Mrs. Hobson, who had brought me here to see him, was my interpreter. I then told Mr. Muffin exactly how I had met Mrs. Hobson and how I had come to hire her, while she earnestly corroborated every detail. Mr. Muffin then adeptly shifted to his own grievances (and, I suspect, the grievances of many of the impoverished people of "part Indian descent"). "Why don't they hire Indians as doctors," he demanded. "Why don't they hire Indians as public health workers? What happens when an Indian applies for a job? They give it to him at the lowest rate!" Why, for example, did we have our well-paid jobs—and why hadn't our jobs been given to some Indian? It was people like him, people like the Natomas, who ought to be given the money to carry on the kind of study we were doing—the money ought not to be given outsiders like us who knew nothing about the situation.

I was tempted to explain how hard Murray and I had tried to teach Indians how social scientific research was done so that they could get their hands on research funds—even though, God knows, we were making scant progress instructing Soobey Fields or Arthur Braveheart. But, instead, I explained concretely that we had applied to the Office of Education for a grant, and they had given it to us. Indians who could do the kind of work for which grants were given could also apply. But this statement brought an outburst from Mr. Muffin. The Natomas and the tribal executive had asked Washington for money many times, but they had received nothing. Then they had discovered that Bill James had subverted their requests. "Can you answer me this," he said in tones of outrage, "why is it that when we took our proposal to the Bureau secretary and asked for funds we didn't get them? And all James had to do is go to the telephone and ask for funds from Washington and he gets them right away?" He then gave me a list of his own qualifications: he "had been some to college"; he had had much experience in life which he would consider equivalent to a master's degree; he now had this church work; he was, in short, a wise and well-educated man quite competent to direct the kind of study we were doing. (In subsequent months, when we got to know a fair number of Gokachi from the "older families," we found that they did not share Mr. Muffin's opinion of his competence. He was a retired mail carrier, eking out a meager living serving as a janitor at the Indian Baptist church.)

Mrs. Hobson now began to take an active part in the conversation. Bending a stern glance on Mr. Muffin she began to quiz him in exactly the tone she had used when she quizzed me about our project. Just what were these Natoma Society meetings, she wanted to know. She had never heard of them (which was odd because she was a member of the Indian Baptist church). Mr. Muffin nervously explained that the Natomas were a group of older Gokachi persons —lawyers, ministers, and some retired—who were concerned with helping the Gokachi people. They had met several times in the churches, but the Gokachi people were afraid to come to the meetings. "*I* would very much like to come," said Mrs. Hobson, determinedly, "I'm very interested in that sort of thing and I'll certainly come to your next meeting here." Mr. Muffin began to look uncomfortable, but Mrs. Hobson did not seem to notice this. "Many Gokachi people are very shy," she rattled on, "they don't understand English or they aren't interested in this kind of thing. But I am interested, and this is just the kind of group I want to join." Mrs. Hobson then told Mr. Muffin some of the things that the Gokachi mothers had told us and that she felt he and the Natomas ought to know. After a while, Muffin interrupted her, saying defensively that there were PTA meetings for that kind of thing. But Mrs. Hobson stood her ground and said that we had told the Gokachi mothers the same thing and that they had said they were afraid to go to the PTA meetings because they could not speak English and were embarrassed. This touched Mr. Muffin, and he seemed for a while to become an entirely different kind of person. He looked at the ground and spoke in a soft and bitter voice, gently scolding the Indian people for not going to the PTA meetings and not interpreting for each other. Then, in an even softer and frightened half-whisper—almost as if he feared that some power might strike him dead—he told us that it was the truth that if an Indian went to school and spoke up for his child, or for another Indian child, the teacher would take it out on the child. He himself only dared to do this now because his children were out of school.

> Only a little while ago a teacher in the small grades told a little Indian boy that the Gokachi were just lazy—the government does so much for them that they won't do a thing. The boy told his parents and the parents came and told me about it. I went to a school board member and complained that the teachers were belittling our children. The school board member promised me that he would take immediate action, but he told me to keep it quiet, because "it could get big." In the end the teacher had to apologize to the father. But the father told the teacher that he ought to apologize to the little child and make him understand. The trouble with the teachers is that they think, "The less the Indians know the better it is for us."

I told Mr. Muffin that I thought he had done a fine thing, and Mrs. Hobson agreed. At this, he cast down his eyes and said "I'm just a citizen."

During the last hour of this "interview" (which lasted more than two hours), I made several attempts to leave, but Mr. Muffin always stopped me with some new question. He and Mrs. Hobson even discussed theological matters for a while, she asking him his opinion on whether or not the meanness of a parent could be inherited by a child. (Evidently in her part-time work with social workers Mrs. Hobson had heard something of the notion of inherited personality defects.) Mr. Muffin replied that on this question he would follow the Bible, which said that a child was born without sin. Consequently, a mean child would have to get his meanness from his surroundings, which usually meant his parents.

When Mrs. Hobson and I finally began to walk off, Mr. Muffin followed us to the end of the long churchyard, keeping up the conversation. Just as we were about to break away, he suddenly fixed me with a malevolent gaze and said, "Take care. You may be called upon to answer questions before the tribal executive just as your husband was." Then, turning to Mrs. Hobson, he said threateningly, "You take care too, Sister Hobson. People may say bad things about you because you are associating with people like Mrs. Wax." At this

I saw red. I had been concerned throughout this weird encounter that Mrs. Hobson would become frightened by Mr. Muffin's accusations and decide that she could no longer work for me. Ignoring Muffin, I turned to Mrs. Hobson and told her gently that if she felt she would be caused any trouble at all by working for me, I would understand if she wanted to quit. "I understand," said Mrs. Hobson. Then she turned on Mr. Muffin and said, "Brother Hobson, if people say bad things about me, I will understand *why* they are saying them and I will not pay them any heed. Like a Christian I will not get angry with them." Then we two ladies walked off, leaving Mr. Muffin standing there.

As soon as Mrs. Hobson and I got back in my car she asked me, "Now just why would a Yuki Indian [meaning Arthur BraveHeart] work to help the Gokachi instead of his own people?" My head was in a whirl, and I said the first thing I could think of, "Well, maybe it's like your sister, who went to Fraser Institute and then took a job working with the Sioux in South Dakota." This answer seemed to satisfy her. Then she said, "I can't understand what's wrong with Dan Muffin—why he takes those views. I went to school with him." Her tone reassured me, since it resembled that which an older sister might take if her adult brother began to behave in a childish manner. When I suggested that we might try to talk to another minister on the next day, she agreed and added thoughtfully, "And I think we ought to talk to Margaret." Margaret, I gathered, was Mrs. Harrison, a lady of part-Gokachi descent, but that part of impeccably old family, and a lady who, I remembered, was supposed to have had some kind of set-to with Chief Mayard and the Gokachi tribal executive committee.

Before calling on Mrs. Harrison, Mrs. Hobson and I called on the Reverend Hunter, the pastor of the church for which Mr. Muffin was caretaker. The Reverend Hunter, though he must have heard much the same things about us as Mr. Muffin had, was very civil. He asked us into his parsonage, which was as modest a dwelling as most of the houses of the poor people, seated us, and listened carefully to what I had to say. I told him what our research project was trying to do and I told him that some people, like Mr. Muffin, seemed to think that we had come to make trouble. Then I asked him what we ought to do.

The reverend Hunter looked uncomfortable, but when he spoke he sounded honest. What we ought to do, he said, is go and see

Mr. Mayard. Then we ought to speak to the people to whom Mr. Mayard sent us, explaining our project and purpose to them. We ought to get the approval of the superintendent of schools (from whom, of course, we already had permission to work), and we ought to see the tribal officials. Especially we ought to go to the Board of Welfare, because they could help us understand the problems of the Indians, and, if they introduced us to the people, the people would accept us. Perhaps it would be best if we did not go to see any of the poor people at all, because they were so uneducated and ignorant that they would just get upset. There would be a lot of gossip, and a lot of stories and rumors would be spread. The best thing for us would be to talk only to the leaders—the people who understand the situation. "Unless you go to the dignitaries, you won't be recognized." In his own life experience, Mr. Hunter told us, he had talked a great deal to the poor, and he was convinced that learning how the poor feel and what they think will not help them. One must work through and with the permission of the people in power.

In a roundabout way he apologized for the rough treatment Mr. Muffin had given us, pointing out that the Indians had good reason to feel suspicious of newcomers like us and to ask that we prove ourselves. Then, like Mr. Muffin, his voice suddenly shifted to an entirely different key, and he spoke with passionate bitterness:

> The Indians feel that they are just on the very bottom of the pile in this country. And every time somebody comes here, it just seems as if they want to push them lower. Even the Negroes are doing better for themselves today than the Indians.

When I asked Hunter what, in his opinion, was the greatest educational need of the young Indian people, he said a good recreational center—something that would help keep them out of the pool halls and beer joints in town. But he added that, if funds were allocated for such a center, "you have to keep the politicians out of it. It should be run by the church people . . . and not by the board of education. To keep a thing clean you have to hire clean people. Christians are interested in elevating people, but the politicians are interested in their own livelihood."

I looked forward to meeting Mrs. Harrison because I had heard a good deal of gossip about her. Mr. Stumpfegger had attacked her in the newspapers. Some members of the Lincoln Project seemed to think that she was a well-intentioned crackpot. But Mrs. Hobson spoke of her with respect.

When I met her, she impressed me as an angry aristocrat. In fact, all the time I worked on this project, Mrs. Harrison was the only person I met who was not afraid of the Establishment or of Bayard Mayard. Her great-grandmother was a fullblood Gokachi, and Mrs. Harrison insisted that "all her life she had thought of herself as an Indian" and "taken up for the Indians." She and her husband, a retired professor, had lived in Ottawa for thirty-five years. They now resided in a handsome house near the university, and my eye was immediately taken by the old and beautiful furniture—and particularly by a handmade chair which, Mrs. Harrison told me, had once been the property of a famous Gokachi leader. She had served on the tribal executive committee for more than ten years, but had resigned the year before protesting the use to which the other tribal officers were putting the remainder of the Gokachi claims monies.

Mrs. Hobson, somewhat to my surprise, began by taking charge of the interview. She asked Mrs. Harrison about her Indian forebears, whether she spoke Gokachi (which she did not), and why she felt that she could "speak for the Indians." She asked, "Is it true that a teacher gets 20 percent more pay by teaching Indian children?" Mrs. Harrison answered these questions in a straightforward manner and in some detail. She went on to tell us that she had taught third grade in a rural school in her youth and how shy and sensitive the Indian pupils were, and she described some of the things she had done to help them. She emphasized how poor many of the rural Gokachi were and how much difficulty they had with the English language:

> I did notice that as the Indian children grew older they would feel bad because their clothes wouldn't be quite so good. One time a teacher asked a boy why his brother wasn't in school that day, and the boy just said, "Barefoot.". . . The other teachers used to come and say, "Oh you dumb Indians." But I'd say, "Don't you speak like that to me!" I'd explain that the Indians had a lot of difficulty and they were slower because they think in Gokachi. The other children who thought in English could answer right off.

She then told us that a friend of hers who was now teaching in the Philbert school wanted very much to take the course in Gokachi (which the Lincoln Project had managed to sponsor as an adult education course), but how could she find the time? Here Mrs. Hobson chimed in: "Even when a [white] person knows only a word or two of Gokachi and speaks it—I can't tell you how good it makes us Gokachi feel. It really does something for us—it makes you feel like the person is interested—it . . ." Her voice choked up and she was unable to continue. Mrs. Harrison said, "And you can just imagine how timid the little Indians are who can't speak the English language."

Mrs. Hobson composed herself and then (again to my surprise) formally asked Mrs. Harrison to explain to us "about that matter that you have been involved in." Mrs. Harrison laughed and began to address herself only to me, but asked me not to quote her on certain matters. She began her story by remarking that the history of the Gokachi had been one long story of the ways in which the white men took the Indian lands. The most recent encroachment is being made by wealthy cattlemen, who covet the small amount of land left to the Indians and use a variety of legal but immoral devices to get it. Some cattlemen, she asserted, get the older Indians to sell their lands and go on welfare. (If one owns sufficient land, one cannot get welfare aid.) Another cattleman, she said, bought up all the land around the tract of a stubborn Indian landholder and put up cattle guards on all the roads. The Indian, whose only means of transportation was a horse and wagon, was imprisoned on his property and was forced to sell his land. She further insisted that a hundred years ago the Indian communities in the hills were economically better off than they are today. The people had more land and more water and they were able to subsist on it fairly well.

As for herself, she had been for many years an active member of the local historical society and of several other organizations whose aim was to assist and uplift the impoverished Gokachi. In addition, she had for many years been a member of the tribal executive committee—of which Mayard, of course, was chief. She said that she had once thought well of Mayard, that he was a good man, genuinely trying to help the Indians. He had even tried, unsuccessfully, to learn something of the Gokachi language. When, in recent years, Mayard had several times said that he wished to resign his position as chief because his duties entailed too much of a sacrifice of time, she believed him. What had really set her off, she said, was bringing in this out-of-state man, Stumpfegger, who wasn't even an Indian, and putting him in charge of an enormous project entailing hundreds of thousands of dollars belonging to the Indians, with the aim of doing something that the Indians didn't know anything about and didn't want done anyway. This, she had felt, was not right.

Before proceeding with her story, it might be well to explain how the Gokachi had come by all this money and what the argument between Mrs. Harrison and Mr. Mayard was all about. About five years before, the Gokachi had won a claims case against the United States government and had received a judgment of over ten million dollars. Of this sum, a large part was distributed as per capita payments to the people who had been on the old tribal rolls or to their heirs. Over a million dollars were paid for attorneys' fees—thus, Lloyd Spear, as one of the attorneys, must have received a large amount of money. This left a residue of several million dollars which, by decision of Congress, was to revert to the tribe. (None of the "fact sheets" handed out by the tribal executive stated specifically how much money was paid out per capita and how much was left as surplus, but most people to whom we talked figured that the residue amounted to about two million dollars.) It was the question of what was to be done with this residue that was causing some of the current fuss.

Mrs. Harrison was convinced that the Establishment's plan to build a model Indian village for the tourist trade did not have the support of the poor people and, indeed, that most of the poor Gokachi did not even know about it. She had voted against the proposal and protested personally to Mayard. When this had not helped, she had written letters to the local newspapers, explaining what was being done. Most of the papers had not printed her letters. She had appealed to a high-ranking official in the BIA, but he had told her not to talk to reporters. Then she had criticized the project at a public meeting. But all her efforts had accomplished nothing, and the construction of the village and amphitheater had proceeded. She had then resigned from the tribal executive commitee, though Mayard had entreated her several times to return. Now, she told me, she felt very discouraged, and she saw little point in continuing her efforts. "You can't fight a big corporation," she concluded.

When I mentioned that Lloyd Spear had castigated Murray at the Natoma meeting, Mrs. Harrison snorted in a ladylike way. Spear, she said, had been Mayard's stooge for years. Not only did he get a small fortune out of representing the Gokachi in the claims case, but Mayard still paid him a substantial sum monthly as retainer to serve as attorney for the Gokachi tribe. Mayard, she said, would occasionally offer to resign from his time-consuming office as Principal Chief. But then Spear would immediately make a long address, describing the greatness and nobility of Mayard and call on everyone present to stand up in signification of a unanimous vote of confidence in their great chief, Bayard Mayard. Naturally, everyone always stood up. But, said Mrs. Harrison, after she made her speech about the money, many people refused to stand up.

She also gave us some helpful information on the Natoma society. *Natoma,* she said, was the Gokachi name for a pagan ceremonial organization. About thirty years ago there had been several such *Natomas,* each of which was led by its own charismatic Gokachi leader. At present there were at least two genuine *Natomas* or dance groups, and Soobey Fields (our leisure-loving research assistant) was the leader of one of them. But the Natoma Society to which Murray had spoken was a different kettle of fish. It had been founded by Lloyd Spear, and most of its members were retired Christian people with a little Indian blood who lived in Ottawa. They did not have the right, Mrs. Harrison said, to assert that they represent "the Gokachi" or that they understood the needs and point of view of the poor Indians, since they had little or no contact with "the folks who lived out in the hills and go to the [pagan] dances."

This talk with Mrs. Harrison helped to explain why certain members of the Natoma Society and the tribal executive had been so hostile to Murray and had showed so little interest in his proposed study of the schools. The tribal Establishment saw itself threatened on two fronts—by the possibility of a poor people's uprising (incited, they believed, by the Lincoln Project) and by a division in its own ranks, as represented by Mrs. Harrison. Little wonder that its members were touchy about the sudden appearance of another group of professors, who went about talking to poor people, and who could, ultimately, be traced to Metropolis University, a place which (Mrs. Harrison jokingly remarked) they considered "a den of iniquity."

27   We Are Attacked

During the month of May, Murray also tried hard to establish good rapport with the local officers and administrators of the BIA. At first his efforts in this direction seemed promising. On one occasion he met with a local Bureau official and a dean of a state college, and both men assured him that they would like to make an accurate survey of the Indian population of the region. Murray was even more encouraged by a subsequent talk with the head of the BIA area office, and with the superintendent of the Indian boarding school. Both of these men appeared to be enthusiastic about getting Murray's professional and financial assistance in such a survey. Murray felt that he could, with the approval of the Office of Education, transfer some of the funds allocated to our project to an endeavor such as this, because we needed some of this information as badly as did the Bureau. He also felt that, if we worked with the Bureau in this fashion, the educational and local tribal officials would shortly perceive that we were what we claimed to be—social scientists studying Indian education, not social activists bent on inciting a revolt against Mr. Mayard.

When Murray explained that the questionnaire would have to be properly structured, the Bureau officials presented him with a great sheaf of questions, a hodgepodge of items from every separate department, and suggested that he structure the questionnaire himself. They also told him that haste was of the essence, because they had already engaged a number of Neighborhood Youth Corps boys to begin interviewing in the following week. So for a week Murray devoted himself exclusively to preparing a compact precoded questionnaire that could be administered by untrained youngsters to Indians who had a small knowledge of English. He turned it in and, to his great surprise, he heard nothing at all. After a couple of days he telephoned Mr. Turley, the Bureau education specialist, and made an appointment to discuss the questionnaire with him.

When Mr. Turley finally arrived (half an hour late) in his office, he was businesslike but polite, making only a few suggestions about changing the questionnaire. Murray told him that we would be away from Ottawa during most of June and that he had arranged for Paul

330

Wiebe, a graduate student from Midwest University, to work with the Bureau on the questionnaire. (Mr. Wiebe, in addition to being a very competent young sociologist, was strikingly Anglo-Saxon in appearance and personality. Murray enjoyed the idea of hiring Wiebe, because several people had told him that his being a Jew had added to the unpopularity of our project. Since no one in his right mind could take Wiebe for a Jew, Murray looked forward to seeing how he would get along with the members of the Establishment.) Murray quickly retyped and amended the questionnaire according to Mr. Turley's suggestions, and Mr. Turley walked off with it, saying that he would be right back. This time he was gone for an hour. When he returned he said that the Bureau expected Mr. Levy to work only in the area office with the filled-in questionnaires. He was not to do any of the fieldwork. Murray explained politely that this would not be satisfactory, because both he and Paul, whose name was *Wiebe,* not *Levy,* would be concerned with the nature of the fieldwork. Mr. Turley was adamant, pointing out that Mr. Levy, as a stranger, might disturb things by making the wrong kind of remarks to some of the Gokachi. Murray retorted that Mr. Wiebe was a fine young man, and that if Mr. Turley met him, he would agree. The issue was finally resolved by the suggestion that Mr. Turley would allow Paul to accompany him when he made his field checks. (Privately, Murray thought this discussion ridiculous, for, so far as he knew, there was no law prohibiting any non-Indian citizen from talking to any Indian citizen.)

By this time it was 3:00 P.M., and Mr. Turley suggested a cup of coffee. Murray said that he would first like to get a roster of the officers of the Six Friendly Tribes. Turley took Murray to an office down the hall and Murray asked the secretary to mail him a copy. She asked for his name and he told her that he was with the Midwest University project, adding jokingly, "Mr. Turley can tell you all the bad things about me." "I haven't seen your FBI file yet," said Mr. Turley in a cool and matter-of-fact tone, "so I really can't do that." Murray says that at this point he suddenly felt very odd, because he realized that Mr. Turley was not joking. He believed that Murray was a criminal.

Over coffee Mr. Turley asked Murray how our project was related to the Lincoln Project. Murray explained once again—though he was getting very tired of doing this—and once again he noted that his questioner was not listening. Then Turley asked in the tone of a police interrogator, "Your wife is Sam Grossdenk's daughter, isn't she?" Murray did not know what to say, for Sam Grossdenk is four years older than I am, and, since he is a Jew and I am a Christian, it is unlikely that he could even be my godfather. Then Mr. Turley said that he was going to lay his cards on the table. He said that he liked Murray personally and felt that he could get along with him. But he had never liked Bill James and he did not think much of "that woman you have working out in Sherwood" (Dr. Reed). He also said that he had worked for four years in a penitentiary and that he had liked the men there and could get along with them even if he didn't trust them. By this time Murray was beginning to feel pretty angry; so, ignoring this remark, he pointed out that as far as he was concerned he was not prepared to accept the results of a survey conducted by untrained interviewers who might not know Gokachi and might not be motivated to do a good job. He also pointed out that the coverage had to be systematic and not random. Then he left, drove home, and wrote up his notes, remarking:

> We do seem to be dealing with a bunch of very worried people, . . . quite kooky on the subject of James and his project. They have placed us in the same camp. The small glow of good feeling that seemed to have developed two weeks ago is quite gone. [M. Wax, 1966: 31 May]

After this experience Murray wrote a letter to Robert L. Bennett, the Commissioner of Indian Affairs, describing our project as well as the survey we had intended in some detail. But although he was acquainted with us, Mr. Bennett did not respond. On 7 June Mr. Turley telephoned Murray to tell him that the Bureau had secured other funds for the survey and would no longer need his assistance. Turley added that he bore Murray "no animosity." He merely worked for "a man" and "followed his instructions."

Early in June, Murray wrote a page of reflections on what might charitably be called the progress of our study. These give a vivid picture of our situation:

> What is notable about my meetings with the Natoma Society, the Gokachi tribal public relations committee, etc. etc. is that when I state my business as the study of education, no one ever displays any real interest in the topic. At Thrashing Buffalo, so many educators and administrators took the attitude that "education is the answer" to any and every problem, and correspondingly they had problems to discuss or questions to raise about education. But here, no one really wants to discuss educational problems, not even Mr. Disaster, who was presented to us as an authority on education, nor even the administrative

officials of the schools. Instead, there is an immediate counterattack: Who are you and by what right do you come here—and what makes you think there is a problem anyway?—the problems of Indian education are no worse than those of the Negroes and rural Whites—and, of course, most of all, a whole series of questions and accusations intended to identify us with and derogate us as members of Lincoln Project.

Also significant is that both the BIA and the tribal officials seem to assume that they can guard the access to the rural Gokachi. They seem to feel that they can somehow prevent us from communicating with the rural folk. For example, James states that when Rudy Nimmermehr was conducting his survey, Joe Dropit (a member of the tribal Establishment) was denouncing Bill and Rudy in the rural churches. And, again, now the BIA insists via Turley that we can only participate in the survey if our staff remains in Pallas [a large city] and avoids the areas of field research. They denounce the people serving as our interpreters (e.g. Soobey), but when I attempt to obtain their recommendations for interpreters, their candidates, they are then shaken, and insist that they will have to meet and discuss the issue.

Plainly, I am clashing here with a southern rural power structure, with its usual roots, on the one hand in powerful industry, and on the other hand in the small petty politicians who somehow make out from the graft.

THE INTERTRIBAL COUNCIL DENOUNCES US

During our absence from Ottawa (we were gone from 11 June to 9 July) the "Deerslayer" appeal was heard in federal court at Ooga City, the state capital. This was the case in which Mr. Gopher, a fullblood Gokachi, had killed a deer out of season and contended, when arrested, that since he was hunting in Indian territory he was within his lawful rights as an Indian. The tribunal took the case under advisement, and a restraining order was issued, barring prosecution by the state. This meant, as the newspapers reported, that the case could be appealed directly to the United States Supreme Court. Murray and I were pleased when we heard about the success of the appeal because it is always heartening to learn that the courts will listen to a poor person. We were also pleased for the sake of Bill James, for Bill seemed to have a great emotional involvement in the case. According to Bill, the Gopher case was the first organized act of legal self-assertion that the poor rural Gokachi had undertaken in a very long time. Had we been aware that this Gopher case was intimately related to the fate of our research project, we might still have been pleased but we would also have been nervous.

Several articles on the case appeared in the national press. These quoted some of Mr. Gopher's droll remarks and part of the testimony given by Bill James and Rudy Nimmermehr, and they also mentioned the presence of lawyers from the American Civil Liberties Union. Even more significant, they made no mention whatever of the tribal Establishment, the chiefs, the Six Friendly Tribes, or the elaborate plans for the Gokachi Cultural Center. The only Indians mentioned were the people who lived in the hills in poverty and obscurity, who wanted to kill deer because their family needed meat.

One week after the hearing, the intertribal council of the Six Friendly Tribes met and, according to newspaper accounts, listened to an address by Vern Waters in which he told the council that he "was concerned with the partisan political actions of our research group." Waters charged that we had started rumors in his community that he and his wife were not qualified to teach the Gokachi children and that we had gone to the school boards seeking jobs for ourselves. He further charged that persons associated with our groups were attempting to assume leadership in the Gokachi tribe and take an active role in OEO projects. He further suggested that the Metropolis and the Midwest University groups were connected with the Gopher case, which he described as an attempt to encourage lawlessness and civil disorder. His day school pupils, he asserted, were now coming to him and saying that they did not have to obey the laws and that they had the right to hunt without a license.

The intertribal council thereupon passed a resolution aimed at restricting activities of out-of-state groups working with the fullblood Gokachi Indians and another resolution to withold funds from these study groups if they did not cease political activity. Members of the council then applauded a speech and denounced marches which threaten the government and persons refusing to register for the draft.

The attack by Waters and the council concerned rather than scared us, for it only expressed in newsprint a hostility of which we had been aware for over six weeks. We knew that certain members of the Establishment hated and feared us and that, come what may, they would do all in their power to get us out of Ottawa. The important point, so far as we were concerned, was whether the Establishment could achieve its ends: frighten our Gokachi interviewers and their respondents so that we could not get data on how the parents felt about their children's education, and frighten the school principals and other educators so that we would be forbidden to enter the schools. We did not think that the administrators in the Department of Health, Education, and Welfare would take Mr. Waters' bizarre accusations and the hostile resolutions of the tribal council very seriously—and in this supposition we were correct. With the dubious wisdom of hindsight, I am now inclined to say that the one point on which we were very naïve was that we did not see the significance of the Establishment's attempt to connect our study of education with the "deerslayer" case.

Murray and I were also considerably reassured by the reactions of the local critics of the Establishment, who seemed to view the proceedings of the intertribal council as idiotic but typical. Indeed, now that we ourselves had been attacked, some people spoke to us much more frankly, and we heard a great deal of interesting gossip. The tribal council, we were told, was self-perpetuating and unrepresentative. Mayard had the ultimate and only legal power, and though he cloaked his decisions behind the executive committee, they were all his creatures and he ran them with great adroitness. It was only several years after events that members came to understand the impact of decisions that had been made. Mayard, we were told, was an artist in the use of surprise, presenting important issues to the council with little opportunity for reflection or study. The two fullblood Indians on the council sat with their heads down and voted affirmatively on everything.

We were also told that Mayard had informed the council that the Lincoln Project was headed by Sam Grossdenk, who (Mayard said) was a communist. In proof of this accusation, Mayard (the story went) related how, when he (Mayard) had visited Russia, he had told the Russians that he was an American Indian. The Russians thereupon asked to see the marks of his chains. This, Mayard asserted, was because Sam Grossdenk had told the Russians that the American Indians were kept in chains. Mayard (we were told) also claimed that, when he had visited Grossdenk's office at Metropolis University, he had seen on Grossdenk's desk a letter from the Communist Party giving Grossdenk instructions.

(When I heard this, I laughed, for if Mayard had made these statements, it would help to explain why Bureau officials had called me Sam Grossdenk's daughter in a tone that implied that this made me a kind of female monster.)

Murray and I considered the situation and decided that our best policy would be to leave Ottawa for a while and let the Lincoln

335

Project and the Establishment fight it out. Dr. Reed was in Berkeley on vacation, Arthur BraveHeart was in Montana directing a workshop for teachers of Indian children, and Soobey Fields (who had not done any work for months) had been dismissed from the project. Nobody, then, was doing much fieldwork except two Gokachi matrons, Mrs. Tucker and another lady, who were continuing to interview the poor Indians whose children attended the rural day schools. I had two other reasons for leaving Ottawa and returning to Midwest: the weather had turned so hot and humid that I could neither work nor sleep; I wanted to write a preliminary report on the poor Indians of Ottawa and also to draft an article on the Head Start programs we had observed and investigated the year before.[1] Murray prepared a newspaper release about our leaving Ottawa, but, as usual, the newspapers did not print it.

Late in July (after we had left Ottawa), the Gokachi cultural center was ceremonially dedicated by the tribal Establishment. Chief Mayard broke ground in his shirt sleeves, assisted by a young lady in Indian costume and by the regional director of the Bureau of Indian Affairs. The *Ooga City Press* described this event in detail and the same issue carried a separate article explaining that the strained relations between the Lincoln Cross-cultural Project and the established leaders of the Gokachi tribe had begun some years earlier when Dr. Sam Grossdenk of Metropolis University had sponsored the American Indian conference at which a resolution was introduced that the present Bureau of Indian Affairs be revamped and replaced by a new commission. The social scientists, the article continued, are charged with trying to form dissenting Gokachis into a civil rights movement, and the tribal officials are looking with suspicion on the activities of a Midwest University group headed by Dr. Murray and Rosalie Wax.

---

1. Murray eventually joined me in preparing the article and it was published under the title of "The Enemies of the People" (Becker, 1968).

28 From Research to Conflict

In the first week of August, Bayard Mayard (who had once attended Midwest University but had not obtained a degree there) wrote to Chancellor Snow, asserting that he had just learned of the activities and resolutions of the intertribal council of the Six Friendly Tribes and that, as an alumnus, he was much disturbed by the bad publicity falling upon his university. He accompanied this letter with copies of the intertribal council's resolutions against us, but disclaimed responsibility for them. The chancellor then asked Murray for an explanation, saying that the main point at issue seemed to be our alleged participation in the deerslayer case, which Mr. Mayard regarded as a sign of the breakdown of law in the region. Murray, at a meeting with the chancellor and other officials of the university, sketched the outline of events and associations in the deerslayer case as best he could, for he had only a bare and mostly hearsay knowledge of what had gone on. He pointed out that our project and the members of our staff had nothing whatever to do with the case. He also said that, so far as he knew, the deerslayer case was not (as Mr. Mayard feared) a sign of disrespect for the law, but a test case deliberately staged after consultation with representatives of the Department of Justice and the American Civil Liberties Union. Thus, it might well be regarded as a triumph for legal processes rather than a sign of lawlessness.

The chancellor and the other administrators were puzzled by some of the accusations made against us, which, to them, seemed pointless and even hilarious. For example, why would university professors like Dr. Reed or myself try to obtain teaching positions in the rural schools near Ottawa? Or why, even should we wish to be so self-sacrificing, should the intertribal council regard this as a crime calling for a grand jury investigation? Those present concluded that one of the major reasons for the council's alarm was the presence on our staff of Dr. Reed, as she had once been a member of CORE (Congress on Racial Equality) and had worked with CORE in Mississippi during the early 1960s.

The chancellor expressed the view that all of this fuss was the result of a complete misunderstanding, in the course of which we had incorrectly been associated with the deerslayer case because Dr. Reed had settled in Sherwood. Indeed, the chancellor evidently saw Mayard in much the same light as we had seen him—before we began to work in Ottawa. Mayard, the chancellor seemed to believe, was an almost fullblood Indian who spoke the Gokachi language. Beginning as a poor and simple Indian boy, he had risen to eminence. A man of admirable character, he identified himself as Indian on every occasion, remained proud of his Indianness, and devoted himself to the cause of the Indians. He regarded himself as the benevolent leader of the Gokachi and used his chieftainship as an opportunity for enlightened philanthropy. The chancellor also seemed to believe that all would be well if we could convince Mayard that our project had no connection with the deerslayer case. Accordingly, he asked Murray to prepare a written outline of the events to which he himself could refer when he took up the matter with Mr. Mayard. Murray did this—though he did not feel as sanguine about the outcome as did the chancellor.

A week later Murray heard from a dean that the talk between the chancellor and Mayard had been most cordial and that Mayard had said that he looked forward to a talk with Murray at which all these misunderstandings could be cleared up. Murray thereupon wrote to Mayard, suggesting a meeting in mid-September when Murray planned to make a week long visit to Ottawa to give instruction to our newly hired research assistant, Victor Hibou, who had done such fine work for us at Thrashing Buffalo. Murray also began to make arrangements to have a number of eminent researchers who had conducted creative studies of schools visit our project, see what we were doing, lecture to the staff, and make suggestions.

In mid-August the *Ooga City Press* printed an article by a Washington correspondent which began by asserting that the deerslayer case had probably been initiated on the advice of representatives of the Department of Justice.

While the article made no forthright or categorical assertions, it insinuated that the Lincoln Cross-cultural Project, our Midwest University Education Project, and the Department of Justice had conspired to instigate and support the deerslayer case and that we were all somehow united in a plot to defy the laws of the state. In addition, it implied that it was Murray who had revealed the unlaw-

338

ful conspiracy between the Department of Justice and the Lincoln Project.

Murray felt dismayed, because he had prepared the memo hastily for the information of the chancellor—and not for newspaper publication. The chancellor had evidently considered the memo harmless, for he had passed it on to Mayard. Then Mayard had used it, apparently to discredit at one blow all of the people or organizations who, he thought, were making trouble for him. Murray wrote a note of protest to the chancellor, enclosing a copy of a letter written by Professor Sam Grossdenk, which corrected many of the misstatements that had appeared in the press about the Lincoln Project and about our project. (Grossdenk had also sent copies of this clarifying letter to Mayard and Spear.) The chancellor thanked Murray for the materials and remarked that he had nothing to do with the newspaper story and that he believed that no harm had been done by it.

I did not share the chancellor's optimism and, besides, I was furious at Mayard for using Murray's well-intentioned letter in this devious fashion.

In the last week of August we began to receive vigorous complaints from Mary Tucker and our other Gokachi field assistant, to the effect that they were beginning to have a great deal of trouble obtaining interviews in the rural areas. More and more people, it seemed, were beginning to believe the rumors that they were working for "the communists." Murray would have gone to Ottawa at once to assist and consult with them but he was scheduled to deliver a paper at the annual meeting of the American Sociological Association and immediately thereafter he had an appointment for a conference with Mr. Mayard. In consequence, he decided that the sensible thing to do would be to attend the conference and then go to Ottawa.

At the meeting of the Sociological Association Murray met an employee of the Department of Health, Education, and Welfare who "let him know" that our project might soon be subjected to a review and site visit by HEW. Bluntly, this meant that we were about to be investigated. Murray did not believe this. First of all, he was scheduled to meet with Mayard the following week. Second, Murray did not think that any higher official in the Department of Health, Education, and Welfare could be so naïve as to believe the accusations brought against us by the tribal Establishment. In consequence, Murray spent most of his time at the meetings talking with other sociologists who had done research in cross-cultural education. He found a number of experienced researchers who expressed an eagerness to visit our project, see what was going on, and talk with and to our staff. So Murray happily made plans to broaden the scope of the project and publicize its value as pertinent and much-needed research in education. Among the professors he considered inviting were Everett C. Hughes, Donald Horton, Irwin Deutscher, Howard S. Becker, and Edgar Z. Friedenberg.

Immediately on his return to Midwest, Murray received a telephone call from Mr. Kroger of HEW informing him that a review and site visit of our project was to take place some time early in October. He also received a telephone call from Mr. Mayard's secretary, informing him that Mr. Mayard would not meet with him in mid-September (as had been arranged) but in mid-October.

There now began for Murray a most arduous six weeks. He felt obligated to put up the best fight he could. It was not so much a matter of his being emotionally or intellectually involved in the project (because from its inception it had been a pain in the neck); nor was it a matter of money, for Murray had tenure at Midwest University and could not easily be dismissed in disgrace; nor was it a matter of professional prestige, for we felt that most of our colleagues would stand by us. Rather, I think Murray worked so hard to save the project because he felt obligated to his staff, to Dr. Reed, Arthur Braveheart, Mary Tucker, and Victor Hibou (whom he had just hired), and because he believed that research should not be stopped because powerful people thought that it threatened their vested interests.

First of all, he was obliged to cancel the visits of eminent researchers in education, for it was from the ranks of these men that some of the site team visitors might be drawn. If we had already engaged them as consultants, HEW could not use them as unbiased "observers." Next, Murray wrote letters to the officers of the various social scientific societies, asking them to inform HEW that their organizations would not look with favor on the liquidation of competent research because of political pressure. Meanwhile he urged me and Dr. Reed (who was still in Berkeley), to complete the preliminary reports on which we had been working—so that they would serve as examples of the kind of research on which we had been engaged. He also managed to make a week-long visit to Ottawa to help and encourage our Indian staff workers, who were encountering difficulties because of the smear campaign against us, and to instruct and confer with Victor Hibou, who hoped to initiate and carry out a rather elaborate research project in the rural schools.

Murray found that the staff members working out of Ottawa were doing reasonably well. Miss Runner, a young woman whom we had recently hired, was continuing to obtain interviews from Indian teen-age girls, and Mr. Hibou, who had been in Ottawa only three weeks, was already taking hold like a professional. But the Gokachi staff members working in the rural communities were in a bad way. They reported that during the past month their Gokachi neighbors had become increasingly frightened and suspicious, and Clementine, Mary Tucker's daughter, had found the going so tough that she had stopped interviewing altogether. The ladies also told us that Vern Waters and Mudwalls Dobie had been going about in the rural communities, denouncing us as communists and, it would seem, voicing threats about what might happen to people who "cooperated with" communists. The newspaper articles which implied that the Lincoln Project and our project were urging people to break the law were also beginning to have an effect, for, as one of the Gokachi ladies put it, "the people to who I talk are educated and read the newspapers."

Even some of the local ministers were warning people about the Lincoln Project and, by implication, our project, and we heard one fantastic tale which had it that the Lincoln Project had acquired a Gokachi typewriter so that it might print a new and sacrilegious version of the Bible. The extent to which this campaign was influencing people is reflected by Mrs. Tucker's anxiously asking Murray, "Does your money *really* come from the U.S. government?" Murray assured her that it did.[1]

Murray returned to Midwest about 19 September and resumed his long-distance phone calls, letter writing, sending off of reports, and conferences with anyone he thought could help us. On the advice

1. The people of Thrashing Buffalo, who are in many respects more "innocent" and "tribal" than the Gokachi, were not frightened of us when Mrs. GoodHorse told them that I and my interpreter, Mrs. WhiteElk, were communists. To them, this meant simply that Mrs. GoodHorse did not like us and was trying to hurt us.

of Dr. Grossdenk, he wrote to John Gardner, then Secretary of HEW, sending Mr. Gardner some of our research reports on the Gokachi project. Dr. Grossdenk also suggested that we regard the site visit (our forthcoming investigation) as an opportunity for other social scientists to become acquainted with what was really going on in Ottawa. This notion gave us a good deal of comfort, and we got a few chuckles out of the picture of some of our colleagues having to listen to long denunciations of us by people like Spear, Stumpfegger, Muffin, Waters, and Dobie. Murray received numerous telephone calls from Mr. Kroger of HEW, who seemed to be proceeding with the arrangements for the site visit in a scrupulously fair manner. Mr. Kroger asked Murray for his suggestions on how the site visitors might proceed (we assumed that he was also asking our accusers). Murray and I discussed this request and we remembered that our first really helpful and convincing insights into the pattern of what was going on in the area had come from Mrs. Harrison. We therefore suggested that the members of the site team talk to her. We thought that it would more or less even things up if the team also talked to some of the people who were most passionately opposed to our work in Ottawa. So we suggested that they talk to Lloyd Spear and Dan Muffin. We reasoned that no sociologist or anthropologist could fail to learn a good deal by talking to Mrs. Harrison and Mr. Spear.

In the last week in September, Murray seriously considered asking our congressman for assistance, but members of the university administration said that such a request could be made more effectively by the university.

Then, on 3 or 4 October, Murray received a telephone call from Washington informing him that the site visit had been postponed from the week of 6 October to the week of 12 October so that it might coincide with a meeting of the intertribal council of the Six Friendly Tribes. When I heard this, I became truly alarmed, for I knew—as well as I knew that I was not Sam Grossdenk's daughter —that if the heads of the tribal Establishment were permitted to call the plays, we—that is, Murray and the project staff—would be sunk. We had seen how the tribal officers had manipulated the American Indian conference, and we had been told many times how they manipulated and controlled the National Congress of American Indians. We had seen, a month before, what Mayard had done with the memo Murray had written for the chancellor. Therefore, we strongly suspected that this maneuver—the taking up of a large part of the site visit by a meeting of the tribal council—was part of a plan to finish us off in grand style. And, judging by their previous behavior, we anticipated that the members of the Establishment would stop at nothing, provided they could get away with it.

Murray and I decided that the best course would be the boldest —to tell Mr. Kroger exactly what we thought the leaders of the tribal council were up to and to lay down the conditions on which we were willing to meet with them. So on 5 October Murray wrote a letter pointing out that the council had already passed resolutions condemning our project without inviting us to be present and without sending us a copy of the resolutions. He predicted that on the twelfth the council would hurl additional accusations against us, pass an even more strongly worded series of resolutions, and then publish its version of these events in the press. He pointed out that we were appearing voluntarily and that we expected to be treated with courtesy and to be allowed to speak our minds. If we were not treated fairly, we would leave.

Meanwhile, the tribal Establishment was making its own arrangements for the reception of the site team. The local school principals and teachers were summoned to a special meeting where they listened to a long address by Lloyd Spear. Spear also arranged personally to conduct the site visitors on a tour of the schools. Though we did not hear about this meeting until the site visit was over, we experienced its effects immediately. Victor Hibou, our research assistant, reported that several teachers in rural schools with whom he had established excellent rapport had told him that he could no longer enter their classrooms. The school board, they said, had ruled against his making observations in their school.

On 6 October, we received a telephone call from an associate dean at Midwest University telling us that HEW had renewed our contract for research in Ottawa until June of 1968. This news was bewildering, for why should HEW renew our contract for six months immediately before it was to conduct an investigation into our research practices? Still, we comforted ourselves with the thought that whatever befell, HEW was not likely to cancel our contract if it had been newly funded. Bureaucratic steps, once started, are hard to stop, and money that has been allocated must be spent.

Our final days before the ordeal were enlivened by another

343

mysterious occurrence. On the afternoon of 6 October, Vern Waters, the school principal who had formally denounced us to the inter-tribal council, called at our project office in Ottawa and asked anxiously for Murray Wax. He found no one there but Arthur BraveHeart's mother-in-law. On being told that neither Murray nor Rosalie Wax were in Ottawa and that they had not been there since the end of July, Waters asked for Dr. Reed. But Dr. Reed was not there either, having been in Berkeley since the end of June. Appearing very distraught, Waters then asked for Arthur, but Arthur was out.

We were, understandably, extremely curious as to what had caused this last-minute failure of nerve in the man who had initiated the attack on us. Our most sensible guess was that something had caused the Establishment to panic and that Mr. Waters had been told that, since he had made the false accusations against us, he alone would have to appease us or take the consequences.

On 10 October we drove to Ottawa and began the four days that, for me, were like a separate and unique section of my life. I felt as if all of us—Murray, our staff members, Mayard, Spear and the tribal and Bureau officials, the site visitors, and our consultant, Professor Deutscher—had all become performers in a massive pageant or ceremony or, perhaps, a ritual battle. All of us knew some of our lines and all of us knew that there were certain scheduled scenes which we would have to get through. But there were many impromptu or unanticipated skits in which we were forced to improvise. Meanwhile, we desperately threw helpful clues to the actors on our side and ruthlessly threw misleading clues to the actors on the other side. Some of the scheduled acts were carried off well by all parties. Others turned into farces, which caused me discomfort, because I did not dare laugh at a supposedly solemn or tragic moment. The strain of being "on stage" for four days was enormous, but it was also intensely exhilarating. It helped me understand why many professional actors are never able to retire.

When we reached Ottawa, Murray telephoned Waters, and Waters suggested that he and Murray have dinner in a local Ottawa restaurant on Tuesday night. (The intertribal council meeting at which we were to make our appearance was to be held on Wednesday morning.) All of the staff were now present in Ottawa because Murray felt it would be a good idea to have everybody there and because Murray himself had a ceremonial notion that we all ought to stand or fall together. Dr. Reed had flown in from Berkeley, and Miss Runner had come—despite pressure from her relatives who were worried about her "working with those communists." Victor Hibou was there, taking a rather stand-offish attitude, because he had joined the project after the trouble started, and, of course, there was Arthur BraveHeart. In addition, we had a new arrival, Sydney Andruff, who, though he knew almost nothing at all about the situation, gave everybody a great deal of advice about taking an uncompromising and principled stand.

In preparation for the site visitors Arthur had on his own initiative decorated the sitting room of our house-office. On one wall was a large, colored print of President Johnson, flanked by two American flags. On another wall was a poster stating, "God Bless America." Over the fireplace hung an ancient print depicting an Indian maiden crossing a stream. These pictures and the window curtains were elaborately draped with red, white, and blue crepe paper.

Late that afternoon we held a staff meeting. Murray explained that the site visitors were going to be professors, like himself, and that the staff members should answer their questions frankly and as best they could. He told us that Mr. Kroger was scheduled to arrive the next day and that Kroger would spend the morning with the Indian Bureau people in Pallas. At one in the afternoon, Kroger would meet with us. After the meeting with Kroger we would eat dinner and drive to Tomahawk Lodge, the resort where the meeting of the intertribal council of the Six Friendly Tribes was to be held.

We then came to what was for Murray and me the crucial business of the meeting, namely, to decide whether we should try to keep the project going in Ottawa (which we knew would be difficult) or leave Ottawa and use the funds to do research on Indian education in some less touchy or explosive areas. So far as we were concerned, the project had been no bed of roses, and we knew that we would not be able to accomplish much research if we continued to be blocked and harassed as we had been for the past three months. Perhaps, then, the sensible thing to do was to take our funds and go elsewhere. (Indeed, from several hints we gathered that some people in the HEW would be enthusiastic about helping us do this.) On the other hand, we were not doing this research only for the sake of research, but as an effort to provide materials and insights that might contribute to the improvement of education for the Indians. This being so, we felt that the decision how we ought to try

345

to continue the research ought to be made by the Indian staff members. When we introduced the question, Arthur spoke strongly in favor of staying in Ottawa. Victor Hibou said that he too would prefer to stay and complete the research project he had begun. Most of us were heartened by this display of spirit, and the upshot was that we decided—as Arthur put it—to "reluctantly stay."

On Tuesday morning most of us had nothing to do but keep up our morale. I stayed at the house-office with Arthur, his wife, Victor, and Miss Runner, where we said things to make each other laugh and wondered aloud what was going on in the Bureau offices in Pallas. We knew that Mr. Kroger, the director of the site visit, was there conferring with the Bureau officials and, no doubt, Lloyd Spear. Mr. Kroger, Murray felt, was a reasonably intelligent and perceptive man, and we anticipated that the more the Bureau people and Spear harangued Kroger, the more easily he would see what was going on and the kind of people we were up against.

Mr. Kroger, who had said that he would meet with all of us at our Ottawa headquarters at one o'clock, called and said he would not arrive until two. He came at 2:30. Thereupon he and Murray withdrew to the decorated sitting room for more than half an hour. When they came out, we all looked at Murray, and he looked tired and discouraged. Then Mr. Kroger sat down with the staff and asked Elsie, Arthur, and Victor a few questions. They spoke well, Elsie describing some of her findings in the schools and Arthur and Victor describing how Indian students "tune out"—but it was clear to me that Mr. Kroger was not listening. Indeed, his face reflected the expression which Murray and I had seen so often on the faces of the school, tribal, and Bureau officials—the expression of a person who thinks he is being told lies but is too polite to say so. During this uncomfortable half hour, Mr. Waters telephoned and canceled his dinner appointment with Murray for that evening.

Murray told me later that his talk with Kroger had been very difficult. Kroger was convinced that we were in fact political activists and had been doing all in our power to stir up trouble for the properly constituted tribal executive. When Murray denied this, Kroger remarked that he had no objection to political activists but that he disapproved of people who engaged in political action under the shield of social scientific research. When Murray told Kroger that our project had just been funded until June of the following year, Kroger did not believe this either and remarked that there must be some mistake. He then told Murray that Lloyd Spear had arranged to take him on a tour of the community on Wednesday afternoon so that he could talk to school administrators, principals, and teachers about our project.

Fortunately, for us, Murray had made an appointment for Mr. Kroger to meet and talk with Mrs. Harrison on Tuesday afternoon, and Kroger agreed to make a brief call on her. After our "Indian" office in the run-down house, the residence of Mrs. Harrison seemed the height of conservative propriety. More than that, like an aristocrat, Mrs. Harrison minced no words. She immediately took the conversational initiative and instructed Kroger in the nature of Gokachi politics. By the time she had reached the specifics of our project and the indignities to which we were being subjected by both Gokachi and federal officials, she had reduced Kroger to an almost abject state. She told him that no one in the state had charge of Indian education and no one had the right to claim that he could speak for Indians in the schools. (Evidently Mr. Kroger had been told that morning that the tribal Establishment's educational committee had this responsibility.) She also told him that the Natoma Society was not an elected body of Indian representatives (which he had evidently been led to believe) and that they might more accurately be regarded as a mixed bag of reasonably well-intentioned people who gained satisfaction or profit out of claiming to represent the Indians. She also made it clear that the tribal officers were all appointed, that Mayard had been appointed about twenty years ago, and that there had been no elections. Murray was somewhat cheered by the outcome of this conversation, for (as he told me) Mrs. Harrison had shaken Kroger's conviction that the picture presented by the tribal Establishment was the true one. Clearly, if we had allies like her, we could not simply be radical activists pretending to research.

Professor Irwin Deutscher arrived while Murray and Mr. Kroger were talking with Mrs. Harrison. He was dressed in a black turtleneck sweater which made him look a little like a foreign agent. What the tribal Establishment would think of our calling in a foreign agent to help us I could not imagine, but I was beyond caring. Still and all, Professor Deutscher helped us a great deal. He was the one newcomer to the situation who believed what he said, and when, subsequently, he gave us advice, it was always sound and sane.

Since Mr. Waters had canceled the dinner engagement, Murray

suggested that all of us get the best dinner available and then proceed to Tomahawk Lodge, the elegant and expensive resort at which the meeting of the tribal council was to be held. Accordingly, we all drove to a Mexican restaurant in Pallas and had a splendid meal, laughing, joking and teasing each other. This meal was one of the most enjoyable of my life, but it is the one of my field experiences about which I can remember nothing that was said. Since I was not drunk, I must have been what my ancestors called "battle-mad."

29   The Confrontation

Together with WeaselBear, our shaggy Indian dog, and with Irwin Deutscher, our consultant disguised as a foreign agent, Murray and I drove to Tomahawk Lodge. On the way there we continued to fill him in with the details of our project and of its history. For the benefit of the site visitors, with whom we might have less time to talk and who might be less inclined to accept our word for things, Murray had brought with him, not only a briefcase crammed with basic documents, but a large transfer case filled with project reports, field notes, interview schedules, newspaper clippings, and the like. By the time we reached the lodge it was after 11 P.M., and anticipating that no one might be at the desk except for some aged night clerk, or a woman, Murray shouldered his heavy box of precious research materials and started along the walk from the parking lot to the entrance facade. Deutscher followed with his attaché case, while I brought up the rear (as an "Indian" woman) carrying Murray's briefcase in one hand and holding WeaselBear's leash in the other, while she trotted peacefully at Deutscher's heels. On entering the main door, our procession—looking something like "Peter and the Wolf" or perhaps an ancient folktale—was startled to encounter a reception committee. Standing on the carpet of the impressive foyer were the important members of the intertribal council and of the Bureau of Indian Affairs, from Mr. Mayard and the area director on down. They seemed to have been waiting a long time, and they were fatigued in appearance if elegant in their garb. I was dressed in my camping jacket and tennis shoes, but we had not lived among the Thrashing Buffalo for nothing; so we acknowledged this grand reception with sober dignity and gracefully shook hands with all the important men. I even shook the hand of Lloyd Spear and told him I was happy to meet him, although I did catch him, for an instant, looking at WeaselBear with a bewildered expression.

Murray and I were baffled by this red-carpet treatment, but by this time were so stupefied by fatigue that we did not try to understand.

I woke up before dawn and felt very restless. I got dressed quietly, and, taking WeaselBear with me, went quietly out of the palatial lodge and walked around it in the dim grey light. I kept the lodge on my left side, and though I had to make my way over some steep places and walk on some retaining walls, I made it. When I had almost finished our circle we came to a high place from which I could see the lake. Just then the sun began to rise, and the largest flock of wild geese that I have ever seen rose with it, circled once, and then headed south. I prayed very hard—this time that things would turn out well for the young Indians.

At breakfast Murray and I were joined by a man who introduced himself as Dean Richter, then an associate dean on the staff of the provost of Midwest University. Almost at once, Mr. Mayard, who was sitting at a large table with other important men, rose, came to our table, shook hands with Dean Richter, and nodded coldly at us. "We're counting on you to help us resolve this matter," said the dean. "I'll do all I can," replied Mr. Mayard. After he had gone, the dean indicated to us that he felt that the attack on our project had become enmeshed with a much larger struggle within the power system of the state. Perhaps he was right—we never learned any more about it. In any case, it was comforting to know that Dean Richter was there to assist us, especially since Mr. Kroger of HEW seemed so strongly inclined to take the Establishment's views.

The meeting of the intertribal council of the Six Friendly Tribes was held in an imposing conference room. Opposite the doors was a dais where sat the chiefs of the Six Friendly Tribes. Some of them looked like Indians. Others did not; W. C. Rubbers, president of the intertribal council and chief of the River tribe, wore an ostentatious beaded Indian string tie and whooped loudly at unexpected moments. The chief of the Gokachis, of course, was Mr. Mayard.

The meeting opened with an invocation by a Gokachi minister (who was probably the only person present who spoke the Gokachi language), and with the singing of "America the Beautiful." Chief Rubbers led the singing in a raucous and stentorian voice. This annoyed me, and I sang along as loudly as I could, which was even louder than Chief Rubbers. Several of the council members turned around and stared at me as if they were startled that persons accused of radical and civil rights agitating could sing patriotic hymns with such fervor.

Chief Mayard delivered a long and beautifully organized address.

He began with a detailed and meticulously correct chronology of his association with us and with Bill James. He referred to his own interest in Indian affairs and asserted that he had always approved of any project that helped poor people to help themselves or any program that was calculated to improve the lot of the Indians. He said that when the Lincoln Project had been initiated, he had felt that parts of it had considerable merit—for example, the aim of teaching the Indians to use their own language. But after the Lincoln people had begun their program, he had received letters from fullbloods who were disturbed and upset by what the Lincoln people were doing.

Mayard then explained his status as appointed chief and told us that he had resigned about ten years ago. Since then, he, and, by implication, other members of the Gokachi executive committee, had been seeking for some other Gokachi who might serve as chief. At first they had had high hopes that Soobey Fields might be that man. But, continued Mayard, in a tone of regret, Soobey had joined the Lincoln staff, and, as the Lincoln people continued their work, disturbing things began to happen. There were attempts to promote hatred against the whites, attacks on the BIA, criticisms of some of the tribal chiefs. In short, the Lincoln Project was causing trouble in the Indian country, for, said Mayard, it is what people believe—whether true or not—that makes the difference.

In the middle of this unfortunate state of affairs, he continued, Murray Wax wrote that he was coming to Ottawa to do an educational study. Shortly thereafter, Mayard learned that some of the people who had been employed by Bill James were now going to work for Dr. Wax. One of these was Soobey Fields, who had said under oath in the deerslayer case that there were four hundred armed Indians ready to fight the whites over this affair. Moreover, the poor and ignorant Indians began to attend meetings and report all sorts of things—and the source of these disturbances seemed to be the James and the Wax projects. Mayard himself, he said, had talked to Sam Grossdenk all day yesterday about these matters. He had also talked to Chancellor Snow of Midwest University, and the chancellor had been very distressed.

As he approached the end of his speech, Mayard's voice took on a stern and dramatic tone. He told how he had recently met the actor Marlon Brando on a plane bound for Paris, and that Brando had urged Mayard to support and encourage the Indians

351

to demonstrate as the Negroes were doing. Mayard, however, felt that demonstrations like these were un-American and weakened our country. He continued in even sterner tones, "If Metropolitan University and Midwest University want to bring demonstrations to our state, the intertribal council wants no part of it." He also made a reference to meetings held by members of the Justice Department among other tribes and indicated that he wished to know whether HEW was financing a program for outsiders to come into the state and stir up trouble among the Indians.

Murray responded to Mayard's address with a much shorter but equally urbane speech. He began by saying that we were a research and not an action project. He pointed out that grave problems of poverty, education, and alienation existed in Ottawa, problems with which the intertribal council had long been concerned. Businessmen, he continued, have long appreciated the value of outside consultants and of observations and studies made by outsiders. He then outlined in some detail the type of work each member of the staff had been doing, and remarked that we were well aware of how talk could spread in an Indian community. For example, he said, several people had even told us that Mr. Dobie and Mr. Waters were spreading malicious rumors about us.

Sam Grossdenk and Bill James (Murray said) were authorities on Indian Affairs and merited respect. On the other hand, we did not know very much about their project or about what they had done. He concluded by saying that there was nothing secret about our research and that we were not engaged in any conspiracy. We had announced our arrival in the press, sent copies of our publications to Lloyd Spear, and, in every case in which we had visited or observed a school, we had first obtained the permission of the superintendent and the principals, just as we had done in the case of Vern Waters.

W. C. Rubbers, president of the intertribal council, then made a speech. In a loud, hortatory, and angry tone, he asked us members of the Midwest project whether "we knew that 95 percent of the Gokachis can speak as good English as you and I" and that the Gokachis' refusal to speak English "is a pretense." As evidence for this assertion he pointed out that when the census was taken in the state, only two interpreters were needed. He also asked us, in a patronizing tone, whether we were not aware that there were many white people as poor as the Indians. He continued:

I know that since these projects have been started there have been dissident groups organized in the River nation, not collectively, but all going in different directions. Their primary goal is removal of the present chief [himself], to remove the present council, and "to hell" with the Bureau of Indian Affairs. They are saying, Let's go back to 1900, prior to the act of Congress that made Ottawa a state. Someone, somewhere, in some way, is agitating these people.

Mr. Rubbers then called on Vern Waters to make a statement. Since Chief Rubbers had addressed us aggressively, I expected that Waters—our major accuser—would deliver a veritable philippic. But something clearly had happened to him, for he spoke to the assembly as if he expected to be taken out and shot. He began by saying that it had appeared as if we were conducting an action program rather than an academic one. He referred to "charges that had been made," but added, "If we are wrong, a tragedy has occurred." If he had had time, he added, he would have procured affidavits. He continued:

We are going to be forced, unless you can clear the muddy water, to seek a grand jury investigation in our county because we feel laws have been violated. We are going to be forced to ask the Education Association to come in and take a look at this program; and my particular school board and perhaps several others are jointly passing a resolution asking for a federal investigation of the use of these funds.

But he weakened the force of these threats by his timid and servile tone of voice and by adding that Murray and I "were functioning politically or we were not," and "at this particular time I am not convinced, but I am under the impression that you are."

When Lloyd Spear gently encouraged Waters to be a little more specific, he responded by saying apologetically that "perhaps my definition of politics is different than yours." Waters then accused Dr. Reed of asking a school board member for a job, stating that a board member was willing to swear that Dr. Reed had done this. (Why this was supposed to be a political or even a wrong act, we never learned.) He also accused Dr. Reed of telling another school board member that Waters' wife was severe in dealing with her Gokachi schoolchildren. He said that someone had accused him of stealing school funds and of being an Indian Bureau man. He said he had heard that there was a petition being circulated against him. His friends and neighbors, he concluded, "swear that these things are happening and trace them directly to your study group, Dr. Wax, and to the Lincoln Project."

Murray made a courteous and, under the circumstances, very gentle response. He spoke of the nature of an Indian community and remarked that the kind of talk Mr. Waters had heard about was not an uncommon phenomenon. For example, when people had come to us and told us that Mr. Waters and Mr. Dobie were saying unpleasant and untrue things about us, "this had not seemed the kind of thing that anyone takes any action on." As to the charge that Dr. Reed had sought a position on the Ottawa school system, Murray suggested that all one had to do to see that it made no sense was to compare the salary of a professor of anthropology at the Midwest University with that of an Ottawa schoolteacher. And, far from speaking ill of Mrs. Waters' work as a teacher, Dr. Reed had, in her field notes, repeatedly praised Mrs. Waters' abilities and practices. (Ironically, it was Waters who, in Dr. Reed's opinion, was a rather poor teacher, though Murray, of course, did not remark on this fact.)

Mr. Dobie, Murray's other formal accuser, then gave a short address in which he really said nothing at all. At the end he accused us of not complying with the new legislation on civil rights because we had not hired any Negroes on our project, and he suggested that HEW reexamine our application for funds. After Mr. Dobie, each of the chiefs of the other friendly tribes made a speech, some long and some short, the gist of each speech being that, so long as we were *not* agitators or troublemakers, they had no objection to our continuing our research.

Chief Mayard then summarized the proceedings: "If this is really a good program we would like to see it succeed," he stated. He continued:

> My suggestion . . . my recommendation to you, Dr. Wax, would be this: I am going to assume that you are honest . . . that you are intellectually honest to the point that I gather you say you are not a part of a program that is trying to be an action program; therefore, what I would like to suggest is this: I think there would be some people who we could get to work with you . . . who know about your program . . . see what it is. . . . We would hope that you can give us some real help. We have been asking for help. . . . You came in, but I would hope that out of these discussions we find a way that we have been wrong. . . . If we have been wrong, we would lay it on the line . . . we have been wrong. . . . If you have been wrong, we can lay it on the line to you that you have been wrong.

He continued by saying that a bull had been killed in the Sherwood area (where Dr. Reed had been making observation in the school) and that people now believed that our program or the Lincoln program had "caused that action." Many white people, he added, had been given the impression that the Bureau of Indian Affairs was not "doing one thing on behalf of the Indian" and that the federal and tribal governments were not doing anything either. He concluded:

> If you are honest . . . and I am going to accept that you are honest . . . but if you are not we are going to buck you. . . . I think we could provide you with some people who we think are honest . . . and who we think could do the job of answering your questions. We have not been sure you have not been using this as a tool . . . to get your message across . . . because where would all this information come from?

To this cautious concession Murray made the following reply:

> I think Chief Mayard has spoken with the dignity and the wisdom that leads to the Gokachis being known as one of the greatest of the Six Friendly tribes. I am very happy with what he has said . . . and I thank him.

Chief Rubbers then expressed himself as ready to entertain a motion "that we heartily endorse Chief Mayard's proposal in regard to the recommendation he made." The motion was made, seconded, and carried without further discussion.

After lunch Mr. Kroger of HEW told us that the schedule of the site visitors had been changed. Instead of their visiting schools and principals, as had been planned, we would all proceed directly to the examination of our research. This sudden shift of plans threw us offstride, for we were by this time very tired. Murray had, however, sent Mr. Kroger copies of our interim reports, and these, we anticipated, would demonstrate to any social scientist that we had been conducting reasonably well-organized and relevant research. On this point, however, we were mistaken, for the colleagues who were to examine us had not read our reports and so, instead of asking us about our research, they began quizzing us about the framing and procedure of the research project. Answering such questions with style calls for the ability to make profound-sounding, jargon-studded statements and Murray is usually quite skillful at this kind of thing. But I, with a kind of inverse snobbery, have

355

always refused to learn. Now I rued my false pride, for Murray was so exhausted that he answered the site visitors' abstract questions simply and in a straightforward manner and kept referring to reports and documents which, alas, they had not read. Fortunately, Sydney Andruff, one of the research assistants whom we had just hired, proved to possess one outstanding talent—the ability to talk about research on highly abstruse theoretical and methodological levels. He talked so much and so well that the site visitors were overwhelmed. About this time in the interrogation, we suddenly became aware that the visitors were questioning us not about our research in Ottawa but about the research proposal we had drawn up some four years before when we had asked for funds to work on the Thrashing Buffalo reservation. When we pointed this out, everyone was embarrassed, and it developed that our interrogators had been given the wrong research proposal by the Washington office. After this we all relaxed a little and began to discuss our research and our difficulties with some frankness and objectivity. The site visitors and the other representatives of the Office of Education told us many times that we ought to conciliate Mr. Mayard immediately, and they even offered us extra funds, should the conciliation necessitate the hiring of additional personnel.

We slept well that night, and the next day we drove back to Ottawa to tie up loose ends. We met with the staff and determined the limits of our proposed conciliation. These amounted to the resolution that we would hire people suggested by Mayard or the Bureau and really put them to work. After all, Murray and I privately reasoned, such people could not be lazier or less competent than some of the assistants we had hired on the recommendation of our friend Bill James. On the other hand, those of us who were competent and had work to do would proceed with the research much as we had done before we had been interrupted. Next, Murray visited Bill James and told him what had happened, and that evening we had dinner with Professor and Mrs. Harrison. Professor Harrison demonstrated his thorough and experienced understanding of the situation by remarking that all of this official anxiety over conciliating Mayard was unnecessary, as, from this point forward, Mayard would leave us strictly alone. (Professor Harrison was right, for Mayard avoided any further meetings or correspondence with us, and we were never able to carry out a formal conciliation—or hire any protégés of the Establishment. On the other hand, no one interfered with our work or bothered any members of our staff.)

The following morning Murray received a long-distance call from Washington. The caller proved to be Mr. Kroger, who, on returning to Washington, had found that our research contract had indeed been renewed some eight days before, just as we had been informed and as we had informed him. This meant that someone very high in the Office of Education had refunded and reapproved our research in the face of the accusations made against us, and it further meant that the entire, expensive folderol of the site visit and the meeting with the intertribal Council had, theoretically at least, been unnecessary. (On the other hand, the site visit may have served as a means of conciliating Mayard.) Mr. Kroger further assured Murray that the Office of Education would give him even more funds to cover the salaries of the research assistants Mayard might recommend. When Murray came back with these tidings, I began to laugh, for I felt that at this moment in our lives we had reached some pinnacle of idiotic triumph and that nothing quite like this would ever happen to us again. Dr. Deutscher was standing nearby, and I remarked to him that I was now ready to die. He looked horrified. But then I expect that only a crazy gambler could understand how I felt.

We finally managed to communicate with Mr. Waters through a friend, and what Mr. Waters had to say provided a fitting and proper end to our weird adventure. This, in any case, is how his words were reported to us. We must, said Waters, be very big people to behave as we had and not expose his misdeeds before the tribal council. It is difficult, he added, for outsiders to appreciate what goes on in the communities of Ottawa. When Dr. Reed had first come to live at Sherwood, he had been asked to report anything suspicious that she did. This "pressure" he asserted repeatedly, had come from the Bureau of Indian Affairs and from "the courthouse." Some high officials in the BIA then told him that if he framed Dr. Reed he would be given a job in the Bureau paying twice the salary he made as principal of the Sherwood school. So he spread malicious rumors about her and "reported things which were not true." Now he sincerely and humbly hoped we would take his apologies to her, because he had treated her very badly.

30 Comments on the Gokachi Research

Even under the best of circumstances, an impartial study of an institution or social system is going to be perceived by its officials or functionaries as a criticism. When these men are in fact engaged in activities of dubious legality or morality, they will be even more hostile to the conduct of independent research. And this is exaggerated when fear is present, especially the fear that those who have been victimized are organizing themselves to challenge their authority. These kinds of oppressive and explosive situations constitute a dilemma for the would-be fieldworker. On the one hand, his moral sensibilities urge him to expose the injustices which are being perpetrated and to assist those who are oppressed to better their lot. Yet, on the other hand, he is only too likely to be denied entry into the situation or to be evicted from it as soon as officials learn of his work and devise a scheme to prohibit it. Such situations are fascinating laboratories for the social scientist; but even if he can physically enter and remain there, the task of gaining social entry into the most significant circles of action may prove beyond his capabilities. In consequence it should be noted that in fieldwork, even more than in other forms of scientific research, there is ample opportunity for failure, despite the best intentions and the most thorough preparation of the researcher.

In attempting to study these difficult situations, three different strategies present themselves. The first is to enter the situation at a level of such apparent humility or impotence that one does not arouse the interest of authorities who are preoccupied with other more important considerations. Without realizing it, this was perhaps a major asset of my field research within the relocation and segregation centers confining the Japanese Americans. A single young woman without much in the way of formal education or academic status, with virtually no funds, and reporting only to a university project situated far elsewhere, I must have appeared to the center administrators as a creature of the most minor import. And in this judgment they were only too clearly right. Despite my efforts on behalf of the center residents, and even though my assist-

ance was actively recruited by junior administrators who were ap-
palled by the events within the center, I could exercise only a small
effect on basic policies. Even after the centers were closed and the
war was over, I found it hard to present my findings before any public larger than my own academic department and a few friends.

A second strategy is at the opposite extreme. The researcher who
has the support of high officials who have strong political clout is not
likely to be interfered with. Such was in effect our situation on
Thrashing Buffalo, for we entered the reservation with the endorse-
ment of the Commissioner of Indian Affairs, an anthropologist who
strongly believed in the value of independent research. A parallel
configuration exists whenever a high company official himself re-
cruits a team of researchers in order to provide information about
the functioning of his enterprise, or whenever a high government
official contracts with a research team to investigate the operations
of some particular program. In all these situations there are implicit
constraints and temptations as well as moral dilemmas. For the researcher may feel that he should pull his punches and moderate his
criticism in order to repay the assistance from his powerful ally; or,
alternatively, and more venially, some research teams have perceived in the case of government-sponsored research that, while the
contracting agency claims that it wants an independent critical eval-
uation, what it really wants is a positive appraisal which it can present to the Congress as if it were the consequence of an independent
critical researcher.

A third strategy, which is a modification of the second, is to ally
oneself from the beginning with the most powerful group, even if
this be the "Establishment." In general, I have found this mode of
procedure uncongenial and I cannot honestly discuss its merits. Certainly, using this procedure, the researcher ought to have easy access to important varieties of management data, although he may
have severe restrictions on publishing any critical or revealing findings or interpretations. Worst of all, he may find that his alliance has
so branded him that he can obtain very little information from the
victimized peoples at the bottom of the heap.

In the case of our project among the Gokachi, we began with the
misapprehension that the authorities, such as the chief, would have
only minor concern about a project which focused on the Gokachi
children and the public schools. Since the schools were public and
locally controlled and since the standard response which can be

made by any person who wishes to absolve himself of responsibility for Indian misery is that they need to be educated, we figured that our project could not really rouse much antagonism from the top. Indeed, at the time we designed our study and in the earliest months of the study, we were not aware that the Lincoln Project had already aroused so much attention and hostility from the chief and his associates.

If the reader feels that some basic questions have been left unanswered in our narrative, he is right: concerning some of the conflict that developed, we can only guess at the roots, and at the present moment we prefer not to publish wild and possibly libelous speculations. However, just to show the kind of speculation that was aroused, we might mention that one of our staff was convinced that a hidden factor of the highest importance was the presence of low-grade mineral lodes, not presently worth exploiting but of great potential value in a generation; I myself think this speculation far-fetched and not adequate to account for the actualities of the conflict.

Be these considerations as they may, we did have a few initial months relatively free of harassment, and had we known then what we know now, we could have designed our project more efficiently and recruited a team that could have gathered valuable data in a brief period. Instead we worked at a more "Indian" pace, expecting that the Gokachi would have to size us up and hoping that in this interim our Indian assistants would themselves become trained as competent researchers. By the time both these parties were as ready as they would be, the storm had broken upon our heads.

One sort of misapprehension in our design was the notion that we could study the Indian enclave of a small town like Ottawa and move from it toward research on their children in the schools. It took us a while to discover that the Gokachi children were being bussed out of the town to more rural schools, and it took us even longer to realize that, if we wanted to understand the situation and problems of Gokachi in the context of a small city, then we should study that context, in this case the political and economic structure of Ottawa. Murray's initial research design had been almost Red-fieldian in a folk-urban sense: the project was to focus on Gokachi (a) in an "isolated" rural village, (b) in a small town (i.e. Ottawa), and (c) in an urban metropolis (Ooga). In retrospect, in the case of *b,* we would have done better to study Ottawa as a whole and the place of the Gokachi and their children in relationship to it than to think we could detach the Gokachi from their larger social environment. Since the rural Gokachi were surprisingly mobile, both on a daily basis in their lengthy drives from home to work, and on an annual basis in their travels about the region in the quest of work, we were acquiring much valuable information about their lives just by maintaining a research operation in the rural village that appeared so "isolated." What we needed compensatorily to perceive was how the local towns were organized and how they dealt with the Gokachi, and had we been so engaged in research we might have been less vulnerable to the attacks of the chief and his henchmen, for our regular association with town dignitaries would have marked us as respectable types of academic researchers. (Had we planned this kind of project, we would have located ourselves in a "decent" house, bought "proper" furniture, and conducted ourselves like conventional, upper-status researchers. But we had wanted a place where poor Indians and their children could be comfortable in visiting, and we did not care if the respectable folk thought our quarters déclassé. Nowadays, they would be classified as hippie.)

There is a further sense in which our fieldwork was misled by our initial conceptualizations. Despite our experience in Thrashing Buffalo, we still thought too much in polar terms, that on the one hand there were the rural "fullblood" Gokachi in their isolated villages and on the other hand, quite detached from them and unconcerned about their lives, were the tribal establishment (the chief and his allies), who had the benefit of speaking for all Gokachi but were really unconcerned about what was happening to them. Instead, the rural Gokachi were not permitted to be in isolation but were the base of a pyramid of status and power. The rural Gokachi were like the impoverished rural Negroes of the Deep South; while they were derogated and socially segregated, they were also essential to the society and economy of the region, and those who had the political power were intensely suspicious lest these lower classes be encouraged to a state of agitation which would leave the upper sections of the pyramid without support. In short, we were in the situation of so many people who try to help the abused or oppressed—we could not better the condition of one group without decreasing the power (and arousing the ire) of another.

As a final ironic commentary about the Gokachi adventure, there is my own change in status and role. I began my fieldwork experiences as an untrained person serving as the employee of a project director far senior to me in stature. By the Gokachi project, my husband and I were project directors, of senior academic status, and we were proposing to accomplish important parts of the research through the efforts of research assistants. But, whether Indian or white, several of the assistants proved incompetent: one was an alcoholic; one was dedicated and devoted but just not talented or happy in the conduct of fieldwork; and one (whom we do not discuss in this account) was an urban middle-class type who found it impossible to locate and build durable relationships with impoverished Indians. By the end of the project, I was ready to swear that never again would Murray and I place ourselves in the situation of being directors of a large research project. Rather than beat my brains out trying to instruct others in how to perform research, I prefer, if I am to be involved at all, to do the work myself.

Yet matters are not that simple, and some of this expression is nostalgic. For the kind of fieldwork I have described in the accounts of this volume cannot easily be done except by a person who is young and in good physical condition. I no longer have the energy, the stamina, and the dedication to repeat those initial months of fieldwork in the exhausting physical and social conditions of the Gila relocation center. Besides as senior professors in graduate programs of a university, it is Murray's and my role more to train and encourage our students toward such arduous fieldwork than to engage in it ourselves. For the training of my own and others' students, it is appropriate that I assemble this volume.

31   Final Thoughts

FIELDWORK AND SOCIAL SCIENCE

Probably the most important social-scientific point made in this book is that fieldwork is as much a social phenomenon (involving reciprocity, complex role playing, the invention and obeying of rules, mutual assistance, and play) as it is an individual phenomenon (involving observation, recording, testing, analyzing, defining, theorizing, and model building). I repeat, good fieldwork is not something performed by an isolated intellectual or researcher but something created by all of the people in the social situation being studied. Indeed, fieldwork might be viewed as a particular kind of *frontier* situation, in the sense in which this term was used by Robert E. Park ([1936] 1952) and Everett and Helen Hughes (1952). In this frontier situation the achievements of the fieldworker depend to a great degree on the mutually satisfactory devices which "the people" and the fieldworker are able to work out between them. Throughout this book, I have tried to describe the devices worked out by my respondents and myself at various times and in various situations (see especially chap. 4). I do not present these as specific patterns to be followed by the inexperienced fieldworker but as examples of the social creativity and ingenuity demanded of different peoples when they wish, somehow, to do something together.

HOW FIELDWORK CHANGED ME

A colleague has suggested that I reflect on the extent to which I was changed as a person by doing fieldwork. I reflected and the result astonished me. For what I realized was that I had not been greatly changed by the things I suffered, enjoyed or endured; nor was I greatly changed by the things I did (though these strengthened my confidence in myself). What changed me irrevocably and beyond repair were the things I *learned*. More specifically, these irrevocable changes involved replacing mythical or ideological assumptions with the correct (though often painful) facts of the situation. For example, after I learned how the Japanese Americans really felt about the evacuation, I could never approach them or write about them as I had done before. I underwent a similar transformation in the

363

Tule Lake center, when I began to perceive what the superpatriots were really up to. Indeed, after reflecting on how fieldwork changed me, I am now for the first time in my life completely convinced that fieldwork—insofar as it contributes to replacing incorrect notions by correct notions, speculation by fact, or falsehood by truth—is unqualifiedly a good thing.

DISCIPLINED WORKMANSHIP

False, misleading, or downright disgraceful work in the social sciences is not easy to relate to the researcher's sentiments, his moral background, or his personal preference for particular peoples or particular methods or techniques. But it can be and is clearly related to his professional behavior in or out of the field. Thus, the disciplined researcher, whatever his aims or instruments, enters the field with the expectation that he will be obliged to do many things *in spite of* his personal preferences or prejudices. If, for example, he wishes to report on the behavior of a timid or hostile group, he will not base his conclusions largely on interviews with administrators, social workers, teachers, or marginal group members, merely because these persons are voluble, easy to reach, or speak his own language. Conversely, if he wishes to understand why a particular group is timid or hostile, he will not limit his observation and participation to them, but will talk to anyone who can throw light on the situation—be he administrator, policeman, minister, grocer, doctor, industrialist, or politician. If he wishes to administer an achievement test to schoolchildren, he will not ignore the fact that one-third of the children enrolled in the class are not present, being habitual truants. If he wishes to make a general study of the aging, he will not exclude the ill, the poor, and the "lower classes" from his sample when he finds that their responses to his questionnaire schedules are incomplete or eccentric. The true social scientist is not the person who has undergone an educational lobotomy or a moral transformation. Instead, he is a person who does an honest and thorough job, omits no important aspect of a situation, and writes an honest, coherent, and fair report.

HOW DO I INTRODUCE MYSELF?

All fieldworkers are concerned about explaining their presence and their work to a host people. "How shall I introduce myself?" they wonder, or, "What should I say I am doing?"

If the fieldworker plans to do a very rapid and efficient survey, questions like these are extremely important. The manner in which an interviewer introduces himself, the precise words he uses, may mean the difference between a first-rate job and a failure. He should try to obtain the advice and the assistance of an expert, that is, a person who understands and knows exactly how to approach the people who are to be interviewed.

But if the fieldworker expects to engage in some variety of participant observation, to develop and maintain long-term relationships, to do a study that involves the enlargement of his own understanding, the best thing he can do is relax and remember that most sensible people do not believe what a stranger tells them. In the long run, his hosts will judge and trust him, not because of what he says about himself or about his research, but by the style in which he lives and acts, by the way in which he treats them. In the somewhat shorter run, they will accept or tolerate him because some relative, friend, or person they respect, has recommended him to them.

In emphasizing that a fieldworker's deeds are much more important than his words, I am not suggesting that he should not be prepared to make some statement about his interests or some attempt to explain what he is trying to do. But he should keep in mind that, for the most part, his statements are matters of formality or courtesy, and that, in and of themselves, they will probably not convince anyone that he is well intentioned or harmless.

Sensible and circumspect people take time to make observations and judgments. One reason Murray and I had so much difficulty finding a place to stay on the Thrashing Buffalo reservation was that we were anxious and ill advised and did not realize that the Indians needed time to find out for themselves what kind of white people we were. We assured them that we meant well and that we would not bother them, but this is what white people had been saying to them for generations. Once they were given the opportunity to watch, talk to, and test us, many families would have been willing to let us live and work near them. Even as it was, matters did not turn out too badly, for while we were undergoing our rigorous initiation at the GoodHorses', everyone in the neighborhood was watching, gossiping, and, I suspect, chuckling at our predicament. I have no doubt that Mrs. ChargingBear watched the behavior of my husband and myself for many weeks before she suggested that I might find her daughter Rose useful as a guide and interpreter. Rose herself told me that she would not have worked for me had she not watched me

365

and seen for herself that I was not "stuck-up" or "mean"—"like some of the other white ladies."

In the Gila relocation center my carefully prepared self-introductory speeches seemed to make very little initial impact on people. And though I was introduced to my first really helpful respondents, the Murakamis, by an old friend of theirs, I visited them for months and worked hard and honestly on my Japanese lessons before they decided that I was the kind of person before whom they might safely talk about delicate or dangerous topics. My account of fieldwork in Tule Lake demonstrates time and again that the development of a reasonably friendly, and communicative relationship took a long time and almost always involved a period of watchful consideration and judgment on the part of the respondent.

Some research supervisors suggest that a student spend his first weeks in a strange community making a census, calling on all the households and asking a series of predetermined questions. Though this may work well in some communities, I would not advise it as a general rule. For if a fieldworker starts out by acting like a census taker, the chances are that he will be defined as a census taker or as someone who is pretending to be a census taker. This is not likely to enhance his rapport, for most poor people find questions about income, employment, residence, and marital status very threatening. Whyte, for example, found that he got precisely nowhere when he tried to make a door-to-door survey and talk to people about their living conditions. By and large, the fieldworker who is wondering how he ought to introduce himself would do well to remember the old principle that it is not wise to complicate a situation beyond what is necessary. If he feels he must introduce himself, he should try to introduce himself for what he is. The probability that people will not understand him does not matter. He has tried to make a courteous and sensible social gesture.

APPROACHING OFFICIALS

With ordinary folk who do not have vested interests or jobs to protect, a fieldworker may do well to explain his work in accordance with the questions his respondents see fit to ask. When I spoke with Indian mothers, it was sufficient to explain that my *husband* was making a study of the schools and that he had asked me to ask them a few questions about what they thought of their children's schooling. In most cases, this explanation, which on Thrashing Buffalo was often given by my interpreter, brought me a courteous and sometimes a cordial reception. I volunteered little more specific information about my work, since I learned a great deal from the questions the ladies asked me and from the information which they, having decided what I was, then decided was the kind of thing I wished to hear. Incidentally, they rarely asked me anything about the precise nature of my work, and their questions were usually concerned with the difficulties which a child or other relative was having in school or in staying in school.

Many people whom social scientists wish to study today are under the legal or self-appointed "guardianship" of various political, religious, philanthropic, or other custodial organizations or bureaucracies. The more powerful and successful of these guardian groups resent or fear the presence of an outside observer, defining him as critic or competitor or "troublemaker." The less powerful or successful of the "guardians" may greet a fieldworker with embarrassing cordiality, since they view him as a possible confederate in their conflict with the successful groups and organizations. Most dangerous of all—to the fieldworker—are those powerful interest groups or bureaucracies who already feel themselves under attack, for the people who head these groups almost invariably assume that the findings of *any* observer will be used as ammunition against them. And, the world being what it is, they are usually right in this assumption.

In most field situations it is both courteous and politically astute for a fieldworker to call on the heads of the various organizations and groups and explain the nature of his research. But what I would like to emphasize here is that the fieldworker is naïve if (again!) he thinks that most of these important personages will really listen carefully to what he says, much less, believe it. If he comes with a recommendation which they must respect, they will listen with half an ear to his carefully prepared presentation, nod their heads, and then present *their* speech, in which they tell him (1) what a remarkably good job they are doing under difficult circumstances, and (2) how they expect him to conduct himself. If they are against the "Establishment," they will also listen with half an ear and then proceed to give him a lengthy account of the evils they hope he will expose. If he protests that his task is to do research and not to expose graft or corruption, they are likely to smile understandingly, implying that they, of course, understand what he is really there for. Powerful individuals or groups who are convinced that the fieldworker's presence is an immediate or potential danger will, of course, listen to his words but only to use them against him. As soon as they can find a means to eject him from the community they will do so, whether he has said or done anything objectionable or not.

Perhaps the most cogent thing that can be said about a field-worker's interviews with superintendents, chairmen, directors, or heads of bureaucracies is that he can learn a great deal from them but they, at least in a first interview, can learn very little from him. In our studies of American Indian schools, we found that most principals and many teachers immediately asked us for advice on their most pressing "problems" with the Indian children. That they had been teaching Indians for years whereas we had been on the reservation two or three weeks seemed to make no difference. They were baffled and concerned and thought that "experts" like us could help them. Thus, very early in our research, we obtained an excellent picture of how the teachers defined their situation vis-à-vis their pupils. We, for our part, explained that we were only beginning our studies and that we would try to find and communicate the answers to them.

Here again I would like to qualify the suggestion made by some of my colleagues that a fieldworker undertaking a community study should "begin at the top," that is, first obtain the assistance of leaders or other important or powerful people. While I agree that getting the assistance or protection of powerful officials is generally a good idea, too close an association with leaders or "important people" can greatly limit the scope of fieldwork. In some societies the most powerful and influential of the leaders remain behind the scenes, while pretenders and parvenus make the noise and take the blame. In other societies, the fieldworker who involves himself closely with the people at the top may be sure that they will never let him get near the people at the bottom.

"I AM NOT AS OTHER MEN ARE"

That a fieldworker should try to disassociate himself from the kinds of people whom his respondents hate, fear, and distrust, is, of course, natural. On the other hand, the experienced participant observer knows that such a disassociation is only partial and that, if it occurs at all, it usually takes a long time. Moreover, the fact that a host people have come to believe that an anthropologist is a man of reasonably good intent (even though he may be a white man, a *goy* or a *Nasrany*), that he is genuinely trying to help them, is by no means a guarantee that they will thenceforth deal with him in a manner that *he* defines as open, honest, or fair. If, for example, they come to see him as kind, understanding (or gullible), they may make his life miserable, pestering him for gifts or money. Or, if they decide that he is *really* different, they may begin to use him in all manner of ways, some of which will be highly instructive, some of which will waste a great deal of his time, and some of which may be very dangerous. Still, once he begins to encounter problems like these, he may take some comfort in the fact that he is beginning to be "involved in the communal life," and he is going to have to learn how to play his cards, where to draw the line, and, in general, how to make the best of it.

Since my first field experience in Gila (when I knew no better), I have not bothered to put much effort into distinguishing myself from the kind of outsider or administrator whom my hosts disliked or distrusted, nor even from the other kinds of white people with whom I might temporarily be identified. I had learned twenty years before that people developed their own definitions of what I was and what I was doing and that these definitions rarely corresponded precisely with my definition of what I was and what I was doing. Indeed, at Thrashing Buffalo I was variously taken for a teacher, an FBI investigator, a social worker, a professional cowgirl, a Wave recruiter, and a communist agitator. My husband, to my secret amusement, was often assumed to be an ethnohistorian, so that every few weeks some emissary from "an old man who knew all about the old songs and customs" would call and try to arrange a paid recording session. But my husband could chuckle in return, for one of our neighbors, an elderly man, told people he thought I was "holy" because I took so many solitary walks in the hills. (Only people seeking the help of spirits walked in the hills alone, and the truth is that I often did pray on these walks.)

I suspect that the fieldworker who goes about telling his hosts that he is not like other strangers or not like other white men is likely to be taken for an eccentric. The Caucasian fieldworker tempted to do this might ask himself what he would think of an African, East Indian, or Oriental who went about in the United States telling everyone that he was "different" from his own people. In my experience, most people, if they are not professional politicians, vulnerable civil servants, "guardians," or ax grinders, really do not care to know precisely what a fieldworker is trying to do. If he is agreeable, well-mannered, considerate and discreet—or if they can get something out of assisting him or associating with him—they will usually talk with him and, often, help him.

A fieldworker usually goes into the field with a research proposal composed, in part, of hypotheses, well-planned questionnaires, and ingenious tests. But, in point of fact, he does not know what he is going to do. All he knows is what he hopes to try to do. Thus, in introducing himself to his hosts, a fieldworker might do worse than explain what he *would like to do* (concretely, specifically, and soon) and ask for comments and advice. He need not follow the advice, but it should be illuminating.

THE FIELDWORKER AS FOOL

The person who cannot abide feeling awkward or out of place, who feels crushed whenever he makes a mistake—embarrassing or otherwise—who is psychologically unable to endure being, and being treated like, a fool, not only for a day or week but for months on end, ought to think twice before he decides to become a participant observer. He might make a good interviewer or a good "detached" observer, but he does not have what it takes to appreciate the pains and joys of trying to involve himself with the people of another culture. An ideal participant observer is able to see himself as an educated and highly intelligent adult, and, simultaneously, as a ludicrous tenderfoot or *Schlemiel* who knows less about what he is doing than a native child. He is able to accept the laughter and ridicule of his hosts as instructive, not because he is saintly in nature, but because making fun of improper or incorrect behavior is an ancient if painful method of pedagogy. He is also able to live with a sense of his own dangerousness, that is, the knowledge that any of the words or deeds which he considers natural or well intentioned may be interpreted by his hosts as hostile or insulting. Further, he is able, for weeks and months, to function like a sane and reasonable being in a situation which, for him, is largely without pattern or structure. He does not know whom he can trust, or whom he can trust about what, or, indeed, if he can trust anyone about anything at all. He may find, not once, but repeatedly, that he has been misled, cheated, exploited, or blackmailed, and that, in addition, "the community" knows all about this and is laughing at him. In the last case, if he is a really sterling participant observer, he will be able to shake himself, laugh, and realize that slowly but surely he is learning how to stay out of trouble.

Many young people probably possess more of these qualities than they suspect. Anyone who easily learns to speak (not read) a foreign language, who does not mind being laughed at or considered stupid, has the basic orientation necessary for a participant observer. (All rules should be applied with good sense. Fieldworkers *trying* to be funny in situations which they do not understand are truly a lamentable sight. Better to do what comes naturally. It will be sufficiently funny to the host people.)

I have no advice on how to live graciously through the experience of being exploited, hoodwinked, short-changed, blackmailed, robbed, or fooled, except by bearing in mind that every fieldworker could furnish examples which now sound hilarious but scarcely seemed funny at the time he experienced them. I myself have been fooled so many times that I cannot afford even to look at a stone, much less pick it up and throw it at my fellow anthropologists.

One reason why anthropologists are so gullible is that we assume or convince ourselves that we professional scholars are different from the other people who have abused, exploited, or tried to change or "develop" tribal peoples. We, in contrast, are people of good intent, and besides, our work, being "science" or "a contribution to knowledge," is a good in itself. We further assume that a host people will immediately perceive that we are people of good intent and that our work has great value. Or we may assume (in this case correctly) that the host people has been mistreated or abused, and (less correctly) that our work will assist them and (still less correctly) that they will perceive this and be grateful, helpful, and accommodating. It took me two field trips to realize that this chain of assumptions represented a fantasy by which I concealed from myself the fact that I expected something for nothing. The basic reason I went to work in the Japanese relocation centers was that, as a young anthropologist, I *had* to "do a piece of fieldwork," and the basic reason I went to Thrashing Buffalo was that my husband wanted to get a research grant and do a piece of fieldwork. I did mean well, I tried to hurt no one, and I hoped that my work would help the people I was studying and would constitute some contribution to knowledge. But insofar as I pretended to myself that I was motivated solely by good will, by love of science, or by the desire to help the Japanese Americans or the Indians (rather than by the status opportunities and salary that accompanied the job), I deceived myself, and if the "natives" sold me a gilded brick, a gilded brick was what I deserved.

It may be that fooling himself and being fooled by his hosts is an essential part of "the fieldworker's condition." It may also be an essential part of increasing his "understanding." Many a fieldworker idealizes the people he is about to study and he also idealizes either himself or the nature and value of his fieldwork. Learning better is an essential part of his development as a fieldworker. I went to the Gila center believing that all of the Japanese Americans held much the same sentiments toward the United States as I did (for if they did not, how could I argue that the evacuation was unjustified?). I also believed that they would be pleased that someone was making a record of what they were doing and what was happening to them. I went to the Thrashing Buffalo reservation believing that the white man was responsible for all of the Indians' difficulties, and Murray and I believed that the Indian elders were very dissatisfied with the education their children were receiving and would welcome a study of the BIA Schools. Learning what the Japanese Americans or the Indians really thought about their situation was an essential part of our beginning to understand the situation. (Ironically, at Tule Lake, which might otherwise be called a very difficult investigational situation, many people were pleased to have a sympathetic observer and reporter around.)

I find it difficult to reproach myself or my fellow fieldworkers for our disposition to regard the people we intend to study as good, honorable, and innocent. Indeed, at my age I find it touching that there are still so many of us who assume that poor or abused people can be kind and charitable instead of desperate and grasping, that it is only our own society that is full of selfish, greedy, and bigoted individuals, and that strangers are somehow going to treat us fieldworkers more kindly than do our own people. Some of my reluctance to criticize comes from hard experience. I know that there are many societies that have developed elaborate and ingenious devices for relieving any stranger of his money and of his general confidence in human nature. I also know that no respondent or stranger has ever treated me as vilely as have some of my fellow social scientists. On the other hand, I know that one cannot live with human beings in the field or out of it without trusting them. The great feat in most field expeditions, as in life, is to find the areas in which a mutual or reciprocal trust may be developed. That these areas will be new or odd to both hosts and fieldworker is very likely. But it is in these areas of mutual trust and, sometimes, affection, that the finest fieldwork can be done, even if, as I have remarked elsewhere, one can learn a great deal from people one dislikes or from people who dislike one. In any case, one may live in hope of developing the kind of relationship which Lowie had with the Crow, whom he could always throw into gales of laughter by remarking pompously: "All white men are evil. Only I am good."

BIBLIOGRAPHY

Adams, R. N., and Preiss, J. J., eds. 1960. *Human organization research: field relations and techniques.* Homewood, Ill.: Dorsey Press.

Angulo, Jaime de. 1950. Indians in overalls. *Hudson Review* 3, no. 3. Reprinted in *Hudson Review anthology,* ed. Frederick Morgan. New York: Random House, 1961.

Becker, Howard S. 1951. The professional dance musician and his audience. *American Journal of Sociology* 57:136–44.

————. 1953. Becoming a marihuana user. *American Journal of Sociology* 59:235–42.

Becker, Howard S., and Geer, Blanche. 1957. Participant observation and interviewing: a comparison. *Human Organization* 16:28–35; 17:39.

————. 1958. Problems of inference and proof in participant observation. *American Sociological Review* 23:652–60.

Becker, Howard S.; Geer, Blanche; Hughes, Everett C.; and Strauss, Anselm. 1961. *Boys in white: student culture in medical school.* Chicago: University of Chicago Press.

Becker, Howard S., et al., eds. 1968. *Institutions and the person: essays presented to Everett C. Hughes.* Chicago: Aldine.

Benedict, Ruth. 1948. Anthropology and the humanities. *American Anthropologist,* 50, no. 4, pt. 1:583–93.

Bensman, Joseph, and Vidich, Arthur. 1965. Social theory in field research. In *Sociology on trial,* ed. Maurice Stein and Arthur Vidich, pp. 162–72. Englewood Cliffs, N.J.: Prentice Hall.

Berk, Richard A., and Adams, Joseph M. 1970. Establishing rapport with deviant groups. *Social Problems* 18, no. 1:102–17.

— Berreman, Gerald D. 1968. Ethnography: method and product. In *Introduction to cultural anthropology*, ed. J. Clifton. Boston, Mass.: Houghton-Mifflin Co.

Boas, F. 1911. *Handbook of American Indian languages*. Smithsonian Institution, Bureau of American Ethnology, Bulletin 40. Washington: U.S. Government Printing Office.

Booth, Charles. 1967. *Charles Booth on the city: physical pattern and social structure*. Selected writings, ed. Harold W. Pfautz. Chicago: University of Chicago Press.

— Bowen, Elenore Smith (pseud). 1964. *Return to laughter*. New York: Doubleday & Co.

— Bruyn, Severyn T. 1966. *The human perspective in sociology: the methodology of participant observation*. Englewood Cliffs, N.J.: Prentice Hall.

— Bucher, Rue, et al. 1956. Tape recorded interviews in social research. *American Sociological Review* 21:3.

Burridge, K. O. L. 1960. *Mambu: A Melanesian millennium*. London: Methuen & Co.

Callaway, Henry. 1870. *The religious system of the Amazulu: izinyanga zokubula, or divination, as existing among the Amazulu, in their own words*. London: Publications of the Folklore Society, no. 15.

Carpenter, Edmund. 1965. Comment on research among Eskimo. *Current Anthropology* 6, no. 1:55–60.

Chadwick, Owen. 1964. *The reformation*. Baltimore: Penguin Books, A 504.

— Cicourel, Aaron V. 1964. *Method and measurement in sociology*. New York: Free Press of Glencoe.

Codrington, Robert H. 1891. *The Melanesians: studies in their anthropology and folklore*. Oxford: Clarendon Press.

Cohen Morris. 1931. *Reason and nature*. New York: Harcourt Brace & Co.

Collier, John, Jr. 1967. *Visual anthropology: photography as a research method.* New York: Holt, Rinehart and Winston.

Davis, Fred. 1959. The cabdriver and his fare. *American Journal of Sociology* 63:158–65.

Diamond, Stanley. 1964. The politics of field work. In *Reflections on community studies,* ed. Arthur J. Vidich, Joseph Bensman, Maurice R. Stein. New York: John Wiley and Sons.

Doughty, Charles M. 1888. *Travels in Arabia Deserta.* New York: Random House, 1936.

Douglas, Jack D. 1970. The rhetoric of science and the origins of statistical social thought: the case of Durkheim's *Suicide.* In *The sociology of sociology,* ed. Edward A. Tiryakian. New York: Appleton-Century-Crofts.

Dumont, Robert V., Jr. 1971. Learning English and how to be silent: Studies in American Indian classrooms. In *Functions of language in the Classroom,* ed. Vera P. Johns, Courtney B. Cazden, Dell H. Hymes. New York: Columbia University, Teachers' College Press.

Dundes, Alan. 1968. *Every man his way: readings in cultural anthropology.* Englewood Cliffs, N.J.: Prentice Hall.

Durkheim, Emile. 1897. *Le suicide: Etude de sociologie.* Trans. John A. Spaulding and George Simpson. New York: Free Press, 1951.

Epstein, A. L., ed. 1967. *The craft of social anthropology.* London: Tavistock Publications. Social Science Paperback, SSP20.

Evans-Pritchard, E. E. 1940. *The Nuer.* Oxford: Clarendon Press.

———. 1951. *Social anthropology.* London: Cohen & West. Reprinted with additional essays as: *Social anthropology and other essays.* New York: Free Press of Glencoe. Paperback edition, 1964, FP 90987.

Filstead, William J., ed. 1970. *Qualitative methodology: firsthand involvement with the social world.* Chicago: Markham Publishing Co.

— Freilich, Morris, ed. 1970. *Marginal natives: anthropologists at work.* New York: Harper and Row.

Freuchen, Peter. 1931. *Eskimo.* Trans. A. Paul Maerkerranden and Elsa Branden. New York: H. Liveright.

————. 1954. *Ice floes and flaming water.* New York: Julian Messner, Inc.

————. 1966. *Peter Freuchen's book of the Eskimos.* Ed. Dagmar Freuchen. Cleveland and New York: The World Publishing Co.

Gans, Herbert J. 1962. *The urban villagers.* New York: Free Press of Glencoe.

Geddes, W. R. 1961. *Nine Dyak nights.* New York: Oxford University Press, PB36.

— Glaser, Barney G., and Strauss, Anselm L. 1967. *The discovery of grounded theory: strategies for qualitative research.* Chicago: Aldine Press.

Gluckman, Max. 1963. Malinowski—fieldworker and theorist. In *Order and rebellion in tribal Africa,* pp. 244–52. New York: Free Press of Glencoe.

Godolphin, Francis R. B., ed. 1942. *The Greek historians,* vol. 1. New York: Random House.

Goffman, Erving. 1961. *Asylums: essays on the social situation of mental patients and other inmates.* Garden City, N.Y.: Doubleday and Co., Anchor Books A277.

Göhre, Paul. 1891. *Drei Monate Fabrikarbeiter und Handwerksbursche.* Leipzig: Grünow.

Gold, Ray. 1952. Janitors versus tenants: a status-income dilemma. *American Journal of Sociology* 57:486–93.

— Golde, Peggy, ed. 1970. *Women in the field.* Chicago: Aldine.

—Gorden, Raymond L. 1969. *Interviewing strategy, techniques and tactics.* Homewood, Ill.: Dorsey Press.

Grodzins, Morton. 1949. *Americans betrayed: politics and the Japanese evacuation.* Chicago: University of Chicago Press.

Haak, Ronald O. 1970. Co-opting the oppressors: the case of the Japanese-Americans. *Transaction* 7, no. 12:23–31.

Hammond, Phillip E., ed. 1967. *Sociologists at work: essays on the craft of social research.* Garden City, N.Y.: Doubleday, Anchor Books A598.

Healey, Alan. 1964. Handling unsophisticated linguistic informants. *Linguistic Circle of Canberra Publications,* series A, Occasional papers, no. 2, Canberra.

Helm, June. 1966. *Pioneers of American anthropology.* Seattle: University of Washington Press.

Henry, Frances, and Satish Saberwal, eds. 1969. *Stress and response in field work.* New York: Holt, Rinehart & Winston.

Herodotus (484–25 B.C.). The Persian wars. Trans. George Rawlinson. In *The Greek historians,* vol. 1. ed. Francis R. B. Godolphin. New York: Random House. 1942.

Hughes, Everett C. 1943. *French Canada in transition.* Chicago and London: University of Chicago Press.

―――. 1960. The place of fieldwork in the social sciences. In Buford H. Junker, *Fieldwork: an introduction to the social sciences.* Chicago: University of Chicago Press.

Hughes, Everett C., and Hughes, Helen M. 1952. *Where peoples meet: racial and ethnic frontiers.* New York: The Free Press of Glencoe.

Hughes, Everett C.; Becker, H. S.; Geer, B.; and Strauss, A. 1961. *Boys in white: student culture in medical school.* Chicago: University of Chicago Press.

Janes, Robert W. 1961. A note on phases of the community role of the participant observer. *American Sociological Review* 26:446–50.

Jones, Emily L. 1963. The courtesy bias in South-East African surveys. *International social science journal* 15, no. 1:70-76.

Jones, Gwyn. 1968. *A history of the vikings.* New York: Oxford University Press.

Jongmans, D. G., and Gutkind, P. C. W., eds. 1967. *Anthropologists in the field.* New York: Humanities Press.

Josephus, Flavius (ca. A.D. 37–95). *The great Roman-Jewish war: A.D. 66–70.* Trans. William Whiston, rev. D. S. Margoulioth, ed. Wm R. Farmer. New York: Harper 1960.

— Junker, Buford H. 1960. *Field work: an introduction to the social sciences.* Chicago: University of Chicago Press.

Kael, Pauline. 1965. *I lost it at the movies.* Boston: Little, Brown & Co. Bantam edition, 1966.

Keesing, Felix M., and Keesing, Marie M. 1956. *Elite communications in Samoa: a study of leadership.* Stanford: Stanford University Press.

Kroeber, A. L. 1923. *Anthropology.* New York: Harcourt, Brace & Co. 1948.

Kroeber, Theodora. 1961. *Ishi in two worlds.* Berkeley: University of California Press.

―――. 1970. *Alfred Kroeber: a personal configuration.* Berkeley: University of California Press.

La Farge, Oliver. 1947. *Santa Eulalia: the religion of a Chuchumatan Indian town.* Chicago: University of Chicago Press.

— Langness, L. L. 1965. *The life history in anthropological science.* New York: Holt, Rinehart & Winston.

Lawrence, Peter. 1964. *Road belong cargo.* New York: Humanities Press.

Leach, Edmund R. 1967. An anthropologist's reflections on a social survey. In *Anthropologists in the field,* ed. D. G. Jongmans and P. C. Gutkind. New York: Humanities Press.

Lécuyer, Bernard, and Oberschall, Anthony. 1968. Sociology: the early history of social research. In *International Encyclopedia of the*

Social Sciences 15:36–53. New York: Macmillan and Free Press.

Lee, Dorothy D. 1949. Being and value in a primitive culture. Reprinted in *Freedom and culture*. Englewood Cliffs, N.J.: Prentice Hall. Spectrum Books, 1959, S-6.

Leighton, Alexander H. 1945. *The governing of men: general principles and recommendations based on experience at a Japanese relocation camp.* Princeton: Princeton University Press.

Lerner, Daniel, ed. 1959. *The human meaning of the social sciences: original essays on the history and application of the social sciences.* New York: Meridian M64.

Lévi-Strauss, Claude. 1962. *The savage mind.* Chicago: University of Chicago Press. 1966.

Liebow, Elliot. 1967. A field experience in retrospect. In *Tally's Corner: a study of Negro streetcorner men,* pp. 232–56. Boston: Little Brown.

Lindesmith, Alfred R. 1965. *The addict and the law.* New York: Random House, 1967, V-384.

Lowie, R. H. 1937. *The history of ethnological theory.* New York: Farrar and Rinehart, Inc.

———. 1959. *Robert H. Lowie ethnologist.* Berkeley: University of California Press.

Lurie, Nancy Oestreich. 1971. Two dollars. In *Crossing cultural barriers,* ed. James B. Watson and Solon T. Kimball. San Francisco: Chandler.

McCall, George J., and Simmons, J. L., eds. 1969. *Issues in participant observation.* Reading, Mass.: Addison-Wesley, 7027.

Maine, Henry Sumner. 1861. Ancient law. London: Murray, 1912.

Malinowski, Bronislaw. 1922. *Argonauts of the Western Pacific.* New York: E. P. Dutton and Co., 1961, D74.

———. 1967. *A diary in the strict sense of the term.* New York: Harcourt, Brace and World.

Maquet, Jaques J. 1964. Objectivity in anthropology. *Current Anthropology* 5:47–55.

Markham, Felix, ed. and trans. 1952. *Henri de Saint-Simon: Social organization, the science of man and other writings.* New York: Harper and Row, 1964, TB1152.

Marriott, McKim. 1955. Western Medicine in a village of northern India. In *Health, culture, and community,* ed. Benjamin D. Paul. New York: Russell Sage Foundation.

Maybury-Lewis, David. 1965. *The savage and the innocent.* Cleveland, Ohio: The World Publishing Co.

Mead, Margaret, ed. 1966. *Writings of Ruth Benedict: an anthropologist at work.* New York: Atherton Press.

Mitchell, Robert E. 1965. Survey materials collected in the developing countries: sampling, measurement, and interviewing obstacles to intra- and international comparisons. *International Social Science Journal* 17, no. 4:665–85.

Morgan, Lewis H. 1851. *The League of the Ho-De-No-Sau-Nee or Iroquois.* New Haven: Yale University Press, 1954.

—Nash, Dennison. 1963. The ethnologist as a stranger: an essay in the sociology of knowledge. *Southwestern Journal of Anthropology* 19, no. 2 (summer):149–67.

Neill, Stephen. 1964. *Christian missions.* Baltimore: Penguin Books, A628.

Nimuendajú, C. 1942. *The Serente.* Los Angeles: Publications of the F. W. Hodge Anniversary Publication Fund, vol. 4.

———. 1946. *The Eastern Timbira.* Los Angeles: University of California Publications in American Archeology and Ethnology, vol. 41.

Oberschall, Anthony R. 1965. *Empirical social research in Germany, 1848–1914.* The Hague: Mouton.

Opler, Morris. 1942. Studies of segregants at Manzanar. Unpub. Ms., Bancroft Library, University of California, Berkeley.

Osgood, Cornelius. 1953. *Winter.* New York: W. W. Norton.

Parent-Duchâtelet, Alexandre, J. B. 1834. *On prostitution in the city of Paris.* 3d. ed. 2 vols. London: Burgess, 1857.

Park, Robert Ezra. 1936. Human ecology. *American Journal of Sociology* 42:1–15. Reprinted: Park 1952: 145–58.

————. 1939. Symbiosis and socialization: a frame of reference for the study of society. *American Journal of Sociology* 45:1–25. Reprinted: Park 1952:240–62.

————. 1952. *Human communities: the city and human ecology.* Collected papers of Robert Ezra Park, vol. 2, ed. Everett C. Hughes et al. Glencoe: Free Press.

Park, Robert Ezra, and Burgess, Ernest W. 1921. *Introduction to the science of sociology.* Chicago: University of Chicago Press.

Payne, Stanley. 1951. *The art of asking questions.* Princeton: Princeton University Press.

Pehrson, Robert N. 1957. The Bilateral network of social relations in Könkämä Lapp District. Indiana University Publications, Slavic and East European Series, vol. 5.

Polo, Marco. *The travels of Marco Polo.* Trans. Ronald Latham. Harmondsworth, Middlesex: Penguin, 1958.

Polsky, Ned. 1967. Research method, morality and criminology. In *Hustlers, beats and others,* pp. 117–49. Chicago: Aldine.

Powdermaker, Hortense. 1966. *Stranger and friend: the way of an anthropologist.* New York: W. W. Norton and Co., 1967, N410.

Radin, Paul. 1933. *The method and theory of ethnology.* New York: McGraw-Hill.

Reinertsen, Priscilla. 1969. Report on a sociological pioneer: Einert Sundt. *Journal of the History of the Behavioral Sciences* 5, no. 4:360–64.

Reining, Conrad. 1962. A lost period of applied anthropology. *American Anthropologist* 64, no. 3, pt. 1:593–600.

Reischauer, Edwin O., and Fairbank, John K. 1958. *East Asia the great tradition,* vol. 1. Boston: Houghton Mifflin Co.

Rohner, Ronald P. 1966. Franz Boas: ethnographer on the Northwest Coast. In *Pioneers of American anthropology,* ed. June Helm. Seattle: University of Washington Press.

Roth, Julius A. 1962. The treatment of tuberculosis as a bargaining process. In *Human behavior and social processes,* ed., Arnold M. Rose, pp. 575–88. Boston: Houghton-Mifflin Company.

————. 1962. "Management bias" in social science study of medical treatment. *Human Organization* 21:47–50.

————. 1963. Information and the control of treatment in tuberculosis hospitals. In *The hospital in a modern society,* ed. Elliot Friedson, chap. 10. New York: Free Press of Glencoe.

Roy, Donald. 1952. Quota restriction and gold bricking in a machine shop. *American Journal of Sociology* 57:427–42.

————. 1959–60. Banana time: job satisfaction and informal interaction. *Human Organization* 18:158–68.

Rubruck (Ruysbroek), Willem van. *The journey of William of Rubruck to the eastern parts of the world, 1253–55, as narrated by himself with two accounts of the earlier journey of John of Pian de Carpine.* Trans. William Woodville Rockhill. London: Printed for the Hakluyt society, 1900.

Schneider, Louis, ed. 1967. *The Scottish moralists.* Chicago: University of Chicago Press.

Schwartz, Morris S. 1964. The mental hospital: the research person in the disturbed ward. In *Reflections on community studies,* ed. Arthur J. Vidich, Joseph Bensman, Maurice R. Stein. New York: John Wiley & Sons.

— Schwartz, Morris S. and Green, Charlotte. 1955. Problems in participant observation. *American Journal of Sociology,* 60:4. Bobbs-Merrill Reprint.

Seeley, John R. 1967. Social science: some probative problems. Crestwood Heights: a transaction, in *The Americanization of the unconscious*. Philadelphia: Lippincott Co.

Shibutani, Tamotsu. 1966. *Improvised news: a sociological study of rumor*. Indianapolis: Bobbs-Merrill.

Sjoberg, Gideon, ed. 1967. *Ethics, politics, and social research*. Cambridge: Schenkman.

Skolnick, Jerome H. 1967. The setting, method, and development of the research. Pp. 23–41 in *Justice without trial*. New York: Wiley.

Smith, Marian. 1959. Boas' "Natural History" approach to field method. In *The anthropology of Franz Boas*, ed. Walter Goldschmidt. Memoir No. 89 of the American Anthropological Association, Vol. 61, No. 5, Part 2 (October, 1959).

Snellgrove, David and Hugh Richardson. 1968. *A cultural history of Tibet*. New York: Praeger.

Stein, Maurice R. 1964. The eclipse of community: some glances at the education of a sociologist. In *Reflections on Community Studies*, eds. Arthur J. Vidich, Joseph Bensman, & Maurice R. Stein. New York: John Wiley.

Stringfellow, William. 1966. *My People is the enemy*. Garden City, N.Y.: Anchor Books, 489.

Suttles, Gerald D. 1968. *The social order of the slum*. Chicago: University of Chicago Press.

Tacitus, P. Cornelius (A.D. 55–120). A.D. 97–98. Germania. Trans. H. Mattingly. In *Tacitus on Britain and Germany*. Baltimore: Penguin Books, 1948.

Thomas, Dorothy Swaine, and Nishimoto, Richard S. 1946. *The spoilage: Japanese-American evacuation and resettlement*. Berkeley: University of California Press.

Thomas, W. I., and Znaniecki, Florian. 1918–20. *The Polish peasant in Europe and America*. Boston: Badger.

Turnbull, Colin M. 1962. *The forest people.* Garden City, N.Y.: Doubleday and Company. Anchor Books N27.

U.S. Army, Western Defense Command and Fourth Army. 1943. *Final report, Japanese evacuation, 1942.* Washington, D.C.: U.S. Government Printing Office.

Verdet, Paula. 1969. Social science and the social scientist. Manuscript, Montieth College, Wayne State University, Detroit.

— Vidich, Arthur J. 1955. Participant observation and the collection and interpretation of data. *American Journal of Sociology* 60, no. 4: 354–60.

— Vidich, Arthur J., and Bensman, J. 1954. The validity of field data. *Human Organization* 13:20–27.

Vidich, Arthur J.; Bensman, Joseph; and Stein, Maurice R., eds. 1964. *Reflections on community studies.* New York: John Wiley & Sons.

Villermé, Louis R. 1840. *Tableau de l'état physique et moral des ouvriers employés dans les manufactures de coton, de laine et de soie.* 2 vols. Paris: Renouard.

Wax, Rosalie H. 1943–45. Field notes, Japanese American relocation centers.

———. 1950. The development of authoritarianism. PhD dissertation, Department of Anthropology, University of Chicago.

— ———. 1952. Reciprocity as a field technique. *Human Organization* 11:34–37.

———. 1953. The destruction of a democratic impulse. *Human Organization* 12:11–21.

— ———. 1957. Twelve years later: an analysis of field experience. *American Journal of Sociology* 63:133–42.

———. 1961. A brief history and analysis of the workshops on American Indian Affairs conducted for American Indian college students, 1956–1960, together with a study of current attitudes and activities of these students. Mimeographed. United Scholarship Service, Denver.

Wax, Rosalie H. 1962–63. Field notes, Thrashing Buffalo reservation.

———. 1966. Field notes, Ottawa education study.

———. 1968. Participant observation. In *International Encyclopedia of the Social Sciences* 11:238–41.

———. 1969. *Magic, fate and history: the changing ethos of the Vikings.* Lawrence, Kansas: Coronado Press.

Wax, Murray. 1962–63. Field notes, Thrashing Buffalo reservation.

———. 1966. Field notes, Ottawa education study.

———. 1967. On misunderstanding *Verstehen:* a reply to Abel. *Sociology and Social Research* 51, no. 3:323–33.

Wax, Murray; Wax, Rosalie; and Dumont, R. V., Jr. 1964. *Formal education in an American Indian community.* Supplement to *Social Problems* 11:4.

Webb, Beatrice. 1926. *My apprenticeship.* New York: Longmans, Green, and Co.

Webb, Sydney, and Webb, Beatrice. 1902. *Problems of modern industry.* London: Longmans, Green, and Co.

———. 1932. *Methods of social study.* New York: Longmans, Green, and Co.

Weber, Max. 1892. *Die Verhältnisse der Landarbeiter im ostelbischen Deutschland.* Verein für Socialpolitik, Schriften, vol. 55. Leipzig: Duncker und Humblot.

———. 1909. Zur Methodik sozialpsychologischer Enqueten und ihrer Bearbeitung. *Archiv für Sozialwissenschaft und Sozialpolitik* 29: 949–58.

Westley, William A. 1953 Violence and the police. *American Journal of Sociology* 59:34–41.

———. 1956. Secrecy and the police. *Social Forces* 34:254–57.

Whyte, William Foote. 1943 *Street corner society*. Chicago: University of Chicago Press, 1955.

————. 1967. Models for building and changing organizations. *Human Organization* 25, no. 1–2.

— Williams, Thomas R. 1967. *Field methods in the study of culture*. New York: Holt, Rinehart & Winston.

Wright, Rolland H. 1966. The stranger and the urban world. Manuscript. Social Sciences Division, Monteith College, Wayne State University, Detroit.

INDEX